Fighting the Good Fight

Other Works By George J. Marlin

The Quotable Chesterton (1986)

More Quotable Chesterton (1988)

The Quotable Fulton Sheen (1989)

The Quotable Ronald Knox (1996)
(with Richard Rabatin and Jack Swan)

The Guidebook to Municipal Bonds
The History, the Industry, the Mechanics (1991)
(with Joe Mysak)

The Quotable Paul Johnson (1994)
(with Richard Rabatin and Heather Higgins)

The Politician's Guide to Assisted Suicide,
Cloning and Other Current Controversies (1998)

General Editor
The Collected Works of G.K. Chesterton

Fighting the Good Fight

A History of the New York Conservative Party

George J. Marlin

Introduction by Richard Brookhiser

ST. AUGUSTINE'S PRESS
South Bend, Indiana
2002

1 2 3 4 5 6   08 07 06 05 04 03 02

Library of Congress Cataloging in Publication Data
Marlin, George J., 1952–
    Fighting the good fight : a history of the New York Conservative Party/
    George J. Marlin ; introduction by Richard Brookhiser.
       p. cm.
    Includes bibliographical references and index.
    ISBN 1-58731-251-4 (hardback : alk. paper)
    1. Conservative Party of New York State. 2. New York (State) – Politics and
    government. I. Title.
JK2295.N74 M37 2002
324.2747'03 – dc21   2002003360

Printed on acid free paper.

Printed in the Czech Republic by Newton Printing Ltd, London, UK. www.newtonprinting.com

My efforts are dedicated to

Michael G. Crofton
Homo civilis, misericors, aequus et integer
and

Jack Swan
(1927–1998)
Knight of the Holy Ghost, he goes his way
Wisdom his motley, Truth his loving jest;
The mills of Satan kept his lance in play,
Pity and Innocence his heart at rest.
– Walter De La Mare

Contents

Foreword

In the past few years, numerous books have been written on the rise and success of the conservative political movement in the United States. In reading them, I was troubled that only passing references at best were made to the only legally recognized conservative political party in the nation: The Conservative Party of New York State. It is my hope that *Fighting the Good Fight* will contribute to establishing the Conservative Party's rightful place in the history of American conservatism.

Founded in 1962 to counter the liberal Rockefeller-Javits domination of New York's Republican organization, the Conservative Party has for four decades lived up to its charter to serve political ideals first. Throughout its history, the Party has been the guardian of working-class New Yorkers, men and women who subscribe to the belief that to be good citizens it is essential to love family, neighborhood, country, and God, and just as important to respect an ethic of hard work.

After the 1964 Goldwater debacle, it was the Conservative Party that refuted the prevailing view in liberal circles that the movement consisted of nothing more than a bunch of redneck crackpots. The 1965 mayoral candidacy of William F. Buckley Jr. not only proved that the Conservative Party mattered in the electoral politics of the most left-wing city in the nation, but it also helped regain respectability for the conservative movement nationwide. It was a revival of sorts. Nearly as important, Bill Buckley proved that politics could be fun. As the liberal columnist Murray Kempton wrote: "The process which coarsens every other man who enters it has only refined Mr. Buckley."

In its early years – and in its losses as much as in its victories – the Conservative Party confirmed the view of political analyst Kevin Phillips that there was a new, emerging majority in New York's and America's voting patterns.

Thanks to hundreds who agreed to run on the Conservative line and especially to the 1970 election of James L. Buckley to the United States Senate, an electoral coalition was cemented between inner-city ethnic Democrats and rural and suburban Republicans, all of whom were disgusted with excessive taxation and runaway government spending. Often unspoken but always significant was the passion of both groups for the preservation of their own culture in their own towns and neighborhoods.

The Conservative Party earned the votes of these discontented citizens because it stood for a consistent set of principles that addressed their concerns and championed traditional cultural beliefs.

Throughout its forty-year history, the Conservative Party has made sure New Yorkers have had a choice at the ballot box and has provided the margin of victory for numerous Republicans and Democrats who were willing to go against their party bosses and promote conservative positions. New York's conservatives proved to the nation's conservatives that it was possible to win in the most liberal state in the country, and to paraphrase the famous song: "If you can make it there, you'll make it anywhere." Dedication and hard work can win conservative victories throughout the country, which is why President Ronald Reagan has said that: "The Conservative Party has established itself as a pre-eminent force in New York Politics and an important part of our political history."

In this book I try to tell the story how two men of vision, J. Daniel Mahoney and Kieran O'Doherty, had the guts and fortitude to put together the organization required to establish a new political party in New York. It tells the story of principled people who joined the cause with no interest or expectation of financial gain and went door to door to collect tens of thousands of signatures on petitions required by law to establish a new party. This book tells the story of how dedicated men and women, on shoestring budgets, often under great political and economic pressure to abandon their cause, changed the political landscape of New York State.

I'm not only pleased to have been able to tell this story, I'm also proud to have played a small part in it. In many ways I grew up with the Conservative Party. As a teenager in 1965, I handed out flyers on street corners in Brooklyn and Queens for Bill Buckley. In 1966, I worked out of a storefront in Flushing Queens for gubernatorial candidate Paul Adams and for local conservative nominees. In 1969, I distributed scores of "DUMP LINDSAY" bumper stickers. In November of 1970, I stood in the crowd at the Waldorf Astoria Hotel when Senator-elect James Buckley declared, "I am the voice of the new politics." And it was certainly one of the greatest honors of my life when in 1993 I was able to follow in the footsteps of William Buckley and accept the Party's nomination for the office of mayor of the City of New York.

I hope that I have done justice to the story of the thousands of men and women who were responsible for making the party a reality in 1962 and to those who during the next forty years proudly carried the Conservative Party banner into battle.

I must offer my very special thanks to my wife, Barbara. Without the untold hours she put into assembling the manuscript, this work would never have been completed.

I am grateful to those who assisted and guided me in the preparation of this book. For their critiques of the manuscript at various stages of its completion, I want to thank the following: Brad Miner, Pat Foye, Herbert Parmet, and J. Freedley Hunsicker.

I am also most grateful to Richard Brookhiser for agreeing to write the introduction. He was kind enough to take on the task as he was facing the publication of his new book, *America's First Dynasty: The Adamses, 1735–1918*.

Thanks go to Mike Long and Serphin Maltese for sitting for hours of interviews.

Heartfelt thanks as well go to the following friends: Joe Mysak, William F. Buckley Jr., Richard Rabatin, Robert Royal, Allen Roth, Paul Atanasio, Joe Darden, Nelson Warfield, Charles Woram, Rev. John Bonnici, Rev. George Rutler, Msgr. Michael Wrenn, Rev. Gerald Murray, Rev. John Coughlin, William Gavin, Michael Barone, Bonnie Siddons, Michael Uhlmann, Austin Ruse, Mrs. Eileen Long, Laura A. Schreiner, Shaun Marie Levine, James F. Kelly, James M. Gay, and Eileen M. Long.

In addition to the Conservative Party Papers that are housed at the research library of the State University of New York at Albany, four books were tremendously helpful in tying together the history of the party: J. Daniel Mahoney's, *Actions Speak Louder: The Story of the New York Conservative Party*, which covers the first six years and was indispensable in describing the organizational period of the party and its early successes; *The Unmaking of a Mayor*, Bill Buckley's delightful memoir of his 1965 run, provided valuable insights; Kevin Phillips's *The Emerging Republican Majority*, whose analysis of the shifting coalitions in New York had an important impact on my thinking; and *The Ungovernable City: John Lindsay and His Struggle to Save New York* by Vincent J. Cannato, published in 2000, offered outstanding work on the failure of liberalism in New York. Mr. Cannato's research was an essential resource in the writing of the chapter in this book that cover the Sixties. I believe his book will become a classic on New York politics, one that will stand proudly next to Robert Caro's *The Power Broker*.

I am also thankful to the following members of the Conservative Party who helped me in researching the party's history: Alice Gaffney, Barbara A. Keating, John McGloine, James P. Molinaro, Thomas Bolan, Anthony Rudmann, Leo Kesselring, Jack O'Leary, Tom and Viola Hunter, Jim Brewster, Mark Goret, John Andrew Kay, Daniel F. Fitzgerald, George F. McGuinness, Howard Lim, Stephen C. Miller, Al Hollands, Thomas E. Griffith, Vincent Downing, and Gerard Kassar.

My colleagues at The Philadelphia Trust Company had to put up with me during the writing of this book, and I am grateful to: Michael G. Crofton, Richard Sichel, Gerard Yandoli, Mary Walker, Matthew Walker, Joel Harpel, Tom Praiss, Barbara Civitella, Thomas Kelly, Marilyn Novak, Lindsay Lombardi, and Bill Lamb.

Finally, I offer my profound gratitude to two professors from Iona College: Dr. Larry Azar, emeritus professor of philosophy, who introduced me to the concepts of natural law, common good, and subsidiarity, and Edward F. Leonard, emeritus professor of political science and former Conservative Party candidate for lieutenant governor, who taught me the practical applications of subsidiarity.

I acknowledge my indebtedness to each of these people. I hope their kindness is vindicated by the present work. I, alone, am responsible for any errors, inaccuracies, or follies in what follows.

George J. Marlin
New Hyde Park, New York
February 2002

Introduction

I do not come to *Fighting the Good Fight*, George Marlin's encyclopedic and entertaining history of the New York Conservative Party, with perfect historical objectivity. The first campaigning I ever did was selling Buckley/Adams candy bars on my suburban street in Irondequoit, New York, for the Conservative Party ticket in 1970. I interrupted some neighbors weeding their dandelions, made a few sales, got some encouragement, and felt very civic-minded.

George Marlin had a harder time. In Chapter 5, his account of the 1965 New York mayor's race, he quotes without comment a passage from *The Ungovernable City*, Vincent Cannato's history of the Lindsay administration. John Lindsay, the great white hope of liberal Republicanism, was in an earlier three-way race against Democrat Abe Beame and Conservative William F. Buckley Jr. Cannato describes an outer-borough altercation. "[Sid] Davidoff" – then a Lindsay campaign aide, later a deputy mayor – "attacked a teenager named George Marlin . . . while Marlin was handing out 'Buckley for Mayor' literature in Flushing, Queens." They played rough in Noo Yawk in 1965. When Marlin ran for mayor himself on the Conservative Party line twenty-eight years later, they still did.

Any reader of this book will have trouble imagining its author as a teenager. Surely he was there, as an adult observer, when the founders of the party held their first confabulations, or when Malcolm Wilson took Nelson Rockefeller on his first listening tour of upstate in 1958. Marlin has both an antiquary's love for the minutiae of history, and an intellectual's desire to understand it. He records the vote totals of every major election, and the names of all the significant party faithful; he also seasons his narrative with analyses by academics and professionals like Michael Barone, Herbert Parmet, and Daniel Patrick Moynihan, to say nothing of himself. When you finish *Fighting the Good Fight*, you won't know everything Marlin knows about New York politics – that would be impossible – but you will know more than you did.

The paradox and the mission of the New York Conservative Party are simply stated. New York is one of the bluest of what we have learned, since 2000, to call blue states. Only a few – West Virginia, Maryland, Hawaii – elect more Democrats, and as the years pass New York's Democrats become more and more liberal. Yet New York is sown with red counties and neighborhoods – in the outer boroughs, the suburban lawn-belts, and the gun-and-truck countryside. There are parts of hippie/redneck upstate where half the bumper stickers say "Visualize World Peace," and the other half say "Charlton Heston is *My* President." Not only that: New York's long record of liberal misgovernment can, from time to time, make its blue citizens faint of heart, and susceptible to red arguments.

The Conservative Party exists to give those arguments expression and influence, and it has had notable successes. There were glorious, high-profile losses, such as Bill Buckley's run for mayor. Murray Kempton described him reading "his statement of principles in a tone for all the world that of an Edwardian resident commissioner reading aloud the 39 articles of the Anglican establishment to a conscript assemblage of Zulus." There were impressive victories, followed by impressive service – Jim Buckley, who won in 1970, gave New York six years as a 24-carat senator.

There have also been problematic victories. Alphonse D'Amato won three elections to the Senate, and his protégé George Pataki looks, as of this writing, as if he will win his third election to the governorship. Both men replaced egregious liberals – Jacob Javits, Mario Cuomo – and both had solid conservative achievements. Yet both men moved steadily and relentlessly to their left as time passed. When did they cross the line from buying time to selling out? Did the Conservative Party rebuke them sufficiently? Could it?

New York Mayor Rudy Giuliani posed the Conservative Party a different challenge – not the hero-mayor of September 11, but the liberal crime-stopper of September 10. The year Giuliani won his first election, the Conservative Party – and the author of this book – tried their best to beat him. It's easy to see why. Giuliani was (is) a deep-dyed liberal on many social issues, from abortion to gay rights, and though he talked a better game on taxes and spending, he had no obvious affinity for those issues. At the same time, he was also utterly serious about crime, and New Yorkers were dying in the streets. How does a party of principle cope with someone who attacks it from two directions at once? Does it fight for principle, or for the city? Can it do both?

It is no easy feat to keep a political machine (for that is what every political party is) true to its principles in a largely hostile environment for four decades. New York State badly needs conservative ideas. When the Conservative Party was founded, New York was still the Empire State; California had only just passed it in population, and the economy was diverse and strong. Now we have slipped behind Texas, and our economy is the rusty undercarriage of the rust belt. *Fighting the Good Fight* is a photo album of a lively past. But it also shows New York conservatives of the future how hard their task has been, and will be; and that, if they persist, they can do some good.

Richard Brookhiser
February 2002

Chapter 1

The First Listening Tour
A Short History of New York Politics

In May of 1958, two men climbed into a battered Buick in Westchester County, New York, to begin a driving tour of the state. Behind the wheel was Malcolm Wilson, 42, a member of the state assembly from Yonkers, and in the seat beside him was Nelson A. Rockefeller, 50, scion of the Eastern Establishment and gubernatorial hopeful.

The two men could hardly have been less alike, and neither of them imagined then as they began their journey to meet and greet New York's Republican leaders – assemblymen and senators in Albany, party chairmen in most of the state's sixty-two counties, and rank and file members and voters in cities, towns, and villages from Islip to Ithaca and Bear Mountain to Buffalo – that they were beginning an intense and patchy partnership that would last for sixteen years and transform New York politics.

Rockefeller would be elected four times, and Wilson would come to be known as "the eternal lieutenant governor," although he did succeed Rocky – albeit briefly – when the "perpetual governor" resigned in 1973. That's a very considerable political impact in itself, but you can argue that the help the conservative Wilson gave to the liberal Rockefeller led directly to the founding of the Conservative Party in 1962, since without the sober Wilson's competent counsel the ebullient and erratic Rocky might never have become such a successful politician, might never have spawned the "Rockefeller Republicanism" that convinced a diverse group of conservative New Yorkers that something had to be done to keep the Grand Old Party honest.

Wilson was a chain-smoking Navy veteran of World War II, a middle-class Irish Catholic who had worked his way through Fordham University and whose Jesuit-trained mind had earned him a reputation as a superb legislative writer and thinker during twenty years as a state legislator.[1] Nobody knew more about the complexities of state government than Malcolm Wilson; nobody could grasp the intricacies of the budget process better than he. And he was a nice guy to boot; a devoted husband and father; a quiet, decent man. But he was ambitious too, and when Rockefeller had appeared at Wilson's office a month before – and after three hours of chitchat – the younger man had decided the smart thing to do, the *political* thing, was to hitch his wagon to this WASP thoroughbred and see how fast and far they could run together.

"He convinced me," Wilson would recall later, "that he wasn't the flaming liberal some people had said."

For his part Wilson convinced Rockefeller that he needed to head upstate if he was really serious about winning the Republican nomination for governor, and Rocky *was* serious, although in his mind becoming governor of New York was just a first step towards becoming president of the United States.

Rockefeller, heir equally to the opulence of vast wealth and the obligations of noblesse oblige, was a non-smoking veteran of Washington politics, having served in the past three administrations: Franklin's, Harry's, and Ike's. Yes, he was on a first-name basis with all of them. What he lacked in knowledge of New York State's political infrastructure, he more than made up for with media savvy and available cash. He'd handled wartime propaganda in Latin America – with the help of George Gallup, no less – and nobody knew more about how to schmooze with the press than Nelson Aldrich Rockefeller; until Bill Clinton, nobody could seem quite so sincere being insincere as he could. Rocky philandered with the press as freely as he did with young ladies, but he was sensible enough to know that his success in New York politics depended upon an alliance with the brilliant Yonkers assemblyman.

So off they went.

"No baggage carriers, no sycophants, no P.R. men – nothing but us," Wilson once said, and then with a chuckle added:

"And I paid for it personally."[2]

It was a long trip – they covered thousands of miles together – and in between stops Wilson gave Rocky a not-so-short course on the history of Empire State politics.

The Goo-Goo Legacy

Nelson already knew a lot of that history (a version of it anyway), since his family had made so much of it. The Rockefellers had dominated New York's Republican Party (not to mention the state's economic and cultural life) for more than a century, and it was no surprise that Rocky turned out to be every bit as liberal as the Rockefeller family saga suggested he would be.

They did not call themselves liberal though. The Rockefellers preferred *progressive*. But beginning with John D. Rockefeller, Sr., the family's broadminded view is better described as *Social Darwinism*. During his recitation to Rocky, Wilson probably skipped over this part, the dark side of the "good-government" Mandarins, or "Goo-Goos" as they were known.

But the truth is that like other wealthy families – the Carnegies, the Eastmans, the Harrimans – the Rockefellers established philanthropic foundations that supported numerous questionable causes. Some may seem (and some surely were) inoffensive, including the Southern Education Conference, Riverside Church, and the Institute for Medical Research, but beneath the respectable façade was a very disgraceful skeleton. For example, Planned Parenthood and its founder Margaret Sanger were recipients of the financial aid of all these families, as was Long Island's Eugenics Laboratory. Indeed, these groups depended on the financial generosity of the Goo-Goos. Contemporary feminists who lionize – if not to say *canonize* – Sanger as the great, early champion of women's rights conveniently ignore her advocacy of eugenics. Birth control and abortion were important to Sanger not simply because they liberated women from male domination (or so it is said), but because they were such effective tools for purifying the race. In the April 1932 issue of her journal *Birth Control Review*, Sanger wrote that in order to "increase the general intelligence" in America, the government must undertake a program of what she called "segregation and sterilization." Certain "dysgenic" groups would be given the choice of either internment (segregation) or tubal ligation (sterilization) in order to insure that their "objectionable traits" not be passed on to subsequent generations. Some choice. Those who opted for segregation – a group Sanger assumed was "an enormous part of our population" (and included "five-million moral and mental degenerates," who presumably would have no choice) – were to be housed on "farmlands and homesteads." And for how long would they be segregated? Sanger's chilling proposal: "for the period of their entire lives." As she succinctly put it elsewhere, what was needed was "more children for the fit, less from the unfit, that is the chief issue of birth control."

To Nelson's father, John D. Rockefeller, Jr., Sanger was a "heroine."[3]

And this was neither an extreme nor an isolated example of Goo-Goo patronage of those whose mission was to prove the physiological and cultural superiority of Anglo-Saxons. Their wealth and power were brought to bear on the promotion of the "science" of eugenic research as well as the politics of immigration reform. The new immigrants from Ireland, Italy, and Eastern Europe were more than simply distasteful to the Goo-Goos, they were a repulsive and dangerous assault on every aspect of American life, and as the "responsible class" it was the Goo-Goos' sacred duty to repel the invaders.[4] The Reverend Frank Marling of Manhattan's Second Avenue Presbyterian Church declared: "The vast hordes flocking to this land strike at our national life, which we count most precious, while the ballot gives them power which they know too well how to use."[5]

Theodore Roosevelt of New York and his friend Henry Cabot Lodge of Massachusetts, two men who epitomized the Progressive Era, mourned what in a 1916 book author and socialite Madison Grant had termed: *The Passing of the Great Race*. Teddy Roosevelt called his friend Grant's work a "capital book," and another fan would later write to Grant that, "The book is my Bible." Which is high praise indeed coming from Adolf Hitler. Grant was convinced that what he called "native American stock" would continue to predominate, but just to be sure he favored – and succeeded in helping to pass – the most restrictive immigration laws in American history. "Even if present in equal numbers," Grant wrote:

. . . one of the two contrasted types will have some small advantage or capacity which the other lacks toward a perfect adjustment to surroundings. Those possessing these favorable variations will flourish at the expense of their rivals and their offspring will not only be more numerous, but will also tend to inherit such variations. In this way one type gradually breeds the other out. In this sense, and in this sense only, do races change.

This is Darwin with a heavy dose of Malthus.

Brooks Adams (the grandson and great-grandson of presidents, and with Lodge and Roosevelt one of the "three musketeers" of American progressivism) convinced his more politically successful friend Roosevelt to champion the sterilization of the "criminal class." Roosevelt did, and he also scolded the less-enlightened Goo-Goos for committing "race suicide." (Specifically, he was upset that Harvard graduates were producing only one-half to two-thirds of their original number. Madison Grant's confidence in Anglo-Saxon supremacy depended upon large WASP families.) "Someday," Roosevelt wrote to Charles Davenport, director of the Eugenics Record Office, "we must realize that the prime duty, the inescapable duty of the good citizen of the right type is to leave his or her blood behind him in the world."[6]

For his part, Davenport received numerous grants from the Rockefellers, including one earmarked to study feeble-minded inmates of state institutions with an eye toward taking "more vigorous steps to diminish the number of them who are reproduced through bad heredity."

To implement these views, the third musketeer, Henry Cabot Lodge, introduced in the United States Senate draconian legislation sponsored by the Immigration Restriction League. Lodge, a former Mugwump (one of the dissident Republicans who supported Democratic presidential candidates they considered more reform-minded than GOP nominees), hectored his congressional colleagues about their underestimation of the threat to America posed by the "immigration of people of those races far removed in thought and speech and blood from the men who have made this country what it is."[7] These laws were based on the notion that Anglo-Saxons were the only true Americans.

These "Yankee" Republicans championed various progressive causes throughout the late nineteenth and early twentieth centuries. On the positive side, they were the first conservationists and succeeded in creating America's national-parks system and in constructing most of its great museums of natural history. Later on, however, their Puritan heritage led them to support Prohibition, which has been described as a veiled attempt "on the part of those [the Yankee Republicans] seeking Protestant political supremacy."[8]

New York's progressive Republicans led by Roosevelt, Charles Evans Hughes, and Henry L. Stimson, viewed their movement as a means of managing the industrial, political, and cultural upheaval sweeping the nation. Their hope was to maintain their privileged role as the ruling class without alienating the mob.

Stimson, secretary of state in the Hoover Administration and War Secretary under Franklin D. Roosevelt, summed up the progressive Republican position:

> To me it seems vitally important that the Republican Party, which contains, generally speaking, the richer and more intelligent citizens of the country, should take the lead in reform and not drift into a reactionary position. If, instead, the leadership should fall into the hands of either an independent party, or a party composed, like the Democrats, largely of foreign elements and the classes which will immediately benefit by the reform, and if the solid business Republicans should drift into new obstruction, I fear the necessary changes could hardly be accomplished without much excitement and possible violence.[9]

By the end of the World War I, with the Harding-Coolidge "Return to Normalcy," the progressive Republican movement declined, and many of those who adhered to its principles moved to the Democratic Party. With the election of Al Smith as governor of New York in 1918, New York's Democrats cemented an alliance of "intellectual" progressives and neighborhood ethnics and dominated the state's political life for twenty-two of the next twenty-four years.

Great Awakenings

It could not have been easy for Nelson Rockefeller to hear any part of this from a veteran politico such as Malcolm Wilson. To Rocky, leadership was an aristocratic responsibility, a right and a duty of the Rockefeller family, and like his progressive forbearers forbears, Nelson was bred to hold career politicians in contempt.

"He loves businessmen," Manhattan Republican boss Vincent F. Albano would say after closely observing the Rockefeller style.

"He thinks people in politics are not bright – why didn't they go into private industry and make it?"[10]

Nelson believed in the *New York Herald Tribune*'s brand of liberal, eastern Republicanism, which is to say: "concessive on domestic issues where New Deal reforms were concerned and broadly international as well as rather specifically Anglophile in foreign affairs."[11]

Wilson, on the other hand, viewed the political world from a significantly different perspective. He entered the legislature at an early age because he wanted to give something back to the neighborhood, parish, and family that provided him with the virtues he needed to attain a slice of the American pie. It has been said that he "stood as a practitioner of what has been called the 'Great Tradition' of politics; maintaining justice through a healthy tension of order and freedom."[12]

Opposed to the "social engineers," he championed the Roman Catholic concept of *subsidiarity*, which maintains that "human life proceeds most intelligently and creatively when decisions are made at the local level closest to concrete reality."[13]

Wilson also sensed political opportunities in the growing discontent he detected within the ethnic strongholds of New York's Democratic Party. He would have agreed with historian Herbert Parmet's observation that years of domination by liberal Democrats had begun to alienate the political allegiances of inner-city Catholic voters:

> . . . the Smith and Farley rebellions, the condemnation of Franco by liberals, opposition of reformers to machine politicians, the party's association with left-wing labor unions . . . inevitably colored the election returns. [Franklin] Roosevelt's greatest losses were among the Irish.[14]

The post-war era brought additional Catholic defections. Polish and other Eastern Europeans blamed the Democrats for the "sell-out of Yalta," and the Catholic Church's opposition to communism did nothing to help Democrats who posed for snapshots with "Uncle" Joe Stalin. It was the beginning of a new Great Awakening that would culminate in the election of Ronald Reagan in 1980.

But in early 1958, Assemblyman Wilson had simply envisioned himself as the Republican nominee for governor. He had paid his dues to the party, had distinguished himself as chairman of the Codes Committee, and had come to believe it was time the Republicans turned to a Catholic to head the ticket. But Wilson was also cognizant of his one great weakness: money, or rather the lack of it. There was no way he could muster campaign funds sufficient to match the resources of the Democratic incumbent, millionaire Averill Harriman. All the pundits expected Governor Harriman to run the kind of well-financed, well-organized race that would establish him as an early claimant to his party's 1960 presidential nomination. Wilson saw no way he could compete.

So it was that he came to embrace the long view, came to side with Rockefeller, and came to be rewarded with the second spot on the Republican ticket. He chose to believe his new friend Nelson's dream: that Rocky would be in the White House by 1965 at the latest, and that he (Wilson) would become governor through succession. It was the backdoor approach, to be sure, but it was his best – if not to say his only – shot at fulfilling his own dream of becoming New York's chief executive. And he did enter the governor's mansion through the backdoor, although it took nearly a decade longer than he had hoped, and then his stay was all too short.

But back to chauffeur Wilson's 1958 sightseeing tour. It was not just a drive to meet political leaders; it was also the first course in Rockefeller's education about New York State's political, cultural, and economic diversity.

"During our automobile trips," Wilson recalled, "[Rocky's] eyes were opened to the range and beauty of the wide areas of our state: the smaller cities, the towns and villages, the breathtaking beauty of the Finger Lakes area and many of our state parks, and the South Tier counties out to Westfield on Lake Erie at the extreme western edge of Chautauqua County. That experience was immensely helpful to him when he undertook his responsibilities as Governor."[15]

Rockefeller learned about agriculture in the logging camps of Glen Falls, Lake Placid's maple companies, and Steuben County's dairy farms. He learned about the era's high-tech industries at the Xerox, Eastman Kodak, and Bausch and Lomb labs in Rochester. He saw the Steuben Glass works in Corning. He toured the General Electric Research and Development Center in Schenectady and the steel factories in Lackawanna. He watched shipping on the St. Lawrence Seaway, the Great Lakes, and the Erie Canal, and he marveled at eastern Long Island's aviation construction industry. He saw a New York that in 1958 was at the apex of its economic might.

He was wide-awake now, and much of the enthusiasm he showed in his campaign was utterly sincere.

The Political Landscape

New York was the leading industrial state in the nation, with a population of 16.7 million and, more important in terms of its influence on the nation's politics, it possessed the largest block of electoral votes at forty-three. Twenty-five of America's top fifty companies were headquartered in New York, and nearly 2 million people were employed in manufacturing. The state's industrial base was diverse, both in terms of size and importance: apparel and textiles topped the list followed by printing, food production, various kinds of machinery, diverse chemicals, fabricated metals, and transportation equipment.[16]

Rockefeller learned during his visits to forty-nine of the state's sixty-two counties, that there were in reality three New Yorks:

* The ever-bustling Greater City of New York – the "Naked City" with its 8 million people in five boroughs. Greater New York was the nation's leader in economic activity. Twenty-six percent of all employment was in manufacturing with printing, publishing, and apparel leading the way. And the city's arts and culture, especially in television production, made it the world's communications hub.
* The rapidly growing suburban areas of Nassau, Rockland, Suffolk, and Westchester counties. In 1946, the combined population of the suburbs stood at 1.25 million. By 1960, thanks in large measure to home loans provided by both the GI Bill and the F.H.A., the area skyrocketed 133 percent to a population of nearly 3 million. The boom came from second- and third-generation descendants of the immigrants who had so frightened the Rockefellers a half century earlier. These Italian-American, Irish-American,

and other hyphenated Americans, many of them World War II veterans, began raising families and commuting every day to New York City.
* The other fifty-three upstate counties, with 6 million people and some of most gorgeous real estate anywhere in America. Buffalo, Rochester, Elmira, Syracuse; the northern St. Lawrence region and the Mohawk Valley; the Capital District (Albany) and the Mid-Hudson Area. The whole of Upstate New York was as economically diverse as any region in the United States. It had heavy industry, manufacturing, high-tech R&D, agriculture, and dairy. There were glass factories, paper mills, electronics facilities, pottery kilns, mines producing iron ore, hydroelectric power plants, textile mills, furniture makers, craftsmen making rugs and footwear.[17]

Rockefeller also learned that religion, race, and ethnicity continued to define New York society. In 1958, one in four immigrants in the United States resided in New York State. Huge numbers of Austrians, Germans, Irish, Italians, Poles, and Russians helped shape the state's diversity.[18]

But Wilson made very sure that Rockefeller got to know the make-up of the State Republican Party – that after all was the main point of their trip. The many hours driving gave Wilson ample time to lecture Rocky on the leadership, membership, and recent history of the State Republican Party.

The Republican Depression, from La Guardia to Dewey

Out of power in the 1920s and 1930s, New York Republicans joined the chorus of New Dealer "me-tooism." They did not oppose FDR's programs but insisted that Republicans had the experience and expertise to run those programs more efficiently and competently than members of the president's own party. In foreign policy they were staunch internationalists and supplied various Wall Street "Wise Men" (including Stimson, John McCloy) to FDR's State Department.

Almost immediately after FDR's victory over Herbert Hoover in 1932, Suffolk County's Republican chairman, W. Kingsland Macy, organized a successful coup and ousted the conservative friends of Hoover who had run New York's Republican organization, most notably Ogden L. Mills and Ruth Baker Pratt. Although Macy's attempt to undermine Republican Assembly Speaker Joseph A. McGinnis and the remaining party structure was initially unsuccessful, the conservative grip on party leadership was broken. For a time anyway. The reins of power would be recovered quickly by conservatives . . . only to be lost again in a single, disastrous stroke.

As the 1934 mid-term elections approached, upstate Congressman Bertrand H. Snell (who held the position of House minority leader), declared war on the Democrats, thundering that "the purpose of the Roosevelt Administration is the imposition of a Russianized form of government."[19]

Objecting to Macy's move to the left, his finagling of Republican state legislators to support state-specific "Little New Deal" programs such as the Temporary Emergency Relief Administration, and his move to give the 1934 Republican gubernatorial nomination to Democrat Samuel Seabury (a direct descendant of the first American Episcopal Bishop, who led the special investigation of corruption charges against Mayor Jimmy Walker's administration in 1931–1932), the Republican old guard turned to a candidate "who symbolized the spirit of uncompromising courageous opposition to the whole Roosevelt socialistic program" – the "Master Builder" Robert Moses.[20]

Moses had served as Governor Al Smith's secretary of state and, in the 1930s, as chairman of the Triborough Bridge Authority, as NYC Commissioner of Parks, as chairman of the State Council of Parks, and as Long Island State Park commissioner. He built most of the roads, tunnels, bridges, and parks New Yorkers utilize to this day, and the public revered him in his own day.

When the 1934 Republican State Convention met in Rochester, the conservatives took control, ousted Macy as chairman, and adopted a platform that the *World Telegram* described as "an uncompromising denunciation of the New Deal."[21]

But the popularity of both FDR and incumbent Governor Herbert Lehman and the unexpected ineptitude of Robert Moses as a candidate (he was described as setting "some kind of record for antagonizing people"[22]) proved to be a formula for a Republican catastrophe. Moses received 1,393,638 votes, but that was just a bit more than a third of the votes cast, and the party as a whole suffered the greatest defeat in New York State history. Lehman, whose margin of victory was 808,000 votes, carried upstate counties never before won by a Democrat. The Republicans lost control of both houses of the state legislature for the first time since the election of 1912.

In the aftermath of the disaster, liberal Republicans such as Macy, Kenneth Simpson of Manhattan, and Edwin Jaeckle of Erie County, seized the opportunity to realign the party and as historian Richard Norton Smith has described it, they "emerged to pick up the pieces and fashion a more liberal alternative to the New Deal and its local arm under Lehman."[23]

It was these Republican leaders who forced the party to swallow the radical left-winger, Fiorello La Guardia, as their New York City mayoral candidate.

The "Little Flower" is generally remembered for his eccentricities, such as attending fires, breaking the "artichoke racket," reading comics on the radio during a newspaper strike ("Gather round children and I will tell you about Dick Tracy"), and leading symphony orchestras. But there were other sides to this complex and ambitious man. As historian Thomas Kessner writes, "La Guardia [had] one open vice – he loved power. His lust for power colored his campaigns, his treatment of underlings, his aspirations for higher office, and ultimately it made an irascible, brittle, and deeply frustrated man of him."

La Guardia "sought power without apologies." He was called the "Little

Napoleon" or the "Midget Mussolini" and was accused of running "government by tantrum." He trusted no one and would easily turn on long-suffering advisers. For him, victory was all. When a shaken aide reported to La Guardia that their people were stuffing ballot boxes, he replied, "We must fight fire with fire – all is fair in love, war, and politics. They are stealing, cheating, and murdering us, and we must fight them on their own grounds."

La Guardia, who betrayed his Republican sponsors and endorsed FDR in 1936, introduced "questionable accounting schemes to cover the services that he had introduced." Deficits were dismissed as "entirely a bookkeeping transaction;" current expenses were switched "from tax levy funds to bonded debt;" and current bills were rolled over into the following year's budget. (By the way, it was exactly these kinds of financing gimmicks that brought the city to default in 1975.)

Thomas Kessner concludes: "By the time he left office, the city had been transformed into the colossal metropolis: it was saddled with debt, an infrastructure too expensive to maintain comfortably, dangerously expanding citizen expectations, and snowballing bureaucracy."[24]

It was these same Republican leaders who turned, in 1937, to Special Rackets Prosecutor Thomas E. Dewey as their candidate for district attorney in New York County. He was reluctant to run, but just five minutes before the municipal deadline for filing – and after his sixteenth scotch – he was persuaded to seek the office.[25] In November he handily beat Democratic opponent Harold Hastings, receiving 326,000 votes – 60 percent of the total cast.

A native of Michigan, Dewey stayed in New York after graduating from Columbia University Law School. He joined the U.S. attorney's office in 1931 and was later appointed by Governor Lehman as "Special Prosecutor for the Investigation of Organized Crime in New York City."

Dewey successfully prosecuted racketeers, destroyed Murder Incorporated, convicted mobster Lucky Luciano, and was memorialized in the film *The Racket Busters*, which starred Humphrey Bogart and Bette Davis.

Kenneth Simpson subsequently engineered Dewey's nomination for governor, and the crusading prosecutor came within 64,000 votes of beating liberal icon Herbert Lehman. Dewey received a remarkable 49 percent of the vote to Lehman's 50.1 percent.

In 1940, Dewey went to the Republican National Convention in Philadelphia with 360 first-ballot votes committed to him for the presidential nomination. Although his support rapidly faded and shifted to former Democrat Wendell Willkie, Dewey's showing was impressive.

Running for governor again in 1942, the Manhattan prosecutor clobbered Democratic gubernatorial nominee John Bennett and was elected to the first of three terms as governor of New York.

And what sort of Republican was Thomas Edmund Dewey? Some conservatives involved in New York politics admired Dewey's political acumen yet recognized his shortcomings. F. Clifton White, who served as executive secretary of the Republican Party, party chairman of Tomkins County, and deputy commissioner of Motor Vehicles during the Dewey years (and who later managed the conservative Draft Goldwater Committee and was a consultant in Conservative Party candidate James Buckley's successful campaign for the U.S. Senate) wrote that "if Dewey had one major shortcoming, it was his own lack of ideology. He was a pragmatist first and foremost, a man who believed in good government – honesty, integrity and getting things done efficiently."[26]

Organizationally, Dewey was a realist. From the moment he was elected, he made sure he gained a firm grasp on the State Republican Committee. *New York Times* political reporter, Warren Moscow, observed that Dewey:

> . . . assumed complete control of his party. County leaders who opposed him were broken by cold, hard-bitten use of the patronage of the governor's office. Legislators suffered a similar fate. He brooked no interference . . . for nearly a quarter of a century [Dewey] was the cold, efficient, behind the scenes boss of the Republican Party and the state. He directed the election of legislative leaders, passed on nominees for the judiciary selected statewide tickets. . . . His domination of the party was more complete that Charles F. Murphy's had ever been in Tammany Hall.[27]

Because of his control over the state legislature, Dewey had what amounted to a "pre-veto" system. In order to avoid the public appearance of squabbles that would arise if he might have to veto bills or budget line items, he simply informed the leadership which bills would live or die in committee.

There were several levels to Dewey's success.[28] Out in the political cold for so long, many Republicans were only too happy to fall in line to get their meal tickets. It was not a good time for conservatives.

Governor Dewey led the charge nationally to win control of the soul of the Republican Party from "Mr. Republican," the conservative Robert Alfonso Taft of Ohio. Republicans were hungry to retake the White House, and, as one commentator has put it, "Dewey's promise of 'me-tooism' in the realm of social justice, is also a factor, indeed an essential one, in his success." Many Republicans relished the thought that they might appropriate for their party what had been a winning issue for Democrats.

Dewey brought many like-minded men onto the political scene: liberal Republicans such as Irving Ives, William Rogers, Herbert Brownell, Hugh Scott, Louis Lefkowitz, and Jacob J. Javits. They in turn showed him their gratitude. To a man they frowned upon Democrats who tolerated inner-city political bosses and ethnic-urban political machines. They longed for the return of the progressive

Republican elitism of the early twentieth century. Here's how Javits summed up his personal view:

> Even had I not been repelled by the corruption of Tammany politics in New York City, I doubt that I could have allied myself with the party whose national power depended to a great extent on a regional political and social system that kept black citizens in a state of subservience and often fear. As I saw it then, northern Democrats who castigated southern racism while reaping political benefits (such as congressional committee chairmanships) from the Democratic majorities provided by the Solid South, were not entitled to the mantle of liberalism they claimed as their right.[29]

Not for nothing has Tom Dewey been called the "father of the tradition of progressive Republicanism."[30] Like Nelson Rockefeller, Dewey has been aptly described as a "pragmatic liberal" or a "positive liberal."[31]

They earned this label because they held the following beliefs:

* All problems may be solved, and the solutions require a big, activist government.
* The executive branch of government has the main responsibility for leadership.
* The executive branch must trump legislative majorities, because they are *provincial* whereas the executive is *enlightened*.[32]

Pennsylvania Senator Hugh Scott (who served as U.S. Senate minority leader and chairman of the Republican National Committee) was grateful for Dewey's role:

> The rise of the moderates in the party was due as much to Dewey in New York as to any other factor. He was a young man with new ideas, who had proven that he alone among Republicans could command a heavy vote in the urban, Democratic areas of his state. Dewey's influence and alliances led to a strengthening of moderate forces in other states, for example, Kuchel in California, and Hatfield in Oregon. Most of the new moderates in the party took their cues from Dewey in New York.[33]

On the National level, Dewey and his liberal colleagues in the northeast controlled Republican National Conventions from 1940 to 1952. They were aided by old progressive party organizations in Michigan, Minnesota, Oregon, and California.[34] These were the Republicans who constantly made concessions to the New Deal and Fair Deal programs. They accepted "the inevitability of gradualism," always with the justification that they were better qualified to run the programs.

In New York, those who were promoted by Dewey to important positions (for example, Assembly Speaker Oswald Heck, state senate majority leader – and future U.S. Senator and 1954 gubernatorial candidate – Irving Ives, Assembly Ways & Means Chairman Abbott Low Moffat) were "forward looking and opposed to the old guard."[35]

As a result of the booming war economy, Governor Dewey built up a surplus to the tune of $623 million. Instead of cutting taxes and returning the people's money, he had the legislature pass a law creating the Postwar Reconstruction Fund to which the surplus was transferred. The money was used to finance and expand various government social welfare programs and building projects, many of which were originally created by Lehman's "Little New Deal" for New Yorkers.[36]

On one occasion, Dewey commented that the "very clumsy Republicans" who attack "the Welfare State" only succeed in strengthening the Democratic hold over popular loyalties.[37] Dewey's preferred approach was to listen to liberal Democratic calls for enhanced government progress and, just when the opposition thought that it had hold of an appealing issue, to endorse the proposal, first tailoring it to fit *his* party's needs, and then secure its adoption by the legislature as a *Republican* measure.[38]

One or another conservative Republican did occasionally attempt to put a brake on the governor's programs, especially after Dewey's second presidential defeat in 1948. Some were growing weary of Dewey's constant hectoring of conservatives to "stop belly aching about the past" and begin realizing that government can't be a "cold and impartial empire." His constant reminder to conservatives to read the GOP's 1948 platform was equally irritating. "It must mean something," Dewey told them. "Unless it was designed to deceive, its various sections say and mean that we are a liberal and progressive party."[39]

When he introduced his 1949 budget that called for increases in the gasoline, business, and income taxes, Dewey sounded like a typical big-spending liberal: "My only criticism of this budget is that we are not doing enough," he told the political wags.

State Senator Walter J. Mahoney of Buffalo and five other Republican members found the courage to oppose the tax increases and to demand budget cuts. To the surprise of many, Dewey could not crush the revolt. Forced to give in, he cut $48 million from the budget, withdrew the proposed increase on gasoline and the 10 percent state income tax increase.

Although talked into running for a successful third term in 1950, Dewey lost his zest for the job. He did, however, use his clout at the 1952 Republican National Convention to stop his old nemesis, conservative Robert Taft, from receiving the presidential nomination. Committed to Eisenhower and working with local leader Frank Kenna, Dewey crushed Taft support in Queens County and delivered the New York delegation to Ike.

When Governor Dewey decided not to seek a fourth term in 1954, he hand-picked as his successor Senator Ives. Dewey was confident Ives would carry on his brand of progressive Republicanism. In a hard-fought battle against the Democrats' Averill Harriman, Republicans lost the governor's mansion in the closest state election in history. Harriman won with 49.6 percent to 49.4 percent for Ives. The difference was a razor thin margin of 11,000 votes. Dewey's choice for Attorney General, Jacob Javits, did beat Franklin D. Roosevelt, Jr., and the state legislature remained in Republican hands.

Of Morals and Machines

Even as Nelson Rockefeller was listening to Malcolm Wilson's lectures on the state's Republican history, a cultural revolt was brewing among a significant portion of New York's voting population. Left-wing politicians, bureaucrats, and commentators who believed that only economic influences shaped political decisions overlooked the revolt, but it was coming, and its implications were profound. They could not grasp "that our society is what Michael Novak calls a *trinitarian* polity. The underpinnings of this country are not merely a productive economic system and a representative political system, but also a system of moral and cultural values."[40] Novak joined a growing list of historians and sociologists who emphasized "that the energies shaping public life are emotional as well as rational, cultural as well as economic."[41]

More recently, political analyst Michael Barone, in *Our Country: The Shaping of America from Roosevelt to Reagan,* has rejected the liberal view that America's political history is the "story of progress on the road from nineteenth-century laissez-faire and isolationism to twentieth-century welfare statism and internationalism."[42] He argues that the person qua person makes a difference in the course of history, that actions based on cultural standards have had substantially greater impact on the political landscape than have economic factors. "The voting bases of the traditional Democratic and Republican Parties," Barone writes, "were primarily cultural; both drew allegiance from Americans who saw them not as promoters of their economic status, but as a protector of their way of life."[43] Although economics almost always plays some role in a person's political decisions, an individual's cultural foundations cannot be ignored. No matter what the struggle – Jeffersonians versus Hamiltonians, Jacksonians versus Whigs, or North versus South, and no matter what the controversy, immigration restriction, prohibition, civil rights, Vietnam, abortion or drugs – each has had significant cultural implications.

There exist in New York society cultural elites (progressive Republicans and reform Democrats) who are contemptuous of conservative, working-class values. Their ideological positions are not necessarily a function of wealth or schooling, but rather a shallow sophistication that rejects the populist position that people should be relied on to govern themselves. "Pessimism about people's ability to do well at [self-governance]," writes Jeffrey Bell in his 1992 work *Populism and Elitism*, "leads to a belief that the people should delegate the setting of standards to various elites – elected officials or, more often in recent years, judicial and bureaucratic elites appointed by the elected officials and accountable only tenuously to the people."[44]

The neighborhood has often been the target of social experimentation, because neighborhoods – and the conservative values that they preserve – instinctively resist attempts by elitists to manipulate human behavior. Andrew Greeley has suggested that elitists view the neighborhood as "a regression to more primitive and pre-modern ways of living. The neighborhood asserts the importance of the primordial, the local, the geographic, the familial against the demands of the bureaucratized, rationalized, scientific, corporate society. . . . The neighborhood is rejected by our intellectual and cultural elites because the neighborhood is not modern, and what is not modern is conservative, reactionary, unprogressive, unenlightened, superstitious, and just plain wrong."[45]

To grasp the change in political allegiance taking place in conservative, working class neighborhoods, it is essential to consider briefly the condition of the Democratic Party in 1958, the year in which W. Averill Harriman – banker, aviator, railroad executive, presidential advisor, ambassador, playboy, and polo star – was about to complete his first term as New York's forty-eighth Governor.

As noted above, he knew that to be taken seriously as a presidential contender in 1960 he had to have a spectacular re-election victory. This he believed was within his reach. After six years of Republicans in the White House, all the polls indicated that the Democratic Party was headed toward large gains in the mid-term elections.

But as we have also noted, a shadow was falling between the old-time Democrats, who represented the neighborhood clubhouse, and the liberal elite, who believed in reform at any cost. The party was experiencing its own cultural crisis, and it appeared that the upcoming Democratic State Convention would be a battleground.

During the first half of the twentieth century, Democratic political machines ruled most of urban America. Daniel Patrick Moynihan, pundit and politician, has written that the Irish have a genius for organization. The Irish drafted the blueprints for most of the big-city political machines, and – being Roman Catholic – they were spontaneous advocates of subsidiarity. They built from the bottom up: neighborhoods were organized block by block, through parishes, clubhouses, saloons, and candy stores. This was the system that provided services and dispensed patronage, contracts, and franchises to the faithful.

New York City's much-maligned Tammany Hall stands as the premier example of a political machine. At its best Tammany was represented by the likes of professional pol George Washington Plunkitt (1842–1942), who made the city work through "honest graft"; at its worst by Boss William Tweed (1823–1878), who made the city work almost entirely for himself and a few cronies. Plunkitt helped thousands of immigrants assimilate into mainstream American life. Tweed, ultimately unable to govern, found his lease on city hall terminated with a jail sentence.

Decades before the birth of the "poverty industry" and public-policy specialists, the machine pols realized that the job of local government was to provide basic services. Their compassion was apolitical; ideology did not enter the picture. But the need to forge alliances did. As more than one historian pointed out, the system worked because immigrants trying to gain a foothold in their new country received aid without losing their dignity.[46] George Reedy, President Lyndon B. Johnson's Press Secretary, correctly noted that "one of the great strengths of the political machines was their treatment of poor people as human beings rather than 'cases.'"[47]

Tammany's Charles Francis Murphy (1858–1924) was the very model of the boss. He remained in power for decades because he felt a sense of civic responsibility to his wards. The reformers, who tried to claim the credit for saving the cities, were in Plunkitt's words, "short-lived morning glories." The good government patricians' hold on office has always been brief. Instead of rolling up their sleeves and mixing it up with the people, they have appointed blue-ribbon committees to study charter reform.

Tammany Hall on the other hand, as even *The New York Times* admitted in 1923, "wore human spectacles." The Goo-Goos failed because they "attempted to deal with . . . municipal government as though it were a private corporation, and they a board of directors whose only aims were efficiency and economy. [They forgot] that a city administration must have a heart as well as a head."[48]

It was the "Charles Murphy Institute" that permitted men like Al Smith, Robert Wagner, and James Farley to become major players in the political process. Murphy explained it this way:

> Formerly, it was difficult for young men of talent and ambition to get into public life. They were discouraged at every step by those already in who wished to keep the influence within as narrow bounds as possible. I encouraged the selection of young men for public office, particularly for legislative positions, encouraged them to develop their talent, to keep free from demoralizing influences, to speak their minds, do what was right and develop character and a reputation which would do credit to themselves and reflect favorably upon the organization and my leadership. These young men went out into public life and made good. . . . They gave you a different viewpoint of what Tammany Hall is and its aims and aspirations.[49]

The reign of Boss Murphy begat Al Smith, and it was Smith who as governor of New York managed to implement a state agenda that embodied the principle of subsidiarity. Unlike the progressives, he was not embarrassed to deal with politicians and to bargain for programs that enhanced the quality of life in the neighborhoods. His record shows it, featuring as it does the construction of hospitals for the indigent and mentally ill, a state teachers college, a network of parks, 5,000 miles of roads, as well as social legislation that eliminated sweat shops, regulated child and female labor, established a forty-eight-hour work week, created workmen's compensation and widow's pensions, and instituted a primary system.

Urban policy analysts Edward Banfield, James Q. Wilson, and Daniel P. Moynihan all agree that urban political machines have tended to reflect an ethnic group's values and social standing.[50] Boss Murphy was naturally conservative and understood the needs and culture of the neighborhoods. His machine was built on meeting the needs of the diverse immigrants throughout the city. After a 1911 fire at the Triangle Shirtwaist Company killed 146 young women, Murphy's support for Al Smith's safety code legislation was, in analyst Michael Barone's view, "based more on political demands than socialist theory."[51]

The machine reached the height of its powers in the 1920s. Yet even as they savored the presidential nomination of one of their own – Al Smith – the seeds of their destruction had been planted. The passage of the 1921 and 1924 Restriction Acts on immigration, the result of pressure from nativists and liberal Republicans, cut off the machines' lifeline. The New Deal brought in the social engineers, who were ruthlessly willing to repress the party's traditional organization. When Al Smith walked out of the 1936 Democratic convention, he was accused of sour grapes. But in a speech that fall, he revealed the real reason he bolted: "The Regulars were out on a limb holding the bag, driven out of the party, because some new bunch that nobody ever heard of in their life before came in and took charge and started planning everything."[52]

New York's Democratic Party emerged in the late 1940s and the 1950s as the home for social engineers. Searching for a new intellectual liberal hero, they stumbled across Adlai Stevenson of Illinois, an odd choice. Stevenson had earned gentlemen's C's at Princeton and at Northwestern Law School and was more a socialite than an egghead. Except for the *Social Register*, he was not a particularly voracious reader.

Furthermore, he wasn't all that liberal: he opposed national health insurance, opposed revision of Taft-Hartley, opposed increases in the minimum wage and Social Security, and avoided civil rights issues. Stevenson was, however, embraced by the new generation of reformers because he was, "the first leading Democratic politician to become a critic rather than a celebrator of middle-class culture – the prototype of the liberal Democrat who would judge ordinary Americans by an abstract standard and find them wanting."[53] Liberal journalist Jack Newfield admitted in 1989: "Stevenson was a curious kind of hero. He was not a champion of the workers or the little guy. . . . Stevenson's appeal resided more in his intellect and wit, his patrician gentility, his melancholy dignity."[54] His cultural elitism and contempt for the conservative blue-collar worker engendered a new generation of political progeny who grew up not with the fragmented local politics which Franklin Roosevelt had grown up with, but instead with the centralized national politics which had grown up with the large central government produced by Roosevelt's New Deal and wartime policies.

Carmine De Sapio, Tammany Hall's Grand Sachem, looked forward to a 1958

Democratic State Convention that would further enhance his reputation as kingmaker. This Lower East Side Italian-American, who picked up the machine's pieces after the 1950 resignation of Mayor William O'Dwyer, anticipated re-electing a governor and electing a U.S. Senator in 1958.

To consolidate his power, De Sapio implemented the "big tent" theory. He supported neighborhood regulars in local races while encouraging liberals to run in statewide races. In 1954 he was responsible for the election of Harriman, and he organized Robert F. Wagner's mayoral victories in 1953 and 1957. De Sapio viewed himself as nothing more than a political mechanic. "The extent of his ideological commitment may be measured by his pronouncement to the Holy Name Society Communion Breakfast of the New York Sanitation Department that 'there is no Mother's Day behind the Iron Curtain.'"[55]

At the 1958 state Democratic convention in Buffalo, De Sapio pushed Manhattan District Attorney Frank Hogan for the U.S. Senate nomination. In his judgment, the ticket needed an Irish-Catholic to balance the WASP Harriman and the Jewish candidate for Comptroller, Arthur Levitt.

Although Harriman and Wagner initially supported Atomic Energy Commissioner Thomas E. Murray for the spot because he had a background in foreign affairs, they were neutral at the convention since there was nothing really wrong with the Hogan candidacy.

Liberal reformers, including Eleanor Roosevelt and Herbert Lehman, however, were appalled by the "boss-controlled" convention. Hogan's nomination and Harriman's passive acceptance of the "balanced" ticket were unacceptable. Ethnic ticket balancing to the reformers was a corrupt act.[56]

Revenge of the Liberal Republicans

While the Democrats were battling, Nelson Rockefeller was moving rapidly to lock up the Republican nomination.

Although others within the Republican ranks fancied themselves gubernatorial material – Malcolm Wilson, of course, but also Assembly Speaker Oswald Heck, staunch conservative Senate Majority Leader Walter Mahoney, and former National Republican Chairman Leonard Hall – none could put together the financial wherewithal to run a credible race.

Rockefeller's association with the Roosevelt and Truman administrations did not make him a favorite of upstate New Yorkers, but opposition was neutralized by Malcolm Wilson's support, by the dim prospects of battling Rockefeller money, and by the gloomy predictions of a Democratic landslide. In August, when the Republican state convention met, Rockefeller, whom many inside Republicans labeled "a New Deal Democrat in Republican clothing," was unanimously nominated.

Rockefeller hit the ground running with the best-financed campaign organization in the state's history. "When he went upstate before conservative audiences,

Rockefeller hammered away at the Harriman administration's deficit spending. But the Democratic stronghold of New York City provided a milieu that drew out the many facets of his political personality. There he campaigned as a liberal drawing on the connections and alliances his family had established in three generations of living and giving."[57]

It was the race of the millionaires with Rocky (as he was now known) spending a record breaking $1.8 million to Harriman's $1.1 million. Nationally syndicated columnist Stewart Alsop, described the race this way: "The voters of the New York State are being asked to choose between a couple of extremely rich Siamese twins."[58]

While both men adhered to a common liberal creed – strong on activist government and civil rights – Harriman was the weaker of the two candidates. "Unwilling to stand up to De Sapio and the party machine, but reluctant to offend the party's influential liberal wing, Harriman was a victim of his own equivocation, berated and bullied by both sides."[59]

In the fall, hordes of liberal Democrats deserted their party's ticket. Nelson Rockefeller adhered to his pollsters' advice to run as a "personality" not as a Republican. Columnist Mary McGrory put it best: "Rockefeller has been the life of the party this fall but he's desperately hoping voters don't remember which party."[60] Rocky attracted disenchanted Democrats by describing his liberal vision of New York.

Although nationally Democrats picked up thirteen slots in the U.S. Senate, forty-seven house seats, and nine governorships, Harriman lost to Rockefeller by more than a half-million votes. Republican Kenneth Keating beat District Attorney Hogan in the Senate race by a much narrower margin. Nelson Aldrich Rockefeller would now possess the power to continue what he called "New York's proud progressive tradition of services to our people."

Chapter 2

Athwart History

The Rebirth of American Conservatism

At the end of the Second World War, the conservative political movement was in a shambles; it was – to paraphrase the old joke about the Holy Roman Empire – not conservative, not political, and not a movement. When critic Lionel Trilling published his much admired book, *The Liberal Imagination* (1950), he gleefully observed that:

> In the United States at this time liberalism is not only the dominant but even the sole intellectual tradition. . . . [T]he conservative impulse and the reactionary impulse do not, with some isolated and ecclesiastical exceptions, express themselves in ideas but only in action or in irritable mental gestures which seem to resemble ideas.

Trilling was wrong, but he wasn't far wrong.

As the good professor seemed to suggest, there were some conservative activists, but they had yet to recover from the staggering electoral losses and humiliations suffered during the Depression. The post-war world was in transformation, however, and no change would have quite the impact, both politically and culturally, as the rediscovery of a "conservative" intellectual tradition and the birth of a true Conservative Movement.

The Rising Phoenix

You must recall just how bad it had been. Back in 1932, Republicans had lost not only the White House but also thirteen Senate seats and ninety seats in the House. In the 1934 midterm elections, when the incumbent president's party would have been expected to lose seats, the party of FDR bucked the trend, and Republicans lost nine more Senate and nine more House seats, hitting a low of just twenty-five in the Senate and 117 in the House.

Then it got worse.

The New Deal was in high gear as the 1936 elections came to a climax. FDR received 532 electoral votes to Kansas Governor Alf Landon's eight. Congressional Republicans managed to lose seven more seats in the Senate (falling to a 76-16 minority) and twenty-one more seats in the House (which made them a whopping 331-89 minority). When the new government convened in January of 1937, President Roosevelt had a veto-proof Congress, and the Republicans were an impotent minority, seemingly on the verge of extinction.

But like Icarus of Greek mythology, FDR overreached. Deciding to seize on his apparent invincibility, he quickly proposed a plan to pack the Supreme Court with justices who would not derail any New Deal programs, no matter how antithetical to tradition those programs might be.

February 5, 1937. That was the date on which he proposed his court-packing plan, and it may very well be the date on which a new conservatism was born. A spontaneous coalition between conservative southern Democrats ("Boll Weevils" or, as a short-lived political party, Dixiecrats) and the few remaining Conservative Republicans derailed the New Deal Express.

By 1938 there was a definite change in the political landscape. In the mid-term elections Republicans gained seven Senate seats and seventy House seats. The conservative Republican phoenix was rising from the ashes of New Deal liberalism.

Among those elected that year was a man who was unquestionably the most formidable member of the 1939 congressional freshman class, Senator Robert A. Taft. The son of President (and Chief Justice) William Howard Taft, Bob Taft was a man of intelligence and integrity, and, in this turbulent political era so dominated by liberal Democrats, he would prove to be a remarkable public servant, remarkable especially for his conservatism.

Throughout his 1938 campaign, Taft demonstrated to the voters of Ohio that the New Deal had failed to restore prosperity.

"In the mistaken belief," Taft declared, "that government can remove all poverty, redistribute all wealth and bestow happiness on every citizen, measures are proposed which must destroy American democracy."[1]

He defeated incumbent Democrat and New Deal supporter Senator Robert J. Buckley. In remarks following his victory, Senator-elect Taft made clear to the press that he had won because of his pointed analysis of New Deal failures:

> There has been some suggestion that the result of the November election in Ohio was determined by local issues. As a matter of fact [I] based my whole campaign on an anti-New Deal platform. We did not criticize merely New Deal methods. We openly asked the people to repudiate the basic principles which the New Deal adopted during the last two years, the principles of planned economy and government regulation of commerce, agriculture, and industry and the arbitrary power to carry out such a program.[2]

Taft was immediately accepted as a member of the inner-circle of the Senate, and with Democrats Harry Byrd of Virginia and Richard Russell of Georgia, he controlled the flow of legislation and led the Congressional revolt against the New Deal. As political analyst Samuel Lubell pointed out, Roosevelt's third- and fourth-term victories "obscured the fact that the last major measure of a New Deal nature which he was able to get through Congress was the Wage and Hours Law in mid-1938."[3]

While Taft and the other conservatives – Republican and Democrat – succeeded on the congressional level, they could not get the national Republican Party to embrace the insight that their legislative coalition was simply a reflection of the electoral mood in the nation at large. Three times Taft lost the Republican presidential nomination to the liberal wing of the party, due mostly to the power of the so-called Eastern Establishment. Party leaders looked upon the congressional conservatives as whining, moralistic cowboys who preferred to "die with their boots on" rather than win elections. The East Coast wing depicted themselves as the sort of middle-of-the-road Republicans who could be victorious at the polls, as the *only* Republicans who could win nationally. Hence they turned to Alf Landon, Wendell Willkie, and Tom Dewey as pragmatic candidates whose liberalism was clearly what American voters wanted. Who could possibly beat FDR but an FDR manqué?

Then in the 1946 mid-term elections – campaigning with the slogan "Had Enough?" – a few conservative Republicans attempted to appeal to an American electorate weary of so many years of Democratic rule. They succeeded. Republicans picked up thirteen seats in the Senate and fifty-five in the House, and for the first time in fourteen years took control of both branches of Congress.

During the sessions of the 80th Congress, conservative Republicans cut the national budget, reduced income taxes, and passed the Taft-Hartley Act, which ended the closed shop and contained the "right to work" clause.

This same Congress approved the Marshall Plan and supported the Truman Doctrine in the fight against communism. And after President Truman admitted in July of 1947 that there were some 3,000 disloyal federal workers, the Republican-controlled House Un-American Activities committee began to examine Communist influence in government and the media. The HUAC record was uneven at best, but it did lead to the August 1948 testimony of Whittaker Chambers. His evidence, which included the revelation that State Department employee Alger Hiss was a spy, shook the very foundations of the Washington establishment.

Although the 80th Congress had a fine conservative record, this was not enough to put Senator Taft over the top at the 1948 Republican National Convention. As we noted in Chapter One, the liberals who controlled the proceedings handily re-nominated New York's Governor Dewey, and wrote a "progressive" platform to support his second failed candidacy. Sensing there were significant differences between the members of the 80th Congress and the policies expressed in the Republican platform, President Truman called a July 26 special congressional session from which he demanded the enactment of "liberal programs – civil rights, price controls, the Wagner-Taft-Ellender housing bill – which Truman had been pushing and which were mentioned in Dewey's Republican platform."[4] As expected, the newly powerful congressional coalition of conservative Republicans and southern Democrats stopped passage of the measures, and thus gave Truman the opportunity to run against, as he called it, the "Do-Nothing" Congress. Even with the Henry Wallace Progressives and the Dixiecrats deserting the Democratic Party, Dewey's "me-tooism" failed to excite the nation, and Truman won election in his own right in the greatest upset in American presidential history.

Right Minds at the Right Time

Conservatism is not simply a vision of politics, even if politics is the sphere in which the word is most commonly used. As political conservatives were beginning to win races for everything from county clerk to United States Senator, there were other conservatives actively attempting to define what we mean by *conservative*.

In late 1944, for instance, Fredrick Hayek's *The Road to Serfdom* was published in America for the first time, after having created a sensation in Britain. Hayek, who was to win the Nobel Prize for Economics in 1974, promoted this fundamental insight: "Planning leads to dictatorship, the direction of economic activity necessitates the suppression of freedom."[5] On the front-page of *The New York Times Book Review*, journalist Henry Hazlitt declared that *The Road to Serfdom* "is one of the most important books of our generation."

Also in 1944, Felix Morley, William Henry Chamberlain, Henry Regnery, and Frank Hanighen founded a conservative weekly newsletter, *Human Events*, which by 1946 had nearly 3,000 subscribers.

In 1946 Henry Hazlitt's *Economics in One Lesson* appeared and had a wide circulation. Hazlitt's premise was the essence of simplicity:

> The art of economics consists in looking not merely at the immediate but
> at the longer effects of any act or policy; it consists in tracing the conse-
> quences of that policy not merely for one group but for all groups.

The "Chicago School" of conservative economists (associated with the University of Chicago), who were influenced by Hayek and Ludwig von Mises, began to present eloquent defenses of the free market. Frank Knight's *Freedom and Reform,* published in 1947, was the School's first salvo. As one commentator has summed up the Chicago view: "Through economic liberty we recognize the limits of human knowledge; in state planning we ignore those limits."

In 1947, Henry Regnery opened a publishing house dedicated to issuing books "which didn't necessarily fit the liberal ideology which so dominated publishing as to constitute a particularly effective form of censorship."[6]

Richard Weaver's *Ideas Have Consequences* was published in 1948. Dense but rewarding, Weaver's book argued that the world is real and men are free, and that the decline of civilization was due fundamentally to "unintelligent choice." The plethora of narcissistic choices had brought us to the edge of moral anarchy, in other words, to relativism.

But the high-water mark of renascent conservatism came with the publication in 1953 of Russell Kirk's monumental *The Conservative Mind*.

Kirk's tome (now in its seventh edition) is a sweeping history that from its first publication gave coherence to the conservative philosophical and political movement, where, perhaps, none had existed before. Kirk laid out his vision of the fundamental principles of conservatism:

* Belief that divine intent rules society as well as conscience; that political problems, at bottom, are religious and moral problems.
* Affection for the proliferating variety and mystery of traditional life, as distinguished from the narrowing uniformity and egalitarianism and utilitarian aims of most radical systems.
* Conviction that civilized society requires orders and classes; that society longs for leadership.
* Persuasion that property and freedom are inseparably connected, and that economic leveling is not economic progress.
* Faith in prescription and distrust of, in the phrase of Edmund Burke, "sophisters and calculators." Man must put a control upon his will and his appetite. Tradition and sound prejudice provide checks upon man's anarchic impulse.
* Recognition that change and reform are not identical.[7]

In its July 4, 1953, issue, *Time* magazine devoted its entire book section to *The Conservative Mind*. "Kirk tells his story of the Conservative stream," wrote reviewer Max Ways, "with the warmth that belongs to it. Even Americans who do not agree may feel the warmth – and feel, perhaps, the wonder of conservative intuition and prophecy, speaking resonating across the disappointing decades."

Although conservatism as a force in America was beginning to take root, there was still much disarray. On the political level, Robert Taft lost his party's nomination for the final time to Dwight D. Eisenhower. This was in 1952, and the Dewey crowd was still very much in control of the party's machinery, and once again the platform reflected the views of "pragmatic liberals."

On the philosophical and policy side, the new Conservative Movement was really a collision of factions, so much so that it was difficult to promote a consistent message to the public. Members of the various conservative groups often disliked members of other conservative factions, and rather too much time was spent taking shots at one another.

One group consisted of *libertarians* who subscribed to nineteenth-century "classical liberalism," which puts "emphasis . . . on consent, that is, if two people agree to do a thing, and if the thing is not harmful to another, their agreement should not be prohibited by any authority other than their own wills."[8] Members of this group included, to one degree or another, Henry Hazlitt, Milton Friedman, and Murray Rothbard.

Then there were the *traditionalists*. Men such as Richard Weaver, Russell Kirk, Eric Voegelin, Frederick Wilhelmsen, Leo Strauss, and John Hallowell were members of the Traditionalist wing of the Conservative Movement. Influenced by Plato, Aristotle, Aquinas, and Edmund Burke, their principles were succinctly described in Hallowell's 1934 work *The Moral Foundations of Democracy*:

* There exists a meaningful reality, an "orderly universe" independent of the knower.
* Man can, by use of his reason, discern the nature of reality.
* Knowledge of what man should do in order to fulfill his human nature is embodied in what has traditionally been called the "law of nature" or the "moral law."[9]

A third group, many of whom were uncomfortable with the term *conservative*, were the *anti-Communists*. Dominated by incredibly brave men and women who broke with the Communist Party or the extreme left wing, the list of anti-Communist intellectuals included Max Eastman, James Burnham, Frank Meyer, Sidney Hook, Eugene Lyons, Ralph De Toledano, William Henry Chamberlain, and the aforementioned Whittaker Chambers, author of the era's most influential memoir, *Witness*. This group consisted of both admirers and detractors of both HUAC and Senator Joseph McCarthy.

New York: Center of the Right

It was a thirty-year-old dynamo named William F. Buckley Jr. who successfully organized and consolidated these scattered voices under the masthead of a new journal, *National Review*. Buckley had burst onto the national scene with the publication of *God and Man at Yale* (1951), a work that criticized his alma mater for giving lip service to "academic freedom," while permitting the School of Liberal Arts to be dominated by socialists and atheists, whose views were inimical to freedom. At Yale, Buckley had served as editor of the *Yale Daily News* and was star member of the Political Union, Yale's Debating Society. After a brief stint in the CIA, Buckley was determined to apply his writing and debating skills to promotion of the conservative cause. With the demise of the *American Mercury* and the *Freeman*, many prominent conservatives agreed that a new national publication was needed. Buckley's first

thought was to purchase *Human Events*, but then former *Time* Editor, William S.
Schlamm, convinced the young Buckley to found a brand-new "Journal of
Conservative Opinion."

After his family agreed to put up $100,000 in 1953, Buckley worked for the next
two years to raise the additional capital needed to launch the new publication. The
fund raising prospectus made it clear that the magazine's function was "not solely to
review the attack against the left but to consolidate the right."[10]

To survive internal squabbles that destroyed magazines like the *Freeman*,
Buckley structured the parent corporation with two classes of stock:

> Class A common stock, with no par value but with voting rights; and Class
> B, nonvoting but with a par value of $1 a share. These latter were sold in
> sets of twenty, together in each case with a debenture (face value $100,
> market value $80), which package was priced at $100 in the fond hope that
> it would be worth $120 at maturity. Class B was designed to be sold to the
> public; the Class A shares – all of them – were purchased by and vested in
> Buckley alone.[11]

This approach gave him full editorial control and, presumably, the ability to resolve
disputes.

Buckley was able to attract to the magazine's masthead notable writers and
thinkers from every segment of the Conservative Movement. Among them were:
Whittaker Chambers, Frank Meyer, Willmoore Kendall, James Burnham, Brent
Bozell, Max Eastman, Morrie Ryskind, Ralph De Toledano, Eugene Lyons, Richard
Weaver, and Erik von Kuehnelt-Leddihn. Buckley rented an office on Manhattan's
East Side, and *National Review* appeared on newsstands for the first time in
November of 1955. In his "Publisher's Statement," Buckley declared that the purpose
of *National Review* was to "stand athwart history, yelling stop, at a time when no one
is inclined to do so, or to have much patience with those who do."

Commuting between his home in Sharon, Connecticut, and his Manhattan apartment, Buckley was fast becoming a visible member of New York political, intellectual, and social scenes. Politically, he witnessed the New York Republican Party's growing domination by "moderates" Jacob Javits, Louis Lefkowitz, Kenneth Keating, and
Leonard Hall. Buckley's opposition to this brand of Republicanism was well known.
As early as 1953, he wrote in his prospectus for potential *National Review* investors:

> Middle-of-the-Road, *qua* Middle of the Road, is politically, intellectually,
> and morally repugnant. The most alarming single danger to the American
> political system lies in the fact that an identifiable team of Fabian opera-
> tors is bent on controlling both our major parties – under the sanction of

such fatuous and unreasoned slogans as "national unity," "middle-of-the-road," "progressivism," and "bipartisanship."

As Nelson Rockefeller began campaigning for the gubernatorial nomination, Buckley's was one of the few voices raised in criticism of Rocky's Republican credentials. The August 2, 1958, issue of *National Review* pointed out that Rockefeller:

> . . . has been shielded from questions and has ducked debate. His campaign has consisted entirely of his publicized reports, grandiose claims of delegate support, the emission of pleasantries and the circulation of a [Republican state chairman] Morhouse poll proving that Rockefeller is a well-known name. . . . Between now and the convention, the delegates may want to know just where Rockefeller does stand politically. They may even want to discover the nature of that brand of politics which Liberal journalists are hailing as 'Rockefeller Republicanism.'

This attack was the first conservative salvo in the war for the soul of New York's Republican Party. It was to be an important theater in a war that was to be fought in the state and the nation for the next twenty-two years.

But it was not Buckley's first move to reform New York's political life. In January of 1957, more than a year before Rockefeller had made public his intention to purchase the soul of the Republican Party, Buckley had met with several conservative activists to discuss how the Right might counter the Left's influence on New York's GOP. Attendees Thomas Bolan, Karl Ettinger, Jeremiah Millbank, Jr., Gerrish Milliken, and, of course, Buckley wondered if it made sense to promote the creation of a New York State Conservative Party.

In a January 22 memo addressed to "All Concerned," Buckley summarized their meeting, which had "discussed the possibility of a modest attempt at right wing political action in New York State." The third point of his memo was key:

> The time may have come to attempt to establish a counter-part to the Liberal Party in New York. We feel that such a party could exert a considerable influence upon the conventions of the Republican Party.
>
> a) A prodigious effort should be made this year to round up the signatures necessary to put that party (let us, for the purpose of this memorandum, call it the Conservative Party) on the ballot.
>
> b) Such a party, once having been constituted, should, as a matter of course, endorse all Republican nominees *with the exception of*

the one or two most objectionable from a conservative point of view. For example, in 1956 the Conservative Party would probably have endorsed all Republicans except Jacob Javits. The purpose of such a procedure would be to establish, after the first demonstration, the size of the hard conservative vote – which vote, if it is large enough, would be a formidable weapon to level at the Republican Party in future nominating conventions, whenever the temptation arises to nominate objectionable candidates. Simultaneously, the Conservative Party would be using the Republican apparatus to roll up enough votes to keep it constantly on the ballot, since a vote for the Conservative Party would, in all but a single or two instances, be a vote for Republican candidates; thus, also, the Conservative Party would not isolate itself from the major viable and potentially right wing party in New York State, the Republican Party.

c) We would not articulate in any detail whatever the ideological position of the Conservative Party, as to do so would have a sundering effect among Now York conservatives as we squared off on such issues as the tariff, segregation, public schools, etc. The Conservative Party's platform would be as indefinite as the platform of the Liberal Party. It would merely be known that we represented, – in effect, the right wing of the Republican Party, just as the Liberals represent the left wing of the Democratic Party.

d) It is felt that we can profit by studying the composition of the board of directors of the Liberal Party. The head of it is an intellectual who has had political experience, Adolf Berle. Second in command is a professor well known in the education world, with a considerable following of his own, George Counts. It was suggested, accordingly, that Mr. Raymond Moley would make an excellent chairman of the Conservative Party. Other persons whose names were mentioned who might be interested in the proposal included Godfrey Schmidt, General A.C. Wedemeyer, Robert Morris, Mrs. Preston Davie, Ludwig von Mises, Henry Hazlitt, David Grimes, William J. Casey, René L. Wormser, to mention a few.

The Third Party Idea

Unlike most other states in the nation, New York has long given official status to "third" parties. What's more, the state's election laws allow those parties to "cross-endorse" candidates of the Republican and Democratic Parties, meaning that two or more parties can nominate the same candidate and that the votes cast on each of those lines are added together:

> In New York the combined practice of multiple nomination and multiple ballot placement, has had the effect of (1) facilitating the attainment by minor parties of official party status; (2) placing minor parties in the position of holding the balance of power, thereby nullifying the "winner take all" theory of minor party demise; (3) undermining the "wasted vote" theory of minor party demise; (4) allowing voters the luxury of supporting a major party's candidate without supporting the candidate's party; and (5) protecting and enhancing the power of the minor parties and their leadership.[12]

Succumbing to pressure from "Goo-Goos" and other political reformers, who did not want to cast their ballots for a party that in their judgment had been corrupted by "bossism," New York began giving ballot access to splinter parties. Among the earliest third parties was the Prohibition Party (1892), which was followed by the Socialist Labor Party (1896–1904), the Socialist Party (1900–1938), the Independent League (1906–1916), the Progressive Party (1912–1916), and the American Party (1914–1916).[13]

New York's rules permit any individual who can obtain at least 20,000 valid signatures of registered voters with any party affiliation to establish an independent party. If in a subsequent gubernatorial election that independent party's candidate receives at least 50,000 votes, the party is officially recognized and automatically receives a spot on the ballot in every election for the next four years.

When law mandated the use of voting machines in the 1930s, the recognized minor parties received separate ballot placement. The machine ballots made it easier for the smaller parties to cross-endorse major party candidates while maintaining their identity and their ability to reach the 50,000 votes needed in each gubernatorial race, the ongoing requirement for their continued existence.

Other electoral regulations were lax. Until 1947, a candidate could file for any party's primary. In 1942, for instance, radical left-winger Vito MarcAntonio (who had ties to the Communist Party and led the American Labor Party) filed petitions in both the Democratic and Republican primaries – and won. To put a halt to these raids, the election law was amended whereby one had to be a party member to enter a primary unless the party's leaders specifically authorized an exception. Named after its sponsors, the 1947 "Wilson-Pakula" Law was intended to maintain the independence of the two major parties, but in actuality it created legal cover for "cross endorsement" agreements. In return for specified patronage or policy favors, the minor party leadership agrees:

> (1) not to contest its *own* primary; (2) to authorize the entry into its primary of only one candidate from the major party, the one backed by the major party organization; and (3) to fight any insurgent within its own ranks who tries to upset the arrangement with a primary challenge. In making such agreements possible, the 1947 law thus enormously enhanced the power and prestige of minor parties and their leaders (such as the late Liberal leader Alex Rose). Indeed, by formalizing and legitimizing the annual bargaining sessions, the law enhanced the power and prestige of the leaders of *all* parties, major and minor alike. The "Wilson-Pakula" act also permitted major party candidates who lost their primary to remain as a candidate on the minor party line.[14]

In more recent New York history, third parties began to gain status during the Depression years. The American Labor Party (ALP) was founded with the approval of President Franklin Roosevelt in 1936. Roosevelt believed he would pick up votes on this line of extreme left-wingers, socialists, and progressive Republicans who could not bring themselves to vote on the line of the corrupt "Tammany Hall controlled" Democratic Party. The left-wing, anti-Communist founders of the ALP – David Dubinsky of the International Ladies Garment Workers Union, Sidney Hillman of Amalgamated Clothing Workers, and Alex Rose of the Millinery Workers, all of whom had lost control of their unions to Communists for a short time in the 1920s – wanted to wean their membership away from Communist influences by utilizing this new political party. In 1936, over the objections of top Democratic Party officials Jim Farley and Edward Flynn, the ALP endorsed the re-election efforts of FDR and Governor Herbert Lehmann. The party polled an impressive 275,000 votes.

Designated as a permanent party, the ALP made a deal in 1937 with Manhattan Republican leader Kenneth Simpson to endorse Republican "fusion" candidate Fiorello La Guardia, as well as various Republican candidates for city council.

This political move contributed heavily to La Guardia's re-election and frustrated Democratic bosses who expected to take back city hall. La Guardia, who won by 453,000 votes, received 482,700 votes on the ALP line, in itself the margin of victory.

While the ALP was savoring its victories, the Socialist Party, now effectively run by Communists, lost its official status in 1938 by failing to receive 50,000 votes for its gubernatorial candidate. The Communists thus displaced turned their eyes on the ALP and quietly began infiltrating the party through registration and election to leadership positions. Since actual third-party registrations are often miniscule compared to votes actually cast on the party line (thanks to crossover voters), it was not difficult for the Communists to quickly gain significant control. In 1940, Dubinsky and Rose barely carried enough votes at their state convention to nominate FDR as their presidential standard bearer. By 1944, conceding that the Communists now dominated the party, most of the unions pulled out of the ALP and founded the New York State Liberal Party. Although their candidate for governor lost to Tom Dewey, they received enough votes (177,000) to become a permanent party, a status they have never lost. When former U.S. Vice President Henry Wallace was nominated by the ALP for president in 1948, the last large union still supporting the party, the Amalgamated Clothing Workers, pulled out. The ALP never recovered from the Wallace endorsement, although it struggled along for six years. In the 1954 governor's race, it received fewer than 50,000 votes and went out of business. The demise of the ALP did not, however, stop the growing influence of third parties throughout the 1950s.

When New York City Mayor William O'Dwyer resigned to become Ambassador to Mexico (and to escape indictment) in 1950, the Liberal Party cut a deal with Tammany boss Carmine DeSapio and as part of the bargain got to name the mayoral candidate. Liberal Party leader Dubinsky tapped his gin-rummy buddy Judge Ferdinand Pecora. In return the Liberal Party agreed to endorse whomever the Democrats nominated on the statewide ticket.

Although the deal demonstrated the growing clout of the Liberal Party at the bargaining table, it eventually backfired. Acting Mayor Vincent Impellitteri was offended that his Democratic Party had not even considered him as a serious candidate to retain the office he had inherited. To get back at them, he organized a one-time independent party, the Experience Party.

When Boss DeSapio offered a Supreme Court judgeship to the acting mayor so that he would go away, Mayor "Impy" turned the proffer into a political issue, namely bribery. Impy was the first mayoral candidate in city history to be elected without the endorsement of a major party. Receiving 1,161,000 votes, he easily beat Democratic-Liberal Pecora (935,000 votes) and Republican Edward Corsi (382,000).

Third parties *had* to be taken seriously in the State of New York. In the 1958 election, in which Nelson Rockefeller was elected on the Republican line, one of his running mates, comptroller candidate James Lundy, lost his race by 1,485 votes. The margin of victor for Lundy's opponent, Democrat Arthur Levitt, was the nearly 300,000 votes he received on the Liberal Party line. In fact, most Democrats – and an occasional Republican – grabbed the Liberal line, fearing defeat without the cross endorsement. The Democrats' rush to secure the Liberal nod was obvious in the 1958 elections:

* In the 41 congressional races, 31 Democrats took the Liberal Party endorsement.

* In the 58 state senate races, 47 Democrats took the Liberal Party endorsement.
* In the 150 assembly races 113 Democrats appeared on the Liberal line.

When Bill Buckley and his friends met in January 1957, they were cognizant of the influence splinter parties possessed in New York. They reasoned that an organized Conservative Party might be able to position itself to influence the Republican Party. They believed that if successful, the Conservatives would be the right-minded "tail" that would "wag" the Republican "dog."

After Buckley sent out his January 22 memo, meetings were held with Brooklyn conservative activist Eli Zrake. It was believed that Zrake had the organizational skills to handle the political nuts and bolts necessary to achieve party status. Negotiations with Zrake continued with the new publisher of *National Review*, William A. Rusher. Plans to move forward ended abruptly, however, when the thirty-nine-year-old Zrake suffered an untimely death from a heart attack.

Still the die was cast, or as Bill Buckley might have said: *Iacta alea est.*

Chapter 3

Thunder on the Right

The Founding of the Conservative Party of New York, 1960–1962

Nelson Rockefeller was sworn in as governor on January 1, 1959. "New York," he proclaimed, "is a big dynamic high powered state and it wants a big dynamic high powered man for its governor."[1] Rocky was not noted for his modesty. The would-be president's task was now to hit the ground running: to convince the entire nation that he was not a stodgy Republican. This he would accomplish by implementing grandiose plans for the redesign of New York State.

The truth is an American politician can wreak utter havoc so long as he is unafraid of issuing debt. The fearless Rockefeller began his first term by pushing through the legislature something called the "Housing Finance Agency." One new agency does not a massive bureaucracy make, of course, but HFA was just the first of 230 agencies and authorities created during Rockefeller's tenure. In the end, Rocky's numerous bureaucratic innovations would incur $12 billion in debt.

As the size of the state's general operating budgets began dramatically to increase, so did the need for more taxes to fund the expenditures. Governor Rockefeller was to earn the distinction of having requested more tax increases than any governor in state history. No fewer than eighteen tax bills were enacted between 1959 and 1973.

Immediately upon taking office, Rocky began to practice a kind of fiscal sleight of hand. After blaming his predecessor, Averill Harriman, for the state's woes, the new governor piously called for reestablishment of sound fiscal policies based on "pay as you go" and the "minimum use of bond financing." Under the cover of such rhetoric he then called for a tax increase of $277 million. This additional revenue was actually needed to balance Rockefeller's first budget, which called for increased expenditures of 13 percent over Harriman's last fiscal year. The revenue was to come from hikes in the cigarette, gasoline, and income taxes. While Rockefeller rationalized these increases as necessary to "meet pressing social needs," the higher income taxes actually hurt the poor by adding 300,000 low-income families to the tax rolls.[2] And so-called "sin" taxes are always regressive. The Republican-controlled legislature, which had resisted similar tax increases during the Harriman years, sheepishly approved the new chief's revenue package.[3]

Rockefeller and his supporters were delighted with the legislative victory. With tax increases out of the way early in the first term, the spending binge could now begin. Indeed, the state's full-faith-and-credit debt jumped from $897 million in 1959 to $988 million in 1960. Debt service on state general-obligation bonds skyrocketed to $428.6 million in 1960, up from $250.3 million the year before. General fund expenditures were up 13 percent: up to $1.8 billion in 1959 and then to $2 billion in 1960.[4] The governor's personal staff grew from sixteen under Harriman to twenty-seven just in Rocky's first year in office.

And then there were the task forces. Rockefeller created sixteen in 1959 alone. The most important of them was a government operations commission chaired by Martin Ronan, whose report gave the governor a blueprint for reorganizing state government, notably by expanding the governor's power.

In 1960, Rockefeller publicly stated: "It is fiscal folly to borrow during periods of rising income because it is less expensive to pay for construction out of current revenues than to issue bonds."[5] But this was a ruse. To maintain the illusion of a "pay-as-you-go" front, the governor utilized inaccurate revenue projections, tax deferrals, and accelerated payment schedules – all fiscal gimmicks designed to achieve on paper the state constitutional requirement of a balanced budget.[6] To circumvent the constitutional mandate that General Obligation Debt be submitted for voter approval, Rockefeller started using various existing and new state agencies to issue debt to pay for his building schemes. Government agencies and authorities have independent power to issue long-term bonded debt for various projects, and principal and interest on these bonds are not paid by direct state taxes but by user fees, hence they are exempt from constitutional limitations. The Triborough Bridge Authority, for example, would meet operating costs and debt-service payments by charging tolls. Rockefeller would persuade the board of the agency to construct a building that would then be leased to the state. The lease payments, which coincidentally covered the principal and interest due on the bonds issued to finance the building, would come out of the state's General Operating Budget. Although the state is technically obligated to pay off the agency's bonds according to the terms of the lease, it is not considered a general-obligation debt, and therefore – again technically – voter approval is unnecessary. Thus was Rocky able to have his cake and eat it too.

Of course the state General Operating Budget only *appeared* to be balanced. "The Democratic comptroller, Arthur Levitt, was highly critical of the state's cash-basis budgeting system, and the attendant flexibility that this system offered the governor to meet the constitutional requirement of a balanced budget by manipulating reserve funds, using one-time payments, accelerating expenditures, rolling over expenditures, and employing other devices at the end of a fiscal year."[7] In 1963, Levitt finally informed the public:

"In truth the [Rockefeller] administration is *not* on pay as you go and never has been."[8]

Rockefeller was a quick study. He learned and mastered every means at his disposal to force his will on the state. To spend money, he frequently resorted to utilizing the "Message of Necessity" which enabled him to ram through legislation that the legislature had no time to review. "The device was designed for emergency use and allowed immediate consideration of new bills, free from the normal requirements that they age three days on legislators' desks."[9]

Rockefeller believed that this flurry of activity in New York would so impress the nation that he would ride a wave of acclamation right into the White House. Reflecting on the presidency he once remarked:
"When you think of what I had, what else was there to aspire to?"

1960 and the End of Conservative Patience

Some believed Rockefeller's January 1, 1959, inaugural address would have been more appropriately delivered on the steps of the Capitol in Washington, D.C. Rocky was two-thirds of the way through the speech before he mentioned the words: "New York." Anti-Communist in tone, the governor's little sermon made him seem the very model of a cold warrior:

> Our neighborhood is the world. . . . It is divided, essentially, between those who believe in the brotherhood of man and the fatherhood of God – and those who scorn this as a pious myth.[10]

In fact, during Rocky's first term it often seemed as though he were competing with the federal government. Indeed, when it came to spending on various programs, he very much wanted to beat the feds to the punch.

In February 1962, Rockefeller would deliver the prestigious Godkin Lecture at Harvard University. His topic was the "Essentials of Free Government and the Duties of the Citizen." Describing the role of the states, the governor took great pride in the fact that New York had raised the bar higher than Democrat-controlled Washington, D.C., required:

> *In education*: State aid to elementary and secondary education in the State of New York totaled $753 million in the 1961–1962 fiscal year, or $87 million more than the President required of the Congress for the whole nation in 1961 . . .

> *In civil defense*: The $100 million for the New York program, made law in the special session of the State Legislature in the fall of 1961, is equivalent to approximately one-third of the program enacted in Washington the same year for the entire nation.

In power development: The State Power Authority of New York has built more hydroelectric generating capacity on the Niagara and St. Lawrence Rivers in the past ten years, with the funds of private bondholders, than all the hydroelectric dams of the TVA system.

In housing: While the federal housing program enacted by the Congress last year authorized the sum of $5 billion, I recently proposed a New York State housing program which for New York City alone would involve the identical sum of $5 billion – these funds to be supplied through the newly created State Housing Finance Agency at no cost to the taxpayers.[11]

But beginning back at the time of his inauguration Rockefeller used his newly acquired media visibility to torment the heir apparent to the 1960 Republican presidential nomination, Richard M. Nixon. When the U-2 spy plane crashed on May 1, 1960, Rocky publicly criticized the Eisenhower Administration, warning about the "missile gap" and calling for an immediate increase of $5 billion in defense spending. Then he really threw fat on the fire. "I am deeply concerned," he pompously stated, "that those assuming control of the Republican Party have failed to make clear where the party is heading and where it proposes to lead the Nation."[12]

By now Rockefeller had realized that the 1960 presidential nomination was beyond his reach. Nixon had spent eight years faithfully standing-in for Eisenhower and had labored in the Republican vineyards. Republican leaders across the nation were solidly for Nixon. Even Rocky's friends on Wall Street supported the vice president. The moneychangers figured they could gain access in a Nixon Administration, since Nixon needed their money. Whereas Rocky had so much of his own wealth he could afford to ignore them. Rockefeller was savvy enough to realize all this, but he simply could not resist publicly embarrassing Nixon. As he told a friend, "I hate the idea of Dick Nixon being president."[13]

In mid-July, Rockefeller made it known to Nixon that he was unsatisfied with the Republican platform, and that the two needed to meet. Rockefeller threatened to make his displeasure public unless the two leaders could work out compromise language. Fearing that a floor fight at the Republican National Convention would hurt his chances in the fall, Nixon agreed to a face-to-face session; he even allowed Rockefeller to choose the time, the place, and even when and how the media would be notified.

Two days before the opening of the convention in Chicago, Nixon met Rocky for dinner at the governor's thirty-two-room apartment at 810 Fifth Avenue. They worked until 3:00 A.M., and in the end Nixon agreed to fourteen amendments to the platform, including a more liberal plank on civil rights.

The "Compact of Fifth Avenue" was subsequently rammed down the throats of the platform committee. President Eisenhower saw the changes as direct criticisms of his administration. He was annoyed.

Conservatives were furious. Senator Barry Goldwater, rising icon of conservative activism, referred to the deal as the "Munich of the Republican Party."

Rockefeller, of course, was ecstatic. He was the big winner, and his coup appeared to have no downside. If Nixon were to win in November, Rocky could take credit for moving the party to the center, which is to say in a liberal direction, and if Nixon lost, he would point out that Nixon didn't move far enough or fast enough to the left. What Rockefeller didn't recognize, however, was that his clever maneuvering galvanized the growing political Right, especially in the western and southern states. "Every movement needs a villain," wrote *National Review* publisher William Rusher. "For the GOP Right Nelson Rockefeller was it."[14]

Calling in a slew of IOU's, Nixon managed to pacify a convention insurgency by irate conservatives, many of whom were ready then and there to nominate Goldwater for president. As he withdrew his name from consideration, the Arizona senator insisted that the party unite behind Nixon and support the Republican platform "over the blueprint for socialism presented by the Democrats."

But he also issued a call to arms:

> We must remember that Republicans have not been losing elections because of more Democrat votes – now get this – we have been losing elections because conservatives often fail to vote. . . . This country is too important for anyone's feelings; this country in its majesty is too great for any man . . . to stay home and not work just because he doesn't agree. *Let's grow up conservatives.* . . . [I]f we want to take this party back – and I think we can some day – let's get to work.[15]

Conservatives throughout the nation heard the Senator's message loud and clear – even, if not especially, in "liberal" New York.

Although Rockefeller had pledged undying loyalty to Nixon, he managed to sit on his hands during the fall campaign. He prevented the Republican National Committee and the Nixon organization from handling any New York activities, and although he delegated his own people to oversee New York's efforts for Nixon-Lodge, it's fair to say they didn't exhaust themselves during the campaign. Indeed, there was precious little done to help Nixon in New York.

The 1960 presidential election was the closest in the twentieth century. Nixon lost the election nationally by 118,550 votes. John Kennedy carried New York by 383,666 votes, and his margin of victory was the 406,176 votes received on the state's Liberal Party line.

On election night, the Rockefeller entourage clicked champagne glasses. They had it all figured out: New York was the powerbroker in Republican politics, and Rockefeller was the presumptive presidential candidate in 1964 – 1600 Pennsylvania Avenue, here we come!

It's what the Greeks called hubris. It's what destroys ambitious politicians. The tumultuous history of the sixties would take Jack Kennedy, humble Dick Nixon, and bring Nelson Rockefeller to within a heartbeat of the presidency . . . but no nearer.

The Conservative Party of New York

Six days after John F. Kennedy was elected the thirty-fifth President of the United States, a young lawyer named Dan Mahoney had lunch at a Wall Street watering hole with several Republican colleagues. They complained bitterly about how little Governor Rockefeller had done for the national ticket. They argued about the advisability of leading a revolt in New York's Young Republican organization, of doing something to express their discontent with the party hierarchy. At one point in the discussion, Mahoney's brother-in-law, thirty-four-year-old Kieran O'Doherty, wondered aloud why they didn't just start a conservative political party in New York?[16]

Party founders J. Daniel Mahoney (left) and Kieran O'Doherty at a Conservative Party annual fundraiser.

There was a pause, and then some laughter. Third parties seemed almost comical, and anyway they were Republicans, right?

Mahoney wasn't so sure. He knew what was on his brother-in-law's mind: Back in 1958 they'd seriously discussed such a project but had concluded then that the political atmosphere was not yet ripe. Just now – with Rockefeller pushing the Republican Party to the left both locally and nationally – the atmosphere was so ripe it had begun to reek.

Later that day as the brothers-in-law spoke on the telephone, O'Doherty said bluntly:

"No conservative can stomach a Rockefeller-Javits Republican ticket. Rockefeller is riding high toward the 1964 Republican presidential nomination. At least we could fly the flag and we might really accomplish something."[17]

When Mahoney got to his home in Forest Hills, Queens, home that evening, he was carrying a copy of New York's election law under his arm.

"Kieran and I are going to start a Conservative Party," he informed his wife. Kathleen Mahoney, known for her sharp, biting wit, replied: "Have you got time for dinner first?"[18]

J. Daniel Mahoney was born in 1931. He'd graduated *magna cum laude* from St. Bonaventure University in Oneonta, New York, and was a Kent Scholar at Columbia Law School. After a three-year stint in the Coast Guard, he joined the prestigious Wall Street firm of Simpson, Thatcher and Bartlett, married Kathleen Mary O'Doherty and began raising a brood in Forest Hills that would grow to include five children.

Bill Buckley described Dan Mahoney as "relaxed, humorous, wise and a peerless conciliator." On the other hand, he thought of Kieran O'Doherty as "intense, fascinated by politics, prodigiously informed, with an *infinite capacity for righteous indignation.*"[19] A product of the street corners of New York City's Queens County, O'Doherty graduated *cum laude* from CCNY and, like his brother-in-law, received his law degree from Columbia. Kieran's Irish father, Edward (of County Donegal), brought up his children in a politically charged household. Loyal to the Irish cause of independence he had, until 1928, been an active member of the Irish Republican Brotherhood. Growing up in this atmosphere helped develop the trademarks of both Kieran and Kathleen: keen wits and sharp tongues.

At twenty-five, O'Doherty had been a devotee of Senator Taft of Ohio, and had worked successfully in 1952 to elect eight Queens delegates pledged to the great man. It was a bitter first experience in hardball politics. At the Republican National Convention he'd witnessed the very delegates he'd helped bring to the convention renege on their promised support. The young man realized that "tolerant," "open-minded" liberals like Governor Dewey tolerated no opposition and exerted whatever pressure was necessary to force the delegates to switch to Eisenhower.

O'Doherty also attended the 1960 Republican Convention and campaigned unsuccessfully for conservative Congressman Walter Judd of Minnesota, who was touted as a possible vice-presidential nominee. Upon his return home he took on the position of vice-chairman of the Research and Writing Committee of New York State Independent Citizens for Nixon-Lodge. Since inaction was the Rockefeller approach to the New York Nixon campaign, O'Doherty had plenty of free time to get to know and to grumble with other New York Nixon loyalists.

It was to these men and women that Mahoney and O'Doherty turned to discuss their pet project. Among them were: Robert M. Saunders, 34, the former chairman of the Executive Committee of the Independent Committee for Nixon-Lodge; Richard R. Doll, 28, a Manhattan investment counselor with a B.A. and M.B.A. from the University of Michigan, who was the personnel director of New Yorkers for Nixon; Paul Franklin, 32, a Yale-educated investment analyst, who served as Manhattan coordinator for Nixon-Lodge; and Paul Cheney, a lawyer educated at Duke University, who was a board member of the New York Young Republicans and the Young Americans for Freedom, and was a veteran of the Independent Committee as well.[20]

This "gang of six" met every other week and began to organize a schedule for the launch of their venture. The New York State Conservative Political Association was incorporated to serve as the legal umbrella, and Richard Doll and Bob Saunders began drafting a political prospectus.

The Prospectus

Mahoney and O'Doherty were introduced to William F. Buckley Jr. and conservative public-relations man Marvin Liebman by lawyer Tom Bolan. All were enthusiastic about the prospect of a new party. Buckley was happy to see another "dream walking," and both men recognized that a third party would be an outlet for irate conservatives throughout the state.

The Doll-Saunders prospectus, a forty-page document completed early in the summer of 1961, opened with a letter dated July 4 and signed by the gang of six. The letter began with a statement of purpose emphasizing that this was not a national movement, that their actions were limited to New York:

> We are New Yorkers; and our plans center on that state. Perhaps in no other state has the conservative voter been more completely disenfranchised. Witness the plight of the conservative voter in New York State who approaches the critical 1962 gubernatorial and senatorial elections with the foreknowledge that the Republican Party, the normal vehicle of conservative political policies; will offer him the uncherished opportunity to cast his ballot for Nelson Rockefeller and Jacob K. Javits and their brand of modern welfare statism. His distress is more keenly realized upon consideration of the signal influence of the New York Republican leadership in the shaping of Republican Party policy on the national level. All too fresh in memory is the scene at the 1960 Republican national convention in Chicago when the about-to-be nominated candidate for the Presidency, Richard Nixon, felt compelled, in the face of Rockefeller's divisive criticism of the outgoing Administration, to court his favor by whipping regular Republicans, basically conservative in view, into line behind a repugnant, liberal-oriented platform.

In sum, liberal New York Republicans have ridden to power with conservative assistance, and proceeded to wage highly successful political war upon the conservative faction within the Republican Party. It is high time this anomaly was ended. The New York State Conservative Political Association is dedicated to that objective.

The letter pointed out that a Conservative Party could tip the balance of power in the 1962 elections. Furthermore, if a party candidate received 50,000 votes, there would be two important long-range effects: "(1) the Conservative Party would be on the New York ballot to stay, an essential strategic position for continuing political influence; and (2) heart and hope would be given to the conservative cause throughout the nation."

They also reminded conservatives who resisted organized dissent that:

> It is equally true . . . that conservatives cannot bring real influence to bear upon the Republican Party unless, at the margin, there exists the possibility of organized conservative dissent from a liberal-dominated Republican Party. Let those who reject this analysis consider the perennial liberal Republican assessment of the conservative "backbone" support of that Party: "No concessions to them; they have nowhere else to go." This view was explicitly voiced, for example, by Senator Javits at the 1961 New York County Republican Committee Lincoln Day Dinner. And given the advisability of organized dissent as a tactic of limited political warfare, it goes without saying that New York, headquarters of the unceasing liberal effort over the past twenty years to infiltrate and capture the Republican Party, is the ideal place to initiate this tactic.

Pledging dedication to their cause, the original signers concluded the letter with a call to arms:

> The signers of this prospectus are deeply, enthusiastically dedicated to the creation of The New York State Conservative Political Association, and to the promising and important objectives which it would be uniquely able to subserve. But we are interested in first-rate candidates, first-rate campaigns, and real political influence. We are not interested in a conservative debacle. Accordingly, we cannot proceed further without the promise of widespread support from the key members of the conservative community to whom this prospectus is addressed. It is our confident hope that you will see fit to lend assistance to this critically important political endeavor.

The prospectus contained an organizational section that described the initial steps of action: the formation of a state organization; the solicitation of members, the creation of county organizations, funding and campaign plans and draft by-laws.

National Review Senior Editor Frank S. Meyer, the ex-Communist author of the 1961 work *The Molding of Communists* agreed to pen the "Declaration of Principles." This eloquent statement stressed the need for strong anti-Communist principles, the need to scale back oppressive tax burdens, and the need to end policies that were transforming America into a socialist state and violating the inherent dignity of the human person. The Declaration concluded with a call for the termination of government support of special privileges to special groups through:

> freeing the working man, industry and the community at large from the imperial domination of the trade-union bosses, by reducing their monopoly power to a level compatible with the rule of law;

> freeing the farmers from bureaucratic regulation as dependent wards of government, by eliminating in gradual states the entire crop control, price control, and subsidy program;

> freeing the energy of American industry, by eliminating specialized subsidies and governmental favors;

> freeing the consumer (who is all of us) from the pressure of constant inflation, which is largely brought about by the curbs of special privilege on American productivity and by the cost of the non-productive bureaucracy which enforces these curbs; and

> returning the control of education to the parent and the local communities; and returning the content of education to the fundamental principles of our civilization and the fundamental skills of an educated man.

To attain these goals, the founders pledged their "unswerving loyalty and determination."

The prospectus was sent to a select list of potentially interested parties. Bill Buckley also sent a cover letter with a prospectus to his mailing list of prominent New York conservatives, urging them to join the operation. Positive replies of support came from *National Review* Senior Editor, William F. Rickenbacker (son of the World War I flying ace), novelist Taylor Caldwell, Mrs. Alfred Kohlberg and NYU Law School professors Sylvester Petro and Betel Sparks.

Through Ed O'Doherty, Dan and Kieran met Fordham University Law Professor Charles Rice. Kathleen Mahoney, who went to grammar school with Rice, joined the men when they called on Rice at his Garden City home. Rice, who recently retired from the University of Notre Dame Law School, signed on and proved to be a valuable player directing the fledging association through the New York election law maze. In later years, Rice would joke that he joined the cause solely to get "this nut and his political party out of my living room."

Funding was becoming an important concern. Unlike the Rockefellers, the

Mahoney-O'Doherty family did not have unlimited wealth. To finance the organizational phase as well as the 1962 fall campaign, the founders told the readers of their prospectus that they would need about $350,000.

Jim McFadden, assistant publisher and art director at *National Review*, volunteered to help design the initial fund raising mailing. It was agreed to wait until after the 1961 New York City mayoral elections to make the first drop. Later that date was pushed to early 1962, in the belief that it's easier to get donations in January than during the holiday season.

This gave the founders ample time to communicate with those who replied to their prospectus and appeal, and to develop an organizing committee for the Conservative Association. They met with former New Jersey Governor Charles Edison, son of the inventor, who agreed to help.

Those who eventually joined Mahoney and O'Doherty on the masthead of the "Conservative Association" were Tom Bolan, Anthony Bouscaren, Dan Buckley, Paul Cheney, Dr. James Foster, Alex Hillman, Earle Holsapple, Frank Meyer, Commodore Frederick Reinicke, Charles Rice, and Godfrey Schmidt.

On November 15, 1961, Long Island's *Newsday* leaked the Conservative Association's plans with the headline "N.Y. Rightists to Form Anti-Rocky Party." When they read reporter John Cummings *Newsday* story, the founders had their first experience with the ways in which the left-wing press spins myth. According to Cummings, an anonymous source had told him that a meeting at the offices of *National Review* had been held and that, after a few phone calls, $10,000 of seed money had been committed to implement plans to "make Rockefeller and Javits stop licking the liberals' boots." The story concluded with the tip that an additional $1 million would be raised to finance the movement.

The AP wire picked up the story and *Newsday* had follow-ups. Sensing trouble, the Rockefeller machine asked the well-known conservative Republican Majority Leader of the State Senate Walter Mahoney to urge all conservatives to rally around the governor.

Although the founders wrote a letter to *Newsday*, pointing out the errors in their story (particularly concerning the pledge of $1 million), they declined interviews. They preferred to maintain a veil of mystery until the venture was officially announced.

Meanwhile, to enhance the fledgling party's legitimacy, Mahoney got the okay from a friend to use 120 Liberty Street in lower Manhattan as a mailing address. A telephone answering service was hired and stationery with the organizing committee on the letterhead was printed. In an attempt to save scarce dollars on the cost of incorporating the party, Rice approached former Young Americans for Freedom chairman Robert Schuchman, who had formed something called the Freedom Party in 1961. It was his hope to create mischief in the elections, but his plans never got off the ground.

Schuchman agreed to turn his corporation over to the Conservative Association, and Rice immediately re-registered the Freedom Party as The Conservative Party, Inc., with the Secretary of State's office in Albany.

On February 15, 1962, over 50,000 New Yorkers, identified as conservatives, were sent a letter and a brochure containing the Declaration of Principles. Here are excerpts from that letter:

> New York's conservatives have no vote in state-wide elections. The reason is simple. Both major parties in our state are now dominated by the liberals.
>
> These elements have saddled the Republican Party with the leadership of Nelson Rockefeller, the New Deal's legacy to the G.O.P., and Jacob Javits, the only "Republican" in the Senate with a 100% A.D.A. voting record. . . .
>
> We propose direct political action to break this strangle hold: a Conservative Party which will run candidates for Governor and Senator in the 1962 New York election. . . .
>
> We are faced with a choice between time-honored Republican principles and a party leadership that spurns them. The Rockefeller-Javits leadership, confident that conservative New York Republicans are a captive vote, is leading the party in an unabating march to the left. Real party loyalty demands that we stand by Republican principles and combat the New York leadership that has abandoned them. . . .
>
> *Our only alternative is to run independent conservative candidates for Governor and Senator in 1962. . .*
>
> The Conservative Party, Inc. has been formed for this purpose.
>
> We plan to mobilize a statewide organization that will be ready next fall to restore conservatism as a respected political force in New York. We are launching our organizing drive with this appeal to a select nucleus – thousands strong – of active New York conservatives.
>
> The impact of the Conservative Party will extend far beyond the 1962 election. Under the New York election laws, our 1962 campaign will give the Conservative Party a permanent place on the New York ballot. The Conservative Party's endorsement will become essential to Republican victories in New York statewide elections, just as the Liberal Party's endorsement is considered essential by the Democrats. . . .
>
> We have no union treasury or manpower at our disposal. Nor can we enlist the indirect support of wealthy foundations, or hire a corps of public relations experts, to promote our cause. But we do have a common conviction that ours is a time of national crisis, and we know that New York's conservatives are ready to do their part to meet this crisis.

We therefore ask you to *fill out and return the enclosed card,* which will advise us of your answer to four critical questions.

(1) Will you sign the Conservative Party nominating petition which we will circulate next fall?

(2) Will you join the local club which we will establish in your community shortly after this mailing is completed?

(3) Are you interested in a position of leadership in this movement?

(4) Most important of all at this time, will you *make a financial contribution to The Conservative Party, Inc.*?

The liberals tell us that ours is the age of collectivism; that the efforts and beliefs of individual men and women are no longer significant. We intend to prove that free men who are deeply anxious for the future of their country can stand up and be counted with decisive effect.

It all depends on you.

While waiting for the returns on their mailing, it was becoming obvious that the governor was not going to tolerate any opposition. No one was going to be permitted to interfere with the Rockefeller juggernaut to the White House. "While Dewey wooed the conservatives, Rockefeller ignored them. Finally, when he recognized the conservative threat as real, Rockefeller chose to fight."[21]

At a Brooklyn Lincoln Day dinner, Jacob Javits took the first public shot at the fledging movement by accusing the promoters as possessing "freakish ideas . . . wholly-out of step with the twentieth century . . . crackpot ideas."[22] In the pages of *Newsweek*, Rockefeller took his turn at denigrating the cause: "[Conservatives] are like cattle that aren't going anywhere. They are scared and they'll fly off in any direction."

To counter the saber-rattling on the left, a formal press announcement along with the Declaration of Principles went out to the state's news outlets on Friday, February 23. Papers throughout the state picked up the announcement. But it was a *New York Daily News* lead editorial on Monday, February 26, that put the movement on the map:

As most voters are aware, there are some states in which you can detect little if any difference between the Democratic and Republican parties. New York State is one of these.

Therefore, it seems noteworthy and newsworthy to us that a group of Republicans has formed what it calls the Conservative Party, Inc., with offices at 120 Liberty St., New York 6, N.Y. . . .

Gov. Nelson A. Rockefeller and Sen. Jacob K. Javits between them, says the Conservative Party, have sewed up the Republican Party in this state and are rapidly hauling it leftward, so that "New York's conservatives have no vote in statewide elections."

Therefore, the new group intends, if it can raise enough money, to run independent conservative candidates next fall for Governor and Senator. The explanation: The Rockefeller-Javits elements must be made to realize that so long as they abandon Republican principles in pursuit of liberal backing, they will be denied the support of the conservative Republicans who constitute the backbone of the party.

This editorial in no way commits *The News* to The Conservative Party, Inc., or any candidates it may put into the field.

But we will say that we're glad to see the new group organize, and we hope it may succeed in building a sizable fire under Messrs. Rockefeller and Javits . . .

The voters are entitled to a real choice as between party principles when they cast their ballots. . . . If the new conservative political organization can force the GOP to give them such a choice, we think it will perform a genuine service to the voters and to the Republican Party itself.

To the astonishment of the professional fundraiser, the February 15 appeal had a 14 percent return and took in over $40,000.

With the seed money thus raised, and permanent office space rented at 350 Lexington Avenue, Mahoney and O'Doherty decided to take the next, risky step – each asked his respective law firm for an unpaid leave of absence for the remainder of 1962. Mahoney had a large family to feed and knew his firm was not thrilled by his request. Indeed, it was by no means sure the firm would take him back in 1963.

Nevertheless he took the leap. Kieran O'Doherty was a bachelor, so he did not share his brother-in-law's family concerns, but his situation at work was even more problematic. After a confrontation with senior partner Jack Wells (a loyal Javits Republican who would serve as the senator's 1962 campaign manager), O'Doherty realized prospects with the firm of Royall, Koegel, and Rogers were dim. Nonetheless, he too took the plunge.

With the die cast, the founders moved in early April into their new digs and began the organizational work required to get their project off the ground. After much family discussion, it was agreed that Kathleen Mahoney, once she found suitable help to care for the children, would join them as a full-time office manager. Paul Franklin, a signer of the prospectus letter, and Jim McFadden's brother Ed also took on full-time unpaid positions as Director and Assistant Director of Organization.

While writing an Organizational Manual, Ed McFadden worked on the mailing list that would be utilized to create the grassroots. Three people in every county, who returned back blue volunteer cards, were sent an organizational manual, and one received a mailing list of identified conservatives in their political subdivision.

The manual was a "how-to" book that included a charter application and boilerplate by-laws. The level of interest was encouraging, by the time petitions were to be circulated, 112 chartered Conservative Party clubs were operational.

New York State has the most complex and onerous collection of election laws in the nation. Over the years they were designed to confuse and to make sure that the "ins" kept power and the "outs" stayed in the cold. To master the election-law maze, Mahoney, O'Doherty, and Rice were fortunate to be introduced by novelist Mary Bancroft to James Leff. A long-time confidant of the last of the Tammany Hall bosses, Carmine DeSapio, Leff became one of the leading election law lawyers in the state. Within minutes after meeting him they realized that their recent cram courses in election law were no match for Leff. After convincing him to join their cause, they asked if taking on the entire Republican State Organization was an exercise in windmill chasing. Leff's reply was prophetic: "There are plenty of steps that could be taken that would make things awfully hard for you... but the Republicans aren't used to this kind of challenge and they are awfully cocky. Your ace in the hole will be the incompetence and over-confidence of the New York Republican Party."[23]

Before the August 11 petition drive began, however, the party leaders had to assemble a slate of state-wide candidates for governor, lieutenant governor, comptroller, attorney general, and United States senator. Dedicated individuals had to be found who did not fear and could withstand political pressure and retribution from the Republican establishment.

During this period, the Republicans were not sitting still. The party's state executive committee passed a resolution on June 14 that "No Republican can be a member of a splinter party and at the same time be a Republican." They warned the faithful to beware of "political pied pipers who could only betray those whom they lured into their political adventure. . . . the irreconcilables obviously committed to a rule or ruin course."

In the name of the Conservative Party, Inc., State Committee, Frank Meyer wrote a scathing four-page reply to Republican leaders that was released to the press on Thursday June 21:

> . . . [The Republicans] know perfectly well that the Conservative Party has not come into being because of the whim of a "few individuals." They know that it represents hundreds of thousands of New York voters who have been unable to make their considered beliefs felt at the state level because of the domination of the state machinery and the convention system of the Republican Party by an entrenched liberal cabal, whose members are little more than carbon copies of the Wagners, Lehmans, and Eleanor Roosevelts who control the New York Democratic Party. The Conservative Party is the handwriting on the wall for the liberal dictatorship over New York Republicans.

Therefore, the bluster to hide their panic – bluster copiously larded with hypocrisy. For what else can it be called but hypocrisy when Republicans with a record of 30 years of dogged defense of the Constitution against the attacks of Franklin Roosevelt and the legion of his successors are sanctimoniously scolded for daring to raise the banner of resistance to liberal oligarchy.

And by whom? By Nelson Rockefeller, who served his political apprenticeship under Franklin Roosevelt and Harry Hopkins; and who having learnt nothing since that apprenticeship and forgotten nothing of it – recently told Newsweek: "This country hasn't had a sense of purpose and direction since Roosevelt." . .

Or what about Jacob Javits and his heart-rending appeal for party loyalty? Senator Javits was launched into political life under the sponsorship of the Liberal Party, the very party which the resolution of the State Committee brands as "a splinter party" with "tragic" and "paralyzing potentia. . . .

These are the men with whom the state machine of the Republican Party has saddled us – in defiance of the beliefs and sentiments of the overwhelming majority of New York Republicans. . . .

They accuse the Conservative Party of embarking upon a "rule or ruin" course, of being composed of hard-bitten "irreconcilables."
We are not out to ruin the Republican Party; we only want to make it possible for the Republican Party to shake loose the tyranny of liberal interlopers . . .

The First Conservative Candidates

The first meeting to interview potential candidates was held on June 11 at the Waldorf Towers apartment of former Governor Edison, who was now a member of the state committee. Joining Edison, Mahoney, and O'Doherty were William F. Buckley Jr., Eddie Rickenbacker, Marvin Liebman, Paul Franklin, and Alex Hillman. Foreign Policy expert and LeMoyne University Professor Anthony Bouscaren (who had already joined the state committee) and Donald Rogers, financial editor of the *New York Herald Tribune*, were favored as the "dream" ticket.

After a serious discussion, the prospects decided to decline the honor, but Rogers did agree to join the state committee. Days later, the founders received their first jolt of political reality; the *Herald Tribune* ordered Rogers to resign his party position or face unemployment. Bouscaren, giving into Syracuse political pressure, also resigned several weeks later.

Former senator Joseph H. Ball of Minnesota, who lost his seat in 1948 to Hubert Humphrey, was sought out as a potential candidate. The Senator, whose name appeared on the original mailing list, had contributed fifty dollars and was intrigued by the idea. But he too took a pass, due to his age.

"You have a new party," he told the state committee. "You ought to have young men, new faces, as your candidates."

Robert Thompson Pell, a sixty-year old cousin of Rhode Island Senator Claiborne Pell, was a retired U.S diplomat who served under permanent U.S. Representative to the Vatican Myron Taylor, agreed in late June to be the Conservative Party's first senate candidate. The Harvard-educated Pell, who after retirement from government service had served on the editorial board of *America*, the Jesuit magazine, and as an adjunct professor in international relations at Fordham University, announced his acceptance in a strongly worded statement dated June 28:

> The Conservative Party . . . has asked me to be their candidate for U.S. Senate. I have accepted their call. . . . I believe passionately in democracy. I believe equally vigorously that democracy can only survive if there is discussion and debate of the fundamental issues of our time in the foreign and domestic fields. Now there can be no discussion and there is less debate if the Republican Party becomes the craven image of the Democratic Party as it has become in New York with Nelson Rockefeller in Albany and Jacob Javits in the U.S. Senate.

Within days after the announcement, the founders realized there were serious differences between them and Pell on how the upcoming campaign was to be run. Unable to reconcile their disagreements, Pell agreed to withdraw on July 20th.

The clock was running, only a few weeks remained before the August 11 petition drive was to begin. On Wednesday June 27, light began to appear at the end of the tunnel when Syracuse State Committee member John McCarty told O'Doherty that the president of an Onandaga County steel fabricating company, David Jaquith, could be their man for governor.

David Jaquith, 1962 candidate for governor.

Although Jaquith's first reaction to McCarty's proposal was that he was nuts, after some thought, he agreed to further discussions. On July 2, O'Doherty flew to Syracuse, discussed the possibility with Jaquith over a private lunch, and heard him speak publicly at a local business association meeting.

A forty-four-year-old father of three, Jaquith, appeared to meet the bill. He had a fabulous résumé: He was president of Vega Industries, chairman of the Manufacturers Association of Syracuse, an elected Syracuse commissioner of education, a founding director of the local Republican Citizens Committee, a member of numerous charitable boards, and a director of the Merchants National Bank and Trust Company of Syracuse. A graduate of Princeton, he was pursuing part-time doctoral studies at the NYU Graduate School of Business.

Always watching the election clock, they convinced Jaquith to come to New York City for further meetings – but he couldn't get there until July 9. Panic set in when after a long meeting at the party's Lexington Avenue headquarters, Jaquith said: "I'm interested, but I want to give it some more thought."

To the relief of all, the next day, July 10, Jaquith called and said: "I've decided to do it Dan. If you've got a pencil handy, you'd better take down some telephone numbers. We're going to have to stay in pretty close touch."[24]

The formal announcement was made on Friday, July 13th. In a powerful acceptance statement he blasted the Rockefeller Administration's fiscal record and assailed the governor's ambitions:

> I have been a lifelong Republican and place high value on Party loyalty. To me, party loyalty means loyalty to principles, not to persons, and certainly not to unreprehensible [sic] leadership. True party loyalty demands the repudiation of leadership which abandons principle for personal political gain.[25]

The New York Times actually gave the story two columns but they implied an extremist label with the sub-headline "David H. Jaquith of Syracuse, A Follower of Goldwater, Is Chosen as Candidate." In a *Syracuse Herald Journal* July 16th editorial, executive editor Alexander Jones, praised Jaquith and the Conservative Party and concluded that he believed "the Conservative Party here will serve as a needed brake on [Rockefeller] constantly increasing state budgets. . . . Personally I do not care how generous the governor is with his own money. What I object to is his being so profligate with mine. . . . I hope [the Conservative Party] sticks the needle in real deep and makes the Republican Party realize its function is not to outspend the Kennedys."

With only thirteen days to go before a July 27 rally at Long Island's Garden City Hotel, four more spots had to be filled to round out the ticket. For weeks Kieran O'Doherty, now chairman of the state committee, had been traveling the state to meet and interview potential nominees. Frantic calls were made and numerous meetings were held, and by Thursday, July 23, two more statewide candidates were announced: For comptroller, the Conservative Party chose Thomas D. Cole, 62, of Lockport. Cole, a Presbyterian, was president of Lockport Mills. A veteran of World War I, he served as president of the area's Chamber of Commerce and of its Community Fund, and was the former president of the Cotton Insulation Association and Cotton Batting Manufacturing Association.

For attorney general, the party chose Frederick S. Dennin, 39, of Lake Placid. Dennin, an attorney, was a graduate of St. Lawrence University and Albany Law School. Married with five children, he was the president of the Ogdensburg Catholic Lawyer Guild, and in his acceptance speech he described himself "as a life-long conservative Democrat in the *Al Smith tradition. . .*" He went on to express his deep concerned that the leadership of both of New York's traditional parties "has been steadily drifting to the Left. . . . Accordingly I deem it both an honor and obligation to accept the candidacy tendered me by the State Committee of the Conservative Party of New York."

That left just two important slots still unfilled: candidates for the United States senator and lieutenant governor of New York. As the deadline for filing candidacies approached, the state committee was stumped about whom to designate for the latter, but it realized it had the right man for the Senate very close at home: Kieran O'Doherty. For some weeks various members of the state committee had been pressing Kieran to take on the job of opposing Javits. O'Doherty was reluctant, because he believed an older person would be more suitable. Besides, he liked being chairman. But conservatives in Syracuse, having heard O'Doherty on the stump during his numerous visits to the area, had begun a stampede to nominate him. So O'Doherty relented and Dan Mahoney was elected to succeed him as state chairman. Charles Rice was chosen as vice chairman.

The First Conservative Party Rally

Over seven hundred people paid two dollars apiece to participate in the first Conservative Party rally at the Garden City Hotel on Long Island. Attendees carried placards announcing their home areas, waved flags and wore black or orange buttons urging a vote for Conservatives. David Jaquith told the crowd that it would be a miracle if they won but added: "Miracles do occur and I will do my utmost to prove it. Win or lose, I don't expect our efforts to be in vain, because if it only serves to restore the franchise to conservative voters in New York it will have been worth it."[26]

Kieran O'Doherty, in his maiden speech, pursued an anti-Communist line calling for the U.S. to "break relations with the Soviet Union and all other Communist dominated nations." While attacking the recent U.S. Supreme Court decision forbidding prayer in schools, the crowd roared "Impeach Warren,"[27] a reference to then Chief Justice of the U.S. Supreme Court, Earl Warren. Chairman Mahoney introduced the notables seated on the dais, which included the ticket and Philip Herzig of Great

Neck, James Blake of Lido Beach, Daniel Buckley of Rockville Center, Charles Rice of Garden City, and James Fortuna of Cold Spring Harbor. Mahoney urged members to reach deep into their pockets and to give generously to the baskets being circulated, and he asked his audience to give up their vacations to solicit signatures for the nominating petitions.

The rally was a success and newspaper coverage the next day was fine. Both *The New York Times* and *Newsday* ran two column stories and photos. It was interesting to note that the *Times* article, which featured a photo of O'Doherty, had a sub-heading which read: "Manhattan Lawyer, 35, Says He Would *Heed Goldwater*." It seemed like the liberal *Times* already considered "Goldwater" a pejorative term.

Before the blank petitions went to the printer, the lieutenant-governor spot had to be filled. As time was running out, Dan Buckley suggested his Rockville Center neighbor, NYU Graduate School professor, E. Vernon Carbonara. O'Doherty located his number in the phone book, called, and made the pitch. Carbonara, recalled hearing of the movement and writing a small check in reply to an appeal, said he might have an interest. Wasting no time, Charles Rice and Dan Mahoney went to his home on the evening of Thursday, August 1, and after a fruitful discussion Carbonara reluctantly agreed to run. Sensing that the professor's wife opposed the candidacy, they decided at 2 A.M. to get the word out to the press immediately. Having Carbonara's name in the papers, they figured correctly, would prevent any cold feet.

The Petition Drive

On August 11 the real work began: the circulation of petitions. To petition the state to create a party, the minimum number of signatures of registered voters required is 12,000. Also, contained within the 12,000, there must be a minimum of fifty signatures from each county in the state. This is not an easy task. The petition itself must be carefully designed to contain every bit of information required by law. Each county has a different petition. If there is one typo, the entire petition can be legally thrown out. The person going door to door canvassing for signatures must get each registered voter to sign the petition exactly as the voter is registered. This means that if the voter registration card filed with the Board of Elections shows a middle initial and the signer omits it, the signature can be ruled invalid. Furthermore, affidavits at the bottom of each petition page must be filled out very carefully by the subscribing witness: one tiny error – a wrong date or an incorrect election district – can invalidate all of the dozen signatures gathered on the page. Charles Rice, serving as chairman of the Party Law Committee, sent a fourteen-point memo on petitions dated August 3, to all supporters. Reading just a few points from Rice's memo will convey why gathering petition signatures is confusing and intimidating:

> * You cannot be a subscribing witness unless you have voted at some time in
> New York State. You need not have been registered to vote in 1961 in order

to be a subscribing witness, even though you must have been so registered in no order to sign the petition. Therefore, it is possible for a person to be eligible to be a subscribing witness, and yet, not be eligible to sign the petition as a signer. . . .

* If you find no other signers, get the signatures of your spouse and other members of your household, if eligible. But remember that a subscribing witness cannot sign the sheet he witnesses; he must sign another sheet and have it witnessed by someone else. . . .

* If you want to use your petition sheet in a county other than that printed on the sheet, you may do so if you cross out the printed county, insert the name of the county in which you use the sheet and initial the change. Remember, do not put signatures from persons now residing in different counties on the same sheet.

Yes, the election law is designed to induce failure.

Although 12,000 signatures are the minimum required, the goal was 40,000. Achieving the higher number would provide a cushion if the Board of Elections or the courts ruled out any signatures.

Panic set in on August 28 when the total number of signatures that reached headquarters was only 728. A bulletin was rushed out with this message: "The Conservative Party petition drive is failing." Kieran O'Doherty, his brother Neil and Ed McFadden hit the road the remaining weeks to supervise the drive upstate. John Strauman, Regina Kelly, and Mary Allison Ryland, full-time volunteers, worked with Rice and Leff and a young lawyer named Fred Reuss to organize and clean up the arriving petitions.

Ex-paratrooper Jim Ryan of Staten Island volunteered to drive around the state dropping off literature. On the morning of August 30, Mahoney checked out a garbled message that an upstate volunteer was dead. It was Jim Ryan. He was killed in an auto accident on the New York State Thruway heading to Syracuse. Here's Mahoney's description of what followed:

> I called Jim's father to express my sorrow, and the party's, as best I could. I was prepared for anger, anguish, bitterness, almost anything, at the other end of that telephone. But the call had to be made. I was not prepared, however – could not have been prepared – for the quiet strength and dignity of John Ryan, Jim's father.
>
> Mr. Ryan was very anxious that I feel no responsibility for his son's death. He stressed that Jim was "very dedicated" and strongly desired to do everything possible to qualify our petition. Mr. Ryan shared his son's convictions. He only hoped that Jim's death would not have been in vain.
>
> Some announcement had to be made to the party. We wrote the following memorandum for general circulation:

James Ryan, a twenty-seven-year-old former paratrooper from Staten Island, was killed in an automobile accident on the New York Thruway last night. He was driving to meet Kieran O'Doherty in Syracuse. Jim had volunteered his entire vacation to our petition drive.

The wake will be held in Staten Island Friday night, and the funeral mass Saturday morning. Anyone wishing to attend should consult Mr. Robert Sensale, 212 WO4-6780, Extension 72.

I talked to Jim's father on the telephone earlier today. He was resigned to the will of God. He told me several times that his son was "very dedicated." Then he asked me how the petition drive was going, and said he hoped his son's dedication wouldn't be wasted.

It won't be.

And it wasn't. Jim Ryan's death seemed to galvanize energy and dedication all over the state. From that day forward our petition drive caught fire. For the first time, we sensed an outside change to make the grade.[28]

A slew of volunteers worked around the clock to complete the drive: New York City Attorney C. Charles Burns traveled to obscure parts of the state to circulate petitions. Ed Kahn of the Bronx, Nassau's John Sheehan, Don McGowan, John McFadden and Walter Zaleski of Brooklyn, Noel Crowley and Ed Wasiak of Queens, Marilyn Baumeister of Dutchess County, John Miller of Suffolk County, Carroll Griffith, Bob Sensale, Joe Kennedy of Staten Island, Bob and Frances McCauley of Albany, Chuck Lewis of Rochester, John Ferris of Syracuse, Norm Hunter of Rockland County, Warren and Jean Morton of Scarsdale, Al and Carolyn Gage of Columbia County – these and so many others exhausted themselves for the cause.

Twenty thousand man-hours were put into the petition drive that included 44,606 signatures that were to be filed and 3,500 suspect signatures that were held back. Fearful that some volunteers were Republican shills who may have committed fraud on the petition sheets to ensure rejection of the drive by the election board, Jim Leff purposely left the signatures out of the filing.

As the process was being completed, the founders realized they had also run up $60,000 of debt. World War I flying ace Eddie Rickenbacker and Reed Chambers put together a dinner that yielded $2,000. Governor Edison came up with an additional $1,000. A friend of *National Review* publisher Bill Rusher, Earle Holsapple, would open his checkbook whenever the wolves were at the door. Regina Kelly and Mary Ryland insisted on loaning their $500 savings for college tuition. All of these sacrifices helped keep the headquarters open and the petition drive alive.

County activists were assigned quotas. Robert Blake, finance chairman in

Syracuse, sent out a letter on September 14 "requiring each and every member to raise a minimum of twenty-five dollars. . . . You are correct," Blake concluded, "in assuming that we will graciously accept more."

New York election law concerning independent nominating petitions states: "The sheets of such a petition shall be numbered consecutively, beginning with number one at the foot of each sheet. . . . When bound together and offered for filing, shall be deemed to constitute one petition." Since any minor error, even the misnumbering of a page, could throw out the entire petition, Leff was very careful during the final reviews of the petitions. To make sure the letter of the law was carried out, Leff and Reuss bound the petitions in one volume. The final product contained over 5,000 pages, stood forty-four inches tall, and weighed over 207 pounds.[29]

The night before the drive to file, Fred Reuss slept in the office protecting the petitions. At 9:30 P.M., Friday, September 21, after a final check of the pagination, Leff, Rice, and Reuss left for Albany in two limousines, their treasure protected by two armed guards ready if necessary "to shoot it out with Rock's goons on the Thruway."[30]

Twelve hours later, the petition was filed with the office of the secretary of state. When Leff asked clerk John Ghezzi to time stamp the petition, Ghezzi replied, "What do I look like, a freight handler?" The deed was done! A statement released from headquarters at 10 A.M. stated:

> The nominating petition of the Conservative Party has been prepared with painstaking care. It meets every requirement of New York's highly exacting election law. The Conservatives of New York have shown, unmistakably, that they are fed up to the teeth with the meaningless, no-choice elections which the liberals have inflicted upon the voters of New York at the state-wide level.

The Republican Response

Throughout the process, the Republicans were not idly sitting by as their party's future was being challenged from the Right. As early as June 6, Jacob Javits introduced Senate Resolution 196 to suspend the FCC's equal time requirements with regard to third parties. His intent was to prevent the triumph, as he put it, of "the Radical Right parties of New York, similar in philosophy to the John Birch Society." In fact, it is more likely he wanted to make sure he didn't have to face off in televised debates with O'Doherty. The resolution failed to pass the Congress. Nevertheless, it was becoming obvious that the Republicans would play dirty in order to keep the Conservative Party from succeeding.

The *Syracuse Post Standard* confirmed this in a July 29 story:

> Republican state leaders have reached a high-level policy decision to spare

no effort to keep the Conservative Party off the election ballot this fall. The risk is too great. "Our position," a GOP spokesman said, "is that the Republican Party will be better off if they (the Conservatives) aren't on the ballot. The leaders feel that they (the Conservatives) can't do as much damage if they aren't on the ballot." Additionally, the Republican leadership feels "if they can knock them out now, it will eliminate trouble in future years."

When state Republican chairman L. Jud Morhouse (who was to be convicted in 1966 of bribery charges) heard of the Conservative Party filing, he rushed out a memo to his county leaders, ordering them to canvass the petition signers and provide reasons for Republicans to repudiate the signatures. Attached to the memo was a remarkable document that described potential reasons in an affidavit form for signatories to claim they were misled.

The suggested recantation began: "I do not now nor did I ever intend to support the persons sought to be nominated by the purported petition of the Conservative Party to be candidates for public office at the coming election to be held November 6, 1962." This basic mea culpa was to be supported by sundry reasons proposed by Morhouse and his brain trust:

1. To help organize a new party but not to support candidates;
2. To oppose Rockefeller only;
3. To oppose Javits;
4. To oppose Rockefeller and Javits but not oppose Republican candidates;
5. To pressure the Republican Party to nominate Conservatives;
6. Only to influence Republican platform;
7. Represented that petition supported by regular Republican organization;
8. To organize Conservatives and not to promote candidacies;
9. To oppose Liberal Party but not to hurt Democratic or Republican Party;
10. To fight communism but not to oppose Republican or Democratic Party;
11. To promote Americanism and not to encourage John Birch Society support
12. To oppose Welfare State and giveaways but not to nominate candidates.

In a September 25 press release blasting these tactics, Mahoney published the text of a telegram he sent to Governor Rockefeller. It read in part:

When the Conservative Party last February first announced its intention to place candidates for statewide office on the ballot in New York this November by petition, you commented: "The greater citizen participation we have in public affairs the better." Senator Javits likewise stated: "Of course, any citizen has a perfect right to pursue any political course he feels is right." . . .

It is therefore with considerable shock that the Conservative Party today received dozens of reports from Conservative Party workers across the state that threats and coercion are being used by Republican workers to secure canned affidavits for use in an attempt to invalidate Conservative Party petitions. We cannot feel that you would either initiate or condone the tactics being used in some counties. We urge you promptly to instruct Republican State Committee and all local Republican Committeemen to discontinue the use of coercion or threats in the investigation of Conservative Party petitions. . . .

Incidentally, we note that apparently no similar attempt is being made to invalidate the petitions filed with many fewer signatures by the Socialist Workers and Socialist Labor parties. It seems Rockefeller and Javits do not object to competing with socialists, but do not dare compete with conservative candidates who believe in limited spending and limited taxation.

To comply with specific provisions of state election law, Morhouse had until October 1 to file specific objections, mostly to do with fraud, in order to successfully challenge thousands of signatures. Republican Party workers and elected officials were ordered door-to-door to convince their friends and neighbors that they had been conned by the Conservatives.

Reacting to the hardball tactics being employed, the *New York Daily News* ran an editorial titled, "Call Off Your Dogs Rock." The *Buffalo Courier Express*, in a lead editorial, insisted that the "Right of Petition Must Not Be Abrogated."

During this tense period, Jim Leff was always cool and confident: "Never underestimate the incompetence of the Republican state leadership. They don't know what they're doing. They'll never break our petition." He was right. Activist Jean Morton of Scarsdale called Kathleen Mahoney at 2:30 P.M. on October 1, to report that she heard on the radio that the Republicans had decided not to pursue their challenge. Upon hearing the news, Dan Mahoney called *The New York Times* and received confirmation. Morhouse lamely admitted "it would take too long to prove the case in court."

Chairman Mahoney told the political world that "the tough little Conservative Party today won its first knockout over the mighty Rockefeller forces. . . . [M]omentum . . . is already in force above and beyond our wildest expectations. We are sure that hundreds of thousands of New Yorkers will rally to our standard and demand a return to the historic principles upon which our nation was founded and grew strong."[31]

The Conservative Party first conceived by J. Daniel Mahoney and Kieran O'Doherty in November 1960 had become a reality.

The First Election Campaigns

Shortly after the champagne corks were popped another reality set in: Election day was only five weeks off. Although burdened with debt, the new party had to shift gears into campaign mode.

Fortunately, throughout the petition drive process, gubernatorial candidate David Jaquith had been doing his best to maintain a public presence. When it was announced that Senate Majority Leader Walter Mahoney (known for his conservative sympathies) was to be keynote speaker at the State Republican Convention, Jaquith wrote to him a letter of condolence. In it he pointed out that Mahoney must either repudiate the conservative principles upon which his own career had been built or repudiate the liberal premises of the Rockefeller-Javits Republican. That or he could rely on meaningless banalities in order to tie together his divided party. Jaquith concluded his letter by stating: "Seriously we do sympathize with your problem. Rockefeller and Javits will be listening to every word you say. But so will the Conservatives, the backbone of the Republican Party."

On September 27 Mahoney sent a letter to all club chairmen outlining the next steps. A tape of Jaquith's appearance on a Barry Gray radio show was made available, and the chairmen were urged to keep track of free time afforded by the local media to Republican and Democratic candidates for statewide office, because by law Conservative Party candidates were entitled to matching free time. Mahoney reminded them of the party's desperate financial straits; that half the paid staff was to be laid off at the end of September. He stressed the importance of ticket sales for an upcoming Madison Square Garden Rally on Saturday, October 20th. To conduct a coordinated, carefully planned campaign, Mahoney announced that Frederick M. Reuss, Jr., of Queens had joined the staff on a volunteer basis to serve as Campaign Manager. Mahoney closed his letter with this appeal:

> Now that the grueling work of our petition campaign is behind us, we must maintain the pace of our efforts in order to stage a spectacularly successful Madison Square Garden rally and get out a maximum Conservative Party vote on November 6. I know you don't need any exhortation to maintain the pace of your efforts.

Earlier in the year when Rockefeller realized that the potential opponent he feared most, New York City Mayor Robert Wagner, was not going to run, he was certain of victory in the fall. Hearing that his Democratic-Liberal opponent was to be the milquetoast U.S. Attorney Robert Morgenthau (son of FDR's secretary of Treasury), his confidence soared so high that he feared no political risk in announcing the separation from his wife of thirty-two years, Mary Todhunter Clark. Rockefeller's handlers began to boast that his margin of victory would exceed a million votes, and that there would be a stampede to nominate him for president in 1964.

The Conservatives, however, had other plans. Even with their limited resources, they began to chip away at Rockefeller's record, hoping to tarnish his vote-getting appeal.

In a six-page Conservative Party brochure titled "Answers to Key Questions by David H. Jaquith," the candidate addressed the reasons for the party's existence, described its philosophy, and his major criticisms of Governor Rockefeller:

1) He apparently believes that increased State government activity is the solution to every human or personal problem. As an editor friend of mine has commented – "The people of this state are paying dearly for the privilege of being a testing ground for ideas and programs designed to attract the attention of every fringe group which may have some voice in the 1964 national election." In short, he has a special benefit program of some kind for everyone except the taxpayer.

2) He campaigned in 1958 on a promise to improve the business climate and increase job opportunities within the State, and has done almost nothing in this area except talk. Any informed industrialist will tell you that the legislated costs of doing business in New York State are much greater than in neighboring industrial states. The Governor appointed a very able committee to make recommendations for the programs to stimulate economic growth and then refused to adopt the recommendations. If this situation continues uncorrected we will have a mammoth exodus of industry from the State within the next few years.

3) My ultimate criticism is that in just four years under his administration State expenditures have increased 48.9% and income tax collections have increased 55.4% over the biggest figures of the prior Harriman administration – and this year's budget was balanced only by the fiscal legerdemain of borrowing against next year's income.

Rockefeller, stung by Conservative Party criticisms of his handling of state finances, the growth in back-door borrowing, and the myth of "Pay-as-you-go" budget practices, felt compelled late in the campaign to make this statement: "There won't be any tax increase. I won't let you down."

As election day approached, the governor made even stronger statements. In Jamestown, Rocky told a crowd that "we're gong to keep this state on a pay-as-you-go basis and we're not going to raise taxes again." In another speech he said:

"I can say to you categorically that there will be no increased taxes in the next four years."

Jud Morhouse sent out a confidential note to his henchmen describing "28 fiscal and business moves" that proved Rocky's "conservative fiscal side." Ever the hypocrite, Morhouse did warn that the data "must be used cautiously and should not be published because we do not want to emphasize the conservative side so much that we lose other votes."[32]

U.S. Senate candidate Kieran O'Doherty also took to the stump. He blasted President Kennedy's plans to meet Soviet Premier Nikita Khrushchev in November in the City of New York. O'Doherty charged that "in view of the faltering incoherent foreign policy which the Kennedy Administration has followed, all that such a conference could produce would be further Western capitulation and retreat."[33]

O'Doherty loved torturing Jacob Javits. The day after Senator Javits gave a speech explaining, "Why I am a Republican," O'Doherty attacked his opponent's Republican credentials, charging in a talk at Hunter College that "Javits has always occupied a left-wing position which has no appeal for traditional Republicans or Al Smith Democrats." He continued:

> From the day he began his political career in 1946 as a Congressional candidate endorsed by the Liberal Party, to the last Senate session when Javits' voting record won a 100% rating from the ultra-liberal Americans for Democratic Action, Senator Javits has always occupied a left-wing position which has no appeal for traditional Republicans or Al Smith Democrats. This explains his miserable showing in the 1956 Senate race, when Javits ran more than 1 million votes behind President Eisenhower.
>
> The only issue which Javits and his Democratic opponent James Donovan will offer the New York electorate in this: which of these men will be the more willing servant of the New Frontier? Javits, who supported President Kennedy on Medicare, the creation of an urban affairs department, and almost every other key issue that has come up over the past months, may well win out in this pseudo-contest.[34]

Jaquith, meanwhile, continued to dance on Rockefeller's head. In Syracuse on October 13, he pointed out that Rocky was juggling the books to make his present budget appear balanced. He indicated that $99 million was obtained by speeding up tax collections from various banks and corporations. Campaigning later in the day in central New York, Jaquith charged that Rockefeller is a "political Pied Piper luring the people of New York State down the roadway to another massive tax increase."[35] On October 14, appearing on WNSW's Channel 5 in New York City, Jaquith was asked whether a vote for the Conservative Party is a wasted vote. He replied:

> Conservatives in New York State have been throwing away their votes at the State level for at least twenty years. If we do not take the opportunity now to cast a vote in opposition to big government, big spending, high

taxes and the welfare state, we may not again have such an opportunity in the next twenty years.[36]

The Conservative Party also realized that voters were beginning to focus on cultural issues. In 1962, the Supreme Court ruled that the voluntary recitation of the non-sectarian regents prayer in New York public schools was a violation of the First Amendment provision that "Congress shall make no law respecting an establishment of religion."

The Conservative Party was the only New York party to support an amendment to the U.S. Constitution to return prayer to our public schools. When Rockefeller was the only member of a fall Governor's Conference who failed to support a similar resolution calling for a constitutional amendment, Jaquith went after him. Speaking before a dinner meeting in Garden City, Mr. Jaquith pointed out that "millions of parents within New York State have been profoundly disturbed at the effect of the Supreme Court's decision prohibiting non-sectarian, non-coercive prayer in our classrooms." He called upon Governor Rockefeller to explain, "why he, alone, among all the Governors attending the recent Governor's Conference failed to support a resolution to this end."[37]

Jaquith also challenged Governor Rockefeller to "explain why the State Education Department in New York State has undertaken to interpret the Supreme Court's decision abolishing the regents prayer on the broadest possible basis, rather than has been the situation in virtually every other state, on the narrowest possible basis. When our school boards are advised that it is perfectly proper to sing the Star Spangled Banner," he continued, "but not to recite the same words as a prayer, we think the height of absurdity has been reached."[38]

Sensing widespread support for their position, the Conservative Party printed a campaign brochure dedicated to the issue with the bold headline, "Is There No Room For God In Our Schools?"

The Madison Square Garden Rally

Back at the Lexington Avenue headquarters, Dan and Kathleen Mahoney and the staff worked sixteen-hour days fund raising, organizing campaign schedules, grinding out press releases, and designing and distributing literature and campaign posters.

Manhattanites Charles Grace, Herbert Wellington, and Harry King were most generous when the fall campaign was in a pinch. But to keep the party alive until January when the next major donor appeal could be made, energies were focused on the Monday, October 22, Madison Square Garden Rally.

To attract a crowd to fill up the 18,000-seat Garden, Mahoney lined up the members of the ticket, William F. Buckley Jr., Charles Edison, and Frank Meyer. In an October 16 memo to all club chairmen, Mahoney stressed that the rally was the single most important event of the campaign. "If there are empty seats at the Rally," he

Scene from Conservative Party Madison Square Garden Rally, October 22, 1962.

reminded his membership, "your Candidates, your Party, and you will be embarrassed. The liberal press will see to that."

Adding to the woes of selling tickets and filling up the arena, the White House announced on the morning of October 22 that President Kennedy would address the nation that evening at 7:15. For weeks events were brewing 90 miles from our shores in Cuba. In his address, the president informed Americans that contrary to its assurances, the Soviet Union had been building missile and bomber bases in Cuba. Kennedy announced that a blockade of all Russian shipping to Cuba would commence on October 24.

Shortly after the president's speech had ended, Mahoney and Rice arrived at the Garden. They were crushed. It was 7:45, and only three hundred people had arrived. The rally was scheduled to begin at 8:30, and Mahoney expected the worse. But in the last twenty minutes, thousands began to work their way into the arena. Having stayed in front of the TV to hear Kennedy, most people rushed over at the last minute, and in the end the crowd was estimated between twelve and fourteen thousand.

Bill Buckley warmed up the crowd with his biting analysis of JFK's speech:

> The President informed us that at the moment Cuba has acquired the
> weapons to deliver nuclear devastation. . . . What is Kennedy's reply? That

no more weapons, than those the Cubans now have, will be permitted to enter. The Cubans will not, so long as Mr. Kennedy is President, be permitted to accumulate more than their fair share of nuclear weapons. Fair play for Cuba, our President believes, who staggered America tonight with the information that what Gromyko had told him last Thursday turned out to be false. Gromyko will be reported to the United Nations.[40]

Then Kieran O'Doherty vilified the Javits record:

He stood with the labor union barons and opposed the Taft-Hartley bill which was passed over Truman's veto by an overwhelming majority of both Republican and Democratic Congressmen. He voted against passage of the Mundt-Nixon bill, and was the only Republican to vote against the 1948 appropriation for the House Un-American Activities Committee. He called for the dissolution of that committee. He urged the repeal of the McCarran Internal Security Act. This, mind you, on the heels of the Hiss affair and other revelations of grave weakness in our internal security mechanism. . . .

When the Supreme Court outlawed prayers in our public schools and indicated that our entire character as a God-fearing nation was in jeopardy, Javits commented that there is "plenty of opportunity afforded to parents to inculcate religious faith in their children at home and at weekend religious schools."[41]

The crowd went wild when Jaquith was introduced. When he was finally allowed to speak, he skewered Nelson Rockefeller:

As the Governor goes around the State playing Santa Claus with our money, he lists in meticulous detail for each community how many millions of dollars more he is spending for them than did his predecessor, and how much more he plans to spend in the future – and yet he has the effrontery to claim that taxes will not be increased. This, in my opinion, is a deliberate fraud on the people. No one with an iota of intellectual honesty can . . . see anything other than a massive tax increase – on top of the two we've had already – or a massive new tax program. . . .

Mr. Morgenthau's suggestion that we deliberately run our State into debt is so foolish and stupid that it isn't worth discussion – but at least Mr. Morgenthau is open and honest about what he plans to do. This, incidentally, is the only difference in programs or platforms which I can see between the two traditional party candidates – Morgenthau wants to spend even a little more money than Rockefeller, but he wants to send part of the bill to our children, while the Governor continues to pretend that nobody is going to have to pay more in the future for the good things he is promising everybody.[42]

Even though the rally was a huge political success, it incurred a financial loss of $20,000. It was worth it, however, because it lifted the morale of the faithful. The next issue of *National Review* gave the best summation:

> This one had everything: a blaring band to stir the blood; powerful spotlights transfixing the speakers or playing over the bunting-draped arena; homemade standards from seemingly every borough and suburban community of the city; and – above all – a delighted and good-humored crowd that roared its answers to every rhetorical question.
>
> When it was over, the impression that remained most forcefully was of the faces of the crowd: young, for the most part; not crabbed or bitter, but good-natured and firmly determined. For these people, one felt, there was work to do.

In mid-October, the party managed to air around the state, a few radio ads. There was a ten-second spot; a twenty-second spot; and a one-minute spot. Here's the twenty-second ad:

> Alerting all New Yorkers – you are threatened at home by big government and abroad by world Communism. The Conservative Party recognizes these two dangers and pledges to fight them on every front. Vote Conservative Party in November. Vote Row F for Freedom.
>
> The Conservative Party offers New Yorkers a chance to make their vote count this November 6. You will, at last, have a choice between liberal and conservative ideologies – big government or limited government. Protect your freedoms. Vote Conservative Party November 6.[43]

Although the constant clamoring of Jaquith and O'Doherty, for candidate debates had fallen on deaf ears, they did manage to get time on "Direct Line," the League of Women Voters show.

Nationally, conservatives began to get involved. The Americans for Constitutional Action endorsed Kieran O'Doherty, and in an election-eve issue *National Review* published Jaquith's "Why I'm Running Against Nelson Rockefeller."

In the final days of the campaign Jaquith did a tour of the Hudson Valley and Capital District areas where he lashed out at Governor Rockefeller for vetoing a residency bill which would have required people to live in New York State one year before being eligible for welfare. Jaquith believed that "all communities able and willing to handle their welfare programs from their own resources" should do so, and that they should be totally free from state control over welfare policies. "Communities," Jaquith declared, "should be encouraged to adopt a common sense approach to local welfare problems."[44] In Albany and Syracuse, on October 27 and 28, Jaquith assailed Rockefeller's dismal fiscal record and hit hard at the governor's refusal to debate.

Kieran O'Doherty wrapped up his campaign criticizing Kennedy's foreign policy moves. At a Staten Island Conservative Party rally he told the crowd that "the Kennedy Administration's policy toward Castro Cuba, which showed such promise of reversing our position of accommodation and conciliation towards international Communism, has taken a very marked turn for the worse. In return for a Soviet promise to remove from Cuba the offensive weapons which constitute a severe and blatant challenge to our very existence as an independent nation, we appear ready to pronounce a 'Monroe Doctrine in reverse': a guarantee of a Communist sanctuary in Castro Cuba."

Continuing his analysis, O'Doherty concluded:

> It is vital that this unwarranted departure from historic American policy be subjected to the most searching scrutiny and debate. No plea for "national unity" can cause our national leaders, and particularly the leadership of the Republican Party, from protesting this sudden decision on the part of the Kennedy Administration to scrap the Monroe Doctrine. That Doctrine was never more sorely needed than it is today.[45]

Finally, it was Monday, November 5 and the bleary-eyed standard bearers, collapsing from exhaustion, shook the last hands, distributed the last pieces of campaign literature, and awaited the verdict of the voters.

Chapter 4

Let the Party Begin
Conservatives Make Their Mark, 1962–1964

As nearly 6 million New Yorkers went to the polls on November 6, 1962, the leaders of the Conservative Party were holed up in the Vanderbilt Suite of Manhattan's old Biltmore Hotel awaiting the returns. Someone handed out mimeographed copies of a little ditty called, "Conservative Victory Song," meant to be sung to the tune of "Yankee Doodle Dandy":

> 1
> We Conservatives are going to town
> In the New York State elections
> We're out to win a victory
> Row F is our selection!

> 2
> So come Conservatives rally round
> Regardless of your party
> Row F will bring us victory
> In the New York State elections!

> 3
> O'Doherty is on our side
> Javits better run and hide
> Dave is sure to rout the Rock
> Like David did Goliath!

The crowd cheered when the networks announced that David Jaquith would reach the coveted 50,000-vote threshold and make the Conservatives a permanent party. That much they learned because the news media – ever ambivalent about an incumbent – could not ignore a "Rockefeller" story, but as the evening wore on the faithful learned an important lesson about the objectivity of the liberal press: most broadcast

Early party supporters: Joe Leopoldi, Dr. Henry Paolucci (1964 U.S. Senate candidate), Flo Leopoldi, Helen Parisette.

news outlets simply ignored the Conservative Party and its candidates in the vote totals they reported.

The morning papers weren't much better. They projected that no Conservative candidate would attract 100,000 votes. *Newsday* pegged the *unofficial* Jaquith vote total at 97,357 and the votes for O'Doherty at 57,472. Dan Mahoney was initially disappointed, but his spirits – and those of the other founders – were buoyed up as the *official* tallies trickled in over the next few days, because the true vote totals were much better than anyone had expected. Gubernatorial candidate Jaquith's final count was, in fact, 141,877; O'Doherty's senatorial total was 116,151. (The difference between their respective totals could be attributed to the fact that Jaquith picked up more support in his hometown of Syracuse.) As the figures were analyzed, Mahoney realized there were other reasons for optimism:

	Rockefeller Rep.	Morgenthau Dem.	Morgenthau Lib.	Jaquith Cons.
Outside New York City	**2,003,294**	**1,191,528**	**80,978**	**91,693**
Bronx	175,086	228,391	38,747	8,196
Brooklyn	305,453	382,812	51,327	12,381
Manhattan	211,937	225,823	36,577	7,650
Queens	341,512	255,626	32,575	19,274
Staten Island	44,305	25,563	2,471	2,683
New York City Total	**1,078,293**	**1,118,215**	**161,697**	**50,184**
State Total	**3,081,587**	**2,309,743**	**242,675**	**141,877**

Early in the year, the Nelson Rockefeller campaign had boasted that the governor would win re-election by a margin of 1 million votes. By November 6, that number was revised down to 800,000. In the end the governor's margin of victory was only 529,169 votes, and that was 43,865 less than his margin of victory over Averell Harriman four years earlier. The Conservative Party was undoubtedly responsible for the drop in Rockefeller's total. Political pundits agreed that Rocky's vote-getting ability had been tarnished, and that the Rockefeller juggernaut to the White House had hit a bump in the road – if not a brick wall.

And there was more good news. Although the fledging party received fewer votes than the Liberal Party in statewide totals, the Conservatives actually outpolled the Liberals upstate: 91,693 to 80,978. In New York City, they beat the Liberal total in the borough of Staten Island. And most important of all, the Conservative Party, which was Row F on the November ballot, outpolled the Socialist Workers Party, Row D, and the Socialist Labor Party, Row E, and this meant that for the next four years the Conservatives would move up to Row D, right beside the Row-C Liberals.

Governor Rockefeller probably lost his appetite for breakfast over the next couple of mornings as he read the reactions of the print media:

* Associated Press: "The state's Conservative Party, only a few months after its birth, has emerged as a potential counterforce to New York's 18-year old Liberal party. The Conservatives could claim two clear-out accomplishments in Tuesday's balloting. 1. Their candidates received more than twice the number of votes required to assure the party a place on the ballot for the next four years. 2. The . . . votes given David H. Jaquith, the Conservative candidate for governor, were a key factor in Gov. Rockefeller's failure to better the . . . vote plurality by which he won his first term in 1958."

* Clayton Knowles, *The New York Times*: "With the minor party count still proceeding, the Conservative vote stood at 126,131, but it seemed likely to top 140,000. . . . The party, starting from scratch this year, rolled up this vote with its own ticket, made up of political unknowns. Both the American Labor and Liberal Parties earned their places on the ballot by backing the late Franklin D. Roosevelt at the peak of his career. Each had help in getting started. Both exerted great influence over Democratic policies."

* *New York Daily News* Editorial Page: "Governor Nelson Rockefeller won re-election easily, though by a reduced plurality. . . This, we think, was chiefly because of the new Conservative Party. Its nominee for Governor, David H. Jaquith of Syracuse, polled 120,000-plus votes, presumably nearly all Republican – meaning Rockefeller and his fellow 'liberal' Republicans had better pay some serious heed to Jaquith & Co. from here on."

* Lyle C. Wilson, National UPI Writer: "Twenty, maybe ten years from now, the establishment of the Conservative Party, Inc., (CPI) in New York may clearly show up as the most pregnant political event of 1962. . . . The founders of CPI are Republicans who assert their purpose to compel Republican national and New York State conventions to consider conservative preferences when nominating candidates for national state tickets . . ."[1]

In his Monday, November 12 nationally syndicated column, Ralph De Toledano predicted a diminished political future for the governor:

Mr. Rockefeller, of course, suffered from the Conservative Party's gains.

Running as an incumbent and against an unknown Democratic contender, he polled 55,000 fewer votes than he did in 1958 – when he was the challenger who unseated the nationally known Governor Averell Harriman. Mr. Rockefeller also ran far behind Republican Senator Jacob Javits, who was able to carry solidly Democratic New York City.

The Conservative Party, therefore, was able to rob the governor of the big vote he needed to make him the prime contender for the Republican Presidential nomination in 1964. One of Mr. Rockefeller's biggest assets is that he comes from New York, with its 43 electoral votes. To deliver those votes, if he wins the nomination and opposes President Kennedy, will not be easy. Many of New York City's Democrats who voted for him last week will return to Mr. Kennedy.

If the Conservative Party continues to organize on a precinct level it will be able, come 1964, to deny New York's vote to any Republican Presidential candidate it opposes. In a Presidential race, it will be able to hold the balance of power. . . .

The big "if" is: Will New York's Conservatives spend the next two years building up their party from the precinct level? Or will they sit back, leaving the dull but vital work of organization to others while their leaders make speeches about conservatism? It is easy to stir up enthusiasm before elections. But the day-to-day drudgery is what wins them.

De Toledano had hit the nail on the head; the real work was just beginning. Mahoney, for one, believed the party should strive to endorse acceptably conservative candidates of the traditional parties and to withhold endorsements or run separate candidates whenever the Republican and Democratic candidates were unacceptable. The Conservative Party's primary goal was not to elect its own nominees but to use political leverage to influence the Republican Party to nominate more conservative candidates.

As for 1963, Mahoney was concerned that local leaders proceed with caution in local elections. He did not want limited resources to be wasted. "There may be some situations in 1963," he wrote his activists, "which will have unusual political significance and will therefore merit our participation, but we ought to be very cautious about involvement in the elections."[2]

Building for the Future

In 1964 the state's congressional delegation, its entire state legislature, and a United States senator were all up for election, and this could mean tremendous opportunities for the Conservative Party. Dan Mahoney also hoped to send a number of volunteers to the Republican National Convention as Goldwater delegates.

To achieve these goals, the founders would now have to organize a true statewide party: county-by-county, city-by-city, and town-by-town. The Conservative Party *Incorporated* had to make the transition to become the Conservative Party of *the State of New York*. To maintain its status, the party now had to take on the difficult task of building a structure that continued to comply with state election law, and one that would do everything possible to maintain its ballot status. Because of quirks in the election law, there were technical concerns that had to be addressed immediately:

> Under New York law, voters enroll in a political party by filling out enroll-
> ment forms throughout the year. But enrollments are tabulated after
> Election Day and become effective only for the succeeding year.
> Accordingly, there would be no Conservative Party enrollment during
> 1963, and no constituency to elect county committees or a state commit-
> tee under the Election Law.[3]

To resolve this problem it was agreed that interim committees would be elected. The state committee would temporarily consist of Conservative club chairmen, while each County Committee would be represented by club members. Under New York law, state committee members, elected from every assembly district, represent the party on statewide matters and elect the state chairman. The County committees represent the party on the local level and elect county chairmen.

To help manage the growth of the party's various committees, Mahoney created regional vice chairmen (John Ferris, E. James Geater, Robert McCauley, and James Young were the first) to oversee upstate activities. To help handle the ongoing need for party spokesmen, Frank Meyer became chairman of the International Affairs Committee, Kieran O'Doherty served as head of the National Affairs Committee, and Dave Jaquith headed the State Affairs Committee.

After moving the party into new Manhattan digs at 141 East 44th Street, Mahoney began working on a political action manual for Conservative Party activists. The manual was intended to help the committees and clubs to plan program activities as well as to provide background information concerning the party's political purposes as well as its structure. The thirty-page primer did just that: it outlined political strategy, tactics, and organization. It also served as a "how-to" book for enrollment drives, club programs and activities, and gave advice on developing membership, handling fund raising, and conducting meetings. It discussed community involvement, voter canvassing, and media contacts. Mahoney reminded the faithful that the party's future success was in their hands. "Your hard, unremitting work during the days immediately ahead," he wrote, "will make the Conservative Party a mighty influence in the political affairs of this state and nation, and could be instrumental in electing a conservative President of the United States."

The party's new leaders read Mahoney's plea and went to work. In New York City, Ed Cuff (Brooklyn), Dave Jordan (Queens), Carroll and Pat Griffith (Staten Island),

Charlie Witherwax (Manhattan), and Bob Reilly (The Bronx) took over the reins of their respective committees. In addition to the regional vice chairmen, a youthful crew (mostly in their thirties) took control of the upstate county organizations: Tom Moore in Orange County, Al Gage in Columbia County, Art Lyons in Putnam County, Dick Holsapple in Dutchess County, and Bill Griffith in Rockland County. By the time New York State published its annual *Legislative Manual* in late 1963, the party was able to list chairmen for every one of the counties in New York State. This was largely thanks to the Herculean organizational efforts of Charles Rice. In contrast, the nineteen-year-old Liberal Party listed only fifty chairmen.

Not surprisingly, emphasis was placed on enrollment. In 1963, the entire structure of the party would be based on primary elections of state and county committeemen and women. To have a legally recognized county organization, a minimum of 25 percent of the required number of county committee slots had to be filled. (This is not as easy as it sounds, and even the major parties fail to fill the slates in every county.)

For purposes of party structure, New York election law recognizes the assembly district as the state's basic political sub-division. Each assembly district elects two state committeemen, and local county committeemen are expected to be elected from each of the assembly Districts approximate 82 election districts. Again, this is no easy task for the established parties, let alone for a struggling new party.

Mahoney's political action manual provided the road map to achieve these ends – but it required a lot of legwork on the part of local leaders to travel those roads. By the end of 1963, Conservative Party activists had successfully enrolled 10,329 members. Before the next year was out, that number would more than double.

Acting in the Present

Party leaders also realized that to be taken seriously, there had to be ongoing efforts to be heard on state and national issues. Mahoney instituted a weekly memorandum to local chairman that included copies of all press releases issued by the party. The local committees were encouraged to forward these press releases to news outlets in their areas and to write weekly letters to local editors of newspapers, magazines, and broadcast media.

Mahoney also made sure that the party sent representatives to various forums throughout the state. In February 1963, for instance, Dave Jaquith testified on the proposed 1963 state budget before the New York Senate Finance Committee and the New York Assembly Ways and Means Committee. Among his comments that day were the following:

> First you should recognize this budget for what it is – the most recent product of the biggest spending administration this State has ever known – a budget 61% higher than the biggest budget of the prior Democratic administration – a budget whose magnitude represents the philosophy of

a Governor whose answer to every problem is increased government spending – a budget which assumes that everything the State is doing this year must be continued next year, and usually expanded a little – a budget with some special program for everybody, as part of the Governor's attempt to buy himself into the White House with our money.

The most disturbing aspect of the budget is that proposed spending is more than $350 million in excess of normal revenues for the year, assuming no change in our revenue structure. Consider the trend. Last year State *revenues* under the existing tax structure exceeded spending by about $42 million. For the current year, *spending* will exceed revenues under the existing tax structure by about $149 million. The budget you are now considering calls for spending of $353 million in *excess* of what will be produced by our present tax structure. Even if the Governor's new tax proposals were to be adopted, expenditures would still be $219 million in excess of normal revenues.

If you don't bring this trend to a halt, where do you think we will be in another two or three years? The only common sense solution is to reject the free spending proposals of ambitious politicians and fuzzy-headed do-gooders and resolve now to live within our current income, with no ifs, ands, or buts, and with no more resort to gimmick financing or any other fiscal subterfuge.[4]

The Conservative Party also issued its first legislative program, which consisted of recommendations based on conservative principles for the enactment of legislation by both bodies of the state legislature. There were proposals to improve the business climate, to institute a welfare-residency law, to return power to local school boards, and to prohibit unemployment claims by striking union members. This legislative program would be refined and expanded, and then released each year to the members of the legislature. In the early sixties, the Conservative Party was the only New York party to issue an annual platform.

The Conservative Party also took an active stand on various social issues, most notably in response to the U.S. Supreme Court's decisions on school prayer. In *Engel v. Vitale* (1962), the court rendered a 6 to 1 opinion that a "non-sectarian" prayer written and approved by the New York State Board of Regents could not be voluntarily recited in classrooms at the beginning of the school day. The court ruled that it violated the "establishment clause" of the First Amendment. Justice Hugo Black, the court's leading liberal, concluded that "a daily class invocation of God's blessing . . . is a religious activity. . . . [T]he establishment clause . . . relie[s] on the belief that a union of government and religion tends to destroy government and degrade religion." One year later (June 1963), in *School District of Abington Township v. Schempp*, the U.S. Supreme Court took its previous decision another step further. The Court declared unconstitutional a Pennsylvania law that required at least ten verses from the Bible to be read daily – without comment – in all the state's public schools. In his majority opinion, Justice Tom C. Clark, another liberal, told the nation that not only does the establishment clause forbid laws that "aid one religion" or "aid all religions," he also stated that "to withstand the strictures of the establishment clause" all laws must be limited to having "*a secular legislative purpose.*" In his lone dissenting opinion, Justice Potter Stewart was prophetic: he concluded that the decision would lead not to religious neutrality, but to the "establishment of a religion of secularism."

Francis Cardinal Spellman, Archbishop of New York, was "shocked and frightened" by the decision, and stated that it "strikes at the heart of the Godly tradition in which America's children had so long been raised." Former president Herbert Hoover, called for a constitutional amendment "confirming the right to religious devotions in all government agencies."

As liberals throughout New York fell in line to support these decisions – and many politicians, including Governor Rockefeller, tap danced around the issue – the Conservative Party saw an opportunity to strike.

Charles Rice wrote a position paper on school prayer. Objecting to the Court's misguided, abstract assumptions and "a misbegotten concept of government neutrality in matters of religion" the paper concluded:

> The New York Conservative Party strongly urges that the school prayer decisions ought to be reversed by an appropriate constitutional amendment which, while avoiding coercion of all, will affirm that, in accordance with our heretofore unbroken national tradition, it is a legitimate function of government to recognize the existence and supremacy of God. It is this affirmation of the Divinity which basically differentiates our cause from that of our Communist enemy. It is plain that this nation ought not to continue its present policy of unilateral military disarmament. Nor, we submit, ought it to indulge in the unilateral disarmament of the spirit which would attend the replacement of our religious heritage by a new agnostic public creed.
>
> The school prayer decisions, and the future inroads on religious liberty which will come in their wake, give the lie to the affirmation in the Declaration of Independence that the "Creator", and not the state, is the source of human rights. With George Washington, we believe "Reason and experience forbid us to expect that national morality can prevail in exclusion of religious principles." With the vast majority of American people, we believe that our character as a nation under God must be preserved and that the pretensions of those who would deconsecrate this nation must be

emphatically and permanently rebuffed. Only if we continue to draw upon the religious wellspring of our greatness, can we hope to fulfill our destiny as a nation.[5]

Taking forceful stands on controversial social issues would become an important part of the strategy to enhance Conservative Party support.

William Rickenbacker, meanwhile, represented the Conservative Party in testimony before the U.S. House Ways and Means Committee, during which he articulated the party's views on federal taxes. When asked to describe his "ultra-conservative" beliefs, Rickenbacker snapped back: "I'm sorry Congressmen, I have no competence in this area. I don't represent the *Ultra-Conservative* Party of New York."[6]

To promote the conservative cause, Kieran O'Doherty made regular appearances on the "Long John Nebel Show," and in May of 1963, he moderated a Conservative Party-sponsored meeting at Manhattan's Town Hall on "Cuba: A Conservative Critique." A capacity crowd heard panelists Gen. Albert Wedemeyer, Ralph De Toledano, Frank Meyer, and former Cuban ambassadors Earl Smith and Spruille Braden engage in a spirited discussion. The party's announcement of the event had this to say:

> The American people are becoming increasingly disturbed with the Kennedy Administration's complete failure to come to terms with the threat posed by Castro Cuba to the Western Hemisphere. The brutal crackdown on Cuban freedom fighters; the complete disenchantment of the Cuban exile community with our government; the systematic "management" of news concerning Cuban developments; and the mounting evidence of Cuban-based Communist penetration throughout Latin America are producing a sense of real alarm concerning the Administration's policy, or lack of policy, in the Caribbean.
>
> At Town Hall on May 7, the Conservative Party intends to provide a systematic, detailed criticism of American policy towards Cuba, and to propose concrete measures looking towards the termination of Communist control of Cuba at the earliest opportunity. In view of the critical significance of this problem, and the distinction of the panelists who will address their attention to it, we hope to make a very important contribution to the public discussion of the crisis in America's policy toward Castro Cuba.[7]

The party officially endorsed Senator Gordon Allott's proposal calling for a provisional Cuban government to be established at the American naval base at Guantanamo Bay.

The Conservative Party struck a coup when it announced in June that New York State Senate Majority Leader Walter J. Mahoney had agreed to serve as the featured speaker at the party's first anniversary dinner in September at the Biltmore Hotel. Thaddeus Dabrowski, chairman of the Flushing Queens Club, was to serve as dinner chairman, and he told the press: "It is particularly significant that Senator Mahoney, a leading Republican, should agree to speak at our dinner. We have always admired the Senator, and now we see that admiration justified as he stands above partisan politics."

The anniversary dinner was attended by 750 guests, and featured master of ceremonies William F. Buckley Jr., who introduced Senator Mahoney. Mahoney's comments gave the political wags plenty to carry on about. In part he said:

> The Conservative Party of New York State is in business, it's a going organization, and we Republicans had better face up to that fact!
>
> Now, facing up to that does *not* mean that the Republican Party should roll over and play dead. As a leader of my party, I would not be faithful to my obligation if I let any group, Conservative Party or otherwise, which works outside the legal framework of our party, dictate Republican policy.
>
> I don't think that is what you really want, either. The Democrats for years have rolled over and played dead for the Liberal Party – and that is precisely the reason why so many lifelong Democrats, fed up with years of outside Liberal domination, voted Conservative last Fall and are here in this room tonight. . . .
>
> Translating this into political realities, I would caution you, as the sinews of the Conservative Party, from permitting your aspirations into becoming a "spoiler" movement.
>
> You did not invite me here tonight without expecting that I would attempt to express my thoughts. In *that*, I will not disappoint you.
>
> As I see it, you have three alternative tactical courses you can follow:
>
> 1. You can try to go your own way, attempting to elect your own candidates for office.
> 2. You can selectively support conservatives and moderates in the major parties, while concentrating on trying to defeat ultra-liberal candidates of whatever persuasion.
> 3. You can use the skills you gained and the morale you built up over the past year in an effort to influence the direction of the Republican Party in the next decade. Obviously, you will never have much chance of influencing the Democratic Party under conceivable conditions.
>
> Beyond the thoughts I have expressed this evening, I will not try to advise you. I am sure you *know* my feelings, but the decision must be yours. For in seeking political power, you must be prepared to exercise it for the good of all of the people.[8]

The Senator's appearance at the dinner, as well as telegrams received from New York Congresswoman Katherine St. George and Congressmen J. Ernest Wharton and John Pillion confirmed the growing stature of the Conservative Party. But although some Republicans were signaling the need for an alliance, Rockefeller and his supporters were plotting to fatally wound the Conservative Party before it could do further damage to the governor's plans to capture the presidency.

Rocky's Meltdown

In February of 1963, Republican Assembly Speaker Joseph Carlino sponsored a bill that if passed would have required all political parties to achieve at least 125,000 votes in the governor's race in order to retain their status as a recognized political entity. So much for the historic standard of 50,000 votes. The bill was approved by the assembly, and every Republican member of that body supported it.

Although Dan Mahoney and the Conservative Party leadership did not fear that the bill would put them out of business come election day in 1966, they did feel compelled to fight the proposal, if only to show the Conservative Party's clout. Calls were made, and Senator Mahoney, who ran the senate with an iron fist, said he would be "surprised" if the bill ever reached the senate floor.

In the span of one week in July, Rockefeller made speeches in Albany, Massena, and New York City. Rocky made it clear to his audiences that he feared his "good friend" Barry Goldwater was becoming a "captive candidate of extreme right wingers on the far conservative edge of the Republican party."[9] Rocky feared that "the Republican Party is in real danger of subversion by a radical, well-financed and highly disciplined minority" that Rocky was sure were set to embark "on a determined and ruthless effort to take over the party, its platform and its candidates on their own terms." Objecting to the recent takeover of the National Young Republicans by conservatives, he accused them of "tactics of ruthless rough-shod intimidation" and of using "the tactics of totalitarianism." Rocky pushed the envelope even further:

> These people have no program for the Republican Party or the American people except distrust, disunity and the ultimate destruction of the confidence of the people in themselves. They are purveyors of hate and distrust. . . . There must be an alternative. But in the sound instincts of the American people, that alternative will never be found in a party of extremism, a party of sectionalism, a party of racism.[10]

Rocky showed his true colors: only *his* concept of the Republican Party was valid; alternative opinions were *extreme, racist, distrustful,* and *totalitarian.* The Central New York Citizens Committee for Goldwater immediately issued a statement insisting that "honest men and women are differing with Governor Rockefeller [and] they are not – repeat *not* – extremists."

Dave Jaquith also went after the governor:

> The disastrous decline in Governor Rockefeller's political fortunes over recent months is the obvious cause for this act of political desperation. He is determined to force the Republican Party to join him in a bid for minority group votes from the urban centers of the northeast, or wreck the Party for refusing to bend to his will.
>
> Governor Rockefeller is clearly willing to smear any Republicans who disagree with his vote-buying political strategy as "racist." It is precisely this sort of demagoguery which will prevent reasonable, decent solutions to the racial question. Moderation, a sense for the inherent limits of legal compulsion, and a respect for our constitutional traditions are the requirements of the hour, and it is the Republican Senate leadership which will provide them – not the maverick Rockefeller-Javits brand of A.D.A. Republicanism.[11]

Reacting to Rockefeller's attack on New York's Conservative movement, *Look* magazine (with a circulation in 1963 of 7 million) stated:

> The Conservative Party is legally locked on the New York ballot through 1966 – "up there like Telstar," beams one strategist – and ready for use in protest against any Republican Presidential nominee who does not please the right. The GOP cannot ignore it. Only Rockefeller, or a candidate of like liberalism, has a chance to swing New York's big vote against Kennedy. But if the Conservative Party has the will and the way to throw the state to Kennedy, the GOP must find a candidate able to pick up a bundle of new votes in other states. Who is he? The question comes with a built-in answer: Goldwater, whose backers believe that he really could take the Solid South and Texas from the restless old Democratic pros.[12]

Nineteen sixty three was an "off-year" in the election cycle, and in New York there were no major statewide races, only local races for town supervisors, district attorneys, and county and town legislators. In New York City, the mayor was not up for election, but there were special elections for the newly created councilman-at-large seats in all five boroughs. Because liberal Democrats dominated New York's city council, the position of councilman-at-large was instituted in order to foster diversity.

Under the new at-large rules, the top two vote getters in each county would be elected. The assumption was that the number one vote getter would be a Democrat but that second place would go to a Republican or a Liberal. In this way minority political voices would be heard in the council. The question for the Conservative Party here – as it was throughout the state – was whether to simply endorse or to actually propose candidates.

There were some easy decisions: Dave Jaquith was endorsed for re-election at the Syracuse Board of Elections, and Dutchess County Chairman Dick Holsapple was endorsed by the Republican and Conservative parties for Pleasant Valley supervisor. In Onondaga County (the greater Syracuse area), local Conservative Party leaders decided not to field candidates. In a September 12 newsletter, County Chairman John Ferris made these remarks:

> The Conservative Party in Onondaga County, after consideration of local political conditions and extensive discussions with our state organization, has reached a decision not to enter candidates in the forthcoming general elections. We are satisfied that, in the overall, the Republican Party in Onondaga County has established itself as a bulwark against the liberal Rockefeller Republicanism at the state level. We have generally been pleased with the activities of Onondaga County legislators at Albany.[13]

But other decisions were not so clear-cut.

Among the most difficult judgments were those concerning elections in Nassau County. Assembly Speaker Joe Carlino, who also served as Nassau's Republican County boss, had decided the best way to fend off the Conservative Party was to cut a deal with the Liberal Party. In return for a few patronage plums, the Liberals had agreed to endorse every Republican running for election in the County, regardless of the candidate's philosophical views. Liberal Party leader Herbert Carr pressured fifteen Liberal Party candidates into declining their own party's nominations, and then allowed Republicans to fill their vacancies on the ballot. Carlino informed his slate of Republicans that they were now also Liberals.

Reacting to the deal, the Conservative Party put up a few selected candidates on Row D. The Town of Hempstead, America's largest township and the nerve center of Nassau's Republican machine, was the main target. Conservative John Sutter challenged incumbent Republican-Liberal Town Supervisor Ralph Caso.

When the November 5 results were tabulated, the Conservative Party's leaders were delighted. Mahoney hailed the results as a "demonstration of mounting Conservative Party strength in New York politics." In Nassau, the Liberal Party delivered only 4,230 votes to Caso, while Conservative Party candidate John Sutter received 17,486 votes. This represented an increase of nearly 60 percent over the Conservative Party's 1962 showing in Hempstead. And compared with the other parties, the Conservative votes in Hempstead showed an increase in total votes cast from not quite 4 percent to nearly 8 percent, and an increase from just over 6 percent to more than 15 percent of the Republican votes cast. "The attempted Liberal Party invasion of the Nassau County Republican Party," Mahoney observed, "has been smashed on the beach."

For the at-large seats in New York City, the Conservative Party endorsed Vito Battista in Brooklyn (founder of the United Taxpayers Party), Conservative Hugh Markey in Staten Island, Conservative Frank Mastandrea in the Bronx, and Joe Modugno, a Republican, in Queens. And the results here were also encouraging. In 1962, the Conservative vote in the five counties of New York City had been 50,184 or just 2 percent of the citywide total. In 1963, stand-alone Conservative Party candidates in four boroughs (Manhattan excluded) received 72,033 votes, which was up 5 percent from the 1962 votes in those counties.

In Staten Island, Markey polled 8,277 votes – a dramatic increase over the 2,683 votes tallied by the Conservative Party in 1962. His tally represented better than 14 percent of the total votes cast and more than a third of the Republican vote cast. He even outpolled the Liberal Party line by some six hundred votes.

Similar progress was made in Brooklyn, where Battista tallied 36,175 votes, against a 1962 Party vote of 12,381. The Conservative percentage of the total Brooklyn vote increased from little more than 1.5 percent to more than 7 percent. And in Queens, 18,705 Conservative votes were delivered to Modugno, which was nearly 11.5 percent of his total vote, and was, by comparison, twice what the Conservative vote in Queens had been in 1962.

Up in Westchester County, a conservative mayoralty campaign in Mount Vernon garnered 3,220 votes, or 12.3 percent of the total cast. In 1962 showing there had been just 525 Conservative votes cast in Mount Vernon. The Conservative numbers were crucial: incumbent Republican Mayor Sirignano lost his bid for reelection by 995 votes.

The balance of the party's activity consisted primarily of endorsements extended to Republican candidates in various upstate races. In virtually every case, the party vote held or improved the percentage of the total vote achieved in 1962. David Jaquith was re-elected as a Republican-Conservative candidate for Commissioner of Education in Syracuse.

The *New York Herald Tribune*'s Tom O'Hara, concluded his analysis of the local elections with these comments:

> The warning from the infant Conservative party in New York State that if Gov. Rockefeller wins the Republican Presidential nomination over Sen. Barry Goldwater (they claim this is not in the cards), they will field another candidate against him.
>
> Whether the party will oppose Sen. Kenneth B. Keating, of Rochester, whose term is up next year, is uncertain. But Mr. Mahoney said he is a sort of "prodigal son" in getting too close to both Gov. Rockefeller and Sen. Jacob K. Javits, another man anathema to the Conservatives. But they applaud his strong stand on the Communist takeover in Cuba.

The Impact of Barry Goldwater

With the November 22, 1963, assassination of John F. Kennedy and the ascension of
Lyndon B. Johnson, there was a dramatic change in the dynamics of the 1964 presidential race. Many agreed with William F. Buckley Jr.'s observation that it was unlikely that the American people would permit the office of president to be held by three
different people in a fourteen-month period.

In New York, F. Clifton White, working out of Suite 3505 of Manhattan's Chanin
Building, was directing the "Draft Goldwater" movement. Dan Mahoney kept in
touch with White's national activities, but his eye was on the New York presidential
primary slated for June 2, 1964. With Nelson Rockefeller's remarriage on May 4,
1963 and his continued spendthrift habits, there might be an opportunity to capture
delegate spots for Goldwater right in Rocky's backyard.

To embarrass Rockefeller, Mahoney urged his troops to send letters critical of the
governor's administration to newspapers in New Hampshire. A report released by the
Conservative Party critiquing Rockefeller's dismal fiscal record was circulated to
newspapers throughout the nation. Utilizing the data, the *Chicago Tribune* labeled the
story, "Rocky Branded a Wild Spender."

The Conservative Party leaders wanted to be helpful to the Goldwater cause in
New York. Although only registered Republicans could circulate petitions for delegates to the Republican National Convention, the Conservative Party could provide an
army of activists to canvass votes. In a January 17, 1964, interview with the *Rochester
Times Union*, Mahoney pointed out that "electing Goldwater delegates in New York
State must be a Republican operation, but we'll have a terrific work force out where
there are contests. You'd need a Soviet regiment to keep our people from working to
elect Goldwater delegates."

Staten Island Conservative Chairman Carroll Griffith and his wife Pat authored a
manual describing a plan of action to elect Goldwater delegates. The strategy they
outlined was simple but sensible:

> I.   This is not a general election, it is a primary. This is our advantage if
> we know how to capitalize on it.
>
> > A. Interest in the primary will be relatively limited; hence, the
> > more easily harnessed by those who are willing to work at it.
> >
> > B. Only those voters who have been cultivated will turn out.
> > Believe it or not, many voted in primaries only because they
> > were asked or to please a friend.
> >
> > C. Every vote counts. In light balloting, one vote per E.D.
> > [election district] can spell victory or defeat.

II. Such a primary is not won by holding picnics, attending rallies, and slapping stickers everywhere. It is won by an intensified, often unseen effort, backed by good literature and extensive person-to-person contact and cultivation.[14]

The handbook described the three types of primary voters: "saints" who favored Goldwater; "savables" who could be persuaded to support him; and the hopeless "sinners" who would vote for anyone but Goldwater. Griffith pointed out that the job of conservative activists was to find the "saints" and "savables," cultivate them, and get them out to vote.

Mahoney was helpful to Clif White and his top deputy Rita Bill in introducing potential delegates. In the Queens Sixth Congressional District he brought an insurgent Republican who ran an independent club in Bayside named Vince Leibel to the attention of the Draft Goldwater leaders. Leibel, a prominent Queens Republican was a strong contender to fill the New York attorney general vacancy when Javits moved up to the U.S. Senate. His chances were killed, however, when Javits decided that as a Conservative, Leibel was ideologically tainted.

Leibel ran one of the ten Goldwater slates that took on Rockefeller's machine, and in the June 2 primary there were Goldwaterite victories: Perry Trimmer won in Erie County; Vince Walsh, Congressman Steve Derounian, and Frank Becker of Nassau were elected; and in Queens County, Vince Leibel won by a *two* vote margin.

Within the State of New York there were incredible opportunities for the party in 1964. Kenneth Keating was up for re-election to the United States Senate, as were the entire congressional and state-legislative delegations.

Kenneth Keating, completing his first term in the U.S. Senate, was a strong anti-Communist, but he toed the Rockefeller line in domestic policy. The Conservative Party had mixed thoughts on whether or not to oppose him, but attitudes changed after the Republican National Convention in San Francisco.

Many New York Republicans, including Senator Keating, returned home after the Convention without having endorsed the Goldwater-Miller ticket. Vice-presidential nominee William Miller was an upstate New York congressman and former chairman of the Republican National Committee. In conversation with Kieran O'Doherty, Miller made it clear that he and Senator Goldwater wanted the Conservative line.

But in order to have a joint presidential ticket, both the Republican Party and the Conservative Party had to put up identical slates of electoral-college voters. Rockefeller operatives killed this effort. Since the Conservative Party could not endorse Goldwater, Mahoney decided to endorse no one. The *New York Times* reported on July 15:

The New York Republican leadership decided today against any joint effort with the state's Conservative Party in the Goldwater Presidential campaign.

A confidential memorandum circulated to key figures in the Republican organization outlined specific legal steps that would be taken to avoid any semblance of campaign cooperation with the small but articulate Conservative group. . . .

According to the confidential memorandum, the Republican party will choose as its 43 Presidential-elector candidates only those who are regarded as certain not to accept the joint endorsement of the Conservative Party. . . . Kieran O'Doherty, chairman of the minor party's National Affairs Committee, indicated tonight that the Conservatives might decide to have no elector slate.

"We would do nothing to jeopardize Barry Goldwater's chances in New York State," he said.

Despite the "victory" of Rockefeller Republicanism with regard to New York's electors, Kenneth Keating remained in a tight spot. His refusal to endorse the national ticket angered conservatives, and one in particular decided to do something about it. William F. Buckley Jr. began to urge Claire Boothe Luce that a good tactic would be to circulate her name as a potential senatorial candidate on the Conservative line.

Claire Boothe Luce was the wife of *Time* founder Henry Luce and had served two terms as a Connecticut congresswoman. She had also done a stint as Dwight Eisenhower's Ambassador to Italy. After some reflection on Buckley's request, she gave the okay. The Conservative Party immediately issued a press release: "Claire Boothe Luce considers Conservative Party nomination."

Senator Keating held a private meeting with David Jaquith and pleaded with him to convince the Conservative Party not to field a candidate against him. Jaquith said he would work on it, if Keating would accept a quid pro quo: endorse Goldwater and the joint electors.

At a Republican unity meeting in Hershey, Pennsylvania, on August 12, Rockefeller insisted that Republicans in New York could never be unified so long the Conservative Party put up former Republicans as challengers in races all over the state. Despite Rockefeller's petulance, Senator Goldwater kept to the high road.

On August 20, Goldwater called Mrs. Luce, who had recently been named co-chairman of the National Citizen's Committee for Goldwater and Miller, and urged her to promote unity in New York. The *New York Times* reported that the "appeal for 'Republicans to back Republicans' was interpreted as a clear request to support Keating even though Keating is not supporting Goldwater for President. . . . Mrs. Luce said her fight against Keating would not destroy Republican unity since it already was destroyed."

Accordingly, Mrs. Luce told the Conservative Party on August 21st that, if it were offered, she would accept the senatorial nomination. Her declaration created a political firestorm. With the Conservative Party Saratoga Springs Convention scheduled to meet in ten days, the Republican establishment moved fast: Rockefeller, Richard Nixon, Tom Dewey, Herb Brownell, and Jacob Javits all leaned on Mrs. Luce, insisting that she bow out of the race.

And she succumbed to the pressure. During an August 30 appearance on an NBC television show, "Searchlight," Mrs. Luce announced her withdrawal from the race. Her statement was cleverly composed:

> I am withdrawing my candidacy for the Senate on the Conservative Party ticket in New York for two reasons; first, because I have decided to concentrate all my efforts in behalf of the National ticket on the Citizens for Goldwater-Miller Committee; and second, because certain New York Republican leaders have recently seized upon it as a means of shifting the blame for party disunity in the state from themselves to the shoulders of Senator Goldwater and his supporters. . . .
>
> I wish to point out here that it has always been within the power of the Governor to eliminate any Conservative Party senatorial candidate from the race. From the beginning, I was clearly given to understand by Mr. Daniel Mahoney, Conservative Party chairman, that if Gov. Rockefeller should agree at any time before the Conservative Party convention to make it possible for Goldwater-Miller to appear on both the Republican and Conservative lines of the ballot (just as Johnson-Humphrey will appear on both the Democratic and Liberal lines), the Conservative Party would not run me or any Conservative Party member against Mr. Keating. I believed at that time and I continue to believe, that this voluntary agreement between the Republicans and Conservatives would increase the number of votes for the national ticket and greatly improve Mr. Keating's chances of victory over Mr. Kennedy. The responsibility for refusing to make this possible now rests with Gov. Rockefeller.[15]

Even though Conservatives were disappointed with Mrs. Luce's withdrawal, all was not lost. Thanks to the national press coverage, the party attained additional stature. Also, there were races throughout the state where the party gained leverage or instilled fear.

The Election of 1964

A senatorial candidate still had to be nominated at the August 31st convention in Saratoga Springs. Some suggested Dave Jaquith. Dark horses included Don Serrell of Garden City and Joseph Joyce of the Bronx. Instead, the party turned to a distinguished scholar, Dr. Henry Paolucci of New Rochelle's Iona College. Paolucci, who had agreed earlier in the year to be the party's standard-bearer in Manhattan's Twentieth Congressional District, happily agreed to make the senate run.

Paolucci, born on Manhattan's Upper West Side, had graduated from CCNY, served as an Air Force flyer-navigator in World War II, and earned his M.A. and Ph.D. from Columbia University after the war. During his career he taught ancient Greek and Roman History at Iona, Brooklyn College, City College, and Columbia University. A prolific writer, translator, and editor, he was a recognized expert on Aristotle, St. Augustine, Machiavelli, and Hegel. Paolucci also proved at the convention that he was a fiery orator who did not shy away from bashing the opposition.

While Rockefeller was working overtime to destroy it, other Republicans were embracing the Conservative Party. Many Republican legislators wanted at least to be friendly with the party, particularly after the publication in February 1964 of the party's first annual rating of legislators. The most significant expression of the party's growing stature was Senate Majority Leader Walter J. Mahoney's acceptance of the Conservative endorsement. Mahoney, who had represented Buffalo since 1937, read the handwriting on the wall, as did Assembly Republican Whip Bruce Manley, who also sought and accepted the Conservative line. A total of fourteen of the thirty-one incumbent Republican senators accepted the Conservative nod, as did twenty-nine Republican assemblymen.

The Conservative Party endorsed candidates against three incumbent Republican state senators, and independent Conservative candidates challenged several Republican Assembly incumbents, including Speaker Joseph Carlino, who was opposed by Nassau County lawyer Mason Hampton.

Early on there were some fine distinctions being drawn. For instance: Long Island Congressman Steve Derounian, a leading conservative, declined the Conservative Party's nomination, stating that since the party was strictly a state organization, it should have no say in electing House members. Signing on to his position were Representatives James Grover of Babylon and John Wydler of Garden City.[16]

In Queens County, Republican boss Frank Kenna ordered his legislative candidates to decline Row-D endorsements. The Conservatives then endorsed a Democrat, Fred Schmidt, over Republican incumbent Anthony Savarese. Fearful of losing their seats, several other incumbents wept and moaned so much that Kenna relented, although only for them.

All other independent Conservatives were challenged in the courts by the Republican organization. Jim Leff, with the assistance of Noel Crowley, fought the challenges. They were successful in all but one case: investment manager Robert Smith, who challenged Liberal-Republican Congressman Seymour Halpern, was thrown off the ballot for two reasons: first, because the defense's legal brief missed the filing deadline by twenty-four hours, and, second, because there was a minor deficiency in the Smith's nominating petitions (the words "Queens County" were missing after the political subdivisions title "Sixth Congressional District.") Although the Election Commission in other challenges to Conservative petitions had rejected objections of this sort, the commissioners contradicted themselves in this case and sustained the Republican challenge.

In Manhattan, the party nominated Suzanne La Follette (former *National Review* editor and cousin of Progressive Senator Robert La Follette of Wisconsin) for the Nineteenth Congressional District. The distinguished black journalist George Schuyler was named to oppose Harlem's congressman, Adam Clayton Powell, and Kieran O'Doherty agreed to run against incumbent liberal Republican John V. Lindsay in Manhattan's famous Silk Stocking District.

Reviewing the statewide strategy, Chairman Dan Mahoney told the media: "In addition to our activity on behalf of incumbent Republicans, we will be mounting a strong drive to elect conservative Republicans in many districts now held by incumbent liberal Democrats or retiring Republicans. This will parallel our effort to elect conservative Republicans, running on Row A and Row D, to the Congressional seats now held by liberal Democrats Stratton, Carey and Murphy.

"The clear majority of Republican state legislators with whom we discussed the matter were pleased to run on our line," Mahoney added. "In some areas, our determination to oppose a liberal Republican incumbent prevented any working alliance. Our general attitude towards regular Republicans is one of cooperation and amity, but the Conservative Party will take an independent position wherever circumstances warrant that action."[17]

Congressman William Ryan was so annoyed that he was opposed by a candidate on the Conservative line (first by Dr. Paolucci and, after he jumped to the U.S. Senate race, by John Comninel), that he read into the *Congressional Record* an article by Walter Kirchenbaum, self-anointed prophet of the Left, called "How Conservative Can You Get?" The piece had been published in what Mr. Ryan called the "very objective" newspaper, *Liberal Party*, and it is proof of just how desperately New York politicians wanted to label conservative activists as wackos.

> A reading of the New York State Conservative platform is like looking at a clock that has stopped. The second hand has stopped somewhere midway between yesterday and tomorrow. . . .
>
> The Conservative Party in New York has no future because it has no faith in the future. Its platform is built on corroded timber. It is a soulless platform and without soul a political platform is nothing but a waste of words woven together to inflame rather than teach. . . .
>
> As the conservatives take to their dinosaurs and ride the countryside warning about the "liberal plot" to take over the country, I, for one, hope they are right. For if it is constitutional government, individual liberty,

victory over all forms of totalitarianism, close to 400,000 liberal New York State voters as opposed to over 100,000 conservative voters know the difference between getting to these goals via positive means as opposed to negative routes. Let the clock tick toward tomorrow without compromise.[18]

In the autumn, Henry Paolucci hit the campaign trail with exuberance. His flamboyant style, sharp wit, and his constant verbal assaults on Senator Keating and Democrat-Liberal Robert F. Kennedy made for lively print coverage.

The Republican strategy for Keating was to encourage ticket splitting. To placate liberals and the "Democrats for Keating Committee", the Senator finally admitted that he will "never, never support Barry Goldwater for President."[19] Bumper stickers appeared urging a vote for "Johnson-Humphrey-Keating." *The New York Times* even agreed, arguing that:

Keating's re-election, if accompanied – as we hope it will be – by an overwhelming victory for President Johnson in this state, will represent the most forceful rebuff New Yorkers can administer to Goldwaterism.

Appearing on the CBS show *Newsmakers*, Paolucci responded to questions about reductions of federal controls and spending, an income tax cut, and the right to prayer in schools with answers seasoned with references to ancient and medieval history. When asked if he though his candidacy would hurt Senator Keating's chances for re-election, Paolucci replied:

. . . I don't care whether it hurts him or not. I am interested in getting Goldwater elected. I doubt that my candidacy will attract more votes from the Republicans than from the Democrats. I wish to attract as many pro-Goldwater votes as I can. I would like to give an opportunity to Democrats who are disgruntled to vote for Goldwater and also for Republicans who are fed up with this liberal acquiescence of Republicans to the one-party system we have had in this state.[20]

At the Conservative Party's Second Annual Dinner on October 21, Goldwater delegate Vince Leibel and Dr. Paolucci whipped up the crowd jammed into the New York Hilton Ballroom. William F. Buckley Jr., once again the keynote speaker, inspired the faithful with a stirring address on the goals of conservatives. He concluded with these words:

I only hope and pray that as times goes by, the Twentieth Century will shed the odium that clings to its name, that it may crystallize as the century in which the individual overtook technology; the century in which all the mechanical ingenuity of man, even when fired by man's basest political lusts, proved insufficient to sunder man's relation to, and dependence on, his Maker. The movement is of you, as American conservatives, by you, and in you. In wishing you luck, I am wishing for myself, and my family, and my country, good fortune, peace, and freedom.

As the campaign was winding down, the party's slate received a tremendous boost with the *New York Daily News* endorsement of Paolucci and O'Doherty over Keating/Kennedy and Lindsay.

But Barry Goldwater, trashed at every turn by northeastern Republicans, was creamed in New York on election day. (Of course, Lyndon B. Johnson won nationally in a landside.) Goldwater received less than a third of the ballots cast in New York and lost the state by nearly 3 million votes. (By comparison, Nixon garnered 47.3 percent in 1960 and lost by only 400,000 votes.) New York Republicans lost seven congressional seats and one seat in the Senate, Keating having lost to Kennedy. The Republicans lost control of both houses of the state legislature for the first time since 1932.

In the state senate, eight Republicans went down to defeat giving the Democrats a 33 to 25 majority. Republican incumbent Hunder Meeghan, who represented the Thirty-Second District in Westchester, lost because conservative Marie Smith received 2,088 votes on Row F. In this case, the Conservatives provided the margin of defeat.

In the lower house, Republicans lost twenty-three seats, leaving the Democrats with an 82 to 62 edge. To add to the misery, both Republican majority leaders, senate and assembly, went down to defeat. Walter Mahoney lost the seat had he held for twenty-six years by the stunning margin of 57 percent to 43 percent. Out in Nassau County, Assembly Speaker Joseph Carlino, who opposed Conservative cross endorsements, also went down in flames, receiving only 43 percent of the votes cast:

Carlino, Rep.	45,843
McDougal, Dem.	52,653
Folanga, Lib.	2,862
Hampton, Cons.	3,109

There were, however, some bright spots for the Conservatives. Paolucci's vote total was 212,216, a 50-percent increase over Jaquith's gubernatorial vote in 1962 and a whopping 75-percent increase over O'Doherty's senate totals that same year.

	Keating Rep.	Kennedy Dem.	Kennedy Lib.	Paolucci Cons.
Outside New York City	2,035,113	1,913,312	130,445	92,245
Bronx	164,953	313,418	34,696	22,820
Brooklyn	305,283	519,701	49,815	33,675
Manhattan	221,689	349,688	35,452	13,313
Queens	335,298	401,489	32,595	42,701
Staten Island	41,720	41,495	1,643	7,462
Total New York City	**1,068,943**	**1,625,791**	**154,201**	**119,97**
Total State	**3,104,056**	**3,539,103**	**284,646**	**212,216**

There were also interesting trends. The party outpolled the liberals in Staten Island and Queens as well as the four major suburban counties of Nassau, Westchester, Suffolk, and Rockland:

	Kennedy Lib.	Paolucci Cons.
Nassau	22,373	29,963
Rockland	2,078	3,355
Suffolk	9,291	15,504
Westchester	11,567	11,780

Local candidacies had begun to establish the party as a stronger force at the local level. There were six assembly races in which the Conservative Party vote was either the margin of victory or came within a handful of votes of being so. Also, thirty-two members of the New York State legislature were elected with the party's endorsement, as was Congressman Robert McEwen from the upstate Thirty-First Congressional District.

The Conservatives managed these achievements despite the fact that they did not have a presidential nominee at the head of Row D, that Kenneth Keating had been endorsed by Goldwater and Miller, and that the candidacy of Robert Kennedy had frightened many Conservatives into voting for Keating.

The 1964 performance proved, as John Chamberlain wrote the week after the election, that the Conservative Party is a "potent leverage group whose vote or endorsement might make or break a GOP candidate for almost any state office."

Chapter 5

Bill Buckley Mugs the Liberals
New York City's 1965 Mayoral Race

In the early 1960s, New York City's reform Democrats began a concerted effort to gain control of their party. These "Amateur Democrats," as James Q. Wilson has labeled them, were in an "ideal situation to recruit candidates on the basis of their commitment to a set of policies. . . . The party would be held together and linked to the voters by a shared conception of the public interest. . . . Private interests, which for the professional are the motive force of politics, the amateur would consider irrelevant, irrational or immoral."[1]

In 1963, reformer Edward I. Koch scored a major upset by beating the last "tiger" of Tammany Hall, Carmine DeSapio, for Greenwich Village Democratic District Leader. Other reformers throughout New York began to take control of their local organizations. The reformers were appalled by what they considered the parochial attitudes of rank-and-file Democrats. "Patronage" had strictly pejorative connotations; clubhouse beer parties and picnics were frivolous.

Surveying the battles between liberal reformers and conservative neighborhood regulars, Daniel Patrick Moynihan concluded, "the divergence is cultural in a broad sense." The reformers, he wrote, "are people with what is called a high rate of upward mobility. Not so the regulars who incline to stay near the old neighborhoods, speaking with the old accents, even after they have become rich and successful. . . . The liberals live in silk stocking Republican neighborhoods and they have virtually no connection with the working class."[2]

Losing assault after assault, the regulars desperately held on to their local patronage – judgeships and bureaucratic jobs in borough halls – but ceded state-legislative, city council, and congressional seats. Reformers such as Elizabeth Holtzman, Robert Abrams, Herman Badillo, Shirley Chisholm, Allard Lowenstein, Steven Solarz, Andrew Stein, Donald Manes, and Ed Koch, began their political careers by challenging "regular" incumbents.

For many liberal Democrats the collapse of Franklin Roosevelt's coalition can only be explained in terms of venality and racism. They are convinced that as soon as their traditional constituencies achieved middle-class status, they thumbed their noses at their benefactors. Speaker Tip O'Neill declared on one occasion: "I go out and campaign among those guys whose parents went to school on the G.I. Bill, got their first house on FHA housing, whose life has been made by these Democratic programs. Then they go out and make $20,000 a year and start voting Republican."[3]

Thomas and Mary Edsall's book *Chain Reaction* asserts that the politics of race has propelled significant numbers of voters out of the Democratic Party.[4] But is this rationale true?

Throughout the sixties conservative working class voters in New York's inner cities began to feel unwanted in the Democratic Party. As James Q. Wilson explains in the *Amateur Democrat*, the reformers fixation on "small-d democracy" and "good candidates," and with integration and other liberal causes "[was] simply irrelevant to the major preoccupations of both the lower classes and those middle-class represen-tatives of ethnic groups."[6] These old-line Democrats were concerned with neighbor-hood crime, the decline of traditional values, quotas, soaring welfare costs, the defense of freedom abroad, and respect for the American flag at home.

Both inner-city working people and the new ethnic suburbanites began to feel alienated from the Democratic Party's ideology and by the constituencies it embraced. "Before the sixties fairness had meant that a person received what his sweat earned him. The family that emerged from Ellis Island to work six days, twelve hour shifts in sweat shops deserved to move up. It had played by the rules. Just so, the less indus-trious did not deserve to do so well."[7] The voters who lived by this commonsense code were frightened by what they perceived to be a new doctrine of "fairness" in the Democratic Party, one that endorsed not equality of opportunity but equality of results. What's more, the reformers themselves labeled this working-class code as racist. But as Senator Joseph Lieberman of Connecticut, a Democrat who was elect-ed by going against the ideological tide of his party, points out:

> The average white voter is not racist. The average white voter is protective of what he has.... There is a sense of injustice here that is beautiful. It's more [the working class saying] "You [Democrats] are making a fool of me. What am I, a chump? I'm breaking my back, my wife is, too. And you're going to give my money to these people who don't even work and are pulling the wool over your eyes. What are you, fools?"[8]

In New York City's 1961 mayoral race, practically nobody saw this discontent sur-facing among white ethnic voters. Although Mayor Robert F. Wagner was reelected to a third term by deserting the "bosses" who created him and embracing the reformers, there was a third-party movement led by Comptroller Lawrence Gerosa that the ethnic neighborhoods found attractive.

Gerosa was elected comptroller on Wagner's ticket in 1953 and again in 1957. But a bitter feud developed between the men during their second term. So in 1961 Wagner dumped Gerosa from the ticket, and this prompted Gerosa to run for mayor independently on the "Citizens Party" ballot. This race "was the culmination of the conflict between the party's culturally conservative wing dominated by Catholics and the liberal wing dominated by Jews."[9] The conservatives lost the conflict, and gave their support to Gerosa, who "won 320,000 votes (14 percent of the total) mostly from Catholics who might have otherwise voted Republican."[10] The base of Gerosa's support came from ethnic voters in Catholic, blue-collar neighborhoods. Gerosa's message – that reformers were driving working-class Democrats out of their party – hit a nerve.

These battles among Democrats did not go unnoticed by the Conservative Party's leaders, who detected some interesting voter trends in the dismal 1964 presidential returns. Dan Mahoney realized that Barry Goldwater's appeal to segments of the New York populace was based on certain cultural issues: on opposition to Communism, support for the war in Vietnam, and skepticism about the Civil Rights Movement. In the ethnic Catholic suburbs and city neighborhoods:

> . . . the restless black ghetto impinged on Catholic trade unions and neighborhoods; rising taxes for escalating welfare bore down on small home-owners; soaring crime rates jeopardized blue-collar and middle-class lives; new sociological concepts hamstrung the police and undermined the neighborhood school; and new hiring policies and political realities disrupted the Catholic political clubhouses and municipal bureaucracies. More than any other Northeastern religious group, Catholics tended to inhabit the socio-economic "combat zone," confronting the Democratic Party with the cruel dilemma of aborting its ideological thrust or alienating the loyalties of its largest bloc of longtime supporters.[11]

It is interesting to note that although John F. Kennedy's share of the Catholic vote in 1960 increased substantially over Adlai Stevenson's in 1956, it did not reach the level garnered by Al Smith in 1928. Smith received 80 percent of New York's Catholic vote while Kennedy got only 60 percent.[12] Richard Nixon actually received a clear majority in most of New York City's working-class Catholic neighborhoods. (It is ironic that Alfred E. Smith, Jr., endorsed Nixon.)

Catholic Political Volatility in New York City, 1954–1960[13]

Assembly District	GOP % of Total Vote for Governor, 1954	GOP % of Total Vote for President, 1956	GOP % of Total Vote for President, 1960
13 Queens (German-Irish)	66	80	64
9th Brooklyn (Scandinavian-Irish-Italian)	60	80	60
2nd Richmond (Italian-Irish)	52	78	58
9th Queens (German-Irish)	64	76	56
1st Richmond (Italian-Irish)	51	75	55
3rd Queens (German-Irish)	55	74	59
12th Brooklyn (Italian-Irish)	50	73	53
10th Bronx (Italian-Irish)	49	70	49
20th Brooklyn (German-Irish)	43	70	45
3rd Brooklyn (Italian-Irish)	49	67	47
8th Brooklyn (Italian-Irish)	40	66	42

Goldwater actually won a majority of New York's white Catholics. In the blue-collar sections of Queens, Staten Island, Brooklyn, and the North Bronx, many Catholic neighborhoods gave solid majorities to the Arizona senator.

Italo-Irish Presidential Voting Trends in The Bronx, New York, 1960–1964[14]

Republican Share of Total Vote for President

Assembly District	1960	1964
10th Bronx	49%	45%
Italo-Irish EDs,* Throgs Neck	60%	65%
Italian EDs, Pelham Bay	56%	56%
9th Bronx	29%	25%
Irish EDs, Bedford Park	44%	42%
8th Bronx	30%	27%
Irish EDs, Fordham	46%	48%
7th Bronx	26%	20%
Italian EDs, 187th St.-Little Italy	40%	44%

*Election Districts (Precincts)

Also, in the substantially Catholic working-class suburbs, Goldwater ran well ahead of his 31.3 percent state total:

Suburban Voting Trends in the New York Metropolitan Area, 1952–1964[15]

	Republican Share of the Major-Party Vote for President			
Town	1952	1956	1960	1964
Upper & Upper-Middle-Class Suburbs				
Scarsdale*	78	72	63	35
Pound Ridge*	80	76	73	44
Upper-Middle-Class Largely Catholic Suburbs				
Pelham*	84	86	73	59
Working Class Suburbs (Substantiall Catholic)				
Orangetown**	68	75	58	41
Babylon***	71	76	55	43
Smithtown***	72	77	57	45
Oyster Bay****	72	73	53	42
Yorktown*	70	72	60	42

*Westchester County; **Rockland County; ***Suffolk County; ****Nassau County

Conservative Party leaders became anxious to test these trends in the 1965 mayoral race, particularly when it became apparent that the new poster boy of the Republican left, John V. Lindsay, was to be his party's standard-bearer.

The Silk-Stocking Challenger

In early 1965, political junkies anxiously waited to hear word from the tenant of Gracie Mansion whether he was going to seek an unprecedented fourth term for the office of mayor of the Greater City of New York. Robert Ferdinand Wagner, Jr., was the last of a breed of city politicians who succeeded at being all things to all segments of the voting population. The son of the revered left-wing U.S. Senator from New York, who gave the nation the 1935 National Labor Relations Act ("The Wagner Act"), Mayor Wagner justly laid claim to the proud banner of liberalism. To placate the Left's insatiable appetite for expansive government, he told them: "I do not propose to permit our fiscal problems to set the limits of our commitments to meet the essential needs of the people of the city." Wagner, A Roman Catholic of German and Irish descent, could also mix comfortably with the Tammany hall crowd, and he instinctively understood the needs of the neighborhood blue-collar ethics.

Sensing that a changing political climate in the sixties might just close the curtain on his balancing act, Wagner stunned the political world in June – just five months before the election – when he announced that he would not seek another term.

When Jacob Javits decided that he preferred to remain in the Senate rather than run for mayor, both he and Governor Rockefeller agreed that John Lindsay, the young congressman representing Manhattan's upper east side "Silk-Stocking" district had the best shot to capture city hall.

John Vliet Lindsay was born in 1921 on West End Avenue and grew up the quintessential WASP. He graduated from Manhattan's Buckley School and prepped at New Hampshire's St. Paul's School. After graduating from Yale in 1943, he joined the Navy, serving in both the European and Pacific theaters. Upon his return to civilian life, Lindsay graduated from Yale Law School and joined the firm of Webster, Sheffield.

Bored with the practice of law, the six-foot-three, blonde, blue-eyed Lindsay turned to politics. By 1952, he was president of the New York Republican Club, and he joined the Eisenhower Administration as special assistant to Attorney General Herbert Brownell. Realizing that Lindsay was a well-bred Progressive Republican, Brownell – a longtime crony of Governor Dewey – took the young assistant under his wing and began educating him in the ways of New York politics.

In 1958, Lindsay returned to New York to seek the Republican nomination in Manhattan's Seventeenth Congressional District. Lindsay was running in an area that was described by Bill Buckley "as probably the most fabled in the United States. It shelters not only just about·all the residential financial, social, and artistic elite of New York but also probably the densest national concentration of vegetarians, pacifists, hermaphrodites, junkies, Communists, Randites, clam-juice-and-betel-nut eaters . . ."[16]

Thanks in part to the efforts of Brownell, the WASP establishment rallied around Lindsay. The incumbent, Republican Congressman Frederic Coudert, was literally scared out of the primary, and Lindsay, "one of the bright hopes of the Republican Party" (as *The New York Times* described him), went on to beat his Democrat-Liberal opponent.

And he became one of the most liberal members of the House of Representatives. By 1964, he was voting with the Democrats half the time, and the left-wing Americans for Democratic Action gave him a rating of 87 percent. Lindsay went out of his way to infuriate conservative Republicans: he sponsored bills to abolish the House Un-American Activities Committee; refused to sign the annual statement opposing admission of Red China to the UN; opposed an amendment to permit prayer in public schools; voted against the reaffirmation of the Monroe Doctrine; and supported all of Lyndon Johnson's domestic initiatives.[17]

Lindsay refused to endorse Barry Goldwater and repudiated the GOP Platform. He would remind his constituents that: "I am not running as a Republican, I am running as Lindsay." His pretentious campaign slogan was "John V. Lindsay – The District's Pride, the Nation's Hope." While Republicans all over the state went down in flames, better than 70 percent of the "Silk Stocking District" voted to return

Lindsay to Congress. The *New York Times* saw Lindsay's "Stature Enhanced by Vote"; The *New York Post* called him "The Big Winner." Analyzing the 1964 results, Lindsay described his party as "a pile of rubble." He lectured that liberals "are among the Republicans who will have to rebuild the party out of the ashes. We hope we can work with other moderate groups throughout the country to return the party to the tradition of Lincoln."

With Nelson Rockefeller announcing in early 1965 that he would seek a third term as governor, and with Javits and Robert Kennedy sitting tight on their senate seats, Lindsay's options for political advancement were limited. After much vacillation, and after Rockefeller promised a substantial financial contribution, Lindsay announced his candidacy for the office of mayor of New York. In a city where Republicans represented less than a quarter of the voting population, Lindsay declared that to build a winning coalition, he would run as a "fusion" candidate.

The last mayoral candidate to carry that particular torch was Fiorello La Guardia. To win three terms, La Guardia had made a deal with all the anti-Tammany Hall reformers, and pledged an administration that would throw out the rascals and reform their corrupt ways. By "fusing" together these various municipal Goo-Goos behind his candidacy, La Guardia was able to beat the Democratic machine. Lindsay loved to wrap himself in the La Guardia mantle.

But Lindsay's call for fusion was a hardly serious. After twelve years in power, the Wagner Administration was not viewed by the public as corrupt – indeed it was relatively scandal-free, and the La Guardia analogy was weak. Lindsay's call for fusion was really just his subtle way of seeking the Liberal Party endorsement. He certainly had no intention of fusing with conservative Republicans.

Lindsay told the Liberal Party screening committee that, "I have been a liberal Republican in Congress. Everybody knows that I have been independent in my decisions. . . . I want a non-partisan city administration and not a Republican administration. I want a fusion ticket with a qualified Democrat and a qualified Liberal alongside myself. . . . I will get as far away from the Republican party as possible."[18] And to guarantee that he would receive the Liberal nomination, the "Good-Government," "Reform," "Fusion" candidate agreed that "liberals would receive one-third of all city jobs and judgeships, a chunk of money to use during the campaign, and the right to name one of Lindsay's running mates."[19]

While Lindsay was taking the city's Republican Party hard to the left, there were some significant changes taking place at Conservative Party headquarters as well. Dan Mahoney stepped down as a salaried employee and went back to the practice of law. He kept the title and some of the duties of chairman, but he hired attorney Martin Burgess as the party's executive director. Burgess would serve in the post for the next two years. These changes did not, however, stop Mahoney and Kieran O'Doherty from focusing on the 1965 election cycle. The U.S. Supreme Court decision that threw out the gerrymandering of New York's legislative districts – on the grounds that they violated the "one-man-one-vote" rule – meant that the entire state senate and assembly would have to run again in November. This presented opportunities for the Conservatives to help recoup Republican seats lost in the Goldwater debacle. Also, the new York mayoral race intrigued them. Just the thought of taking on Mr. Blue Blood Liberal-Republican got their heart rates jumping. First, of course, they needed a suitable candidate.

On Sunday, April 4, 1965, William F. Buckley Jr. was the guest speaker at the New York City Police Department's Holy Name Society Communion Breakfast. In his remarks to an audience that included Cardinal Spellman, Mayor Wagner, Police Commissioner Michael Murphy, and over 6,000 police officers, Buckley included a defense of officers accused of "police brutality." He suggested that the media was wrong in presuming that an excess of force was the norm. Such occurrences were actually rare, and, when they did occur, were often as not justified.

The next day both the *Herald Tribune* and *The New York Times* made a major fuss about his remarks. They claimed that he defended the Selma, Alabama, police who had recently used unnecessary force to break up a public protest led by Dr. Martin Luther King, Jr. By Wednesday, The *New York Post* was reporting that policemen laughed and cheered Buckley's "insensitive" remarks. Reading the news stories, State Supreme Court Justice Samuel Hofstadter sent a telegram to Police Commissioner Murphy, condemning him for permitting police to engage in such deplorable behavior. According to the judge, "5,600 members of the force cheered an attack on National Civil Rights leaders that would have done credit to the most rabid race baiters." Roy Wilkins of the NAACP and Jackie Robinson condemned Buckley.[20]

For his part, Buckley was livid over such shoddy reporting. And so he struck back. He called a press conference during which he played a tape of his speech. He pointed out that in four instances in which newspapers had reported applause, the tape showed there had been none. "A reader would be invited to assume that it was a gathering of sadists who gathered there to celebrate acts of brutality by policemen against civil rights workers,"[21] Buckley said. "The speech was not about civil rights, but dealt with the fact that there is generally much greater concern about the rights of alleged criminals than about the innocent people abused by these criminals."[22] Police chaplain Msgr. Joseph Dunne confirmed Buckley's statement saying that the media version of Buckley's remarks, "was a complete distortion, a very vicious and illicit type of innuendo which was an insult to the integrity of all who were there, including the Mayor."[23]

But the press conference had little effect, and the media headlines continued: "Storm Grows Over Buckley Police Talk;" "Protests Pour in on Buckley Speech." *The New York Post* reacted to Buckley's protest with an ironic editorial: "We Herewith Extend a Non-Apology."

Throughout the ordeal, Buckley learned, as he put it, that "the press cares about the scandal, much less about the subsequent developments tending to dissipate the scandal. . . . [I]f [the politician] desires to say something hazardous, [he] had better come prepared with tape recorder, steno-typist and ideally a motion picture camera-man trained on himself and on the audience."[24]

The Buckley Candidacy

As a result of this brouhaha, Buckley began paying closer attention to city politics, particularly the unfolding mayoral race. Not long after Lindsay announced his candidacy, Buckley penned one of his thrice weekly columns (carried in 1965 by 150 newspapers) titled "Mayor Anyone?" The essay described a ten-point program for any potential candidate. The major issues were covered – crime, drugs, water, finances – and Buckley admitted some of his observations were made "half in fun." When the column was reprinted in the next issue of *National Review*, it caught the attention of political wags, because Buckley's sister, Pricilla – then the magazine's managing editor – included a magazine cover headline that read "Buckley for Mayor." That caption caught the attention of Mahoney and O'Doherty. They knew Buckley would be the perfect foil for the "Silk-Stocking" congressman.

Shortly after Lindsay's announcement, Mahoney appeared on NBC's "Search Light" and made it clear that the Conservative Party intended to field a candidate. Afterwards, he leaned on *NR* senior editor Frank Meyer to poke around and find out if there was actually a chance that Buckley would run. While waiting for a return call, Mahoney confirmed with election lawyer Jim Leff that there was ample time for Buckley to change his record of residency from Connecticut to New York.

Meyer reported back that Buckley was pushing *National Review* publisher Bill Rusher to make the race. But according to Meyer, Rusher had turned down the opportunity. More important to Mahoney was what else Rusher had to say: he believed that if handled properly Buckley could be induced to run. In a conversation with Mahoney on June 4, Buckley was non-committal. But when Mahoney mentioned that there was ample time to change his voting residence, Buckley commented, "Is that so?" The way he said it gave Mahoney hope. And just a few days later Buckley confided to Mahoney that he really was leaning toward seeking the Conservative nomination. He made it clear that if he threw his hat in the ring, he intended to wage a campaign based on ideas and thoughtful position papers. He also made it clear that his candidacy could not interrupt his duties as columnist and *NR* editor. Mahoney was only too happy to agree. Suddenly they were discussing actual strategy. They decided that Marvin Liebman would be the ideal fundraiser and that a research director ought to be hired.

Years later, campaign aid Neal Freeman reflected on Buckley's rationale for making the run:

> He knew before the rest of us that it was going to be a big deal in the sense that it was going to be a transforming event for him and for the conservative movement. He smelled the possibilities there, and he went after them.

What he didn't appreciate was that to run for mayor of a city that large actually requires a little time, that it will interrupt your schedule a little bit. Making concessions to that reality was a difficult personal adjustment.[25]

After a June 10 meeting of Conservative Party chairmen from the city's five boroughs, Mahoney was able to report to Buckley that the nomination was his for the asking.

Buckley quickly moved to set up a campaign apparatus. He turned to his brother Jim to serve as campaign manager. James L. Buckley worked for the Catawba Corporation, the family oil-consulting business, and was a graduate of Yale Law School, where he was in the same class as John Lindsay and his twin brother David.

In fact, Jim served in David Lindsay's wedding party and was a godparent to one of his children. Liebman and Freeman agreed to work on the campaign, and Glen Cove School teacher Jim Griffin agreed to oversee the research efforts. The fledging campaign scored one early coup: it signed on Frederic R. Coudert, Jr., as campaign chairman – the very same Coudert who had lost his congressional seat to John Lindsay in 1958.

Buckley formally announced his candidacy on June 24 at the Oversees Press Club:

> I propose to run for Mayor of New York.
>
> I am a Republican. And I intend, for so long as I find it possible to do so – which is into the visible future – to remain a Republican. I seek the honorable designation of the Conservative Party, because the Republican designation is not, in New York, available nowadays to anyone in the mainstream of Republican opinion. As witness the behavior of the Republican Party's candidate, Mr. John Lindsay, who, having got hold of the Republican Party, now disdains the association; and spends his days, instead, stressing his acceptability to the leftwardmost party in New York, the Liberal Party. A year ago, Mr. Lindsay declined to support the choice of the national Republican Party – and of 27 million Republican voters – for President. Mr. Lindsay's Republican Party is a rump affair, captive in his and others' hands, no more representative of the body of Republican thought than the Democratic Party in Mississippi is representative of the Democratic Party nationally.
>
> The two-party system presupposes an adversary relationship between the two parties. That there is no such relationship in New York Mr. Lindsay makes especially clear when he proposes as running mates members of the Liberal and the Democratic Parties. Mr. Lindsay's Republican Party is a sort of personal accessory, unbound to the national party's candidates, unconcerned with the views of the Republican leadership in Congress,

indifferent to the historic role of the Republican Party as standing in opposition to those trends of our time that are championed by the collectivist elements of the Democratic Party. Mr. Lindsay, described by *The New York Times* as being "as liberal as a man can be," qualifies for the support of the Liberal Party and of the Republican Party only if one supposes that there are no substantial differences between the Republican Party and the Liberal Party. That there should be is my contention. Yet it is as foolish for a Republican who stands in opposition to those trends of our time to enter a Republican primary in New York City as it would be for Hubert Humphrey to enter a Democratic primary in Mississippi. If Mr. Lindsay is opposed to third parties, perhaps he will take the opportunity to invite the Liberal Party to dissolve.

Accordingly, as I say, I have declared my availability to the Conservative Party, thinking to give the people of New York an opportunity to vote for a candidate who consults without embarrassment, and who is proud to be guided by them, the root premises of the Republican philosophy of government, the conservative philosophy of government. . . .

In due course, I shall publicize suggested approaches to some of the major problems that face New York. They will be the result of diligent and, I hope, fruitful study, conducted in consultation with distinguished and experienced scholars and public-minded citizens whose collaboration I shall in due course gratefully acknowledge. The recommendations will be guided by the principles of a free and compassionate society, respectful of the rights of the individual, of the limitations of government and of the needs of community. . . .

I assume that there are many New Yorkers who take seriously the cliché that New York is in crisis, and who are serious enough to recognize that not a blessed reform of any consequence has been proposed by the major candidates. I appeal to them to help themselves and their fellow New Yorkers by voting the Conservative ticket in November.[26]

Listening to the Q and A with the press following Buckley's declaration, Mahoney was initially disappointed and feared some of Buckley's responses might cause his candidacy not to be taken seriously:

PAUL PARKER (WINS-Radio): Bill, are you in this campaign to win it or are you in the campaign to, judging from your statement here, perhaps pick away at what you regard as Lindsay's fraud on the party and –

WFB: No. I am in the campaign to get as many votes as I can get, consistent with maintaining the excellence of my position, so the decision, of course, is up to the people, not me. I will not adopt my views in order to increase my vote by ten people, as you have just seen.

ANOTHER SPEAKER: Do you want to be mayor, sir?

WFB: I have never considered it.

QUESTION FROM THE FLOOR: Do you think that is something that at present should be considered?

WFB: Not necessarily. What is important is that certain points of view should prevail. Whether you or I administer those points of view is immaterial to me, assuming you are a good administrator.

BARRY FARBER (WOR-Radio): But you are asking people to vote for you. If you win, will you serve?

WFB: If elected, I will serve.

BOB POTTS (WNDT-TV): Did you say something about what kind of campaign you will run? You are not going to go out and campaign in the streets?

WFB: No, I will not, primarily because I don't have time. I will spend what time I do have on trying to develop as carefully and responsibly as I can those positions that I want to project and will project them wherever the opportunity lies.[27]

The media reaction was interesting: Although many despised Buckley's views, they found the man to be charming, engaging, and funny. Certainly they figured he would liven up the campaign. The *New Yorker* pointed out that for most in the media, there was a "non-partisan reaction; regardless of what Buckley said they thoroughly enjoyed the way he says it. They seem to be grateful for being spared campaign clichés and relish his wit, vocabulary and Roccoco style."[28] Others had the expected reaction to a political Conservative: the Republican house organ, The *Herald Tribune*, viewed Buckley as a "right wing and ultra-conservative debater." *The New York Times* referred to him as "the leading apostle of Goldwater on the eastern seaboard."

Buckley was officially nominated at the Conservative Party Convention, as were his running mates. Rosemary Gunning of Ridgewood Queens, a leader in the battle to preserve neighborhood schools, was chosen as the candidate for president of city council. For comptroller the party nominated Staten Island accountant Hugh Markey, who had run such a respectable race for councilman-at-large in 1963. The convention also chose Manhattanite and Harvard Law School graduate Harry Middendorf, Jr. (whose brother William was treasurer of the Republican National Committee) as its candidate for New York State's highest judicial bench, the Court of Appeals. As the party's first nominee for the court, he was to face former Senator Kenneth Keating and Democrat Owen McGivern. After losing his senate seat, Keating had joined the firm of Royall, Koegel, and Rogers. Shortly before Keating arrived at the firm, senior partner Jack Wells (who served as Javits's honorary campaign chairman in 1962 and Rocky's 1964 presidential campaign chair) told Kieran O'Doherty, until then a firm associate, that it was time for him to pack his bags and leave.

Buckley requested that the Conservative Party make every effort to field candidates in all the legislative races. James M. Gay (future treasurer of the Conservative Party), who ran for one of those assembly seats in Brooklyn's Sunset Park (and received 16 percent of the vote that November), has remarked that Buckley was very grateful and generous to all who joined his ticket. To Jim Gay, Buckley wrote:

> Just a note to tell you how happy and honored I am that we are on the Conservative slate together. I am very deeply impressed by the quality of the members and leaders of the Conservative Party – as you know.
>
> I hope that in the course of this campaign you will give me the benefit of your experience, and that you will be understanding of my own inexperience. I shall do my best, consistent with the limitations of time and money, to help you; and know you will do the same for other members of the ticket.

Introduced by Henry Paolucci, Buckley gave the state convention's keynote address and he emphatically told the faithful of the gravity of the city mayoral campaign.

> The purpose of politics is to keep men free. It is their freedom that we are seriously concerned to achieve; not politics. By that standard the Conservative Party is the only serious political party in New York, and Mr. Markey, Mrs. Gunning and I its only serious candidates. We seriously desire to do something about crime in New York, and we are so serious in our resolve to do something about it, that we are prepared to face, to try to understand, and to try to do something about the major sources of crime, which are the despair, the demoralization, and the tragic disorderliness of a segment of the Negro community. We are so serious about the necessity to unburden the City, that we seriously propose doing without some of the City's allegedly free services, and will seriously propose explicit economies. We are so serious about the necessity to relieve an allegedly free community of the leverage upon it of a few organized labor unions,

that we seriously propose to take what steps we can to deprive them of their license to paralyze our commercial life and our press. It is concededly a dreadful extension of our duty to have to come to the aid of *The New York Times*; but we propose to do just that. We believe so seriously in the necessity for sound education, that we quite seriously advocate distinguishing between the goals of instant racial integration, and the goal of good education. We are serious about the necessity to unsnarl the traffic in our streets, the bureaucracy in our City agencies; serious about the necessity to plan the sufficiency of water, and the purity of the air.[29]

The speech finally put to bed the issue of Buckley's seriousness.

In a post-convention editorial, *The New York Times* made this tongue-in-cheek observation: "As the ticket making accelerates, one of the more tawdry aspects of New York politics is plainly evident, the 'balancing' for religion, race or both. The Conservatives alone threw caution to the winds and have an all-Catholic, all-Irish ticket this year."

The Great Race

While the Buckley organization was opening its headquarters at 29 West 45th Street, the Liberal Party formally endorsed John Lindsay. One party Boss, David Dubinsky, failing to mention the patronage deal, gave this rationalization for nominating a Republican: "Suppose we elect Lindsay as Mayor of New York City. What lesson does this teach to the other Republicans elsewhere who would like to be elected? They must conclude the way for a Republican to get elected is to act like Lindsay."[30]

Democratic primary voters meanwhile had given the nod to incumbent City Comptroller Abraham Beame for mayor, Queens District Attorney Frank O'Connor for president of the city council, and Bronx Judge Mario Proccacino for comptroller. Asked his reaction to his Democratic opponent, Buckley replied: "The differences between Mr. Beame and Mr. Lindsay are biological, not political."[31]

Perhaps the biggest break Buckley had in the race was the three-week newspaper strike that commenced just as the campaign was beginning. This meant that television debates, where Buckley could excel, became the prime media forum in the mayoral campaign.

It's fair to say that Buckley trounced his opponents in the numerous debates. Lindsay, with his chiseled good looks and sonorous voice, may have sounded great when he was fully scripted, but in the debate format, which emphasized spontaneous wit and a ready command of facts, he came across as dull-witted. The four-foot-eleven accountant, Abe Beame, looked and sounded like an IRS agent discussing an income-tax audit. Buckley's performance was so good, he even caught the eye of Pulitzer-Prize winner Theodore H. White:

On TV Buckley is a star. His haughty face, its puckering and hesitation as he lets loose a shaft of wit, would have made him Oscar Wilde's favorite candidate for anything. In television debate Lindsay is normally flanked by Beame, who wants to talk about budget figures. But when Lindsay can free himself from Beame's figures to loose any of the visions of his task forces, there, on his other flank, is Buckley, puncturing the dream or hope with a witch's shaft of rhetoric.[32]

1965 New York City slate (left to right): William F. Buckley Jr., for mayor; Rosemary Gunning for president of the city council; Hugh Markey for comptroller.

Columnists Rowland Evans and Robert Novak wrote that "Buckley's roguish wit and flashy idiom are made for television and this is a television campaign. As a result, New York's liberal voters are being exposed to larger doses of right-wing ideology than they've ever had before from a mayoralty candidate."

The debates also inspired Buckley himself, and he became a serious contender. When asked if he would be flabbergasted if elected, Buckley replied: "Having heard Mr. Beame and Mr. Lindsay, I would be flabbergasted if I weren't elected."[33]

As the campaign got into high gear, the three mayoral candidates realized they had to change their overall strategies. The Lindsay camp's original plan was to secure the traditional Republican base and to spend most of their energy attracting enough Jewish votes to put them over the top. Given that the Democratic candidate was Jewish, they knew they would have to concede a significant percentage of the Jewish vote to Beame, and so they began to concentrate on attracting the traditional blue-collar or "regular" Democrats. And the Buckley camp thought their candidate could attract Manhattan's white-collar Republicans, who would be charmed by Buckley's style and views. Both campaigns were mistaken.

Buckley's base support was in the outer-borough Catholic, blue-collar neighborhoods, and Lindsay was actually more attractive to the Wall-Street types.

Over at Beame's headquarters, they expected to lose the Jewish vote in
Manhattan, but were stunned when polls revealed that Buckley's popularity was surg-
ing in Brooklyn – Beame's own backyard.

Buckley made sure that his campaign issued serious analyses of issues and policy proposals about each of New York's major problems: crime, finance, taxation, welfare, housing, drugs, transit, education, water, and pollution. As early as July 25, he
submitted testimony to a U.S. House Education and Labor Committee hearing on
poverty. It was an excellent summary of his views on New York's plight.

On the failure of federal poverty programs:

> The poverty program in New York seeks to accomplish, by a variety of
> means, wholly praiseworthy goals which however are not accomplishable
> merely by the infusion of money into poor areas. It is the salient fact of
> life that money cannot in and of itself induce reforms of the kind that can
> take hold of poor areas and bring them up to national standards. Those in
> New York who are poor by our standards, are rich by the standards of other
> societies; indeed, are well off by the standards of our own society meas-
> ured 100 years ago. Those Americans who rose from poverty twenty, forty
> or sixty years ago, did so without the benefit of such programs as have
> currently been conceived. They did so because a spark burned among poor
> people which brought them to deeply desire to depart from poverty. And
> that spark was able to flame because we lived in a mobile society in which
> they could reasonably hope to put poverty behind them, and rise to the
> middle class.

On New York's economic plight:

> New York City is in the grip of an economic hallucination. Increasingly,
> New York looks to the federal government for relief. And yet New York
> sends almost three times as much money to Washington as it receives back
> from Washington. With the result that New York's politicians, who have a
> vested interest in economic ignorance, are all the time suggesting that
> Washington is letting New York City down; whereas, in fact, New York
> City is supporting Washington beyond the economic capacity of New York
> to do so. New York City is becoming a vassal state of Washington. We
> dutifully send to Washington our substance every year and spend our days
> crying to Washington for support for our needy – and for our non-needy.
> If the citizens of New York were suddenly to be released from obligations

to support the needy of Cleveland, Ohio, the bridges and highways of Hartford, Connecticut, the agricultural subsidies of rich farmers in Minnesota, the school programs for Hawaii, we would find ourselves with resources to spare to look after our own needy.

On New York's spiritual and psychological plight:

New York is also under the hallucination that to cure the problem of poverty we need only more houses, more education, and more job opportunities. We do need more and better houses – but we cannot have more and better houses unless we have people disposed to pay for more and better houses, and other people disposed to build more and better houses for less money. We do need more and better schools, but we need more than that people who desire to exploit the existing facilities for education – more people who desire more and better schools. One of our poverty ventures is now bogged down in a situation in which vocational job training is offered, yet fewer people graduate from those schools than drop our from them. We need more and better job opportunities – but we need in order to make those opportunities relevant, a class of people who desire to take advantage of those opportunities that exist, who are willing to work in order to qualify for such opportunities as exist. That is a spiritual and psychological problem, of the kind that neither the large-hearted ambition of Mr. Sargent Shriver, with billions in hand to dispense, can create; nor Mr. Adam Clayton Powell, with tens of millions to dispense in order to cultivate the discontents on which he thrives, can create.

On New York's labor practices:

Labor unions that discriminate against any qualified applicant by reason of race, should be denied the privileges given to labor unions under the National Labor Relations Act. The police of the City should protect the right of every New Yorker who desires to work, whether or not he belongs to a labor union. There are tens of thousands of people in New York who need services of many kinds, who cannot get those services promptly, or at prices they can afford to pay, because of the entrenched privileges of certain labor unions. There are people in New York who cannot get a taxi – because taxis are limited by New York ordinances. There are people in New York who cannot hire the services of apprentice plumbers, and electricians, and bricklayers, and masons, or linotypists, and newspaper distributors – because the labor unions deny them the right to take jobs at lesser stages than those guaranteed by the labor union oligarchy.

On New York's rising crime rate:

> The rising incidence of crime is such as to discourage small businesses that might otherwise take root, and help impoverished areas to help themselves. The little shops and enterprises that spend much of their time wondering whether their merchandise will be there the following day, or whether it will have been removed to a local fence, are unlikely to expand, or to entice, by their prosperity, others to come into the area. There is a nexus between the crime rate in New York, and the poverty in New York, as there is a nexus between the crime rate and almost every other problem in the City.

On the failure of liberal ideology:

> Above all, New York City must recognize that it faces a harsh dilemma. It cannot take creative steps to relieve the problem of poverty, without saying things which are politically objectionable. Politically objectionable to the poor *and* to the rich. Politically objectionable to the electrician who receives $12.00 an hour because he desires to maintain oligopolistic advantages over the labor market; and politically objectionable to the Poor who believe that they can rise into the middle class without any exertion on their own part. It is the obligation of political conservatism to speak the truth, by which men will be made free. The poor of New York should be advised that the reason why they are poor is one part other people's fault, but one part also their own. They are poor because those who are better off seek to take special advantages by reason of their special hold on politics and national legislation. And they are poor because they do not take advantage of such opportunities as in fact are open to them. America has proved that our traditional social system is the best means by which people can rise from poverty. All over the world, there are desperately poor people who have abandoned hope because their governors, wedded to the ideology of central control of the economy, freeze them in their wretchedness. We must resist ideology, and return to the ideals of self-help and community responsibility, and by so doing give grounds for confidence to those who are born poor, that they will not die poor, as ignominious wards of the Federal Government.[34]

Buckley was able to articulate views that professional politicians dared not express because those opinions might upset the racial, religious, or ethnic balance of their support. Bill Buckley's positions in the campaign hit a nerve with the neighborhood blue-collar ethnics, who felt themselves the victims of high taxes, rising crime, and failing schools. In Buckley, they found more than a spokesman. They found a hero. And polls began to reflect his popularity. The first *Herald Tribune* poll published on October 7, had Beame at 45.6 percent, Lindsay, 35.6 percent, Buckley, 10.2 percent, with 8.6 percent undecided.

Buckley's growing popularity and Beame's lead in the polls caused panic at Lindsay headquarters. Concluding that their initial strategy, which was simply "ignore-Buckley," had failed, they decided to concentrate on attracting more Jewish votes from Beame. In early October, Lindsay and the entire liberal-Republican establishment began a crusade to discredit Buckley. He was, they declared, a "Goldwater racist." Senator Javits warned the electorate that a Mayor Buckley would send "people on welfare to concentration camps. . . . I fear for the freedom of New York City."

On *Meet the Press*, Lindsay said Buckley adhered to "a radical philosophy full of hatred and division and violence."[35] "The City," Lindsay solemnly declared, "is a powder keg and Buckley is doing his best to light the fuse." The *Times* accused Buckley of "pandering to some of the more brutish instincts in the community . . ." Which instincts? Why only "fear ignorance, racial superiority, religious antagonism, [and] contempt for the weak."

Timothy Costello, Lindsay's running mate for the city council presidency, demonstrated the disarray in the Republican campaign when he condemned Buckley for propagating "the social doctrine of the Catholic Church," even as he urged New Yorkers to remember that a "vote for Buckley is an anti-Catholic vote."[36]

Buckley, a man with a prodigious sense of irony and humor, found little to amuse him in these false and malicious attacks. So he hit back during one of the televised debates:

> I agree that this is a city of fear, and I believe that John Lindsay is doing everything in the world that he can do to cultivate that fear. Every newspaper in New York is talking about his neat operation of the past five or six days. And that operation is explicitly leveled at the Jewish voters of New York City. Mr. Lindsay has been trying to say to them, in his special kind of shorthand, "Do you realize that Buckley is really in favor of concentration camps?" This single maneuver is intended to take votes away from Mr. Beame on over to himself. . . . [Thus] Mr. Lindsay . . . [characterizes] all my attempts to solve some of the pressing problems of New York as [calling for] one or another form of concentration camps, summoning up all kinds of Nazi versions of horror, aimed especially at members of the Jewish race.[37]

The Buckley campaign also filed a formal complaint against Lindsay with the city's Unfair Practices Committee. The complaint – which was thirty-nine pages long, included thirty-two exhibits, and was signed by Jim Buckley – charged that Lindsay and his associates were, "engaged in an irresponsible and reckless campaign; that they have deliberately intruded a racial issue by charging that it is Mr. Buckley's purpose to attract racist supporters at the conscious risk of loosing violence in New York City; and that they have equally deliberately injected an improper and irrelevant religious issue into the campaign." The complaint then requests that the "Committee investigate these charges, and that you bring your conclusions to the attention of the people of New York City at the earliest possible moment."[38]

Claire Boothe Luce also came to Buckley's defense:

> I am a New York voter, a Republican, a former keynoter at the Republican National Convention and a former Republican Congressman. I resent, and I believe that the people of New York should resent, Mr. Lindsay's extraordinary charges. He charges that any New Yorker who, like myself, favors a vote for Mr. William Buckley is a bigot, or a racist, or is trying to destroy the democratic process. I care deeply for the future of my Party, but I care even more deeply for the future of my Country. Mr. Lindsay's flat refusal to grant the sincerity and good faith of those who oppose him is more in the tradition of a Huey Long or a Senator Bilbo, than of a man who seeks election in a City that prides itself on its liberalism. I believe that both Al Smith and Fiorello La Guardia would be disgusted by Mr. Lindsay's tactics, and would, if they could, urge all Democrats and Republicans to rise up in protest against them.[39]

When mid-October polls showed Lindsay at 42 percent, Beame at 41.8 percent and Buckley at 16.2 percent it appeared that the Lindsay strategy was working, even though Buckley's numbers had nearly doubled. Something about the heat in the campaign had helped the two main ideological opponents, but it was killing Abe Beame, so now it was the Beame campaign's turn to hit the panic button. They too decided to turn their guns to Buckley.

Beame accused the Conservative candidate of running a campaign based on a program of "fear and prejudice, of hatred of neighbor for neighbor."

Now the truth is, Bill Buckley got into the mayoral campaign almost capriciously. His intention had been to articulate the issues, not to win votes, which is why he had wanted a campaign with no frills, and why he had intended to spend no more than a few hours a day actively campaigning. But by the time the race went into the stretch, Buckley had become a full-time dynamo of a candidate. Looking back, his brother Jim said: "Bill did go into this thing as a lark. But I think any sense of it being a lark rapidly disappeared."[40]

At an October 21st Manhattan Center rally, Buckley congratulated supporters on the battle they were waging:

Ladies and gentlemen, I do honestly feel a special admiration for you. Because you have to fight for your principles without the opportunity to defend yourselves publicly. Those of us who have occasional access to the public media – Mrs. Gunning, Mr. Markey, and myself – cannot adequately express your legitimate sense of outrage that you are, in virtue of your valiant efforts to do something for New York, do something for yourselves and for your family, denounced as bloodmongers, as anti-Catholics, as racists....Why should you be despised?

Because your principles inconvenience the spirit of the age. I don't need to tell you what that spirit is. I need only confirm that ours is a spirit of resistance to the effronteries of the 20th century that tell us that because the industrial revolution happened, and because the French revolution conditioned the thought of most of our intellectuals, and because Nietzsche announced that God is dead: that therefore, we are anachronized, we don't exist as relevant human beings.

I am a minority candidate, and I say: you may be a minority, but the whole world hangs on you. You are the strength of our free institutions, the strength of our traditions. I am very proud of you, and I want to identify myself with you, now and for all time.[41]

Mike Long, who was then chairman of Brooklyn's Cypress Hills Conservative Club (and would later become state chairman), remembered how Buckley electrified the conservative base. New clubs began to spring up all over Brooklyn and thousands volunteered to give out literature. At a rally held at the Brooklyn Academy of Music, Buckley spoke to a crowd that overflowed into the street. Dr. Henry Paolucci, whose father died the night before, insisted on appearing at the rally to introduce the candidate. Buckley, grateful for the fiery introduction and for Paolucci's loyalty under the circumstances, asked for a moment of prayerful silence in remembrance of the professor's father. Long, who was sitting in the audience that night, recalls how Buckley broke the moment of silence with the statement, "Now back to the wars." The crowd, Long says, went wild. Applause, cheering, and howls went on for minutes. Long recalls that after Buckley's speech, "the thousands who left the Academy of Music were so wound up, they were ready to go conquer the world."

The campaign was turning into a real street-corner battle. In the outer borough neighborhoods, all sides began to harass the candidates and their supporters. In his work, *The Ungovernable City*, Vincent Cannato reports that Sid Davidoff, a Lindsay campaign aide (who later served as deputy mayor and went on to become one of the city's leading lobbyists) recalled seeing:

policemen wearing orange BUCKLEY FOR MAYOR buttons, and some even joined in booing Lindsay. In this atmosphere, Davidoff believed "we had to be our own enforcers." Mike Long, now head of the New York State Conservative Party, remembers squaring off against Davidoff at a local Republican club in the Cypress Hill section of Brooklyn. Long and his friends had come to heckle Lindsay. Davidoff saw the group as potential trouble and headed their way. The two men faced each other down for minutes, narrowly avoiding a fistfight. Davidoff also attacked a teenager named George Marlin (who would later become the Conservative Party's candidate for mayor in 1993 and head of the Port Authority), while Marlin was handing out "Buckley for Mayor" literature in Flushing, Queens.[42]

As Election Day neared, Richard Witkin of the *Times* told his readers:

> The biggest issue in the mayoral campaign has turned out to be – not bossism, not time for a change, not crime in the streets – but the role of a third party candidate, who, with his flare for arch phrase-making, has sparked much of the controversy and all of the humor of the campaign.[43]

The Election Results

On election eve, the most reliable of surveys, the *Daily News* Straw Poll, considered the race too close call. The poll had Lindsay at 42 percent, Beame at 40 percent and Buckley up to 18 percent. The next night, Buckley and his entourage settled into the ballroom of the New Yorker Hotel for what pundits predicted would be a long evening. Around 9:45 P.M., *The New York Times* was ready to declare Beame a winner by 60,000 votes. Lindsay's Campaign Manager, Bob Price convinced them to wait. Around 11:45, concluding that the trend was for Lindsay, Buckley went to the ballroom to concede.

	Lindsay Rep.	Lindsay Lib.	Lindsay Total	Beame Dem.	Beame C.S.F.*	Beame Total	Buckley Cons.
Bronx	132,252	48,820	181,072	201,101	12,879	213,980	63,858
Brooklyn	231,309	77,089	308,398	343,108	23,252	365,360	97,679
Manhanttan	211,192	80,134	291,326	181,183	12,047	193,230	37,694
Queens	258,932	72,230	331,162	235,478	15,184	250,662	121,544
Staten Isl.	33,625	3,523	37,148	22,239	1,228	23,467	20,451
City-wide	867,310	281,796	1,149,106	983,109	63,590	1,046,699	341,226
Percentage	34.2	11.1	45.3	38.8	2.5	41.3	13.14

*C.S.F.= Civil Service Fusion Party

Like all third-party candidates contesting a close race, Buckley's percentage reflected in the polls dissipated in the election itself. Nevertheless, with 341,226 votes and 13.4 percent – Buckley had a dramatic impact on the election.

Many were disappointed that Lindsay was not stopped. That was, after all, the impetus behind the Buckley candidacy, and Kieran O'Doherty, for one, said that on election night he felt like he had ashes in his mouth. But there was some elation as well, because for the first time the Conservative Party had outpolled the Liberals in the City of New York.

Although left-wing pundits loved to assert that Buckley had actually elected Lindsay, upon closer examination it became obvious this was not the case. Lindsay received a quarter of his vote on the Liberal Party line. Most of those votes came from middle- and upper-class Jewish neighborhoods that normally voted Democratic. Beame, who carried Brooklyn and the Bronx, did well in the lower-class Jewish neighborhoods, and he carried the black and Puerto Rican neighborhoods by a narrow margin.[44]

This was reflected in the Louis Harris Voter Profile Analysis of ethnic preferences in the mayoral race:

Ethnic Group[45]	No. of E.D.s Polled by VPA	Lindsay	Beame	Buckley
Jewish (Manhattan)	7	49.3%	47.1%	3.4%
Jewish (Brooklyn-Bronx)	5	34.8%	61.1%	3.6%
Italian	7	40.7%	40.1%	17.8%
Irish	4	40.4%	37.5%	21.9%
Other Catholic (Central European)	4	33.5%	39.5%	26.2%
German (Lutheran)	2	50.4%	22.5%	26.3%
WASP	5	60.9%	15.9%	22.6%
Negro	5	42.4%	54.9%	1.1%
Puerto Rican	1	24.5%	72.4%	2.9%

Buckley did well in the outer-borough Catholic-Republican neighborhoods:[46]

A.D. #	County	Buckley Percent	% Rep. Registration	Description
94	Bronx	27.1	29.5	Parkchester-City Island-Pelham Bay
23	Queens	26.8	37.9	Ridgewood-Glendale
60	Brooklyn	26.7	36.5	Bay Ridge
64	Richmond	26.7	30.3	Fox Hills-Richmond-Tottenville
25	Queens	24.7	31.9	Woodhaven-Ozone Park
29	Queens	24.1	38.3	Hollis-Queens Village-Bellerose
31	Queens	23.8	35.5	Richmond Hill-Jamaica
27	Queens	23.1	34.5	Bayside-Douglaston-Little Neck
65	Staten Island	22.2	28.2	West Brighton Pt.-Richmond-Travis
93	Bronx	21.6	28.3	Woodlawn-Baychester-Morris Park
61	Brooklyn	21.5	31.5	Brooklyn Heights-Prospect Park
59	Brooklyn	21.4	32.8	Bay Ridge-Bath Beach

On the state level, Row D Court of Appeals candidate Henry Middendorf received 3.9 percent of the vote for a total of 207,387. Democrat-Liberal Owen McGivern, who lost to Keating, also received 3.9 percent on the Liberal line and outpolled the Conservative line by *only* 555 votes.

	Keating Rep.	McGivern Dem.	McGivern Lib.	Middendorf Cons.
Upstate	**2,092,381**	**1,042,618**	**55,586**	**60,745**
Bronx	164,154	161,824	27,158	26,323
Brooklyn	280,184	263,099	42,155	42,667
Manhattan	215,036	161,605	44,543	18,405
Queens	315,187	178,105	36,686	51,031
Staten Island	38,742	16,813	1,814	8,216
Total New York City	**1,013,303**	**781,446**	**152,356**	**146,64**
Total State	**3,105,684**	**1,824,064**	**207,942**	**207,387**
Percentage Total Vote	58.1	34.1	3.9	3.95

In the assembly races, with numerous Republican candidates succumbing to pressure to decline the line, Conservative candidates provided the margin of defeat in eleven races. These results prevented the Republicans from taking back control of the lower chamber. Instead of commanding an 86 to 79 majority, the Republicans sat in the minority with 75 seats to the Democrats' 90.

On the state senate side, the Republicans regained majority control. Conservatives provided the margin of victory in the election of Martin Knorr in Ridgewood, Queens, but they also provided the margin of defeat for Republican John Calandra in the Thirty-Eighth District in the Bronx.

The party also provided the margin of victory in Robert Connor's race for Staten Island Borough president. Republican Town of Huntington Supervisor candidate beat incumbent Democrat Robert Flynn, thanks to the Conservative line.

Conservative candidates ran in 650 races compared to 200 in 1964. Future State Chairman Serphin Maltese, who got active by filling out a post card he received from a *National Review* mailing, ran for the state senate in Queens. Also future Party leaders George McGuiness of the Bronx and Vincent Downing of Queens ran for the assembly on Row D.

The strength and stature of the Conservative Party was immeasurably enhanced by the 1965 performance. At *National Review*'s tenth anniversary dinner two weeks after the election, keynote speaker Barry Goldwater told those gathered that "Running as a Conservative in New York City must be an interesting experience. You're not really a candidate. You are a political Kamikaze. . . . But Bill Buckley ran a great race. I understand at one point, Bobby Kennedy was so worried, he put Staten Island in his wife's name." In closing, Goldwater summed up Buckley's contribution this way: Buckley was, he said, the "man who lost the election but won the campaign."[47]

Chapter 6

Breaking Records
1966–1968

As 1965 came to a close, Dan Mahoney and Kieran O'Doherty felt deeply satisfied with their accomplishments. In three years, the Conservative Party had earned a permanent spot on the state's ballot and had proved that many New York voters yearned for responsible government based on conservative principles.

Yet with all its successes the party also had its share of problems, the foremost being money. The party generally lived on a very modest month-to-month budget. In 1964, for instance, total income was $94,704 and expenditures were $86,990. The annual appeal, the primary source of revenue, raised $43,000 and the anniversary dinner brought in $24,365. With three full-time and four part-time employees, the total payroll was only $21,352, proving that dedicated conservatives were willing to work "on the cheap."

Things improved in 1965: income jumped to $137,663. Thanks largely to all the attention given to Bill Buckley's mayoral race, individual contributions to the party itself rose 150 percent to $29,168, and donations to specific campaigns skyrocketed to $44,390 from $14,294 the year before. This windfall – if you can call it that – helped the party bring down its long-term debt from $21,000 to $5,685.

Despite its tiny budget and small staff, the Conservative Party managed to grow in stature and in membership. When the 1963 enrollments were announced early in 1964, the party was off to a solid enrollment of 10,329. Although this was only a fraction of the party's voting strength, it represented a committed core of regulars upon whom the future of the party depended. In the spring of 1965, the Department of State announced that the Conservative Party had more than doubled its registered enrollment to 21,590. In New York City, the figures jumped from 2,925 to 8,686.

Early in 1966, as Dan Mahoney was beginning to make plans for that year's elections, he was delighted to learn that Party registration had increased again and that the statewide total was now at 30,936. New York City registrations skyrocketed to 15,565 – more tribute to the Buckley race.

Conservative leaders firmly believed that 1966 could be their banner year. Their goals were to oppose Rockefeller's bid for a third term and to outpoll the Liberal Party statewide, which would advance the party to the Row C ballot line.

When Nelson Rockefeller had hinted in May 1965 that he intended to seek a third term, Mahoney wasted no time in making clear the Conservative Party's intentions:

> Nelson Rockefeller is simply a New Deal retread, whose program has been expropriated from the Democratic Party of New York. . . . Accordingly to ensure a real choice to the voters and a thorough review of the record of the Rockefeller administration, the Conservative Party will definitely field a candidate for governor in 1966 if Nelson Rockefeller persists in his announced intention to seek re-election.[1]

Rockefeller had been able to continue his spending spree during his second term, because in addition to owning the Republican Party, he had managed to make the Democratic Party a wholly owned subsidiary of his political conglomerate.

On election night 1964, the Democrats were pleasantly surprised to discover that the Goldwater debacle had given them majorities in both houses of the state legislature. Just how unprepared they were for their new responsibilities became obvious in January when the legislature met to elect the speaker of the assembly and the senate president pro tempore.

The newly elected Democratic members of the legislature found themselves in a party that was hopelessly splintered. There were New York City "regular" members, some pro- and some anti-Mayor Wagner. There were the self-righteous members of the reform movement, and there were the newly elected upstate Democrats, who were more conservative than the New York City contingent and were determined to have a say in party matters.

By the time the legislature met formally in January, all sorts of behind the scenes political maneuvering had taken place. Two old guard Democrats, Bronx boss Charles Buckley and Assemblymen Stanley Steingut of Brooklyn, made a deal with long-time Albany County Democratic boss Daniel O'Connell to push Steingut for speaker and Julian Erway of Albany for senate majority leader. Meanwhile the friends of Wagner had thrown their support behind Brooklyn Assemblyman Anthony Travia and Manhattan Senator Joseph Zaretski.

When the Democratic Conference met on December 22, 1964 at the DeWitt Clinton Hotel, the old guard had the majority of votes, but the Wagner faction refused to make the designations unanimous. And, sure enough, when the whole legislature convened in early January and moved to the business of electing officers, no candidate was able to obtain the necessary votes in either house.[2]

For weeks the Democratic majority was in disarray, and virtually nothing was getting done in Albany. Committees could not be formed, legislation could not be introduced, and the state budget could not be enacted.

After observing this chaos for more than a month, Nelson Rockefeller sensed an opportunity: a chance to spirit his spending agenda through the legislature. And so he went into action. He told Mayor Wagner and his Albany forces that he would supply the necessary Republican votes to support their original team of Travia and Zaretski. Rockefeller did not mind making the deal because he believed he could work with Wagner and his cronies. Besides, it was a golden opportunity to humiliate the junior Senator from New York, Robert Kennedy, who supported the Steingut ticket. Almost as an afterthought, Rocky made it clear he expected Democratic support for the creation of a state sales tax.

And so the political wags were dumbfounded when Syracuse *Republican* Senator John Hughes nominated *Democrat* Joseph Zaretski for president pro tempore. He was elected with the votes of twenty-five Republicans and fifteen Democrats. In the lower house, Anthony Travia was elected speaker with the combined votes of thirty-five Democrats and forty-six Republicans.[3] Governor Rockefeller now had the legislature in his back pocket, and it was one to his liking, which is to say, *liberal*. He no longer had to wrestle with upstate conservative Republicans; he could just make deals with Democrats who were sympathetic to his spending schemes.

When Rockefeller took office in 1959, he gave New York the first $2-billion budget in the state's history. Five years later, he topped that with the state's first $3-billion budget. And by 1966, with the help of his Democratic friends, the budget topped $4 billion.

As alarming as these figures were, they did not tell the full spending story, since appropriations always exceeded the budget. In 1963–1964, the state actually spent $4.2 billion and in 1965–1966, $4.4 billion. Democratic Comptroller Arthur Levitt estimated that total state spending in fiscal 1967 would reach $5.6 billion.

The overspending occurred – then and now – because in the final chaotic hours before the state legislature adjourns, a *supplemental budget* is introduced – and usually passed in the middle of the night. Throughout the sixties, the supplemental budget generally restored all the cuts that had been made in committee to the original budget submitted by governor, and it often included new spending. This kind of fiscal mischief permitted Rockefeller to announce in January 1966 an election year budget of under $4 billion, but gave him $4.8 billion in appropriations before the legislature adjourned.

To meet his constitutional obligation to manage a balanced budget, Rockefeller would employ a surfeit of bookkeeping gimmicks and veiled borrowing. He would delay income tax refunds and "borrow" cash by way of issuing Tax Revenue Anticipation Notes (TRANS) for a short period to give the illusion of a balanced budget.

During the first eight years of his tenure, revenues from personal income taxes were increased 186.4 percent to finance his slew of new programs he created that bloated his budgets, among them: the Office of Atomic Development, the Office of Transportation, the Council of Arts, the Office of General Studies, the Office for Local Government, Water Supply Planning Aid, Aid for Sewage Treatment, the State

Recreation Council, the Office for the Aging, and the Department of Housing Code Enforcement and Identification.

One program the Conservative Party opposed from inception and predicted could someday bankrupt the state was the Medicaid Bill that Rockefeller signed into law on April 30, 1966.

When the 1965 "Great Society" Congress passed the National Health Act, there was more in the law than Medicare for senior citizens. Title 19 of the law established guidelines for a Medicaid Program that states could adopt to provide medical services for welfare recipients. The federal government would cover half the costs, and the states would have to pay the other half.

Seeing this as an opportunity to receive huge sums of federal dollars, Rocky quickly sent a Medicaid bill to the state legislature. Liberal Democrats had a field day – they added numerous amendments that offered coverage not just for welfare recipients but also for those they more broadly defined as "poor." What's more the legislature decreed that Albany would pick up only half of the state's portion of Medicaid costs; the rest of the financial burden would have to be shouldered by local governments.

The Conservative Party complained that "it is doubtful if at any time or in any place any legislative body, with so little study and deliberation, [has ever] passed so inept and ill-considered a piece of legislative lunacy as New York State's brand new Medicaid Law."[4] No one could guess how much it would cost annually. Estimates for year one ranged from Rocky's optimistic $532 million for the first year to a grim $1.9 million. Estimates of those eligible ran from 2 million to 8 million. In upstate New York, many rural counties feared that up to 80 percent of the families in their political sub-divisions would be eligible. Municipalities panicked because they had not budgeted for their mandated quarter share of the costs, nor did they have a tax base sufficient to obtain the needed revenues.

New York's version of Medicaid decreed that a family of four with an after-tax income of $6,000 a year (which seems low today but then was not), who own their home and a car, who have $3,000 in the bank and $4,000 in insurance and who never before thought of themselves as "medically indigent," were now entitled to have all medical bills paid by the people of the State of New York. Medical costs included doctor bills, dentist bills, hospital bills, druggist bills, eyeglasses, and dentures. It included any kind of therapy prescribed by any kind of doctor.[5]

In essence, the law written in April 1966 directed half the people of New York State to pay the medical bills of the other half. The law mandated that welfare officials must seek out potential beneficiaries, and it exempted all relatives from any responsibility for the care of "indigent" family members. It was designed to make dependency a way of life in New York State. And the Conservative Party was a voice in the wilderness warning the public that the program could one day bankrupt both state and municipalities alike.

Back in 1962, when he had felt the heat of the new Conservative Party, Rocky had told the voters, "I can say categorically there will be no increase in taxes the next four years. There will be no need for one." Throughout his second term, the Conservative Party constantly reminded the public of this pledge.

But when Rockefeller proposed his 1965–1966 budget, which Comptroller Arthur Levitt called "most extravagant," it included numerous tax increases, including a state sales tax. This proposed tax would hit tobacco, gasoline, liquor, hotels, and various other services.[6]

To make the tax attractive to New York City legislators, Rockefeller designed it so the city's actual tax increase "would amount only to one percent because the City's own sales tax would be reduced by one percent (from five percent to four percent) before adding the 2 percent state charge. In addition, the city's lost revenue would be restored through increased state aid financed by the stock transfer tax."[7] In other words, to soften the blow in New York City, the governor was content to hit the rest of the state twice as hard.

By the spring of 1966, Rockefeller's popularity was hitting all-time lows. His own polls showed that less than a quarter of the state's voters wanted him elected to a third term. "Husbands have left home with higher ratings than that, Governor," said Rockefeller's pollster. "You couldn't get elected dogcatcher."[8] For a few moments, even the Rockefeller's old friend Jacob Javits thought about challenging him for the gubernatorial nomination. Rocky quickly reminded the senator that his financing of the state party gave him a controlling interest; but to humor Javits, Rocky agreed to support him in the 1968 Republican Convention as New York's favorite son.

Smelling victory in the air, Democrats starting "popping out of the woodwork" to grab the crown. Wannabes included Eugene Nickerson, Howard Samuels, Congressman Howard Stratton, Frank O'Connor, and Franklin D. Roosevelt, Jr. According to most political pundits, the front-runner was O'Connor, president of New York's city council.

A lifelong resident of Queens, O'Connor served as a state senator and as district attorney before being elected to the Council in 1965. Alfred Hitchcock immortalized O'Connor in the 1956 film, *The Wrong Man*, about his brilliant defense in the mistaken-identity case of Christopher "Manny" Balestrero. In the movie, Henry Fonda played Balestrero and Anthony Quayle portrayed O'Connor. When he was re-elected Queens D.A. in 1963 with nearly three-quarters of the vote, O'Connor began traveling around the state, hoping to drum up support for a run against Rockefeller in 1966.

He won the Democratic nomination for city council president in 1965 by beating Daniel Patrick Moynihan by some 90,000 votes. In the election itself, despite the fact that his mayoral running mate, Abe Beame, was soundly defeated by John Lindsay, O'Connor ran ahead of the ticket by over 170,000 votes.

O'Connor seemed to many the odds-on favorite to be chosen the nominee of both the Democrats and the Liberals, but there were a few – a powerful few – who disagreed.

Bobby Kennedy, for one, was in no rush to have a Democratic governor capable of taking control of the state party, and his support for O'Connor was lukewarm at best.

O'Connor succeeded in winning the Democratic line, and made a gesture of unity by agreeing to take one of his opponents, Howard Samuels, as his running mate, but there remained another also-ran, who was not collegial in defeat: Franklin Delano Roosevelt, Jr.

FDR Jr., it may be said, did not inherit his father's political skills. He was, in fact, a ne'er-do-well who thought he was entitled to inherit high public office. As the candidate for state attorney general in 1954, he was badly beaten (in what was otherwise a banner year for Democrats) by Republican Jacob Javits. In 1965 he announced his intention to run for mayor of New York City and was hurt when his party simply ignored him. And by 1966, this friend of the Kennedys, who squired JFK's widow to fashionable functions around Manhattan's Upper East Side, had – on no evidence of any political following – begun to fancy himself the heir to the job his father and his Uncle Teddy had once held.

But though the name had magic the man did not. Nonetheless, the Liberal Party's Alex Rose and David Dubinsky did sense in Roosevelt the chance for a little political trickery. They did not like Frank O'Connor because they believed that "deep down" he was actually a cultural conservative, a Catholic from the neighborhoods of Queens who couldn't be trusted to toe the liberal line. It was no comfort to them when on one occasion O'Connor confessed: "So many ideas I had as a young man I've discarded. . . . I can only repeat that I wasn't born a liberal. I've had to fight my background to become one."[9] If this was meant to placate the Liberal Party, it failed to do so. And having analyzed Bill Buckley's 1965 vote, the Liberal Party's leaders concluded that their continued possession of Column C was in jeopardy, and that an O'Connor endorsement wouldn't help much to retain the line. So they turned to the bitter FDR Jr., who agreed to head up their ticket.

The Battle over Policing

During all this political turmoil, the Conservative Party remained very busy. In addition to searching for suitable statewide candidates, the party leadership decided to take on a cultural battle that was then brewing in New York City.

When John Lindsay took over as mayor in 1966, one campaign promise he kept was his creation on May 17 of a Civilian Complaint Review Board (CCRB) consisting of four civilians and three policemen.

The concept of a civilian board, which was to review allegations of police brutality, had been kicked around in New York since 1950, when a review board consisting strictly of police officers was instituted. In April of 1964, the board became a focus of controversy when a liberal Democrat, Councilman Theodore Weiss of Manhattan's West Side, proposed a bill in the city council calling for a nine-member CCRB. Inspired by the civil-rights marches in the South, Weiss believed it was time to bring the movement to New York by undertaking reforms of the NYPD. When race riots erupted in Harlem in 1964 and 1965, Weiss and others charged the police with insensitivity to minorities. Many liberals thought these allegations strengthened the case for the CCRB. But Police Commissioner Michael Murphy and most of the city's establishment opposed the Weiss bill, and it died in committee.

In his nationally syndicated column, Bill Buckley addressed the issue of "police brutality":

> The point of a civilian board is to interpose some authority between the regular victims of the alleged brutality of policemen, and the police authorities. It is widely felt among the colored population in New York and elsewhere that the police are regularly abusive and that it is hopeless to call the police to account for being so when it is a foregone conclusion that their superiors will consistently side with the police. Thus they seek their own representatives, to serve alongside the police members of the review board, to insure them justice.
>
> The underlying question very seldom surfaces, namely, why should the police be brutal to the colored minority, assuming that they are? An unanswered question because it requires either discreet evasion, to summon statistics which can sound invidious.
>
> The fact of the matter is that crimes in New York are committed by Negroes greatly in excess of the per capita average; so that there are, constantly, more frequent contacts, and more frequent points of friction, between Negroes and policemen, than between whites and policemen. It is perfectly understandable that a people should think of themselves as oppressed and discriminated against if they feel that the eyes of the law are constantly and discriminately upon them. . . .
>
> That pride regularly fanned by the demagogues of dissatisfaction, whose surly spirits feed on supposing that every effort to crack down on crime is a concealed assault on the Negro people.
>
> The dilemma requires considerable tact. Politicians tend to believe that tact requires submission to the line of least resistance, which in New York is to measure the velleity of the majority opposed to a civilian review board, against the martial demands for it by the minority, and come out for the latter.
>
> The tactical advantages of such a policy are at the expense of the community's strategic objectives which are first the restoration of order to the streets of New York, and second, a reconciliation between the races based on a mutual respect, and a mutual recognition of objective realities.[10]

When Lindsay announced the creation of his version of a review board, he appointed his mentor from the Eisenhower Administration, Herbert Brownell, as chair of the screening committee that would select the civilian members of the board. Bill Buckley immediately sent the following telegram to Mr. Brownwell.

> Urgently recommend Vincent Broderick, Michael Murphy, Stephen Kennedy and Francis Adams for consideration of your Committee. Assuming four civilians must be added to police complaint review board, a point which neither the Conservative Party nor I concede, these four former police commissioners should be selected. They combine required experience, integrity and judgment in unique measure. Their selection would redeem Mayor Lindsay's foolhardy campaign pledge with minimum damage to law enforcement in New York City.[11]

Those actually appointed to the board were a very different group. The chairman was NAACP Vice President and ACLU Director Algernon Black, who was to write in his book *The People and the Police*:

> Historically the police have almost always been a reactionary force defending the king and emperor, the nobility and the aristocracy, the institutions of property and repression. Historically they are identified with the upper classes and against the masses. Normally they would tend to defend the employer and the factory against the workers and the unions, the landlords against the tenants, and in Western culture the white people and their power and privilege against those who challenge these. As the police represent authority, they become the focus for all the resentments which Negroes hold against a system of law and property and politics which denies them equality of opportunity and a fair share of the good things of American life.[12]

Reacting to Black's appointment, Bill Buckley said that he was "the most spectacularly disqualified man to investigate a criminal situation in the history of the United States. A man who knows as much about crime as Quakers do about war. . ... He has always backed oddball left-wing causes. A man who wouldn't know the difference between a black jack and a crucifix."[13]

The Conservative Party reacted immediately by objecting to the mayor's capitulation to minority-group demands that Lindsay, rather than the police commissioner, appoint the civilians to the board. The party took the position that Lindsay was violating the city charter, which clearly provides that jurisdiction over such appointments rests with the police commissioner. As Dan Mahoney put it:

> Lest there be any misunderstanding, the Conservative Party reiterates its

absolute and unwavering opposition to Mayor Lindsay's whole scheme to pack the police review board with a non-professional majority. At the outset, this plan was a political expedient designed to woo minority group votes at the expense of effective law enforcement in New York City. It is disheartening that this same pattern continues to prevail as the details of the Lindsay proposals are exposed to public view.[14]

And the Conservative Party was not alone in opposing the board. The President of the Patrolmen's Benevolent Association John Cassese announced that his union, which represented 20,000 patrolmen, was opposed to the mayor's review board and was prepared to spend whatever was needed to eliminate it. Cassese announced that he would commence a petition drive with the intention to force a referendum on the fall ballot.

New York City's Municipal Charter permitted ballot referendums to change the city charter if the sponsors successfully followed a very rigorous petition process. Thirty thousand signatures were needed, presented in much the same way as the complicated forms for establishing new political parties, and had to be filed no later than July 7 with the city clerk. Then another 15,000 signatures had to be filed by September 8.

Although the Conservative Party was initially inclined to support the PBA's densely detailed charter amendment, it was agreed after meeting with PBA leaders that the party would circulate its own more simplified petition. Since legal challenges to the petitions were expected, party lawyers Charles Rice and Jim Leff believed a separate petition would be a good insurance policy to ensure that some form of referendum would appear on the ballot.

The party was confident of success, because 1966 was a politically active year. The Congressional delegation, the state legislature, and delegates for a state constitutional convention were all up for election. Conservative activists could easily carry a referendum petition when they went door-to-door gathering signatures for their local representatives.

The movement was called COPS (Committee on Public Safety) and its membership included William F. Buckley Jr., Hugh Markey, Rosemary Gunning, Kieran O'Doherty, and Charles Edison. The petition drive began on June 22 and in only fifteen days 40,383 signatures were collected and filed in the County Clerk's office. The PBA also filed 51,582 signatures for its charter amendment.

Lindsay blasted the opposition plans as the work of "highly organized, militant right-wing groups." The city's human rights commissioner saw the efforts as an "appeal to basic prejudice and bigotry."[15] Roger Starr, and expert on New York City politics, has concluded that this ideological clash "marked the point at which the Lindsay Administration found that it had picked the strategy of social progress over the strategy of 'good government.'"

Concluding that both the Conservative Party and the PBA petitions were flawed (their legal form was imprecise and both possessed defective signatures – or so it was alleged), City Clerk Herman Katz sued to have the petitions invalidated. Both the New York State Appellate Division and the state's highest judicial review, the Court of Appeals, rejected Katz's objections concerning the legal form of the petitions.

While the courts were reviewing the legality of the signatures on the petitions, Dan Mahoney held a strategy meeting with Conservative Party chairmen from the five boroughs and with representatives of the PBA. The participants agreed that having two amendments on the ballot would lead to voter confusion, not least because on election day those who opposed the CCRB would have to vote "yes" for both Amendments.

On September 28, Dan Mahoney held a final meeting with his five county leaders (Ted Dabrowski of Queens, Mauro Magnami of Brooklyn, Charles Witherwax of the Bronx, and Marie Monplaisir of Staten Island) as well as John Cassese and Norman Frank of the PBA. While the party leaders knew that the rank and file would be disappointed if all their work in gathering petitions was for naught, in the interest of achieving their shared goal they recommended that the party withdraw their petition in favor of the PBAs.

On September 29, Jim Leff made a motion in court withdrawing the Conservative Party's proposed ballot referendum. At a joint press conference with the PBA, Mahoney told New Yorkers:

> As of today, the form of the P.B.A. petition has been upheld by the Court of Appeals, and the City Clerk has certified that an adequate number of valid signatures has been submitted in support of that petition. After extensive consultation with local Conservative Party leaders, the Conservative Party has therefore determined to throw its wholehearted support behind a single ballot question, in support of the broader-based citizens committee which is now leading this fight, and withdraw its own Review Board petition.
>
> There is already an element of confusion in this referendum, because those who oppose the Lindsay Review Board must vote "yes" on the referendum. It would compound that confusion if opponents of the Lindsay board were required to vote "yes" twice, and this would be the case if our petition went on the ballot. The Conservative Party believes that confusion on this vital question would not serve the public interest.
>
> To those who signed the Conservative Party petition, and even more to those who worked so hard through the hot summer months in its behalf, the Party extends its heartfelt thanks. But we know that this tremendous effort was made by Conservative Party workers out of concern over a vitally important public question, and not with a view to narrow party advantage.

It is in this spirit that the Conservative Party has made its decision to withdraw its review board petition. We call upon all New Yorkers who are concerned for the safety of their city and the integrity of their police department to unite behind the Independent Citizens Committee against civilian review boards as we do today, in its historic fight on this crucial issue.[16]

In a September 30 editorial, the *New York Daily News* commended the Party:

To help the voters – in the Nov. 8 referendum on the John V. Lindsay civilian-majority police review board, the Conservative Party has taken its anti-board petition out of the picture.

The Conservatives are as strongly opposed as ever to the board, and as anxious to see the voters give it the axe.

But the Patrolmen's Benevolent Association petition has won in the courts. The Conservatives are pulling theirs out to save the voters the inconvenience of two review-board referendum questions instead of one.

Anyway, don't forget: Because of tricky question wording, you must vote YES to vote AGAINST the Lindsay Board.

Lindsay's corporation counsel was shocked by the move, and he actually tried to get the courts to keep the Conservative Party referendum on the ballot. The city was successful in the Appellate Division but on October 25, two weeks before election day, the Court of Appeals in a 7-0 decision, ruled that the party could withdraw its referendum. On the November ballot, Local Question #1 would read:

Shall there be adopted a local law entitled "A Local Law to amend the New York City Charter in regard to the establishment of a procedure for handling civilian complaints against members of the police department." Inserting a new Section 440, requiring that any board established by the civilian complaint against police department members shall consist only of full time members of the police department or at least one year prior police department service; and providing that neither the Mayor, the Police Commissioner nor any other administrator or officer of the City may authorize any person, agency, board of group to receive, investigate, hear, recommend, or require action upon such civilian complaints, and providing further, that such section shall not prevent investigation or prosecution of police department members for violations of law by a court, grand jury, district attorney, or other law enforcement agency?

The Election of 1966

While this battle was going on, the party also had to assemble a state ticket. When the party held its September 7 convention in Saratoga Springs, it appeared that Paul Adams, the academic dean of Rochester's Roberts Wesleyan College, was the favorite to be nominated for governor. Monroe County chairman Leo Kesselring and Regional Vice Chairman Chuck Lewis had been working the downstate leaders urging them to support Adams. In their judgment, the Methodist father of four, who was a veteran of World War II and a soft-spoken but articulate proponent of conservative principles, would be the ideal man to take on the liberal establishment.

Adams was nominated and received 238 delegate votes to Garden City activist Donald Serrell's sixty-eight votes and twelve votes for John J. O'Leary, who would go on to become the Nassau County Conservative chairman and the county's tax assessor. The convention unanimously endorsed Kieran O'Doherty to serve as Adams's running mate.

Benjamin Crosby, vice chairman of the Alfred E. Smith Conservative Club, treasurer of the Bronx County Organization, and controller for the Sheraton Whitehall Corporation, was nominated for comptroller. In 1965, Crosby was a candidate for the New York City Council, and he had carried petitions in 1962 to help get the party on the ballot.

Mason Hampton, a graduate of Virginia Polytechnic Institute and the Washington and Lee University School of Law accepted the attorney general's spot. In 1964 he had run on the Conservative line against Assembly Speaker Joseph Carlino.

After hearings chaired by Frank Meyer were held, the party adopted a platform that called for the repeal of the state sales tax, the New York City income tax, and the commuter's payroll tax. It also called for the elimination of the recently enacted Medicaid Act and for the creation of a simplified state constitution to be adopted by the 1967 New York State Constitutional Convention that would "affirm State sovereignty and provide a general structure for sound government rather than a patchwork of inappropriate statutory details." The party also endorsed fifteen candidates for delegates-at-large to the 1967 constitutional convention: Francis Aspinwall, Vernon Carbonara, Joan Carroll, David Jaquith, Leo Kesselring, James Leff, Mauro Magnami, Dan Mahoney, James Marrin, Frank Meyer, Henry Middendorf, Thomas Moore, Russ Norris, Henry Paolucci, and William Rickenbacker.

At the conclusion of the convention, Chairman Mahoney stirred up the troops when he read a telegram from Bill Buckley:

> I cannot imagine better auspices for a Conservative candidate. The opportunity simultaneously to reject Franklin D. Roosevelt, Jr., Nelson Rockefeller and Frank D. O'Connor is a confidence of historical opportunities

that dazzles the imagination and leaves one numb with admiration for the prodigalities of nature.

Lawrence Fertig, who served as chairman of Citizens for Adams, and O'Doherty put together a grueling schedule for members of the state ticket. On a shoestring budget of $44,243, the candidates wandered the state in search of the votes needed to outpoll the Liberal Party and to bring an end to Rockefeller's political career.

Adams barnstormed the state, hammering away at Rockefeller's fiscal excesses. To stem what he called the mounting numbers and costs of welfare, Adams demanded a one-year residency requirement as a condition for welfare eligibility, with a provision for emergency assistance for non-residents. On education, Adams proposed a comprehensive review of the philosophy, organization, and administration of education by a newly created panel of experts. He also called for the election of an education commissioner to prevent the state education department from "growing away from the people." Finally he proposed a program to slash state expenditures by 5 percent. Noting that Republican Governor James A. Rhodes of Ohio had cut his state's budget by 9.1 percent in the first year of his administration, Adams argued that at least 5-percent's worth of savings could be found in New York.[17]

Commenting on Adams's policy positions, a *New York Daily News* editorial stated that:

> The Only Cheering Talk we've yet heard in the 1966 gubernatorial campaign is coming from Paul L. Adams, the Conservative Party's candidate. Mr. Adams flatly proposes a 5% cut in state government spending. . . .
>
> This would be only a beginning, Dean Adams adds, if he should become Governor of New York.
>
> There may be slight chance of that coming to pass. But the campaign utterances issuing from Adams, and from Kieran O'Doherty of New York City as his running mate, are music to staggering taxpayers' ears, and we hope to hear a lot more of it.[18]

Although early polls showed Democrat Frank O'Connor in the lead, his campaign operation was a mess. His treasury was nearly empty, and he was able to spend just $750,000 in the final weeks of the campaign – peanuts compared to the millions Rocky was spending. O'Connor tried to prove that his status as a former crime-fighting district attorney did not prevent him from being a liberal, and he made the fatal mistake of endorsing Lindsay's CCRB, thus infuriating neighborhood blue-collar voters who had supported him in the past.

And the New York City CCRB referendum battle was turning out to be a real Donnybrook. Battle lines were drawn and major voices lined-up on both sides of the issue. The liberals created FAIR (Federal Associations for Impartial Review), a group headed by Herbert Brownell, Herman Badillo, and labor lawyer Theodore Kheel. Rallying around media consultant David Garth's slogan, "Don't be a yes man for bigotry: Vote No!" were the American Jewish Committee, the Anti-Defamation League, Americans for Democratic Action, CORE, the International Ladies Garment Workers, the Liberal Party, the NAACP, the New York Civil Liberties Union, the United Federation of Teachers, and the New York State Young Republican Club.[19] Viewing this collection of latter-day Goo-Goos, Daniel Patrick Moynihan wrote in a foreword to *Police, Politics and Race*:

> At the risk of over-generalizing, the Civilian Review Board was a proposal that originated in the liberal upper-middle-class white community of the city as a measure to control the behavior of less liberal, lower middle-class white city employees toward members of the black and Puerto Rican community of varying social classes. . . . Persons not at all exposed to a social problem were acting in ways quite insensitive to the problems of those who were.

Bill Buckley, who served as honorary chairman of Citizens For Adams, and O'Doherty debated Theodore Kheel on *Firing Line*. In a lively session, Buckley forcefully told his audience that:

> The pressures for the civilian review board are primarily generated from a small group of representatives of the non-white segments of the New York City population who have been addressed by demagogues [who] have told them the New York police force is anti-Negro and anti-Puerto Rican. . . . I think the very fact that we are willing to set up a structure as this tends to give the impression that it is and this causes a quite anticipated resentment.[20]

As the battle heated up, the polls began to reflect that the CCRB issue had struck a nerve in the blue-collar neighborhoods of Queens, Brooklyn, The Bronx, and Staten Island. Liberal Democratic Congressmen Hugh Carey of Brooklyn, John Murphy of Staten Island, James Delaney of Queens, and even the Queens Liberal-Republican Congressman Seymour Halpern read the handwriting on the wall and publicly endorsed the abolition of the board.

Nelson Rockefeller, who was spending lavishly on his campaign (a record-breaking total of $5.2 million to be exact) refused to take a position on the CCRB saying it was not his place to voice an opinion so parochial an issue. He did, however, realize that concern about street crime was becoming a key issue. So he started sounding like a conservative: He accused O'Connor of being soft on crime and proposed a tough narcotics program "designed to pursue and jail pushers while forcing addicts into

1966 campaign storefront in Brooklyn.

mandatory treatment. So strong was the measure that it worried many civil libertarians, and Frank O'Connor opposed the program." Rockefeller commercials went so far as to state: "If you want to keep crime rates high, O'Connor is your man."[21]

On October 24, the *New York Daily News* announced the results of its first straw poll: "Adams Surge In City Trims Poll Leaders." While Adams statewide support in the poll was only 7.4 percent (versus Rocky's 39.1 percent, O'Connor's 40.3 percent and Roosevelt's 13.2 percent), his projected vote in New York City was at 9.5 percent. "Conservative candidate Paul Adams" wrote the *News*, "pulling about one straw in six, was the big factor, with Liberal F.D.R., Jr., falling below his city average." While Roosevelt was polling 13.2 percent statewide, his numbers dropped to 11.8 percent in liberal New York City.

Dan Mahoney was unhappy because he figured the Conservative Party would not win Row C on election day. The Liberal Party spent $264,000 versus the Adams campaign's modest $44,000 expenditure, and Mahoney concluded the spending gap would have an impact. And indeed, although the race remained too close to call, on election eve the final *Daily News* poll did have FDR Jr. outpolling Adams by 4 percent, a difficult difference to overcome in a tight election.

But as in all close elections, support for minor party candidates tends to dissipate when voters enter the polling booth. So it was that Roosevelt's vote shriveled as many Democrats went home to O'Connor on Row B. Also, the CCRB battle brought out a surge in the number of neighborhood Democrats who voted "yes" on proposition No. 1 and then expressed their displeasure with O'Connor for deserting them by casting their ballots for Adams.

The results were a surprise to the Conservatives gathered at political storefronts throughout New York City and the state. While Rockefeller pulled an upset victory, he did so with a plurality, receiving only 44 percent of the vote. Early totals also showed that Roosevelt was outpolling Adams by only a handful of votes: 498,710 to 491,367.[22]

The great victory was the overwhelming defeat of the civilian review board by almost a 2 to 1 margin: 1,307,738 vs. 768,492. In Queens, 69 percent voted "Yes" (to abolish), and in Staten Island an astonishing 84 percent voted to abolish. Only in Manhattan did "No" carry the day, with 58 percent.

John Lindsay was humiliated. James Q. Wilson has written that the mayor's political ideology reflected "the segment of the urban middle class which has deserted the police" and "the hypocritical liberal who both wants to maintain law and order and to win votes of the lawless."[23]

Writing about the resentment of the defeated liberals, William Buckley observed that there was "a growing transcendence, of the disabling tendency to view all controversial questions in 'black and white.'"

The election of 1966 gave the Conservative Party other reasons to rejoice: in assembly races the party provided the margin of victory in the race for two seats in Rockland County and one each in Queens County, Monroe County, and Orange County. In Suffolk County, where Republican boss Robert Curcio at first agreed to allow his candidates to accept Row D endorsements and later changed his mind, the Conservative Party candidate, Charles J. Melton, provided the margin of defeat for Republican Joseph DeLizio. Refusing cross-endorsements in Nassau County cost Republicans one assembly seat, and they nearly lost two others. In the Twenty-Seventh Congressional District, which covered Delaware, Orange, Rockland, and Sullivan counties, the 13,946 votes received by Conservative Frederick Roland cost Republican Louis Mills the seat. In the state senate race in Brooklyn's Fifteenth District (primarily East New York), the Conservative Party ran a twenty-seven-year-old ice-cream-parlor proprietor named Mike Long. Long received less than 10 percent of the vote, but the defeat did not deter him from playing a major role in the party.

In total, twenty-three Republicans and three Democrats were elected to the state legislature with Conservative Party endorsement.

In local contests for delegates to the upcoming constitutional convention, the party's endorsement provided the margin of victory for thirteen Republicans and one Democrat. The party also provided the margin of defeat for nine Republicans. In the four races where Republicans endorsed registered Conservatives, Ted Dabrowski of Queens and Ben Crosby of the Bronx lost in close races while Rosemary Gunning of Queens won and Charlie Rice went down by only eight votes in the Bronx. After court battles, a new June 11, 1967, special election was ordered for the Rice race, and he went on to beat Democrat Alfred Santangelo. Rice, who also had the Republican line, actually received 40.2 percent of his 584 votes on the Conservative line.

In fifteen delegate-at-large races for the constitutional convention, thirteen Democrat-Liberals won, as did two Republican-Conservatives: former Lieutenant Governor Frank Moore and New York Farm Bureau Federation President William Bensley. The party savored these two victories because they involved the defeat of two

Republican-Liberals: Lindsay's Corporation Counsel, J. Lee Rankin, and none other than Senator Jacob Javits. Reviewing the results, nationally syndicated columnists Evans and Novak wrote in their post-election column: "Indeed, the Conservative Party, so despised by Governor Rockefeller and his lieutenants at its birth in 1962, is helping force the once mighty New York Republican Party to its knees."

The Liberal Party decided to gloat over the Conservatives by running an ad in the November 23rd edition of *The New York Times* that proclaimed: "We polled approximately 520,000 votes, the largest in our history. . . . We also maintained our hold of our traditional Column C. Had we lost Column C to the Conservative Party, it would have been a blow to liberal-minded people throughout the nation and front page news everywhere."

But two weeks later the Liberals had to eat crow: the State Board of Canvassers announced from Albany the official election count: Conservative Paul Adams received 510,023 votes while Liberal Franklin Delano Roosevelt, Jr. received a total of 507,234. The Conservative Party was to be elevated to Row C.

A jubilant William F. Buckley Jr. wrote to *The New York Times* demanding that they refund the Liberal Party the cost of their ad. An editorial in the Rochester *Democrat and Chronicle* declared: "The Conservative Party is on the move," and *The Buffalo Evening News* agreed: "'C' Is For Conservatives." The *New York Daily News* gleefully told its readers:

> You could have knocked a lot of us over with a feather, to coin a phrase, when the news broke in yesterday's papers that the New York Conservative Party, after all, outpolled the Liberal Party at the elections last Nov. 8. . . .
>
> With the recounts and final checkouts now in, the Adams-O'Doherty combo turns out to have racked up about 3,000 more ballots than Junior Roosevelt & Co.
>
> Thereby, the Conservatives, four short years after first landing on the state ballot, have bumped the Liberals down from Row C to Row D on the voting machines and established their party as a formidable factor in New York State – and City – politics.
>
> The effects cannot but be healthy all around, in our opinion. The Liberal Party's longstanding nuisance value seems certain to be cut far down – if the party itself survives this setback for long. Me-too Republicans, who think the way to win elections is to ape Great Society Democrats, seem sure to be jolted into some reappraisals which may be agonizing but also should do the GOP a world of good.
>
> Many congratulations to the Conservatives, and we hope their party's future may prove every bit as bright as it looks now.

Paul Adams outpolled FDR Jr. in Queens, Staten Island, as well as many other counties in the state, including Monroe, Nassau, Onondaga, Orange, Rockland, Suffolk, and Westchester.

	Rockefeller Rep.	O'Connor Dem.	Roosevelt Lib.	Adams Cons.
Upstate New York	**1,726,262**	**1,264,351**	**288,494**	**285,433**
Bronx	154,349	199,719	42,622	39,926
Brooklyn	263,538	341,106	70,426	69,497
Manhattan	230,261	185,098	49,038	22,210
Queens	280,669	277,658	53,950	87,102
Staten Island	35,547	30,431	2,704	15,855
Total New York City	**964,364**	**1,034,012**	**218,740**	**234,590**
Total State	**2,690,626**	**2,298,363**	**507,234**	**510,023**

While Conservative comptroller candidate Benjamin Crosby did not outpoll Liberal Arthur Levitt (331,467 votes vs. 412,368), Attorney General candidate Mason Hampton with 322,693 votes beat out Liberal Simeon Golar, who received 284,813. In the Court of Appeals, the independent conservative candidate Kenneth Mullane outpolled the two Liberal candidates (Charles Brietel and Matthew Jason) 432,641 to 206,649 and 197,037.

In his January 1967 news bulletin to party activists, Dan Mahoney took great satisfaction in reporting the previous year's accomplishments. "Our splendid performance," he wrote, "was achieved without a 'name' candidate, on a financial shoestring of $44,243, and despite a very hostile press." He warned his membership that they could not afford to sit on their laurels and that in 1967 "they must build on these foundations to strengthen the Party for the challenges that lie ahead. Party communications can and must be improved. Finances allowing, we plan a quarterly bulletin to all active Party supporters commencing next March. Our organization is powerful, but it can be improved, especially in certain upstate areas." He also told them that "A new edition of the Party's political action manual and organization manual, and an updated item of state-wide literature, have already been drafted. Both during the legislative session and at the forthcoming constitutional convention, we will be articulating a strong conservative position on the major issues confronting New York State."

Party leaders also took great pleasure in the knowledge that Rockefeller's dismal 43 percent plurality probably ended his quest for the presidency. If a candidate was unable to win a majority in his home state, how could he be expected to carry the nation? Barry Goldwater confirmed this sentiment in a November 21, 1966, *U.S. News and World Report* Q&A. When asked about Rocky's chances of being nominated in 1968, Goldwater replied: "Oh no. He didn't even get 50 percent of the total vote in his State. In fact, it was a toss-up all the way. I would say, just from outside observation, that the New York Republican Party is in the worst shape of any in the whole country."

The Election of 1967 and Constitutional Revision

In January of 1967, Paul Adams and Kieran O'Doherty delivered the party's legislative proposals for the coming year to legislators in Albany. In a press conference accompanying the release of the conservative agenda, O'Doherty made it clear that he expected the Republican controlled legislature to pay serious attention to the party's ideas outlined in the proposals: cutting the state budget by 5 percent, freezing government hiring and salary increases, requiring all legislation to have price tags, repealing Medicaid, and discontinuing rent control.

Sensing that Adams was flexing his political muscles, the press asked if the party was now going to "purge Republicans who did not go along with them." Although he believed that "Conservatives have more influence with Republicans now than Liberals did with Democrats," Adams added that "the term 'purge' is not in the Conservative Lexicon, but we are going to exert every bit of influence we can."[24]

The Conservatives leadership was determined not to overplay its hand. Nineteen sixty seven was another "off-year" election cycle, and the party did not want to make any rash decisions on local elections that could cause any setbacks. In addition, changes were taking place at party headquarters in Manhattan. After two years of service, Marty Burgess decided to step down as Executive Director to return to the practice of law. James Griffin, who had been serving as Research Director and editor of the party newsletter, was to take over the Burgess spot. Regina Kelly also resigned, and Jean Casko took over as office manager.

The party had ended the year with total income of $136,493; but expenditures were $141,155 and the party's long-term debt grew to $10,874. As Mahoney told the troops: "[W]e have no more important task on the agenda for 1967 than a full scale assault on the Party's pressing financial problems." Once again great things were expected of Treasurer James O'Doherty, who had managed in previous years to keep the wolves from the door.

One stand the party was confident would attract support was its opposition to the revised constitution that was to appear on the November ballot for voter approval.

The new constitution proposed for New York State had taken six months to draft and had cost taxpayers about $10 million. The vast majority of the 186 delegates were liberal Democrats and Liberal Party stalwarts, including: Robert Wagner, William van den Heuvel, Marietta Tree, David Dubinsky, Donald Harrington, and Hulan Jack. The review process mandates an appraisal of the state constitution as a whole, and the law states that delegates "should be permitted to introduce constitutional proposals in form suitable for incorporation in the Constitution or resolution in form sufficient to apprise the Convention of the purposes to be accomplished."[25]

And this is exactly what the liberals did:

* Article X, Section 16 called for the assumption by the state government of

all welfare costs over the next decade. Upstaters would get stuck with the tab for New York City's ever-growing welfare rolls.

* Article IX, Section 1 proposed that state aid to public schools no longer be based on attendance but on pupil registration. In other words, the taxpayers could be paying to educate "drop outs."

* Article X, Section 2 called for the abolition of the popular-referendum requirement on the issuance of state debt. (It was a constitutional convention in 1846 that had codified the Jeffersonian principle that unapproved debt that mortgaged future generations was antidemocratic. A delegate at that convention, Michael Hoffman, summarized the view of the majority with these words: "We will not trust the legislature with the power of creating indefinite mortgages on the people's property. . . . And . . . that whenever the people were to have their property mortgaged for a state debt, that it should be done by their own voice and by their own consent." One-hundred-twenty years later, the Liberals wanted to abolish this protection and lift the lid on reckless and irresponsible spending.)

* Article XI, Section 3, called for the repeal of the "Blaine Amendment" which forbid "the state or any subdivision thereof [from using] its property or credit or any public money . . . directly or indirectly, in aid or maintenance . . . of any school or institution of learning wholly or in part under the control or direction of any religious denomination, or in which any denominational tenet or doctrine is taught." While the Conservative Party did support a revision of the Blaine Amendment that would allow a system of tax credits for parents of children attending private schools, the Conservative delegates to the convention voted for the repeal of Article XI, Section 3, as the only practical way, in the context of the convention's deliberations, to insure beyond question the constitutionality of such tax credits. The Conservatives were astute enough to realize that Assembly Speaker Travia, who served as president of the convention, forced a single package referendum of the revised Constitution in order to blackmail supporters of Blaine repeal into accepting his whole constitution.[26]

After reviewing all the proposed constitutional changes, the Conservative Party urged voters to vote "no" on the November 7, 1967, Ballot Question No. 1, which read: "Shall the proposed new Constitution, adopted by the Constitutional Convention, and the Resolution submitting the same, be approved?"

After taking this stand, Dan Mahoney noticed that he suddenly had a strange coterie of allies. While the Conservatives opposed the constitutional revisions that would give Albany an excuse to spend money like drunken sailors, many liberals opposed the revisions because they feared that Cardinal Spellman would be running the state if the Blaine amendment was repealed. The liberal League of Women Voters, for instance, urged a "no" vote, citing in their campaign literature that the document "fails to give New York the modern charter it desperately needs."

As they reviewed the elections results, the Conservatives were pleased that they had refuted the liberal assertion that the party's strong showing in 1966 was a fluke due entirely to the presence on the ballot of the Civilian Review Board proposition. The proposition to revise the state constitution went down big, with 3,487,513 (72.4 percent) voting "No" and 1,327,999 (27.5 percent) voting "Yes."

In the Nassau County race for chief executive, Republican Sol Wachler (the darling of suburban liberal Republicans) lost to incumbent Democrat Eugene Nickerson by 2,863 votes, while Conservative A. Werner Pleus racked up 57,065, or 10.5 percent of total votes cast.

The Conservative Party candidate for county executive in Suffolk, John Conroy, received 19 percent of the vote, and Conservative Frank A. Schaeffer, with Democratic support, was elected to the Babylon, Long Island, town council. In the few county-wide races, support for the party continued to grow:

* Queens County vote grew from 12 percent in 1966 to 18 percent in 1967;
* Onondaga County grew from 6 percent to 14 percent;
* Rockland County increased from 10 percent to 11 percent.

The party also broke records in the statewide Court of Appeals race. Whereas Henry Middendorf had garnered 3.88 percent in 1965 and Stanley Field 6.6 percent in 1966, the 1967 candidate, Kenneth Mullane, piled up 436,641 votes for a total of 8.78 percent.

Reviewing these totals, the *New York Daily News* political reporter Edward O'Neill made these post-election observations:

> The most significant political development of last Tuesday's election – a development that has given Democratic and Republican pros their biggest electoral hangover in years – centers on the amazing, area-wide showing made by the Conservative Party. In a word, all concede, the Conservatives have now fully arrived as a party of power and prowess.
>
> Up to then, the Dem and GOP chieftains were eager to downgrade the Conservatives despite growing evidence that they were losing large blocs of their own registered voters to them.
>
> The fact that razor-tongued William F. Buckley Jr. tipped the balance in the '65 mayoral contest by drawing 341,226 votes for mayor was written off to "personal appeal."
>
> And last year, when nice but colorless Paul Adams, with no campaign

war chest to speak of, rolled up 510,023 votes statewide for governor, the pros were still skeptical. . . .

But Tuesday's ballots finally turned the pros into believers. . . . Here are the conclusions being drawn by the Republican and Democrat brass: Tens of thousands of their party members are displeased with their organizations and have shown their disapproval by going elsewhere – in this case, to the Conservatives.

The people of New York State, and, more slowly, the city's metropolitan area, want displays of more center and right of center thinking from party leaders and elected officials. In other words, a trend away from the old "liberal" and "progressive" stuff the leaders have been peddling.

The Conservatives are here to stay and, if anything, should grow stronger in future elections. The major parties, like it or not, will have to deal with them. . . .

The Election of 1968

Nineteen sixty-eight was one of the most cataclysmic years in American political history. Theodore White, author of *The Making of the President* series, gave the best overview when he wrote:

In 1968, it was as if the future waited on the first of each month to deliver events completely unforeseen the month before. Thus, on January 1ss of 1968, no one could foresee the impact of the Tet offensive at the end of the month. On February 1st, no one could forecast the student invasion of New Hampshire or the withdrawal of George Romney. On March 1st, no one could forecast the entry of Robert Kennedy into the race, or Lyndon Johnson's withdrawal on March 31st. On April 1st, no one could foresee the assassination of Martin Luther King, Jr. or the riots that followed, or Rockefeller's entry into the race. On May 1st no one could foresee Robert Kennedy's stunning victories in the primaries of Indiana and Nebraska, or his defeat in Oregon – or foretell the course of negotiations in Paris. On June 1st, no one could foresee the assassination of Robert Kennedy in Los Angeles. . . . And so on throughout the political calendar: Rockefeller's last grand flourish in Presidential politics and his understanding with Ronald Reagan, defeated at Miami by Nixon's long range planning and preparation. The bloody climax of the year's politics in the streets of Chicago, while Hubert Humphrey, isolated from reality in his hotel suite, waited for nomination. The campaign, in which three small town boys – Nixon, Humphrey, Wallace – offered leadership to an America perplexed as never before.[27]

Early that year Dan Mahoney was completing his book *Actions Speak Louder: The Story of the New York Conservative Party* (which would be published in the fall by Neil McCaffery's Arlington House press), and he too realized that the 1968 political cycle could be life or death for his six-year-old party. Unrest in the state's major cities and campuses, the failures of the Great Society, and the strategy pursued in the Vietnam War were turning the Conservative Party's natural constituencies further away from the Democratic Party. Yet Mahoney's most pressing problem concerned whom his party and its constituency would turn to in 1968: Richard Nixon or George Wallace. Who would be the man who to fill the void after the collapse of the Great Society? Who would be the right man to provide the voice for the silent majority? Who would be the man who would best forge the realignment of New York's blue-collar workers and ethnic Catholics?

Early party supporters (left to right): back: Clif Riccio, Jack O'Leary, Serf Maltese, Nick Longo, Eric Schiller; front: Mrs. Riccio, Mary Laffler, Terry Anderson.

By spring, Mahoney believed that the off-again–on-again candidacy of Nelson Rockefeller and the non-starting campaign of the new governor of California, Ronald Reagan, made Richard Nixon's nomination inevitable. Mahoney leaned toward supporting Nixon, because he believed that the regular Democrats, driven out of their party by the "elitist heirs" of Adlai Stevenson, would accept Richard Nixon as a president who would protect their interests. Mahoney agreed with historian Herbert Parmet, who described Nixon's appeal to the working class in *Nixon and His America*:

> Nixon personified the children of the New Deal generation who regained confidence in American capitalism. They rediscovered the values that seemed to have gone askew. Nixon keenly reflected the priorities that were

especially important to those we may identify as the working middle class. They saw in Nixon not a figure of glamour at all, but someone closer to the real gut: a guardian of their intent to secure a piece of the American turf, or their idea of the American dream, and to do so without losing out to those who insisted on changing the rules in the middle of the game by grabbing advantages not available to earlier generations. This was not only the coming of age of the great middle-class majority; we must also understand it as a process of acculturation and assimilation by generations of immigrants. They achieved their security, had faith in the American dream, and contributed a conservative, stabilizing force in their context of American traditionalism.[28]

But Mahoney also realized that George Wallace of Alabama, who redesigned himself from Southern racist to national populist, also struck a cord with many of his party's rank and file. Wallace's opposition to elitist ultra-liberals (among academics, politicians, and bureaucrats), as well as his opposition to communism, higher taxes, government waste, welfare, crime, and big business appealed to many conservative leaders. As even super-liberal Teddy Kennedy conceded, "most Wallace voters are not motivated by racial hostility or prejudice." "It is they," he explained, "who bear the burdens of a draft that defers the better off, are unable to afford higher education, but are not poor enough for scholarships." It was they, he went on, who carry the brunt of the taxes for an "established system [that] has not been sympathetic to them."[29] Yes, George Wallace had the potential in 1968 to forge what his biographer Stephen Lesher described as "a new xenophobic political consensus among Americans who chauvinistically venerated their nation while fearing and resenting the institutions governing it."[30]

Buckley for Senator

To avoid a split in the party, Mahoney hoped to rally all his troops around a strong candidate to oppose Jacob Javits, who was up for reelection. Since his record was so far to the left, just to mention the name of New York's senior senator got the blood pressure of Conservatives boiling. On 287 Great Society roll call votes, Javits voted yea 75 percent of the time – a record exceeded by only seven Democratic senators. The National Tax Reform Committee reported that of the two-dozen senators running for re-election in 1968, only one had voted to spend more than Jacob Javits.

One man Mahoney believed could make a strong run against Javits was Bill Buckley's brother, Jim. Mahoney came to this conclusion because he'd had an opportunity to observe this soft-spoken, yet dedicated conservative when Jim served as his brother's campaign manager in the 1965 mayoral race.

When Jim Buckley was first approached about running by Mahoney and Kieran O'Doherty, he was guarded. As a vice president and director of his family's oil-consulting firm, Jim spent a great deal of time traveling abroad, and he did not believe he could take an extended leave of absence. He also feared that he lacked sufficient experience to run as a qualified candidate.[31] Future Party Executive Director and State Chairman Serphin Maltese believed it was Mahoney's low-key powers of persuasion that pushed Buckley to run. Reflecting on his "quixotic" 1968 campaign, Jim Buckley said: "If there had been a risk of my winning, which there clearly wasn't, then I couldn't, as a responsible man, have entered the race in the first place."[32] Buckley decided to seek the nomination because he wanted to:

> . . . ascertain the plausibility of a leverage party, namely the Conservative Party, its purpose having been that of reform: specifically, to re-establish a kind of two-party dialogue of choices. If it's a game plan, it's the Liberal Party's game plan: if the two national parties in this state cannot nominate somebody whom you can endorse, then, in order to be able to yield a measurement as to how desirable your endorsement would have been, you have to run somebody in opposition so that you can measure that latent support. This is what Bill referred to as jury-duty in '65 with the clear understanding that there was absolutely no freakish chance of his ever winning.[33]

On April 2, 1968, the Conservative Party State Committee placed James L. Buckley's name in nomination as its candidate for United States Senator.

Mrs. Marie Monplaisir, Staten Island chairman, nominated Buckley, and Westchester County Chairman Wilson Price seconded the nomination. Monplaisir described Buckley as "the man uniquely equipped to make the United States Senate race in 1968 a genuine three-way contest." She predicted that Buckley's candidacy "will again write a new chapter in New York State political history." Price said in his seconding speech that "we will again offer a distinct alternative to the Liberal philosophy of both Senator Javits and whoever emerges from the Democratic lottery." Jim Buckley was the unanimous choice of the state committee.

At a conference held the following day at the Overseas Press Club on Manhattan's West 40th Street, Buckley accepted the nomination pointing out:

> When I was first asked if I would consider the nomination, I urged the leaders to seek out someone who has had greater experience than I in the discussion of public issues, who has been more deeply involved in politics, and who would be better able to devote his full time and energies to the task of campaigning.
>
> They nonetheless asked me to run and I have agreed to do so because I believe strongly in the principles – the Republican principles – which among the parties in New York State these days the Conservative Party

alone espouses; because there are times when a man must be prepared to serve in the support of his beliefs; because the people of New York deserve better than to be offered no alternative to the unfortunately liberal Jacob Javits' and his Democratic think-alike.

The enterprise on which I have embarked is not quixotic. The Conservative Party has already become a force in the political life of New York which cannot be ignored. It has developed the power to influence the outcome of elections; a power which, judiciously used, could yet liberate New York's Republican apparatus from its obsessive concern for the good opinion of Alex Rose and the fundamentalist liberals of the *New York Times*.

Buckley continued:

In the months ahead . . . we propose to remind the voters of New York that there is abroad in the land an increasingly lively force represented nationally by the Republican consensus and in New York by the Conservative Party which has not despaired of America, and which offers hard-headed alternatives to the panaceas spun in Washington by Senator Javits and his democratic colleagues, and to that morass of contradictions which passes for American foreign policy. . . . In the conduct of our foreign affairs, we should be guided by our own understanding, not U Thant's, as to where our national best interests lie; recognizing that these interests are best served by the maintenance of international order and, by the same token, keeping ever in mind that the Soviet Union continues as a principal threat to that order for the reason that she still intends the collapse of the West by any means that do not invite a direct military confrontation with the West.[34]

Buckley's statewide campaign organization took shape under the direction of James D. Griffin, the party's Executive Director, who was designated Buckley's campaign manager. Griffin enlisted regional and county campaign chairmen across the state whose primary responsibility was to coordinate all campaign activities within their regions and counties. Regional and county campaign chairmen included: Bruce McAllister for New York County; Bill Wells for Kings County; Bob Gambieri for Queens; Tom Cronin for the Bronx; Max Phillips for Nassau; Marie Monplaisir for Richmond; Ed Campbell for Suffolk; Bill Price for Westchester; Bill Griffith for Rockland; Mr. and Mrs. Joe Pulido for Orange; Don Yellen for Dutchess; Paul Kennedy for Delaware; Phil Harris for Clinton, Essex and Warren; John Ferris for Onondaga; George MacPherson for Lewis and Jefferson; Chuck Lewis for Livingston, Ontario, Yates, Seneca, Wayne and Monroe; Pete Hopkins for Madison and the Central Region; Tony Rudmann for Albany and Schenectady; and Doug Frederick for Niagara. Joe Koopman of Amenia (Dutchess) served as field coordinator of the campaign and would be regularly visiting regional, county, and local campaign chairmen. The goal was to open as many storefront headquarters as possible in the fall. Conservative Party state headquarters doubled as Buckley for Senator campaign headquarters and took care of fund raising, research, and scheduling.

The Buckley campaign hit the ground running. On April 23, the American Jewish Congress invited Javits, Buckley, as well as the Democrats fighting for the Senate nomination (Paul O'Dwyer, Eugene Nickerson, and Joseph Resnick) for a "Crime in the Streets Forum." Only Nickerson showed up to face Buckley. Nickerson equated crime in the streets with poverty and lack of education and called for massive federal spending programs. Buckley responded that the "eruption of violence is due not so much to the continuing existence in our society of unacceptable levels of poverty, functional illiteracy, and restricted job opportunities, as it is to certain obsessions and excesses . . . which have destroyed the balance wheels which formerly could be relied upon to assure a substantial measure of stability in an essentially humane society." Buckley condemned "the almost maudlin subjectivity which has found reason to excuse the most vicious transgression to some sort of collective deficiency for which the law-abiding is expected to bear the burden of guilt." Buckley also spoke out against "a tolerance of disorder in the name of social protest which has failed to draw the distinction between lawful demonstrations and those which are aimed at the disruption of vital functions of society," and said that "we find ourselves expanding an individual's moral plight to civil disobedience into a legal right to escape the consequences of that disobedience."[35]

In June, the Democrats chose national party delegates in the New York primary. Supporters of anti-Vietnam War candidate Eugene McCarthy, supporters of the assassinated Robert Kennedy, and supporters of Vice President Hubert Humphrey fought an ugly battle for control of the New York delegation to the Democratic National Convention. On primary day, Tuesday, June 18, the radical left came out in droves, elected McCarthy delegates, and shocked the Democratic establishment by nominating Paul O'Dwyer for the United States Senate.

Born in Ireland in 1907, O'Dwyer arrived in America in 1925, and graduated from St. John's University School of Law in 1931. In the Depression he began his legal career defending the rights of unions to organize. In the forties he defended Stalinist sympathizers Lillian Hellman and Paul Robeson. He made his first unsuccessful run for Congress in 1948 as the candidate of both the Democrats and Communist-controlled American Labor Party. In 1968, his long-time radical affiliations worked in his favor, and he beat out Nickerson, the Nassau County Executive, and Resnick, an upstate congressman.

On June 28, after returning from a two-week, 25,000-mile business trip, Jim

Buckley spoke at the Suffolk County Conservative Party dinner and gave his first reactions to the opponents he would now face in November.

> As things now stand, the voters of New York will be presented with a clear-cut choice between "Jacob O'Dwyer" on the one hand, and truth, wisdom, and the eternal verities on the other. For as a correspondent of the *New York Daily News* so succinctly put it in this morning's edition, there is "no political difference between Senator Javits and Paul O'Dwyer. They both want to give everything away. Possibly Javits, having more experience, could give it away much faster.
>
> This identity of views extends not only to a certain freedom with the taxpayer's money, but to Vietnam as well; Mr. O'Dwyer's victory having given Senator Javits the courage to state the other day, in the forthright manner which characterizes his more important public pronouncements, that "unilateral withdrawal from Vietnam is not unthinkable." I must confess that I am anxious to come to grips with my opponents on this issue.[36]

In August, when most Liberals were shocked over the Soviet Union's invasion of Czechoslovakia, candidate Buckley urged the president to adopt this course of action:

> 1. Terminate immediately all trade between the United States and those Warsaw Pact nations who participated in the invasion of Czechoslovakia.
>
> 2. Terminate immediately the direct flights between New York and Moscow.
>
> 3. Call an immediate meeting of our NATO allies to discuss joint political and economic sanctions against the aggressor states.
>
> 4. Call for emergency meetings of the General Assembly and of the Security Council of the United Nations to act upon the following matters to be submitted by the United States:
>
>> a. resolution to declare that the Soviet Union and those nations who joined her in the invasion of Czechoslovakia constitute a threat to world peace; and
>>
>> b. a resolution to invoke mandatory economic sanctions against those nations equivalent to the sanctions which were invoked against Rhodesia in 1966 – a small nation, I might add, which has yet to threaten the peace of any of her neighbors.

5.   Cancel the pending missile limitation negotiations with the Soviet Union.

6.   Order the U.S. military to proceed vigorously with the development of effective ABM and MIRV missile systems – with special emphasis on the latter.

7.   Withhold recognition of any government which succeeds the Dubcek regime.

Jacob Javits, who entered and won the Liberal Party primary on June 18, took aim at the Conservative Party during an interview on ABC's *News Matters* show on August 11:

QUESTION: Senator, should New York Republicans permit the Conservative Party to endorse Nixon on the Conservative line?

JAVITS: I would hope very much that our party will not compromise itself, its soul and its principles by letting the Conservative Party – which is essentially a spoiling party as far as Republicans are concerned. They're trying to encompass their defeat unless they yield to the Conservatives. It's the very thing that I'm talking about with this Nixon-Agnew business – would be done in New York if we allowed the Conservatives to run our electives. And I hope very much that the – that our party people and the Governor will not fall for that. And knowing them as I do, I'm confident they won't.[37]

Reacting to the Senator's hypocritical comments at an Onondaga County campaign kick-off picnic, Buckley told his audience:

I don't know how closely you have followed the furor caused among the New York Republican leadership by the kind offer of the Conservative Party to endorse the Republican presidential ticket and thereby insure Richard Nixon's victory this coming November.
      It seems that this offer of cooperation ran afoul of the fastidious principles of Senator Javits who somehow sees no problem with his own acceptance of the Liberal Party endorsement or with throwing votes in the direction of Hubert Humphrey who will be on the Liberal Party line with him. Or can it be that the good Senator believes in all sincerity that his own re-election is more important to America than a change of administration in Washington.

At the September Conservative Party Convention, it was Mahoney's intent to convince the party to endorse the Nixon-Agnew ticket by endorsing the Republican Party's electors. His plans became moot, however, when the Rockefeller-Javits Republican organization decided to sell Nixon "down the river" by making it clear that there would be no joint electors with the Conservatives. The Republican State Committee went so far as to extract written pledges from its thirteen electors promising that they would not accept Conservative endorsements. Richard Nixon also sent a personal note to Dan Mahoney asking him to refrain from naming independent electors.[38]

The Republican move may have saved Mahoney an embarrassment, because at his convention numerous leaders were singing the praises of George Wallace. Mike Long has pointed out that Mahoney knew he had a dilemma on his hands: a Wallace endorsement could be a major setback for the party, not least because the liberal press would have a field day labeling the party as racist nuts.

Long has explained how the Conservative Party convention became a serious test for Mahoney. Two of the biggest counties, Brooklyn and Queens, were split between Wallace and Nixon. Even Long, who felt some sympathy for Wallace, understood that the party could not give the former Alabama governor its endorsement. "It would have backfired and severely damaged the party," Long says. So, after lengthy and spirited discussions, a proposal was adopted whereby the Conservative Party agreed to field no electors in November. The party did, however, endorse Nixon, but he received only 60 percent of the state committee vote. There was a general understanding that members were free to support whomever they wanted. "No one at my Cypress Hills

1968 state dinner dias (left to right): Kieran O'Doherty, Father Sweeney, Bill Buckley, Rosemary Gunning, Jim Buckley, James Leff.

Brooklyn Club knew who I was supporting for President," explains Mike Long. "We had literature in the club house for both Nixon and Wallace."

In Long's judgment the party stayed united thanks to Jim Buckley: "His race clearly kept the party together. I believe that if it wasn't for Buckley, the presidential election could have destroyed the Conservative Party."[39]

By Labor Day Buckley's candidacy was beginning to pick up steam. After the campaign was over Buckley admitted that, "once again I learned that there is no such thing as a part-time campaign, at least not for me. But I also learned that I could give a speech, could hold my own in a debate [and] could field reporters' questions."[40]

At a Bronx rally on September 19 he proved just how good he could be. He called Javits "the greatest master of the political shell game in this, or any, generation. What he cannot bury, however, is his record – the record which has made him the darling of the liberal establishment. More than most Democratic Senators, he has been a consistent and energetic supporter of those grand schemes spun in Washington which chip away at our freedoms, inflate our money, and threaten to bury us under an overwhelming load of taxes and bureaucracy."[41]

Buckley also went after Paul O'Dwyer as "the man whom the leaders of the Liberal Party would have nominated had Mr. Javits not been available and eager. He is the man who would pull out of Vietnam at any cost and abandon the South Vietnamese to the tender mercies of the Viet Cong."[42]

At this rally Buckley received the endorsement of both the Republican and Democratic candidates for the Twenty-Third Congressional District, Alexander Sachs and Mario Biaggi. He was also endorsed by incumbent Republican Assemblyman John Fusco (Eighty-Sixth District), Democratic incumbent Assemblyman Ferdinand J. Mondello (Eightieth District), and Republican Assembly candidate Anthony Rizzo (Eighty-Fifth District).

In giving his endorsement to Buckley, Mr. Sachs said: "Mr. Buckley represents the mainstream of Republican philosophy on the issues now before the electorate, whereas Mr. Javits does not." Mario Biaggi, who retired from the NYPD as the most decorated cop in the department's history, called Buckley the "only candidate for this office whose realistic positions on foreign policy, law and order and other major issues of our time warrant his election to the U.S. Senate."[43]

As the campaign progressed, the Conservative Party tried to scrape together a few dollars for the Senate race. Charles Edison signed a plea for donations declaring the party motto is "Help Now! Vote Later . . . [because] we have an opportunity to exert powerful influences on the national elections this fall."

Jim Buckley remembered in later years that: "The campaign was starved for funds. It was October before we could distribute basic campaign materials – leaflets, bumper stickers, posters, and pins. And by the time election day rolled around, we had received and spent $160,000, less than 10 percent of what each of my two opponents had expended, and none of it for statewide television or radio commercials."[44]

As the polls began to reflect Buckley's impact on the race, Senator Javits stooped to race baiting. When asked (on the October 13 edition of WABC's "*Page 1*") his reaction to Buckley's call for Javits to disassociate himself from the Johnson Administration, Javit's replied: "Well, it sounds like George Wallace." Interrogator Milton Lewis followed up:

> LEWIS: Speaking about the Conservative opponent, Senator Javits, Governor Agnew, as you know, is scheduled to speak tomorrow night, Monday night, at a dinner for your Conservative opponent. What do you make of that?
> JAVITS: Well, I said before, and I would like to repeat, Milt, that's an odd one. Nonetheless, I sort of shrug it off, smile at it. I think Governor Agnew is learning the job, how to be a candidate, hopefully how to be a Vice President, and maybe this is part of the process.[45]

The dinner in question was the Sixth Annual Dinner of the Conservative Party of New York held at the Waldorf Astoria, and Buckley and Agnew charmed the audience of eight hundred. After a long and loud standing ovation, Buckley told the crowd:

> New York State still dominates the intellectual and political life of this nation; and if the Conservative Party can demonstrate in this state that the average American voter – the un-organized, non-labeled voter – has an instinctive understanding of the essential requirements of a free society; and if it can demonstrate that the voter still prizes his freedoms more than he does the kind of security offered by a welfare state, then the other political parties will take notice and will once again turn to the traditional values on which American liberties and American prosperity have been based. If we can accomplish this here in New York, then we will have turned the political tide in America.[46]

Governor Spiro T. Agnew, who arrived later in the evening following another campaign commitment in New Jersey, accused the Liberal Party of harboring "far out views." Although he couldn't endorse Buckley, he did manage to wink in Buckley's direction.

In the home stretch, Buckley campaigned hard against Javits in upstate New York. At a speech in Rochester on October 24, he called Javits "a maxi-Liberal and only a mini-Republican . . . I join you in [being] loyal to Republican principle by running against a man who is destroying the party. . . . Jacob Javits is not a Republican in any sense of the word." The next day in Buffalo, Buckley said that it is "not at all surprising" that Javits should be spending the country into ruin. After all, he was first and foremost the candidate of the Liberal Party, and is "only masquerading as a

Republican upstate in order to fool good Republicans into voting for him. . . . Mr. Javits is an avowed Liberal who is proud to be running along with Hubert Humphrey as a Liberal Party candidate."[47]

On election day, Tuesday, November 5, 1968, 6,790,000 New York cast their votes for a presidential ticket and 1,139,402 then crossed over to Row C to vote for James L. Buckley for U.S. Senator. With 17 percent of the vote, Buckley received the highest total ever won by a third party candidate in the history of New York State.

	Javits Rep.	O'Dwyer Dem.	Buckley Cons.	Javits Lib.
Upstate	**2,016,446**	**1,244,032**	**663,737**	**141,026**
Bronx	122,164	161,656	78,486	57,507
Brooklyn	236,061	274,710	130,297	100,259
Manhattan	160,178	227,672	52,533	64,664
Queens	242,959	216,886	181,345	92,544
Staten Island	33,081	25,739	33,004	2,936
Total New York City	**794,443**	**906,663**	**475,665**	**317,910**
Total Statewide	**2,810,889**	**2,150,695**	**1,139,402**	**458,936**

The Buckley voters were registered Republicans and Democrats who consciously voted against their own party's nominees – more than twice the defection that had occurred in 1966 when 510,000 New Yorkers had voted for Conservative Paul Adams.

The Conservative vote in 1968 showed dramatic gains in all key areas of the state. In the New York City metropolitan area, which is to say the city itself plus the four suburban counties of Nassau, Suffolk, Westchester, and Rockland, Buckley's share of the vote jumped to 21 percent from Adams's 10 percent two years earlier. In the suburbs, Conservative strength increased from 15 percent to 24 percent. In Westchester, Buckley received 21 percent of the total vote.

Buckley's upstate share of the vote also doubled. He polled 306,825 votes or 12.4 percent, while Adams's vote was 6.2 percent. In the Central New York region, Buckley received 20 percent compared to Adams's 8 percent in 1966. In the Mid-Hudson region, Buckley's share reached 17 percent compared to 7 percent for Adams.

	O'Dwyer	Buckley
Nassau	130,185	128,893
Rockland	17,243	15,435
Suffolk	70,781	83,223
Westchester	78,468	65,309
Queens	216,782	180,831
Richmond	25,738	33,111

Buckley actually outpolled Democratic candidate Paul O'Dwyer in several major counties and came close in others

In the blue-collar Maspeth-Glendale-Ridgewood section of Queens, a significant portion of Democrat congressman James J. Delaney's district (and the future seat of Geraldine Ferraro), Buckley actually carried the day.

Maspeth-Glendale-Ridgewood 1968 U.S. Senate Results

Javits (R-L)	16,847	36.3%
O'Dwyer	12,249	26.4%
Buckley	17,308	37.3%

Senator Javits, the first Republican statewide candidate to also run on the Liberal Party line, running in effect with the backing of both major presidential tickets (and by labor, the liberal media, and a $3 million campaign fund), secured re-election with less than a majority. He received 49 percent of the vote. "Peace" candidate Paul O'Dwyer, who ran 1.2 million votes behind the Democratic Presidential ticket, secured only twice the vote obtained by Jim Buckley.

A questionable November 7 *New York Times* "analysis," called the 49 percent Javits win (which was down from the 57 percent he received in 1962) an "impressive third-term victory [which] has made the liberal-oriented Republican Party organization in New York healthier than ever." The *Times* went on to report that, "many knowledgeable Republican politicians expressed the view that the reason why Mr. Nixon had done so much poorer than Mr. Javits statewide was his flirtation with the Conservative Party."

The *Times* analysis concluded that the Conservative Party's vote, "although impressively large" may not make the party "a powerful influence . . . so far as statewide elections are concerned" since "initial studies" indicated the vote was "drawn from both Republicans and Democrats – in almost same numbers" and "with the impact almost evenly divided, there is no apparent reason – at least not in a stateside election – for either party to make an alliance with the Conservatives and thus risk defeat in a liberal-oriented state."

The *Times*'s reasoning was flawed. The Nixon-Agnew ticket lost New York's forty-three electoral votes by a margin of 376,000 votes. A 190,000-vote switch (just 3 percent of the vote) would have won the state for the Republican ticket. The appearance of Senator Javits on the Liberal Line undoubtedly switched some votes to Humphrey-Muskie. He certainly hurt Nixon's chances when, in the last week of the campaign, he permitted full-page ads to appear in newspapers throughout the state urging the election of Humphrey and Javits as the "best men." He also hurt the national ticket when he vowed at the end of the campaign that he would "have the damndest fights with a Nixon administration" and vote against a Republican president "60 percent of the time."

On election night at Javits's headquarters, the *Times* reported that, "campaign workers applauded every television report of a Humphrey gain." The *Times* also observed that an interesting local phenomenon in the aftermath of the election was "the gloom found among workers in Javits's and Rockefeller's offices yesterday." "Many had rooted openly for Vice President Humphrey," the *Times* explained, further reporting by way of understatement that these attitudes may have been the factors that hurt Nixon the most in New York.

How many votes would have been added to the Nixon-Agnew total by the ticket's appearance on Row C can never be determined with any accuracy. Certainly the all-out support of the Nixon-Agnew ticket by Jim Buckley in the campaign was designed to encourage a maximum vote by Row C voters on the top of Row A for Nixon-Agnew. However, some erstwhile Democrats might have voted for Nixon-Agnew on Row C but were psychically blocked from voting for them on the Republican line. And there were doubtless some mechanical losses for the Republican presidential ticket from voters who simply voted the straight Conservative line and thus failed to vote for any presidential ticket. The formal appearance of Nixon-Agnew on Row C would probably have had the effect of producing further inroads by the Republicans into the Wallace vote, which was cut down to 349,000 votes due, in no small measure, to the strong Buckley campaign for Nixon-Agnew.

In addition to Jim Buckley's great showing, there was other good election news for Conservatives: Nine assemblymen–including two Conservatives with Republican endorsements – won election by the margin of their Row C votes. Five of these ousted Democratic incumbents, thus making the Conservative Party a key factor in giving the Republicans a 78-72 margin of control in the assembly.

In Queens, the party had a decisive impact. Registered Conservative Rosemary Gunning beat Democrat Robert Whelan. John Flack, who received 32 percent of his vote on the Conservative line, beat Democrat Stanley Price by only 447 votes. Another close race was in the Queens Thirty-Second Assembly District, where Republican-Conservative John LoPresto beat incumbent Jules Sabatino by 22 votes. The 3,621 votes LoPresto received on Row C truly made the difference.

In Nassau County, Conservative Mason Hampton, with the support of the Republican line, lost a very close congressional race to the nationally prominent Liberal Allard K. Lowenstein, the man who was responsible for the creation of the "Dump Johnson" movement and Eugene McCarthy's presidential run. Mason lost by only 2,706 out of a total vote of 195,680. Suffolk County's Charles Jerabak, an enrolled Conservative with Republican endorsement, was also elected to the assembly.

The results from all over the state proved that the Conservative Party was now an important player in New York. In seven years, the party vote had grown from 141,000 to over 1 million. "We in the Conservative Party," Dan Mahoney told his troops, "regard this annually increasing vote as a mandate to continue opposing the tax and spend policies which have brought our state to the verge of bankruptcy, and to continue to present responsible alternatives to the liberal policies which have been so long tried and so desperately found wanting."[48]

Chapter 7

Dump Lindsay!
The Mayoral Election of 1969

Most native New Yorkers have at least one thing in common – the old ethnic neighborhood.

In the Greater City of New York, Poles, Jews, Hispanics, Asians, Irish, Italians, and Germans all get blended together in the cosmopolitan work life of Manhattan, but when they return at a day's end to neighborhoods in Greenpoint, Williamsburg, Jackson Heights, Flushing, Woodside, Bay Ridge, and Ridgewood, they come home to a way of life suffused with their ethnic heritage.

As youths in those neighborhoods, they were parochial and protective of a turf that was often nothing more than a piece of cement sidewalk or a brownstone stoop. There were stickball, punchball, boxball, and scooters made of wooden milk crates. The best stickball players would boast how many sewers they could punch a "Spalding." (Translation: sewer manhole covers are about 75 feet apart, so the small red rubber ball hit two sewers traveled about 150 feet.) Growing up in the neighborhood also meant being instilled with the virtues of family, education, discipline, hard work, and loyalty.

Unfortunately for the city he governed, New York mayor John Lindsay and his administration never grasped the significance of the ethnic neighborhood, never learned – or never wanted to learn – how its citizenry operates. The mayor and his Manhattanite cohorts viewed the outer boroughs as breeding grounds for racism, narrow-mindedness, and rudeness. They never understood that those neighborhoods are self-contained life centers that promote an environment that protects traditional values and repulses state domination of human behavior.

When he entered office, Lindsay believed he could ignore the city's ethnic power brokers and impose on the entire city the sort of social engineering proposed regularly on the editorial page of *The New York Times*. In practice, however, he hit a brick wall. Practically in Lindsay's first minutes in power, the Irish-dominated Transit Workers Union called the first mass-transit strike in the New York City history. It would be a test of the new mayor's mettle, and the politically naïve Lindsay failed – mostly because he approached the unions and their working class members with an attitude of "noblesse oblige," of moral self-righteousness, of arrogance.

Indeed, during his first term Lindsay managed to alienate most of the city's ethnic unions: Irish transit workers, Irish and Italian sanitation workers, Irish police officers, and Jewish teachers. One Lindsay aide, Marvin Schick, blamed the mess on the mayor's "failure to connect with ordinary people or really care about the feelings of others."[1]

Lindsay and his coterie of Upper East Side boy scouts had no clue about how the city actually worked

> Anyone around City Hall knew that Lindsay had no control all the way down the line. He tried to do it all with his top assistants, whom he appointed, who had no followings of their own. And you just can't run a city that way. [When] Bill O'Dwyer was mayor . . . he knew the city and how it works to a "T." He knew the first name of the guy you had to call to get a pothole filled on a particular block out in Brooklyn. . . . Wagner always knew the clubhouse pol or the power broker . . . who was responsible for getting that pothole filler his job in the first place. But Lindsay – he only knew his own assistant. And his assistant – he only knew Lindsay. And nobody knew the pothole filler or how to reach him.[2]

Lindsay's budget director, Peter Goldmark, admitted that: "We all failed to come to grips with what a neighborhood is." Another Lindsay staffer, Nancy Seifer said, "There was a whole world out there that nobody at city hall knew anything about. . . . The guys around Lindsay didn't know what a neighborhood was. If you didn't live on Central Park West, you were some kind of a lesser being.[3]

When the sanitation workers went on strike in February of 1968, the administration didn't catch on that this predominately Italian department was "angry at the City, angry at the changes in working conditions, angry at the apparent preference shown the minorities; they felt like second class citizens ("garbagemen") and wanted to strike almost for catharsis."[4] The typical liberal reaction to the mounting trash, however, was expressed by Paul O'Dwyer: ". . . the middle class of New York may have to live for a little while the way the poor people live all the time."[5] By the ninth day of the strike, with over 100,000 tons of garbage piled on city streets, Governor Nelson Rockefeller intervened in the negotiations, saying he was tired of "government by dilettante."[6]

The Battle for Local Schools

Lindsay also managed to alienate additional outer-borough folks when he took sides in the battle for neighborhood schools.

As early as 1955, the New York City Board of Education was creating plans to integrate public schools utilizing district rezoning and cross-town busing. Future Conservative Party activist Rosemary Gunning established her reputation as a defender of neighborhood schools when she led a Glendale-Ridgewood, Queens parents' revolt in 1959 against the busing of students from the Bedford-Stuyvesant part of Brooklyn. Education expert Diane Ravitch has pointed out that in the late fifties the battle had begun in city neighborhoods "to control their schools and to exclude outsiders who had not earned the privilege of residing in their neighborhoods."[7]

Although John Lindsay promoted "school decentralization," this did not mean he believed in community control of schools. Neighborhood activists became irate when they realized Lindsay merely intended to eliminate certain administrative duties previously handled by the board of education's centralized bureaucracy (located at 110 Livingston Street in Brooklyn). In the late sixties tensions began to increase in neighborhood schools, as white was pitted against black. By 1969, the tension was most evident at Franklin K. Lane High School in the Cypress Hills section of Brooklyn.

Although the Cypress Hills neighborhood was predominately German, Irish, and Italian, Franklin K. Lane High School had been integrated since the fifties. In the early sixties, when a third of the school population were minority students, Lane maintained high academic standards and regularly competed strongly for state merit awards and regents scholarships.

But later in the decade school-board bureaucrats began to weaken Lane's ranking through the imposition of school zoning unit changes and by policies designed to make Lane a dumping ground for students who had failed out of vocational and trade high schools. By 1968 the 3,500-student school building was bulging with over 5,300 students. Over 70 percent of the student population consisted of minorities from neighborhoods outside of Cypress Hills.

When so many of the former vocational students were found to be ill-equipped for Lane's traditional curriculum, physics and chemistry classes were abolished. German, Latin, Hebrew, and Russian language courses were also eliminated, and honors classes in English and Social Studies were discontinued. Many students refused to say the Pledge of Allegiance, and in many classrooms the U.S. flag was replaced by the black-green-and-red "Marcus Garvey" flag, representing black nationalism.

Criminal incidents were on the rise. Gangs of black youths wearing Black Panther garb roamed the school hallways reeking havoc, assaulting other kids, and destroying school and personal property.

On November 27, 1968, 150 black youths who were demonstrating at various Brooklyn schools that week, hit Lane waving knives, chains, and clubs, assaulting teachers and students. On December 18 a young female teacher was assaulted and raped. Violence reached its peak when on the morning of January 20, 1969, a popular teacher, Frank Siracusa, walked outside the school building to discover who had thrown a rock that had smashed his classroom window. He confronted several black students. One of them shot a water pistol filled with lighter fluid at him, and another knocked him to the ground and beat him. A third threw a match that set him on fire. Although he suffered serious burns, the semi-conscious Siracusa survived by somehow crawling out of his burning garments. The criminals responsible for this act were never found.

It was in this atmosphere that a young Conservative Party leader, Michael R. Long, founded the Woodhaven-Cypress Hills Community Association. In his 1972 book, *Race War in High School*, Harold Saltzman described Mike Long as "tall, blonde, and extremely good looking. Long had a charisma that attracted a large following. A dynamic speaker, fiery and dramatic, and claiming to be totally devoted to the salvation of Lane, he became the group's chief spokesman."

Mike Long organized neighborhood residents in protest to the ever-increasing racial violence and in an effort to pressure local legislators and Mayor Lindsay to force the Board of Education to change its zoning policies.

After the burning of Frank Siracusa, tensions mounted so high that the school was closed for three days (January 22–24). When classes resumed there were dozens of policemen stationed throughout the building. Reacting to all this madness, Long's association and the United Federation of Teachers distributed 50,000 flyers to homes and collected 10,000 signatures on a petition that demanded a racially balanced rezoning plan that would restore Lane to the status of an interborough school.[8]

Long led Conservative Party activists and legislators the party had endorsed in a concerted effort to support a plan that eliminated Brownsville and Bedford-Stuyvesant from the local school district. Fearing a community backlash, a number of Democrats also jumped on the bandwagon.

The Association also put pressure on state legislators to pass anti-busing legislation. Mike Long told Assemblymen Battista and Schmidt to "go back to Albany and bring back the neighborhood school. They should go to Albany and demand an end to busing. Albany has to tell Lindsay, we've had it."

> In 1969 the New York State Legislature did indeed pass an anti-busing law which prevented the state education commissioner and nonelected school boards from ordering the busing of students for the purpose of achieving racial balance. This was the law cited less than a year later by Mississippi Senator John Stennis in his campaign to compel the United States Justice Department to apply the same standards of integration to Northern schools as were being applied to those in the South.[9]

On March 27, 1969, a *Long Island Press* headline read "Franklin K. Lane Parents Plan Demonstration at School." Long was quoted as saying: "I'd like to see a thousand of our neighbors there. If we get a tremendous turnout then Mayor Lindsay and the Central Zoning Unit will know who we are when we go there." The March 28 demonstration took place with hundreds of placards that read: "Make Lane a Neighborhood School."

After numerous demonstrations and confrontations, Mayor Lindsay capitulated, fearing repercussions at the ballot box that November. The board of education removed Lane's principal and appointed a committee of professionals and local residents to redesign the zoning unit. Mike Long was appointed to the committee and served with, among others, the professional union contract negotiator Theodore Kheel. According to Long, the "Redesign Committee helped bring peace to the neighborhood, raised the standards of the school and gave ten to fifteen years of life to the high school."[10] Mike Long had his first community victory. This would not be the last time city hall or Albany would hear the booming voice of this street-corner conservative.

Lindsay's Fiscal Follies

While Lindsay deserves some of the credit for calming down New York City during the riots of 1967 and 1968, he nevertheless had the knee-jerk reaction that the cause of the disorder was white racism. As vice chairman of President Johnson's Kerner Commission on Civil Disorders, Lindsay was responsible for the introductory statement in the Commission's final report: "Our Nation is moving toward two societies, one black, one white – separate and unequal."

During his first term Lindsay had also become a patron of the counter-culture movement. On May 14, 1967, Lindsay infuriated thousands of marchers when he skipped the "Support our Boys in Vietnam" parade to accept a book of poems from Russian poet Andrei Voznesensky at Gracie Mansion. In a February 1968 speech at the University of Oregon he told students: "There is obviously much in our capacity to dissent from, to rebel against." He viewed radical student activists as a "prophetic minority." He permitted areas like Washington Square in Greenwich Village to be so overrun by the "beautiful people" that even *The New York Times* ran a critical headline in August 1968: "Derelicts and Hippies are Making Washington Square a Nightmare Area."

In April 1968, Lindsay's schedule permitted only a ten-minute appearance at the tail end of Fifth Avenue's Loyalty Day Parade, but he managed to find ample time to spend with 90,000 anti-war protesters gathered at the Sheep Meadow in Central Park. At the Republican National Convention in August 1968 he declared: "The course we have been following in Vietnam, I submit, has not been one of a great nation."

While *The New York Times* condemned the takeover of Columbia University by radical left-wing students as "hoodlumism," Mayor Lindsay had a more sympathetic attitude. When students were wrecking buildings and destroying the research and files of numerous professors, Lindsay told the city that: "students have a right to protest, to dissent, to demonstrate."[11] At a speech at Columbia in December 1968, Lindsay didn't criticize the student behavior, but expressed sympathy:

> Unreasoning surrender and unreasoning upheaval both threaten to impede
> the urgent, authentically revolutionary work of this generation. . . .
> Whatever the last year has taught us, it has taught that your effort and your

energy may not be sufficient to build a better America, but it is necessary to that effort. I do not come to promise you that all we seek will be won if you continue speaking and acting for these goals – but I do come to say that without you, we cannot win.[12]

Reacting to Lindsay's behavior toward the Columbia riots, Bill Buckley concluded: "Mr. Lindsay has a genius for bringing out the worst in Liberalism."

On the fiscal side, Lindsay's increased budget spending far outpaced the Wagner years. The welfare rolls grew dramatically. In 1960, 4 percent of the population received welfare benefits. That number had doubled by 1965, and by 1969 it had grown to 13 percent. Expenditures for welfare programs rose from $400 million in 1965 to over $1 billion by the end of Lindsay's first term. It was so easy to apply for benefits in New York City that the *Daily News* called Lindsay's welfare commissioner "Come and Get it Ginsburg."

To pay the tab for the incredible growth in spending, the administration used every financial gimmick, including increased nuisance taxes, water rates, and sewer taxes, and instituted the New York City income tax. In 1969, Budget Director Fred Hayes quietly admitted: "We're going broke on $6.6 billion a year."

For many outer-borough New Yorkers, the last insult from John Lindsay was his handling of the great snowstorm of 1969.

On Sunday, February 9, 1969, fifteen inches of snow fell on the city. It was not a record fall, yet the city was paralyzed for days. The Sanitation Department, lacking equipment maintenance money, discovered that 40 percent of its snow removal equipment was broken. Major parkways were unusable for days. Schools couldn't open until Wednesday. Forty-two people died and 288 were injured.[13]

The hardest-hit county, Queens, had unplowed streets as late as Thursday. Kew Gardens resident, Ralph Bunche, who served as United Nations undersecretary, sent a telegram to Lindsay complaining that: "There are no buses, no taxis, no milk, newspaper or other deliveries and there have been no trash or garbage collections since last Friday. . . . As far as getting to the United Nations is concerned, I may as well be in the Alps. This is a shameful performance by the great City of New York, which should certainly condone no second-class borough."[14]

Reacting to the rage of the Queens' citizenry, Lindsay resorted to his usual tactic – political theater. He was sure a walking tour of Queens would have a calming effect just as it had during the Harlem riots. While driving to the borough, the mayor experienced first-hand the problems caused by the unplowed streets when his limo got stuck in the snow. A four-wheel drive city truck rescued him and delivered him to his constituents. His walking tour was really a sliding tour through the slush. In Fresh Meadows a woman shouted at him "get away, you bum." At a Kew Gardens stop another woman told the mayor: "You should be ashamed of yourself. It's disgusting."[15]

In the spring of 1969, New Yorkers lived in a city that had polluted air, filthy streets, traffic tie-ups, pot-holed avenues, and ever-increasing crime. They also endured three teacher strikes, a transit strike, a sanitation strike, police and firemen slowdowns, and a home-heating-fuel strike. Even liberal journalist Murray Kempton (who created the 1969 slogan, "Lindsay – he is fresh, everyone else is tired.") admitted: "The substantive achievement does not exist: under Lindsay, the air is fouler, the streets dirtier, the bicycle thieves more vigilant, the labor contracts more abandoned in their disregard for the public good, the Board of Education more dedicated to the manufacture of illiteracy than any of these elements ever were under Wagner." To all of this clamoring, the best explanation Lindsay could come up with was: "You can just about get things started in four years."[16]

Although Lindsay realized he was not very popular with large segments of the voting public, he also knew that politically he had no other place to go. So at a press conference on March 18, 1969, he gathered together a number of Republican bigwigs (Governor Rockefeller, former governor Dewey, Senator Javits, recently appointed Senator Charles Goodell, and Attorney General Lefkowitz) and announced he was running for a second mayoral term. With a straight face, he told New Yorkers that he "believed that the tide of physical and spiritual decay had been turned." Reacting to Lindsay's rationalizations and puffed-up record, Norman Franks of the Patrolmen's Benevolent's Association said:

> In every area that is central to our survival, the city is literally coming apart at the seams. And as crisis piles upon crisis, as tragedy follows on the heals of disaster . . . the official response at the highest levels has consisted of indecisiveness, procrastination, empty gestures, futile attempts at administrative reform and repeated adventures in brinkmanship.[17]

The Mayoral Race of 1969

Watching Lindsay's follies, Dan Mahoney believed his party could have a major impact on the 1969 mayor's race. Since mid-November, many Republicans, after analyzing Jim Buckley's electoral numbers, began reaching out to Mahoney and establishing lines of communication. Mahoney was receptive to these calls because he now believed the best way to undermine the liberal elements in the Republican Party was to play "a more cooperative role with important elements of the New York Republican Party." Although Mahoney hoped for continued growth in the Conservative Party's own vote totals, he nevertheless foresaw a different use of the potential power of those votes: leverage that would force alliances with select Republican leaders.[18] This was the strategy he hoped to implement in the upcoming mayoral race; if, that is, the right candidate were available.

One man who was totally disgusted with John Lindsay's bumbling, particularly with school issues, was a state senator from Staten Island named John Marchi. Like many others who lived in his borough, Marchi believed that Staten Island, being

Greater New York's smallest and most suburban county, was treated like a bastard child and was often as not shortchanged when it came to city services.

Born on Staten Island in 1921, John Joseph Marchi was educated at neighborhood parochial schools. He graduated with first honors from Manhattan College in 1942 with a degree in political science. After seeing combat in both the Atlantic and Pacific theaters in World War II, Marchi earned a law degree from St. John's University in 1949, and went on to receive a Doctorate of Juridical Science from Brooklyn Law School. Elected to the state senate in 1956, Marchi went on to become chairman of the senate committee on New York City affairs, chairman of the National Advisory Committee on State Urban relations for the Council of State Governments, and vice chairman of the State-Federal Relations Committee of the National Legislators Conference.

As a respected expert on New York City affairs, Marchi knew first hand the ineptness of the Lindsay Administration, and he believed he had to challenge the mayor. Dan Mahoney, his New York City Conservative Party leaders, as well as numerous sympathetic Republican leaders who believed Lindsay could – and would – be beaten in a Republican face-off, concluded that Marchi was their man.

While New York State had 3 million registered Republicans in 1969, the city's portion of that total was very small: only 20 percent. The ethnic breakdown of these 628,000 Republicans was very different from the primarily Protestant upstate suburban and rural party. In New York City, 40 percent of the registered Republicans were Italian, 15 percent Irish, 15 percent German, 3 percent Jewish, and only 24 percent were Anglo-Saxon. Analyzing this breakdown, John Lindsay's consultants knew they had serious problems on their hands if a credible ethnic candidate challenged the mayor.

And John Marchi was the man to do it. In April 1969 he announced his candidacy from the steps of the state capitol in Albany. He chose the Capitol, because he refused to miss important senate business just for the sake of an announcement. Later, a full Republican slate was announced that included Bay Ridge, Brooklyn, Assemblyman Bob Kelly for president of the city council and Queens Assemblyman Joe Kunzeman for comptroller. Vito Batista, the fiery assemblyman from Cypress Hills, Brooklyn (who said the three major issues were "anarchy in the schools, terror in the streets, and runaway welfare") also declared his candidacy for mayor. To avoid a split in the vote, however, Joe Kunzeman agreed to drop out and Batista took the comptroller's spot.

Dan Mahoney was delighted with the proposed slate, all three were bona-fide conservatives, and John Marchi, unlike so many other Republicans, had had the guts to accept the Conservative Party Senate endorsement as early as 1964.

Although neighborhood Republicans had to circulate the petitions to get Marchi on the ballot, Conservative Party activists ran the overall operation. Serphin Maltese, who served in 1969 as Queens County Coordinator for Marchi, said that the campaign was essentially "a Conservative Party movement." Mike Long agreed, calling the Marchi campaign a "Dan Mahoney operation and the first instance in New York where the tail wagged the dog." "Clearly," said Long, "the Conservative Party was a major factor in forcing a Republican Primary."[19]

When a Lindsay-financed public-opinion poll showed that 70 percent of registered Republicans were annoyed with the mayor, his aides advised that he skip the primary and save his campaign treasury for the full campaign in which he would run as a Liberal. In *To be Mayor of New York*, author Chris McNickle describes why this did not happen:

> Lindsay's chief money backers, men like financier John Hay Whitney, publisher of the New York *Herald Tribune* and scion of two of America's most distinguished and wealthiest families, and Gustave Levy of the Wall Street investment bank Goldman Sachs, and a few others, had spent years trying to develop the liberal wing of the Republican party. They did not want to abandon their dream and promised to raise the money Lindsay would need to run a campaign and primary both, so the race was on. No one thought Lindsay could win the Republican nomination, but a respectable showing might keep the wing he represented intact, and provide some momentum for November as well.[20]

To keep the Liberal Party happy, Lindsay chose City Finance Administrator Fiorvante G. Perrotta for comptroller and the Police Department's Chief Inspector Sanford Garelik for president of the city council. Alex Rose of the Liberal Party believed that, with an Italian finance guy and a Jewish law-and-order cop, Lindsay presented a truly balanced ticket.

The Democrats, figuring they would sweep city hall in November, had plenty of candidates willing to run: Congressman Jim Scheuer of the Bronx, Congressman Hugh Carey of Brooklyn, Herman Badillo, the first Puerto Rican elected Bronx Borough president, Comptroller Mario Procaccino, Congressman John Murphy of Staten Island, the PBA's Norman Frank, and even Pulitzer Prize-winning novelist Norman Mailer.

Later in the primary campaign, former Mayor Robert Wagner, bored with civilian life and disgusted with Lindsay, decided to jump into the race. With his entry Carey, Murphy, and Frank, all of whom were vying for the votes of the old Wagner coalition, dropped out.

The Marchi primary campaign, although short on funds, was long on enthusiasm. Conservative Party activists, carrying Republican registration lists, went door-to-door urging voters to come out for their man. The party distributed thousands of black-and-orange bumper stickers that simply said: "DUMP LINDSAY." There were so many cars displaying that slogan that many voters were convinced Lindsay's first name was

"DUMP."

On primary night, with 36 percent of the registered voters coming out, Manhattan's Republican establishment went into shock when an unknown from one of the outer boroughs defeated their man:

	John Lindsay	John Marchi
Manhattan	44,236	12,457
Bronx	12,222	16,132
Brooklyn	20,575	33,694
Queens	26,656	40,469
Staten Island	3,675	10,946
Total	**107,364**	**113,698**

The "street-corner" conservatives were ecstatic, they had beaten Lindsay in four counties. President Richard Nixon and even Governor Rockefeller endorsed Marchi several days after the primary. In defeat, Lindsay's reaction was typical:

"[T]he forces of reaction and fear have captured both major parties. These parties have been captured by the forces of hatred, fear and negativism." He hoped that in the fall election the city's electorate would reject: "this kind of ugliness . . . [and] reject this horrendous appeal to the most basic instincts that human beings sometimes have."

On the Democratic side, a fragmented party chose Mario Procaccino, who won with only 29 percent of the vote. Wagner came in second with 28.8 percent and Herman Badillo was third with 27.9 percent. Norman Mailer, who ran on the issue of making New York City the 50th state, and whose campaign slogan was "Vote the Rascals In," finished last with 5.2 percent of the vote.

While the *New York Post* concluded that the Marchi and Procaccino victories "corroborate the view that reaction is the order of the day and liberalism is in disorganized retreat," Dan Mahoney, Serf Maltese, and the conservative activists now realized they had a problem on their hands: the unexpected victory of Procaccino meant there would be two philosophical conservatives running against Lindsay.

And there were other problems in addition to the possible splitting of the conservative vote: 1) there was no campaign money left, and 2) there was a perception that Senator Marchi was a lackluster candidate, a "loner – almost a mystic."[21] During a July 7, 1969 edition of Bill Buckley's *Firing Line* television show, Dan Mahoney came to Marchi's defense:

Now, he is not a combative kind of fellow. He was written up in the *New*

York Times, when he announced his candidacy as a man with a reputation for integrity and extreme hard work. He is a very knowledgeable man. He knows the problems of the city, and he is very deeply committed with respect to them. I think that over a four-month period, during which there will be very major exposure that the depth, the solidity, the knowledge is going to come over, and that he is going to look to people, all ideology aside, as a man with the capacity to cope with some of the problems we have. . . . I do think that the real integrity and depth and knowledge of this man is going to come over and that as the campaign wears on against a man, Mario Procaccino, who appeals on much the same issues that Marchi does, but in a much more simplistic kind of way, and on the other hand, Mayor Lindsay, who is a terribly glamorous fellow, but not an awfully good mayor, that Marchi is going to look very good.[22]

As the campaign wore on, the reform Democratic movement deserted its party's standard-bearer. Herman Badillo, Al Blumenthal, Manfred Ohrenstein, Andy Stein, Shirley Chisholm, Arthur Goldberg, as well as scores of Democratic Clubs, all endorsed the Lindsay candidacy. These elitist Democrats deserted Procaccino because he, like Marchi, defended the old neighborhood way of life, "the way of life mocked by Woody Allen at a Lindsay gala when the comedian talked of Mario in his undershirt, drinking beer and watching Lawrence Welk on television."[23] Also there was outright bigotry against inner-city Italians like Procaccino and Marchi. Even *The New York Times* reported on this issue:

There is a bias of the upper-middle-income liberal intelligentsia against the lower-middle class, particularly against Italians. You don't read much about that in this country (working people don't write books), but there are Italian jokes and there was a piece in the small New Journal at Yale: The hidden, liberal-radial bigotry toward the lower-middle class is stinking and covered," wrote Michael Lerner, a graduate political-science student and son of columnist Max Lerner. "When a right-wing Italian announced for Mayor in New York, a brilliant professor in New Haven said: "If Italians aren't actually an inferior race, they do the best imitation of one I've seen." Everyone at the dinner table laughed. He could not have said that about black people if the subject had been Rap Brown.[24]

Viewing the race, Brooklyn Congressman Hugh Carey, said that he had "a real Hobson's choice – an incompetent liberal Republican, an inexperienced conservative Republican and an unimaginative conservative Democrat."

Lindsay went after the extreme-Left vote by making his opposition to the Vietnam

War an issue. This secured the endorsement of Bella Abzug, who founded "Taxpayers Campaign for Urban Priorities" to help Lindsay on Manhattan's very liberal West Side. The amazing New York Mets indirectly helped Lindsay by winning the World Series for the first time. Lindsay was able to bask in their post-game, locker-room glory.

To shore up his middle-class liberal constituency, Lindsay put on an Oscar-caliber performance in a TV ad titled, "I Made Mistakes":

> I guessed wrong on the weather before the city's biggest snowfall last winter. And that was a mistake. But I put six thousand more cops on the streets. And that was no mistake.
>
> The school strike went on too long and we all made some mistakes. But I brought 225,000 more jobs to this town. And that was no mistake. And I fought for three years to put a fourth police platoon on the streets. And that was no mistake. And I reduced the deadliest gas in the air by 50 percent. And I forced the landlords to roll back unfair rents. And we did not have a Detroit, a Watts, or Newark. And those were no mistakes.
>
> The things that go wrong are what make this the second-toughest job in America. But the things that go right are those things that make me want it.[25]

Running on the slogan "Marchi Makes Sense," the Republican candidates campaign brochures stressed:

> Senator John Marchi knows this city. As chairman of the senate committee for New York City, he has examined its workings, studied its problems, worked to find solutions. He'll be a no-nonsense mayor who acts swiftly and gets results. . . . Through professional management of every city department – from Education to Welfare – he'll see that New Yorkers get the kind of city services they're paying for.[26]

The on-a-shoestring Marchi campaign, however, was not enough to turn the tide. By election day, it was evident that there would be a huge turnout for Lindsay, voters whom Mario Procaccino called "limousine liberals." Even former mayor Wagner admitted that he would cast his vote reluctantly for Lindsay.

Lindsay received 50 percent of the Jewish vote and the overwhelming majority of the votes of blacks and Puerto Ricans. He squeaked by and was re-elected with 42 percent of the vote:

Lindsay		
Liberal	859,960	36.2
Independent	139,973	5.9
Total	999,933	42.0 percent
Marchi		
Republican	329,506	13.8
Conservative	212,905	9.0
Total	542,411	22.8 percent
Procaccino		
Democrat	774,708	32.6
Civil Service	57,019	2.4
Total	831,727	35.0 percent
Other Candidates	4,169	0.2
Total	2,378,240	100.0 percent

In the council president race, Conservative Bob Kelly received 147,462 votes (7.7 percent) and Vito Bastista polled 168,059 (8.9 percent) in the comptroller's race.

Even though the base conservative vote split between Marchi and Procaccino, there was good news found in these results: 58 percent of the people voted against the mayor, 50 percent of the city's Jews cast their votes for a non-liberal candidate, and Catholics voted 85 percent against John Lindsay.

In addition to carrying his home base of Staten Island, Marchi came in first in Ridgewood, Maspeth, Elmhurst, Little Neck, Douglaston, Ozone Park, and Cambria Heights in Queens, as well as in Bay Ridge in Brooklyn.

Also, when Queens Republican Councilman-at-large, Joe Madugno (who had been elected to his first term with Conservative Party support) refused to denounce Lindsay, the party had run a young accountant named Anthony Spinelli against him. Tony received enough votes to deny Modugno a second term.

The Conservative Party demonstrated in 1969 that an alliance with Republicans could cause havoc for liberal Republicans. Finally, there was the satisfaction in knowing that Lindsay's dream of leading a national Republican ticket was finished. He was, as a *National Review* editorial observed, "consigned to the Republican equivalent of Elba." Just like Rocky before him.

Chapter 8

Isn't It About Time We Had a Senator?
The Election of James L. Buckley

In early 1970, Dan Mahoney was pleased to learn that the latest voter registration figures revealed that the Conservative Party was neck-and-neck with the Liberal Party:
107,372 registered Conservatives to 109,311 registered Liberals. The party's enrollment growth was remarkable when compared with the older Liberal party:

	Conservative Party Enrollment	Liberal Party Enrollment
Fall 1963	10,399	80,201
Fall 1964	21,590	87,828
Fall 1965	30,936	85,125
Fall 1966	54,027	87,596
Fall 1967	71,477	82,889
Fall 1968	106,207	94,000
Fall 1969	107,372	109,372

Dan Mahoney realized the liberal stranglehold in New York had been loosened,
but not broken, and if the party was to sustain growth and achieve new milestones,
keeping the statewide organization strong was essential. Mahoney knew the party had
to do more than exercise political leverage; it had to provide a platform for the projection and promotion of conservative views. Legislative programs, testimony at legislative hearings, policy statements, debates, radio and television appearances, press
releases, letters to editors – all these forums had to be utilized by Party spokesmen to
advertise Conservative positions.

To help meet this end, Mahoney issued a revamped and expanded *Political Action
Manual* in June of 1969. This manual of 200+ pages covered party rules and regulations, basic politics, club activities, petition circulation, campaign strategies and
organizing, party position papers, and a "how-to" appendix that covered everything
from sample welcoming letters to sample press releases.

To help beef up the "bare-bones" staff at headquarters, Mahoney asked Serf
Maltese if he could volunteer on a daily basis. Maltese, the party's Queens County

vice chairman, had ample election law experience and a first-rate knowledge of day-to-day political operations. Mahoney wanted this additional staff support because he believed 1970 might be the year when the party had a serious shot at winning a statewide election on its own.

When Robert F. Kennedy was murdered in June 1968, Governor Rockefeller needed to appoint a successor as stipulated by state law. Whomever he appointed would serve for the balance of the term that was to end on December 31, 1970. The governor waited until September 10, 1968, to appoint U.S. Representative Charles E. Goodell to fill the unexpired term. Goodell, who had represented the mid-western tier of New York State in Congress since 1959, received an M.A. in government and a law degree from Yale University and was viewed by pundits as a safe choice for the seat.

He was considered a typical moderate-to-conservative legislator, but upon reaching the Senate, Goodell tacked hard to the left and became a leading "liberal dove." He supported every left-wing program that came up for a vote and spoke out against and voted against President Nixon at every opportunity. He infuriated not only the White House but many local Republicans as well. Viewing this particular political drama, Mahoney concluded there was a great opportunity for the Conservative Party.

In 1968, Jim Buckley had proved there was statewide a base of 1.1 million conservative votes. But to put together a coalition that might help him – or any other candidate – to actually win a senate seat, it was going to be necessary to pick up some portion of the voters who had cast ballots for Richard Nixon that year. There were 3,007,932 of them out there.

Richard Nixon had seemed to promise blue-collar, ethnic voters that he would protect their interests against the elitist heirs of Adlai Stevenson – those who had control of the mechanics of New York's Democratic Party. And the election results proved that many voters believed Nixon. All the New York City Assembly Districts won by him in 1968 were predominantly working-class Catholic. "In 1960, NYC's German, Irish and Italian Catholics had favored Kennedy by an approximately 5 to 4 ratio, in 1968 they preferred Nixon over Humphrey and Wallace by a ratio of at least 5 to 3 to 1."[1]

The 18 Top Nixon Assembly Districts in New York City, 1968[2]
Percentage Total Vote for President*

Assembly District (Neighborhood)	Nixon	Humphrey	Wallace
49th Brooklyn (Bay Ridge)	61	32	7
50th Brooklyn (Bay Ridge)	60	33	7
58th Richmond (Staten Island)	58	33	9
30th Queens (Elmhurst, Ridgewood)	56	34	10
20th Queens (Cambria, Hollis)	56	36	8
28th Queens (Woodhaven)	55	36	9
59th Richmond (Staten Island)	53	38	9
80th Bronx (Parkchester, Throgs Neck)	50	41	9

The 18 Top Nixon Assembly Districts in New York City, 1968[2] (cont'd)
Percentage Total Vote for President

34th Queens (Sunnyside, Maspeth)	50	41	9
29th Queens (South Ozone Park)	49	42	9
22nd Queens (Douglaston)	51	44	5
85th Bronx (Morris Park, Pelham Bay)	49	45	6
32nd Queens (Steinway, Woodside)	48	45	7
33rd Queens (Astoria, Long Island City)	47	45	8
53rd Brooklyn (Gowanus)	44	47	9
86th Bronx (Baychester)	45	48	7
38th Brooklyn (East New York)	44	48	8
35th Brooklyn (Greenpoint)	41	50	9
Citywide (68 AD's)	34	61	5

The same trend took place throughout the state:

Nixon Percentage Share of the Two-Party Vote for President[3]

County or City	1960	1968
Substantially Italian		
Richmond County	56	62
Oneida County (Utica)	48	54
Substantially Irish		
Yonkers	45	53
Substantially French Canadian		
Clinton County	45	53
Franklin County	49	55

Suburban areas that were dominated by white ethnics who escaped city crime and slums increased their support for Nixon while support for him declined in the more liberal "silk-stocking" sections of suburbia.

Suburban Voting Trends in the New York Metropolitan Area, 1952–1968[4]
Republican Share of the Major-Party Vote for President

Town	1952	1956	1960	1964	1968
Upper & Upper-Middle-Class Suburbs					
Wilton, Conn.	77	79	73	47	66
Scarsdale, N.Y.	78	72	63	35	45
Pound Ridge, N.Y.	80	76	73	44	57

Suburban Voting Trends in the New York Metropolitan Area, 1952–1968[4] (cont'd)
Republican Share of the Major-Party Vote for President

Town	1952	1956	1960	1964	1968
Upper-Middle-Class Largely Catholic Suburbs					
Pelham, N.Y.	84	86	73	59	71
Working-Class Suburbs (Substantially Catholic)					
Orangetown, N.Y.	68	75	58	41	60
Babylon, N.Y.	71	76	55	43	62
Smithtown, N.Y.	72	77	57	45	65
Oyster Bay, N.Y.	72	73	53	42	57
Yorktown, N.Y.	70	72	60	42	60

Analyzing these trends, Mahoney concluded that victory was possible if the party could attract a piece of the Nixon share of the vote and a portion of the 358,864 votes cast for George Wallace.

Mahoney was not alone in understanding these figures and the emotional mind-set of numerous New Yorkers. Political consultant F. Clifton White, who led the 1964 "Draft Goldwater" movement, concurred: political and social forces were converging in New York that could be advantageous for the conservative cause.

Mahoney and White sensed that there was a reaction brewing among New York's middle-class suburbanites and inner-city blue-collar workers against the rhetoric and agenda of the radical New Left and their campus followers. It was a reaction against counter-culture intellectuals such as Robert Wilson, who proclaimed that "fascism is all the values you consider American and Christian." It was a reaction against Betty Friedan, who called the middle-class home a "comfortable concentration camp." It was a reaction against Black Panther Eldridge Cleaver, who described rape "as an insurrectionary act." It was a reaction against those they perceived as affluent, spoiled college brats who called cops "pigs" and threw bags of feces at them while burning their draft cards and proudly displaying Vietcong flags.

Indeed the great divide in 1970 was President Nixon's handling of the Vietnam War. Refusing to surrender to those who demanded instant withdrawal of all American troops, Nixon appealed to and received the support of the "silent majority" for his Vietnamization program of gradual withdrawal. But when part of the strategy to stabilize South Vietnam meant the destruction of enemy supplies and bases in Cambodia, it unleashed the student anti-war movement. On one campus, Kent State University in Ohio, National Guardsmen were activated after the ROTC building was bombed. With students throwing rocks at one squad, several guardsmen panicked and overreacted by firing into the mob, killing four students.

After hearing about the Kent State incident, Mayor Lindsay ordered New York City's flags to be flown at half-mast and said: "The country is virtually on the edge of a spiritual and perhaps physical breakdown."[5] This angered the city's blue-collar workers, and on Friday, May 8, 1970, "hard-hat" construction workers attacked "long-hair" kids by the New York Stock Exchange, leaving seventy injured. On May 20, 1970, over one hundred thousand hard hats and longshoremen marched in lower Manhattan and burned Mayor Lindsay in effigy.[6]

These and other events convinced Dan Mahoney and Clif White that it just might be possible for the "proper" Conservative Party senatorial candidate to receive 40 percent or more of the votes cast. And in a race in which liberals – running on at least two different party lines – would split, the Conservative candidate might end up with a simple plurality and a stunning victory.

The odds of this possibility increased when the Liberal Party, unsure how the three-way Democratic senatorial primary would turn out, endorsed Senator Charles Goodell. The question Dan Mahoney now had to answer was, who is the "proper" senate candidate to field in 1970? For Mahoney and his leaders there was only one candidate – James Lane Buckley.

Divide and Conquer

When he returned from a trip to Indonesia on April 2, 1970, Jim Buckley called *National Review* publisher William Rusher and said:

> "William, you are a political seer."
> "That is true," Rusher humorously conceded.

According to Rusher:

> Jim went on to say that the thought of the ultraliberal Goodell's being elected to a further six years in the U.S. Senate was more than he could bear and that he himself was disposed to seek the Conservative party's nomination and run against him, *provided* there was a serious chance of actually winning in November owing to the aforesaid split in the liberal vote. Did I think there was such a chance?

Rusher's answer was "Yes."[7]

A poll commissioned by Clif White costing $11,000 confirmed Rusher's position. It showed that Buckley could get at least 25 percent of the statewide vote. Analyzing the results, White concluded "We can win." In their April 29th column, Evans and Novak reported the poll's findings and pointed out that the Conservatives "envision Buckley doing as a conservative, what John Lindsay did as a liberal last fall, when he rode in on a minority vote with the majority split between two conservative opponents."

Jim Buckley had spent the first quarter of 1970 traveling to Canada, the Philippines, New Zealand, Australia, and Indonesia. In each of these countries he read stories about how America appeared to be falling apart at the seams. In Darwin,

Australia, he met two Americans who had emigrated there to open a business because they believed "America was coming to the end of the line."

According to Buckley:

> It was during this conversation in late January or early February that I began to think about the possibility of seeking the Senate seat occupied by Charles Goodell. Goodell, who seventeen months earlier had been appointed to fill the vacancy left by Robert Kennedy's assassination, by then had dramatically changed his political views. In so doing, he left an important – I believed a majority – segment of New York opinion unrepresented. I had no thought whatsoever of emigrating from the United States, but I did ask myself what I could do to help keep the predictions made by these new Australians from coming true.
>
> I thought about this all the way back to the United States, considering the prospects of entering the Republican primary and trying for election to the United States Senate as the candidate of both the Republican and Conservative parties. One thing I was certain of, and that is that I would not consider running unless I had a reasonable chance of succeeding. A Senate race is not the sort that anyone will run a second time just for the exercise.[8]

Buckley learned, when he returned to New York, that he was ineligible, under election law, to force a primary against Goodell.

> I [then] considered the possibility of running without the Republican line, as Charles Goodell's change of political course had so angered a great majority of New York Republicans that it was conceivable I could win running solely as the candidate of the Conservative Party.
>
> I had decided that I would make a final commitment only if I could satisfy myself that it was not romantic to believe victory possible; that my candidacy would be taken seriously enough, early enough, by the press to give it the credibility necessary for it to have any chance whatever; and that I could be assured, before I was finally committed, of initial financing of at least $100,000.[9]

The Clif White public-opinion poll helped Buckley make his decision to run, particularly when he realized that a majority of New Yorkers agreed with his support of President Nixon's Vietnam policy.

Serf Maltese recalled that at a series of meetings with Dan Mahoney and key party leaders, Jim Buckley insisted on two things if he were to be a candidate: 1) that Clif White manage the campaign independently, and 2) that there be an additional ballot line that he could run on. The first was easy, but the second was both contro-versial and problematic.

Buckley believed that there were blue-collar Democrats (supporters of President Nixon), who would be unable to bring themselves to vote on Row C. While Maltese agreed that it was possible to pick up as many as 100,000 such votes, not all Conservative leaders were crazy about the idea of creating an additional ballot slot to do so. In the minds of some, the Conservative Party was created as a protest party, and that to establish another transient party line just for this election would be self-defeat-ing. But Mahoney and Maltese agreed with Buckley. In a very close race the extra line could provide the margin of victory.

Reacting to criticism from a few party members who objected to both the inde-pendent operation and the extra ballot line, Mahoney responded: "[W]hy shouldn't Jim have two lines on the ballot the way Charlie Goodell has as a Republican and Liberal? . . . Since Jim has a real shot at winning, he needs an organization which can spend time and money on his campaign exclusively. We just don't have the setup."[10]

Serf Maltese was put in charge of the petition drive to establish the party to be called the Independent Alliance.

While the required number of signatures was easily gathered, filing with the Albany Board of Elections at the last minute was chaotic. During their trip to Albany, Maltese and his Uncle Harry were organizing and numbering the petitions, both on the airplane and then in the cab from the airport. Although the Independent Alliance petitions were not challenged, Maltese and Mahoney did find themselves in court opposing another petition filed by a group trying to create a *Conservation* Party.

Congressman Richard Ottinger, who entered the Democratic senatorial primary, filed for the Conservation Party line as insurance in the fall election. The Conservative Party protested on the grounds that the new party's title would be con-fused with theirs. Mahoney's evidence consisted of news reports (including *The New York Times*) that erroneously labeled Ottinger as the Conservative Party candidate. To further their case, Mahoney pointed out that the court docket listing the case made the same error! With that, the judge knocked the Ottinger party off the ballot.

Despite his losses in court, Ottinger did better on primary day, June 23. On the strength of $1.9 million borrowed from his mother, the Westchester congressman beat Paul O'Dwyer and former Kennedy speechwriter, Theodore Sorenson. The Buckley camp was pleased, since the inarticulate Ottinger's liberal voting record matched Goodell's. Ottinger was a Scarsdale child of privilege, described by *The New York Times* as having done "all the usual Scarsdale things when he was growing up – rid-ing, tennis, swimming, summer camp, Loomis and Cornell, where he was himself something of a playboy, seldom cracking a book, being elected president of Zeta Beta Tau and playing second string polo." Connecting with hardhats was not going to be Ottinger's strong suit.

At the April 1970 Conservative Party Convention, Jim Buckley was nominated for the senate. Paul Adams agreed to take another shot at Nelson Rockefeller, who was running for a fourth term against Democrat-Liberal Arthur Goldberg. Edward F. Leonard, a professor of political science and American history at New Rochelle's Iona College, was nominated for lieutenant governor. Monroe County Leader, Leo F. Kesselring, was nominated for attorney general to oppose incumbent Republican-Liberal Louis Lefkowitz and the radical left-wing Democratic candidate, Adam Walinsky. (Kesselring was vacationing in Spain and didn't learn of his nomination until his return, at which point it was legally too late to decline.) Anthony R. Spinelli of Queens, was nominated for comptroller to run against Arthur Levitt, and the Republican candidate, Buffalo Councilman-at-Large Edward V. Regan. It was Tony Spinelli who gave *The New York Times* magazine the title for its October article on the race when he clumped together the liberal opposition as "Rockeberg, Goldfeller, Ottindell and Goodinger."

While the Conservative Party leaders were focused on their convention, one policy issue that suddenly surfaced and caught them off-guard was abortion. On March 18, 1970, Senate Majority Leader Earl Brydges permitted a no-restrictions abortion bill sponsored by upstate Senator Clinton Dominick to come to the floor for debate. Bryges, an ardent abortion foe who for years had bottled up various abortion bills introduced by Manhattan successors of Margaret Sanger, figured he would get people off his back by permitting a vote on legislation he was certain would be defeated.

After five hours of fiery debate, however, the bill managed to pass with a vote of 31 for, 26 against. Senator Marchi, a leading debater against the bill, was shocked that the bill received such support. "Abortion had barely entered into the public dialogue," he said. "I remember attending the [state] Constitutional Convention of 1967, and there wasn't a single bill on the subject, nor was there any advocacy."[11] Mike Long also admitted the Conservative Party was caught napping: "Abortion was a non-issue up until then. . . . We first put a pro-life plank in the party platform in 1968, and we had a big internal fight about it . . . [because] nobody, and I mean nobody, expected this to become a reality."[12]

When the bill hit the assembly, it was amended to restrict abortions after twenty-four weeks. On March 30, the first vote failed by 3 votes to get the needed majority of 76 votes. Another roll call took place on April 9 and when it was announced, there were now 74 votes for passage, a Democrat from a predominately Catholic area, Assemblyman George Michaels, took to the floor and stated he was changing his vote to "yea" because one of his sons had called him "a whore" for his earlier vote against the measure. With the vote now at 75 for passage, Republican Speaker Perry Duryca chose to use the chair's prerogative to cast a vote when it affects the outcome. With that, the nation's first liberal abortion bill was passed and Governor Rockefeller, whose family foundation had for generations supported the Planned Parenthood agenda, signed it into law on April 11. Looking back on that dark week, Mike Long said: "We didn't really gear up over it because we didn't think it would pass. It came rather fast, and it even took the church by surprise."[13] The party did, however, vow to punish Assemblyman George Michaels and the Republicans who betrayed them on the issue.

Mutiny among the Republicans

As the Buckley campaign began, it was obvious that Republicans around the state were disgusted with Goodell. As early as April 30, State Senator John Marchi, who agreed to be chairman of Republicans for Buckley, called on pro-Nixon Republicans to join him in bolting the party to support Buckley. Marchi attacked Goodell (who endorsed Lindsay in 1969 over the Republican mayoral nominee) for "irresponsible interference" in Nixon's Vietnam policy.

On June 4, Congressman Martin McKneally of Orange County, New York, said he was seriously considering voting for Buckley. "I have absolutely no respect," he said, "for the other fellow at all." On June 11, Elizabeth Tuttle, a Republican state committeewoman, became the first rebel from within the party apparatus to endorse Buckley. In late June, the *Troy Times Record* reported: "Many In GOP Seen Prepared To Endorse James L. Buckley." The *Kinston Freeman*'s June 11 headline read: "Strong Sentiment for Buckley Within Republican Ranks." In Suffolk County, Republican Legislator Louis T. Howard said he would cam-

1970 Attorney General candidate Leo Kesselring with Paul Adams.

paign actively for Buckley. "Charlie's got to go and Buckley's my man."

In the most powerful Republican County in the Nation, Nassau County, which was run with an iron fist by Boss Joseph Margiotta, Hempstead Township Supervisor Fran Purcell told the June 28 *Newsday*: "I'm voting for Buckley and you can quote that in big letters." Looking back, Serf Maltese was convinced that: "Joe Margiotta gave all his candidates a pass in 1970 to support Buckley publicly."

Scores of Republican state and local legislators and Republican Party officials were endorsing Buckley, and Goodell's campaign manager, former Lindsay Deputy Mayor Robert Sweet, admitted that Buckley posed a "serious threat" to Goodell's bid for a full term. So the logical question became: What was Governor Rockefeller, the man who despised the Conservative Party, doing about the defections? It appears that Rockefeller was not very interested in Charles Goodell's future. "I know with certainty," Serf Maltese said in 1999, "that Rockefeller did not want Goodell to win." This was due in part to Lieutenant Governor Malcolm Wilson, who, according to Maltese, was the back door to the Rockefeller camp and made it clear to all that he was for Buckley.[14]

It should be noted that in early 1970 Rockefeller, the historic defender of "progressive Republicanism," felt the winds of change and began to remold himself as a conservative by declaring war on drugs and crime. "With a conservative administration controlling the federal government, Rockefeller [went] further right. He warned of a 'grave financial crisis.' Although no budget that is $1.2 billion over the previous year's can be labeled as an austerity budget, Rockefeller called a halt to new programs and an across-the-board cut in state spending of five percent."[15] He also asked Vice President Spiro Agnew to campaign for him in upstate New York. An amazed President Nixon, recalling the Rockefeller who told him in 1958 and 1966 to keep out of his New York campaigns, stated: "Isn't that something! They're really reading the tea leaves, aren't they?"[16]

Jim Buckley made a three-day fact-finding tour of Vietnam in late June. After inspecting captured Communist weapons from the Cambodian incursion, Buckley told the media in Saigon:

> From what I've been able to learn and observe, it seems clear that the rapidly growing military capacity of the South Vietnamese will soon make it possible to limit combat involved by Americans to volunteer forces. If this assessment is correct, I would strongly urge President Nixon to announce that after the completion of the scheduled withdrawal of 150,000 troops, no draftee will be required to engage in combat in this conflict against his will.[17]

There were still more Republican endorsements of Buckley in July. Delaware County Assemblyman Ed Mason came out for Buckley, as did the Franklin County GOP organization. On July 3, FDR's former congressman, Hamilton Fish, Sr., announced that he was breaking a fifty-year tradition of endorsing only Republicans and supported Jim Buckley. "As an American before I am a Republican," Fish declared, "I urge all Americans, regardless of party affiliation, to vote for Jim Buckley."[18]

By mid-July even a *New York Times* editorial had to admit that Buckley was a "Serious Contender In Three-Way Race." On August 22, liberal columnist Garry Wills (who had once been on the staff at *National Review*), concluded that Jim Buckley "is almost too good to be true and much too good to be a politician. . . . [I]f Buckley goes to the Senate as a supporter of the war, it will be good to have an intelligent one for a change."

Buckley himself began to sense a change in voter sentiment:

> As I criss-crossed New York State during the campaign I was struck by the
> change – or intensification – in attitudes since I had run the same course
> two years earlier. I saw a mounting concern over the outbreaks of social
> disorder. I watched hardhats by the thousands marching down Broadway
> to demonstrate their love of country, their deep belief in its values and
> institutions, and their concern for its future at a time when many of their
> countrymen were burning the American flag and marching under Viet
> Cong banners. I felt the frustration of individual citizens growing in pro-
> portion to the rising level of governmental intrusion into every corner of
> their lives. I talked to hundreds of industrious New Yorkers who found
> themselves increasingly trapped between taxation and inflation, unable
> any longer to plan for their own futures or the futures of their children.[19]

In Washington, the one man who was carefully watching the New York race was
the resident of the White House, Richard M. Nixon. "We are dropping Goodell over
the side," the president said at one meeting.[20] Nixon realized he had to walk a fine
line: he couldn't look as though he were coming out publicly against a fellow
Republican. So he sent Vice President Agnew up to New York with instructions that
he could not publicly use Buckley's name but Agnew could use the line: "Vote for
people who will support the President."

With those marching orders, Agnew laid down his first barrage on September 30:

> Earlier today, I was asked if I would support a member of the radical lib-
> eral clique who is running in New York as a Republican.
>
> I made clear that I will not support a radical liberal no matter what
> party he belongs to. I may not be orthodox, but I am consistent.
>
> The Republican Party embraces a broad range of political viewpoints,
> as I have often pointed out in my speeches, and I have no trouble support-
> ing Republicans who have different political views. But what I believe,
> and believe strongly, is this: When a man consistently opposes a President
> of his own party on the greatest issues of the day; when a man makes pub-
> lic opposition to all his party stands for a major article of his political
> faith; when a man also goes out of his way publicly to reject support of his
> President that has not yet been offered; when a man attempts to curry favor
> with the party's leading adversaries by gratuitous attacks on many of his
> fellow party members; then I think that man has strayed beyond the point
> of no return.[21]

On an October 6 trip to Pittsburgh, Agnew praised "moderate" Senator Hugh

Scott and spoke about the need for diversity in the Republican Party. But then he turned again to the matter of Goodell:

> Well, then, I suspect some may be thinking, how can I make such assertions [about Scott] on the very heels of what has been described as my political excommunication of Senator Charles Goodell of New York last week?
>
> The answer is very simple. Since early 1969 Senator Goodell has sought flamboyantly and ceaselessly to openly divorce himself from our President and from the Nixon Administration. Ever since being named to the Senate to fill a vacancy, he has gambled his political future on public conflict with his own party and his own Administration. I say this: When anyone – of *either* party – constantly disavows, incessantly upbraids, and wages war on his own President in every major issue area, he consciously alienates himself from his party, and thereby forfeits a right to his Administration's support.[22]

On October 10, the vice president hammered Goodell as the "Christine Jorgensen of the Republican Party," referring to the first American who went to Denmark for a sex change operation.

In his 2001 work *President Nixon*, Journalist Richard Reeves reports that in mid-October Nixon "made his first campaign trip . . . to Connecticut with a brief and purposeful stop at the Westchester Airport north of New York City. The President stepped out of the plane for a moment, a crowd waving big "Buckley for Senate" signs ran onto the tarmac, photos were taken, and the Conservative Party candidate had a no-words-spoken endorsement from the Republican president."

Campaign chairman Clif White was also taking strategic shots at the opposition. While Buckley was diplomatically discussing the issues, White was happy to play the heavy. On August 28 he said of Mr. Ottinger: "He apparently thinks we can solve our social problems with the same technique he uses to try to win elections – money, lots of money." White charged further that: "Ottinger's spending in the June primary was extravagant to the point of gross violations of federal campaign spending laws. So too, his proposals for bigger and bigger federal budgets are not only fiscally irresponsible, they come at a time when our best social scientists are acknowledging the futility of federal spending as a solution to the nation's domestic ills. The Ottinger campaign is dominated by the money mystique." Ottinger wants, White concluded, "to be as generous with the taxpayer's money as he is with his mother's."[23]

On September 1, White went after both Ottinger and Goodell:

> The Goodell-Ottinger Twins both appeal to the same narrow constituency. This was clearly demonstrated this week when both candidates accused

each other of hedging on the question of unilateral withdrawal from Vietnam. Each candidate claims that he supported unilateral withdrawal from Vietnam first.

The great majority of New Yorkers are not liberals or New Leftists. The "Goodell-Ottinger Twins" are aiming their appeal to a minority of New York voters. The "Goodell-Ottinger Twins" represent a single point of view, while James L. Buckley represents the majority sentiment of New York voters.[24]

Conservative columnist James Jackson Kilpatrick made a call on White the first week of October to get the latest on the progress of the campaign. Kilpatrick reported:

White said that Buckley was six to eight points behind Ottinger in the polls, which was a little better than he had expected at this point, and he wasn't unhappy about it. What did he need? Money. What else did he need? Organization, especially upstate. White pointed to the Thirty-Third District, down around Oswego, a traditionally conservative district. If he could only get Buckley better known in the Thirty-Third, and get some effective organization in Broome, Chemung, Tioga and Tompkins counties, Buckley could win a clear majority there. Money for TV, and hands to do the work – those were the keys.

I had heard that 75 per cent of New York's Republican committeemen were at least privately for Buckley. What about open endorsements? White beamed over his bow tie. John Marchi, Republican candidate for mayor against Lindsay in 1969, had come out for Buckley. So had Mario Procaccino, Democratic candidate in the same race. And while Marchi's testimonial might be discounted as a consequence of his grudge against Goodell, Procaccino's support would carry substantial weight. For the first time in the history of New York City, both police and firemen had gone outside the traditional two parties: They were openly boosting Buckley. Dozens of members of the New York Legislature had plumped openly for Buckley. The endorsements looked very good indeed.[25]

Meanwhile, Jim Buckley continued to travel the state speaking out on issues and continuing to build a constituency that instinctively opposed the knee-jerk liberalism of his opponents. In a September 25 speech in Southampton, Buckley pursued a Nixon theme when he proclaimed that:

The Silent Majority will be silent no longer. . . . I intend in this campaign to speak for those millions of New Yorkers – that great majority of New Yorkers – who will not stand by and let the wreckers go to work.

The majority of whom I speak includes all the industrious, good-natured men and women of every background. Americans who by and large want nothing more than to live and let live and to be free to go about their lawful pursuits in peace. . . . Americans who know, because they know human nature, that peace and freedom depend on order and that when order is not maintained, there is no peace . . . there is no freedom.[26]

At the Conservative Party's annual dinner on October 12, keynote speaker Bill Buckley, hopeful his brother was going to win, gave this tribute:

Jim wrote me a couple of years ago, when it had been suggested to him that he should run for the Senate, to say with his instinctive modesty, "I can't imagine why I'd be useful to the public, still less why the public should want me." I liked that then, and I like it still more now, in the light of the overwhelming evidence, given by New Yorkers, that they *do* want him to speak for them, on so many of the problems, so very vexing, that are coming up. We used to tease Jim that he was never available for any family function on Saturday, because Saturdays are when people tend to get married, and Jim was always away at weddings, usually as best man, sometimes as usher. His friends felt, instinctively, that they wanted him around at critical periods in their lives. I think that the voters of New York feel the same way about Jim, wanting him in the Senate at this critical period in our lives.[27]

As the mid-October public opinion polls began to reflect that he was coming in dead last, Charles Goodell contemplated withdrawing from the race, hoping thus to ensure the election of the other liberal, Congressman Ottinger. Recalling that Conservative headquarters went into a panic upon hearing of this possibility, Serf Maltese said that a major phone operation was mounted, with conservatives calling Goodell headquarters and urging him to stay in the race.[28]

In a statewide address, two Sundays before election day, Goodell ended the suspense by telling New Yorkers that his conscience demanded he stay in the race. In a post election day interview, Goodell revealed his real reason for staying in the race:

[Goodell asserted] that his withdrawal would have "guaranteed" victory for Conservative Senator-elect James L. Buckley rather than for Democratic Rep. Richard L. Ottinger.

Goodell said he had concluded from a number of polls that his departure from the race "would probably have thrown more votes at that stage to Buckley than Ottinger."

"We analyzed where Buckley's strength was," he said. "Our analysis was that a good portion of it was Republican. A good portion was upstate and suburban.

"And if I had said, 'I'm withdrawing. Please don't vote for me. Vote for Ottinger,' that vote wasn't going to go to Ottinger. It was a Republican vote that would've gone to Buckley. My withdrawing at the stage would have guaranteed the election of Mr. Buckley."[29]

By the end of the campaign, *The New York Times* even took an interest in the Conservative Party. Reporter John Greenfield, when interviewing Dan Mahoney in his home for a *Times* magazine article, appeared amazed to hear the state chairman explain his membership in simple terms: "We do believe, with a sense of nostalgia, in all the old American verities and values. Our meetings have always started with the Pledge of Allegiance. We're not too sophisticated to take pride in our flag. And we're for self-dependence, individual effort, hard work – all the square virtues."[30] In his interview with the *Times*, the forty-five-year old lieutenant-governor candidate, Edward F. Leonard, (who lived in New Rochelle only a dozen blocks from Mahoney's home in Mount Vernon), also appeared to jar the nerves of Mr. Greenfield after the reporter asked why he was running for office. "Certainly he didn't think he had a chance of winning?" Greenfield reported Ed Leonard's reply:

> I could say as a student of history that I know that political upsets happen," he says, pouring shots of Scotch for both of us, "but the reason I'm running is that I'm involved in the party and, if you're serious about it, eventually you have to do your duty and become a candidate . . .
>
> And I'm not just running for this year. We're not just around until tomorrow. We plan to keep on until we can affect a conservative change in both the Democratic and Republican parties.
>
> We're not gadflies, you know, even though it's worked to our advantage to have our enemies consider us as such. They've never taken us seriously." He smiles again: "Just because we're ideological, they can't imagine we're also interested in power. . . ."[31]

As the campaign drew to a close one didn't need to read poll results to know that the Buckley campaign themes – "Isn't it about time *we* had a senator?" and "Join the March for America!" – were catching on with the voters. Supporters from all over New York and the country were sending in donations that totaled over a million dollars. Over thirty dailies backed Buckley including the *New York Daily News, The Post Standard, The Times Union, The Schenectady Gazette,* and *The Knickerbocker News Union Star.*

The Ottinger campaign (whose manager, Steve Berger, admitted early on that it was "a two man race between Ottinger and Buckley") suffered a serious blow on October 18 when *The New York Times* endorsed Goodell:

> The man New Yorkers choose this year to represent them in the United States Senate must be one capable of supplying inspiration as well as intelligence and creativity, a candidate who combines courage with a demonstrated capacity for bold leadership even at the cost of affronting dominant elements in his own party. In our estimation, that need will best be met on Nov. 3 by the return to Capitol Hill of Senator Charles E. Goodell, the Republican-Liberal nominee.

Although, during the debates Goodell and Ottinger tried to take shots at Buckley – mostly by labeling him a political neophyte – Jim Buckley not only carried his own weight but his low-key demeanor proved to New Yorkers that conservatives are not cold-blooded "Simon Legrees." Buckley himself noticed this change in perception among voters:

> I was running for election in what is generally regarded as the heartland of American liberalism, and doing so as the candidate of a party that threw down the gauntlet at the feet of the New York political establishment by frankly designating itself "Conservative." As I moved around the state, it became manifestly clear, far more so than two years earlier, that conservatism had managed to shed its Wall Street, know-nothing, treading-on-the-poor image and had come to be understood as a position manifesting a true concern for the protection of higher values. Because of this I was able to campaign successfully in New York under the label "Conservative" and to speak to the public in terms of a conservative analysis of current problems.[32]

Winning Issues for New York

Besides, Buckley was addressing the tough issues head on, just as his brother had in the 1965 mayoral race. In position papers, policy statements, press releases, hundreds of campaign speeches, newspaper interviews, and press conferences Buckley hit on a vast array of issues confronting the American voter:

Crime and Violence

* Recommended the installation of strong boxes, bulletproof shields, and two-way radios in taxicabs.

* Filed a petition for the disbarment of attorney William Kunstler because of his persistent and public violations of the canons of legal ethics.

* Urged a new sense of toughness in the application of existing laws and penalties – as well as streamlining of procedures – so that the prospect of early, meaningful punishment would once again provide a realistic deterrent to crime.

* Argued for mandatory sentencing for criminals who possess firearms while committing crimes.

Drugs

* Called for the creation of an international commission to develop multinational treaties for the effective control of the international traffic in drugs.

* Advocated firm United States diplomatic measures to cut down the flow of opium and heroin into the country from Turkey and France.

* Supported effective, independent drug rehabilitation programs such as Odyssey House in Manhattan, where former addicts participated in therapy, and insisted that government must encourage diversity and experimentation in developing effective techniques for the rehabilitation of addicts.

* Recommended the establishment of independent courts to handle drug-related crimes with judges specially qualified to handle problems of addiction.

Cost of Living, Unemployment, and the Economy

* Opposed the 40-percent raise in congressional salaries in 1969.

* Supported the concept of a balanced budget in Washington because of the inflationary effects of large deficits.

* Opposed wage and price controls as ineffective and unnecessary.

* Called for a cost of living adjustment in social security benefits and for the elimination of provisions that penalize the elderly who choose to work after they become eligible for retirement benefits.

Environment

* Called for the creation of an independent federal agency which would take over all environmental-related activities now handled ineffectively by scores of federal agencies: the new agency would have the power to determine and enforce minimum standards required to control pollution.

* Advocated tax incentives and tax deductions to encourage the development of technologies needed to recycle industrial wastes, thereby eliminating the major source of industrial pollution and at the same time conserving valuable chemicals and minerals which are now irrevocably lost.

* Advocated intensive federal research to develop new methods of generating electricity in order to satisfy the growing demand for power without increasing pollution or unnecessarily spoiling our landscapes.

* Suggested the burning of combustible trash as a means of generating electric power as is done in many European cities.

Foreign Policy and Trade

* Supported President Nixon's new peace initiative for a cease-fire in Vietnam.

* Backed the President's Southeast Asian policy of gradual and responsible withdrawal with emphasis on building and training Vietnamese forces.

* Opposed the Hatfield-McGovern amendment for a precipitous withdrawal from Vietnam.

* Encouraged the SALT talks for disarmament and arms control, provided that limitations agreed upon are subject to verification.

* Disapproved of the pending trade bill which would impose quotas on selected products in violation of the principles of free trade which benefit all Americans.

Welfare and Housing

* Urged drastic reductions in government-imposed red tape that restricted the effectiveness of welfare caseworkers.

* Called for the restoration of local control of welfare programs designed to help those who cannot help themselves and for the training of able-bodied welfare recipients so that they might enter the labor market.

* Advocated "Open and Honest" direct subsidization of housing for the needy through the use of housing vouchers as an alternative to public programs and controls which impede the private sector.

* Promoted anti-inflationary measures and updated building codes designed to encourage the private sector to meet current housing deficits.

Congressional Reform

* Supported the concept of enforcing ceilings in spending in political campaigns.
* Proposed a constitutional amendment to grant the president a line-item veto.

These and other issues turned out to strike a chord with New York voters.[33]

Election Day Arrives

On Monday, November 2, the final day of his campaign, Jim Buckley looked back on the crusade that shook the very foundations of the liberal establishment:

> While I never felt that my election was assured, after the first few weeks I was confident that I had a chance to win. And as I entered the final week of the campaign, the polls showed me ahead, but by a margin so slender that in its election eve issue, the New York *Daily News* declared the race too close to call. The campaign itself was a blur of rallies and journeys by plan, bus, and car, televised debates, with one event following another in such rapid succession that I had little time to worry about where I stood. All I knew was that I had a chance to present a viewpoint I believe in, and

I took every opportunity to do just that. By election day I was satisfied that
I had done everything I could.[34]

On election day morning, President Nixon's first call of the day was to Bill
Buckley.

"I don't know how you mackerel snappers look at others," the president said, "but
if a quiet Quaker's prayer will help, you've got it. Tell Jim to go to the bar with the
warm beer and relax a couple of hours after the polls close."[35]

That night Buckley supporters gathered in the grand ballroom of the Waldorf
Astoria to await the results. After the polls closed at 9:00 P.M., early results had the
lead going back and forth between Ottinger and Buckley. But at 10 o'clock, Clif
White and a young volunteer voter analyst, Arthur Finkelstein, explained to Buckley
that he was the winner with about 38 percent of the vote. At 1:00 A.M., Senator-Elect
James Lane Buckley of New York declared victory. The spectators in the packed ballroom went wild. About ten minutes later, when the crowd finally settled down,
Buckley told his followers that this "victory in New York would telegraph across the
country the message that Americans want a new course, want new politics, and I am
the voice of that new politics."[36]

	Goodell Rep.	Ottinger Dem.	Buckley Cons.	Goodell Lib.	Buckley Ind.
Upstate New York	**898,215**	**1,191,904**	**1,448,617**	**96,805**	**108,394**
Bronx	41,080	171,958	120,782	25,381	27,543
Brooklyn	78,176	308,421	197,346	44,247	44,780
Manhattan	76,983	220,103	94,883	46,870	30,601
Queens	74,541	257,179	266,393	40,178	29,904
Staten Island	9,684	21,667	51,619	2,312	4,511
Total New York City	**280,464**	**979,328**	**731,023**	**158,988**	**137,339**
Total State	**1,178,679**	**2,171,232**	**2,179,640**	**255,793**	**245,733**

	Total	Percentage
Goodell	1,434,472	23.7%
Ottinger	2,171,332	36.0%
Buckley	2,425,413	40.2%

Chairman Dan Mahoney collected various anti–Conservative Party bromides into
a rah-rah song:

> Three cheers for fear and hatred,
> Division and mistrust.
> When Jim goes to Washington,
> These will be a must.

> Six years of pure repression
> Our liberties will rust.
> Six years for our dear Jim
> To union bust.[37]

Comptroller candidate, Tony Spinelli, who spent $4,000 on his campaign and received 436,584 votes, shouted out to the approving crowd: "Javits next."

Minutes after he completed his victory statement, Buckley received a call from President Nixon who congratulated him on his triumph. The president's communications director Herbert Klein stated that: "Nixon's efforts had a major effect on the outcome of this election."[38]

In the gubernatorial race, Paul Adams's showing at 422,514 votes was below his 1966 total of 510,000, but this could be attributed to Rockefeller's blatant shift to the right. The front page of the *New York Post* titled its lead story, "Rocky's Turn to Right Did It." The article stated:

> Gov. Rockefeller used a time-tested campaign machine, oiled by more than $6 million and a special appeal to conservative voters, to turn back Arthur J. Goldberg's first bid for elective office.
>
> Rockefeller managed to arrange a tacit truce with the state's Conservative Party, a tactic that persuaded many Republicans to push for a ticket of Rockefeller and James L. Buckley, the Conservative Party Senate candidate.
>
> The Republican Governor, who won an unprecedented fourth four-year term in Albany, wooed the conservative Italian and Irish New York City voters to offset the large Jewish turnout here for Goldberg.[39]

	Rockefeller Rep.	Goldberg Dem.	Adams Cons.	Goldberg Lib.
Total Upstate New York	**2,047,256**	**1,237,480**	**315,737**	**84,05**
Bronx	175,178	161,136	16,650	28,815
Brooklyn	297,176	292,014	26,944	49,283
Manhattan	177,453	216,508	14,092	52,007
Queens	345,121	234,334	41,722	46,437
Staten Island	63,036	16,883	7,369	2,475
Total New York City	**1,057,964**	**920,875**	**106,777**	**179,017**
Total State	**3,105,220**	**2,158,355**	**422,514**	**263,071**

Analyzing the Buckley candidacy, loser Charles Goodell made this observation: "He [Buckley] came through as a person of whom a hard hat could say, 'I'll vote for him. He's against the labor laws, he's against all the things we believe in, but he's for safety in the streets and for patriotism.'"[40]

One area that was a
microcosm of the coali-
tion Buckley assembled
was the Ninth Congress-
ional District located in
Western Queens County.
For decades this area,
which encompasses the
neighborhoods of Long
Island City, Maspeth,
Glendale, Ridgewood,
Jackson Heights, and
Middle Village, was a
Democratic Party bastion.
They worshipped Franklin
Roosevelt, John Kennedy,
and the party that gave
them the National Labor
Relations Board and other
programs that enhanced
their ability to attain their
piece of the "American
Dream."

In the 1960s and
1970s the Ninth, whose
ethnic population stood at
59 percent, had more
Irish, Germans, and Itali-

Senator-elect James L. Buckley declaring victory, November 1970. Paul
Adams stands to his left.

ans than any other district in New York City.[41] Disturbed by the decline in traditional
values and by the rise in crime, by riots in the streets, and by an ever-growing welfare
population, voters in the 9th began to shift in their political loyalties.

In 1965, William F. Buckley Jr. received over 25 percent of the vote. Eighty percent of the district voted against the 1966 Civilian Review Board. In 1968, Nixon
received 50 percent of the vote to Humphrey's 41 percent.

The district's long-term incumbent, Congressman James J. Delaney, detected this
trend. Elected in 1944, Delaney was for most of his career returned to the Congress
with substantial electoral majorities. He became dean of the New York congressional
delegation and a ranking member of the House Rules Committee. In 1966, however,
he was reelected with only 53.2 percent of the vote. In a 1968 rematch with
Republican-Conservative John Haggerty, Delaney won with a 49.5 percent plurality.

Fearing defeat in 1970, Delaney moved to the right. His 40 percent American Conservative Union rating moved up into the high sixties.

Delaney shocked the political world in 1970 when he endorsed Jim Buckley's senate candidacy and engineered the cross endorsements of the Republican and Conservative Parties. But he definitely caught the wave: he beat his Liberal Party opponent with 93 percent of the vote.

Buckley, who received only 35 percent of the vote in New York City, garnered 60 percent of the vote in the Ninth Congressional District. This occurred in a district where only 24 percent of the population had family incomes above the $15,000 median. Like Nixon in 1968, Buckley's cultural view appealed to blue-collar ethic voters and he carried their neighborhoods with substantial majorities.

There was other good news on election night. Thanks to Conservative Party endorsements Republicans maintained and expanded their control over both branches of the state legislature. In Western New York, the party provided the margin of victory for an ex-Buffalo Bills football player, Jack Kemp.

Kemp	Flaherty	Kemp	Flaherty
Rep.	Dem.	Cons.	Lib.
82,939	86,142	14,050	4,807
44.1%	45.8%	7.4%	2.5%

Also, the three key legislators who sold out on the abortion bill, Senator Dominick and Assemblymen Michaels and Balleta, all went down in defeat.

Chapter 9

Growing Pains
1971–1974

With the election of James L. Buckley, the Conservative Party had officially – and, to the political establishment, *frighteningly* – transformed its status from mere nuisance to out-and-out rival by virtue of the coalition it had formed between disenchanted blue-collar Democrats and right-wing Republicans. When asked how he did it in a state with a strong liberal tradition, Senator-elect Buckley explained it this way:

> Well, I think that people have consistently underestimated the existing moderate-conservative sentiment in New York State. The sentiment, which was always there and has been ignored, has grown in the last couple of years. And I believe that a substantial majority of New Yorkers definitely feel that we need new approaches to our problems, that the old answers just haven't worked. The political leadership of both parties in this State has tended to chase leftward, stranding large sections of the rank and file – and I stepped into a void.[1]

Richard Nixon also recognized the significance of the Conservative Party victory and invited Mahoney and O'Doherty to a White House meeting to discuss the Buckley race. The White House released Oval Office pictures that appeared in most New York papers with the president and his guests in an intense conversation. To further facilitate relations, in 1971 the Nixon Administration appointed Kieran O'Doherty as a consultant to the U.S. Department of Commerce and Tony Spinelli as the chief of the New York Division of the Small Business Administration.

Things were looking up to say the least, but Mahoney refused to be complacent. In order to manage the challenges ahead, he believed it was time to make at least one serious change at state headquarters. Jim Griffin, who had been serving as party executive director since 1968, began his association with the party as a research assistant in the 1965 Buckley mayoral campaign. A former schoolteacher, Griffin was extraordinarily devoted, and he had worn out several typewriters grinding out first-rate analyses of New York's fiscal, economic, and social ills. But in the role of executive director which required constant contact with party leaders, legislators, street operations and the press, Griffin was less effective, and in recent months Mahoney had found himself turning more and more for help to a young lawyer from Queens, Serphin Maltese.

Born in Corona, Queens, on December 7, 1932, Serf Maltese and his family moved to Manhattan where he attended P.S. 63, Junior High School 64, and Peter Stuyvesant High School. After a stint in the Army, he went to Manhattan College in the Bronx. While returning from an Italian fraternity weekend in the summer of 1950, Serf's friend fell asleep driving a 1952 Plymouth and hit an overpass on Long Island's Meadowbrook Highway. Serf broke both his feet and legs and fractured his skull. Although he had to spend the next year in bed, the Christian Brothers at Manhattan College let him study at home, and he received his diploma with his class in 1958, attending the ceremony on crutches.

While still an undergraduate in August 1955, he married Constance Del Vecchio of Maspeth, Queens. The couple moved to 84th Street in Jackson Heights, where Serf convalesced, completed college, and then went on to Fordham Law School.

In 1961, the twenty-nine-year-old Maltese, then a Democrat, worked for Republican Thomas Galvin, who was running in a special Sixth Congressional District election to fill the seat vacated by newly elected Supreme Court Judge Lester Holtzman.

Maltese had decided to help out Galvin, who would lose the race by only 169 votes, because he considered the Democratic candidate, Benjamin Rosenthal, to be an arrogant Goo-Goo. According to Maltese, Rosenthal and his ilk were "driving ethnic neighborhood types out of the local club."[2] Serf was disgusted with the changes taking place in the Democratic Party.

He may have been a registered Democrat, but he was also a subscriber to *National Review*, and when he received a 1962 letter from editor William F. Buckley Jr. introducing his readers to the formation of a New York Conservative Party, both Serf and his wife returned the enclosed enrollment postcard. On it Serf indicated that he would like to be a member of the new party, and Constance checked the box designated for those interested in becoming a local leader.

When they were welcomed into the new Jackson Heights-East Elmhurst Conservative Club, Serf promptly went door-to-door in Queens – as well as the Bronx and Westchester – soliciting signatures for the petition that was to get the party onto New York's ballot.

Moving to Middle Village, Queens, the Malteses joined Ridgewood's Alexander Hamilton Conservative Club founded by Robert O'Leary, brother of future Nassau County chairman, Jack O'Leary. Because Maltese was a lawyer, club chairman James Morgan made him vice chairman and Constance, an artist, sketched political cartoons for the *Queens Conservative Newsletter*. In early 1964, Morgan moved to West Virginia and Maltese became club chairman.

Maltese was by now an avid conservative. He attended the 1964 Madison Square Garden Rally for Barry Goldwater, where he was introduced to Mahoney and O'Doherty. In the fall he worked strenuously for the Republican presidential candidate in both the Third and Thirteenth Assembly Districts in Queens. Thanks in large measure to Serf's efforts, Goldwater actually carried those areas.

In 1965, Ted Dabrowski became county chairman, and he relied on Maltese to provide advice on election law for local candidates. When Hamilton Conservative club member Rosemary Gunning joined Buckley's ticket as candidate for city council president, Maltese served as her driver, even though he was running himself on Row D for the state senate. It was during this time that he really came to the attention of Dan Mahoney.

It was in late 1969 that Kathleen and Dan Mahoney asked Maltese to get active as an unpaid volunteer in state headquarters. In the spring of 1970, Maltese was appointed to handle the statewide petition drive to get Jim Buckley the independent line on the November ballot. Then at a political function in early 1971, Serf was dancing with Kathleen Mahoney when she told him:

"Dan is going to ask you something, and I hope you say 'yes.'"

What Mahoney asked Maltese was to consider becoming the party's executive director. Maltese realized that he would have to give up the practice of law, but he accepted the offer, and he officially became Director on April 14, 1971.[3]

Battles at the Grass Roots

While the party was still glowing from the Buckley victory, Mahoney hit the ground running in January 1971 by prefacing the party's legislative program with the warning that: ". . . the hard-working New York State taxpayer has had his back to the wall and cannot live with new taxes in 1971 to pay for the follies of 1970."

The Conservatives urged the "bold new concept" of giving localities "priority over their own resources." They said that government and tax resources should be brought back to the local level and the money should be left "where the problems are." Among other measures, the Conservatives advocated adoption of a comprehensive state budget with a five-year fiscal projection and the elimination of the supplemental budget.[4]

On February 17, the party's former candidate for lieutenant governor, Edward F. Leonard, testified before the Joint Finance Committee of the New York State Senate and Assembly and dissected Governor Rockefeller's latest record-breaking budget of $6.8 billion. Leonard made the simple, incontestable point that the State of New York was running out of money:

Gentlemen, something has got to give – either the backs of the taxpayers, or the impetus behind ever increasing state spending. The average hard-working taxpayer in this state cannot afford the new taxes proposed to you this year. He cannot afford to pay more every year for welfare, more for schools, more for wages and fringe benefits for state employees, more for our mounting debt service.

And the simple facts show that if we do not do something about it this year . . . [i]f we do not take the steps necessary to relieve him of his tax burden . . . New York State will be impossible to live in or to do business in.

Whatever you are told by the various pressure groups you will hear today, the taxpayers are not asking for new programs and new spending at any level. They do want you to have the courage to confront fiscal reality, and to curb once and for all spiraling taxes at every level. This is going to require that you as individuals take on the spending pressure groups back home in your districts, and that you do everything possible to give the taxpayers the true facts. It is going to require that all of us be willing to scrap the present system of siphoning money through Albany, and that we be willing to trust the people to run their own affairs.[5]

At the March 3 victory banquet held at the Waldorf-Astoria Hotel, Dan Mahoney told the crowd: "For eight years conservatives dreamed the impossible dream – a Conservative Party victory in the most liberal state in the country." To commemorate the victor, Bill Buckley flew in from Switzerland to pay tribute to his brother. Senator John Marchi, Mario Procaccino, Congressman James Delaney, and freshman Congressman Jack Kemp also gave inspiring addresses to the party faithful.

In May, the Conservative Party and Senator Buckley took pro-active positions in the Forest Hills public-housing-project controversy and got their first sense of the man who would become, after Rocky himself, the cause of much conservative agitation in the decades to come.

In early 1971, one of Mayor Lindsay's top social engineers, Simeon Golar of the City Housing Authority, decided that low-income housing had to be built in middle-class Forest Hills. Earlier in his administration, Lindsay approved thirteen scatter-site low-income housing projects. The mayor characterized these schemes as a "moral imperative."

Although the predominately Jewish neighborhood of Forest Hills had supported the mayor in 1965 and 1969, there was uproar in the community against the housing authority's plan. Protestors lined the streets carrying signs that read: "Forest Hills Doesn't Want Welfare Towers" and "Down with Adolf Lindsay and His Project."[6] The Queens Jewish Community Council told the public that "Mayor Lindsay has shown he is not interested in the Jewish population of his constituency." On May 15, Queens party chairman Ted Dabrowski declared:

Thou shall not build. . . . The people who live in Forest Hills voiced their opposition at the public hearings when those in favor had the opportunity to be heard. Now Mr. Golar says the Housing Authority will start building in July "no matter what" and regardless of the opposition. This "to hell with the people" attitude is typical of the Lindsay administration ever since "I am the Mayor" was elected for his first term. This is still a democracy and the people who should decide whether or not the community favors the housing project and whether it should or should not be built are those persons who conducted the public hearings in the democratic process. Simeon Golar has no right to dictate what the people are going to get whether they like it or not. The voice of the people can still be heard and if it can't be heard in city hall, it can be heard in the polling booths.[7]

Senator Buckley met with Housing Secretary George Romney, who announced that he ordered his agency to give the project an "immediate and thorough review." Viewing Buckley's support of this politically liberal neighborhood, *Newsday* reported that "today it's Buckley, not to Javits that the protestors of Forest Hills appeal in their dismay. They may have been voting liberals in the past, but when it comes to a fight like this, they know which side the Conservatives are on."[8]

Feeling the heat and concerned about his presidential plans, Mayor Lindsay turned to a young Queens lawyer, Mario Cuomo, to study the matter and to resolve the dispute. Cuomo, future New York governor and Conservative Party bête noire, came up with a compromise project that at the time did not placate most of the protesters.

In 1971's "off year" elections, the Conservative Party came out against Proposed Amendment #1 to the state constitution which would have permitted the New York to finance in any community "programs for: the development of adequate, safe and sanitary housing and other types of shelter or accommodations; urban and community renewal; economic prosperity and adequate employment opportunities; health, mental health and environmental health; child care and aged care; transportation and communications; civic, cultural, recreational and other community facilities and services; or any combination of such purposes."[9] In urging its defeat, Dan Mahoney charged that it would "lead to destruction of community identity and saddle the taxpayers with enormous tax burdens." He said it would give the state unlimited power to "revamp" communities and thus affect their growth and character.[10]

The party also urged the defeat of a $2.5-billion Transportation Bond Issue. "We will be mortgaging the future of our children and their children unless New Yorkers vote NO to defeat Proposition #1, the $2.5 billion Transportation Bond Issue," said Executive Director Maltese. He continued:

By passage of this vague Proposition, which lacks schedules of priorities, specifications and safeguards, we can be certain of only higher state debts and higher taxes. Advocates of the bond issue have cited as a reason for passage "that $300 million of the proposed issue has already been included in the current budget." This deplorable action was taken before a vote by the people and that alone should serve as sufficient reason for a NO vote. This fiscal irresponsibility calls for our condemnation and if approved would undoubtedly stand as a continuing precedent in future budgets. We urge overburdened New York voters to call a halt now to new and ever-spiraling taxes and vote NO on the proposed $2.5 billion transportation bond issue.[11]

On November 2, 1971, both ballot issues went down in flames. Sixty-four percent of the voters said "No" to the Community Development Amendment, and 61 percent voted "No" on the Transportation Bond Issue.

In local elections there were a few plusses for the party. In the town of Southampton in Eastern Long Island, Theodore Hulse was elected on the Conservative line as town supervisor. His election ended decades of total Republican control of Southampton. In Yonkers, Conservative Party endorsement provided the margin of victory in three county legislative races. And in Rockland County, enrolled Conservative John L. Dice was endorsed by the Republican Party and was elected to the Clarkstown Council.

There were also two very important difficulties that were not ballot issues but with which the Conservative Party had to contend: first was the move by political leaders in several counties to ban cross-endorsements; and second was Richard M. Nixon's shift to the political left.

After analyzing the 1970 election results, Republican leaders, particularly in Nassau County, were angered by their growing dependence on the Conservative Party in local races. To diminish the Conservative influence, Democratic and Republican county political organizations in Nassau, Suffolk, Monroe, and Rockland agreed to prohibit their candidates from accepting the endorsement of another party. Democrats in these Republican-dominated counties, not seeing any downside, decided to go along with the ban.

Dan Mahoney was livid, and he made it perfectly clear that he considered it obligatory that the Conservative Party enter candidates in every race in 1971 and if necessary in 1972. Mahoney told the Republicans that "this recommendation includes opposition to candidates whom we would otherwise be willing to endorse, but who will not seek or accept our endorsement because of the pressure being exerted against cross-endorsements." Mahoney was determined to run candidates to prove the party's capacity to provide or withhold the margin of victory.

While the bans in Monroe and Rockland County quickly collapsed when local elected officials, fearing defeat at the polls, strongly objected, Nassau and Suffolk held out.

In Nassau County, Republican pressure on Oyster Bay Town Councilman Lewis Yevoli to decline the Conservative line wound up in the courts. Despite the protestations of Republican and Democratic county leaders, Judge Daniel Albert went to the heart of the matter when he stated in his decision: "The obvious purpose of the arrangement between the leadership of the two great political parties is to stem the influence of the more recently formed third parties, such as the Liberal and Conservative Parties."[12]

Judge Albert's decision sustaining the Conservative Party's case underlined the illegality of the pressure tactics being employed by the Republican and Democratic organizations. The court made clear that the state's election laws mandate that nominations be sought and given in open party primaries, that affiliation be made by each candidate in the privacy of his own conscience, including whether or not to accept an additional party endorsement.

In spite of the court decision, the Republican Party leadership in Nassau and Suffolk continued to "gently" persuade most of their candidates to decline Row C. Although 1971 was an off-year election with few races, the Conservative Party managed to make its point by opposing those that would have been endorsable candidates. In Suffolk County, lack of Conservative support caused three Republican Suffolk County Supervisors to go down in defeat. In Nassau, Judge Francis Donovan, a lifelong Republican and incumbent judge for a dozen years, was denied the GOP endorsement because he rejected the cross-endorsement ban and accepted the Conservative Party endorsement. Judge Donovan upset the Republican machine by beating his Republican opponent on the Democratic-Conservative lines.

The other major concern to Conservatives was the Nixon Administration's desertion of conservative principles: his adoption of Keynesian economics (specifically in the imposition of wage and price controls), and his proposed family assistance program and continued expansion of Great Society programs. These and other examples of Nixonian *realpolitik* disappointed many on the right. While many Conservatives supported Nixon's "Peace with Honor" strategy in Vietnam, they deplored his China moves.

On July 16, 1971, Dan Mahoney expressed "grave concern" about the president's intended visit to Communist China. "It is extremely doubtful," Mahoney said, "that any purpose of American Foreign policy can be served by this undertaking. . . . American foreign policy has been based, until now, upon the perception that Communist China is a relentless aggressor in its international policies. Nothing has happened to disturb the evaluation."[13]

Anger over Nixon's policies was brewing, and the August 10, 1971, issue of *National Review* ran this declaration signed by twelve prominent conservatives:

We touch only lightly on the failures of Mr. Nixon's Administration domestically. It is a fact that we continue to have inflation and unemployment, excessive taxation and inordinate welfarism . . .

These domestic considerations, important as they are, pale into insignificance alongside the tendencies of the Administration in foreign policy. Applauding though we do the President's steadfastness in resisting the great pressures upon him to desert Southeast Asia, we note:

1. His failure to respond to the rapid advance of the Soviet Union into the Mediterranean basin,

2. His failure to warn against the implications of the current policies of the West German government,

3. His overtures to Red China, done in the absence of any public concessions by Red China to American and Western causes,

4. *And above all*, his failure to call public attention to the deteriorated American military position. . . .

In consideration of this record, the undersigned, who have heretofore generally supported the Nixon Administration, have resolved to suspend our support of the Administration. . . .[14]

The dozen signatures on the declaration included those of William Buckley, Conservative Book Club president Neil McCaffrey, *National Review* publisher William A. Rusher, *Human Events* editor Tom Winter, and Dan Mahoney.

The "straw that broke the camel's back" for some Conservatives was the expulsion of Taiwan from the United Nations in October. Mahoney, for one, assailed the administration's failure to maintain Taiwan's seat.

In December, continued support of Nixon had become a hot topic at the Conservative Party State Executive Committee meeting. The result was passage of a unanimous resolution suspending support of the president. Dan Mahoney, speaking for the committee, announced that the party was "aligning itself with the broader group of conservative spokesmen who declared their suspension of presidential support last summer, and are currently considering the entry of a candidate in various presidential primaries throughout the nation."[15]

"I have been a member of the group that has suspended its support of President Nixon ever since it came into existence," Mahoney went on. "In view of recent developments, however, the state executive committee wished formally to adopt a position on this question, which is of crucial consequence to conservatives both in New York and throughout the nation."

Mahoney did, however, offer public support to Nixon whenever he could. In fact, the same day the party suspended its support, Mahoney broadcast this reply to a WCBS-TV's editorial calling for the rejection of William Rehnquist's nomination to the U.S. Supreme Court:

WCBS-TV stated, in its editorial opposing the Rehnquist nomination, that Mr. Rehnquist "is qualified intellectually, and has the experience to serve as a judge." This is certainly a modest description of William Rehnquist's superb qualifications for elevation to the Supreme Court. He was first in his class at Stanford Law School, clerked for Supreme Court Justice Robert Jackson, and has been the leading constitutional theoretician for the Nixon Administration for the past several years.

This latter role is the real problem liberals have with the Rehnquist nomination. William Rehnquist clearly reflects and articulates the mounting concern of the American people with a system of criminal justice that does not adequately deter crime or punish criminals. They are equally weary of a Supreme Court that regards itself as a super legislature. President Nixon's promises of reform in this crucial area were a major factor in his election in 1968.

WCBS-TV, and others of like mind, want to call off the democratic system when it operates to their dissatisfaction, as in the case of the Rehnquist nomination. Fortunately for the rest of us, they are unlikely to get their way. I predict a brilliant career for Justice Rehnquist, after an early confirmation.[16]

When Congressman John Ashbrook of Ohio announced on December 29, 1969, that he was challenging Richard Nixon in the New Hampshire primary in order to lead him back to the path of conservative righteousness, the Conservative Party decided to support his efforts.

Dan Mahoney got to know and admire Ashbrook through their American Conservative Union board membership. (Ashbrook was a founding member and first chairman of the ACU.) A Harvard graduate, Ashbrook practiced law and was publisher of the Ohio newspaper the *Johnson Independent* before being elected to Congress in 1960. In 1968 he had broken ranks with the Ohio delegation to the Republican National Convention, which was committed to favorite-son Governor James A. Rhodes, and cast his vote for Nixon. He had supported Nixon because the former vice president had "promised to disperse federal power, cut the budget, shun economic controls, dismantle Great Society programs, outgun the Russians, deny loans to countries trading with North Vietnam, tighten the economic noose around Cuba and keep Red China out of the U.N."[17] But by 1972, Ashbrook believed the record clearly showed that Nixon had deserted many of those views, and that an Ashbrook candidacy would give the conservatives a rallying point to remind the White House that the Right could not be taken for granted.

The Ashbrook Challenge and Nixon's Triumph

On January 25, the Conservative Party endorsement of Ashbrook was made formal.

Mahoney told the media that a unanimous resolution of support had passed the Executive Committee:

> We are deeply grateful that Congressman Ashbrook has stepped forward to provide political expression for the widening conservative discontent with the performance of the Nixon Administration, and we wholeheartedly support Congressman Ashbrook in this courageous effort. The Ashbrook candidacy is the only effective protest against the wayward policies of the Nixon Administration on national defense, Red China and Taiwan, runaway spending and deficits, wage-price controls and welfare. Congressman Ashbrook deserves the support of all those who, like the Conservative Party of New York State, are determined not to be conscripted by silence in support of Nixon policies of Nixon policies with which they thoroughly disagree.[18]

"The Ashbrook campaign in New Hampshire," Serf Maltese says, "was primarily a Conservative Party operation. None of the 'Making of the President' books give us the credit." The gang of twelve that signed the declaration to suspend support of Mr. Nixon, agreed that Serf Maltese was the right man to go to New Hampshire and organize the Ashbrook challenge.

Maltese arrived in New Hampshire with a dozen New York volunteers three weeks before the March 7 primary. The volunteers quickly realized that the Ashbrook "campaign" had done no advance work. "We had to set up a headquarters, get phones, furniture, etc. ASAP," recalls Maltese. Although funding was promised, no money had yet arrived, so Maltese used his own credit card to finance the Ashbrook campaign. "I had a $5,000 line of credit on this new card I had received in the mail, so I used it to the max. I was never reimbursed and it took me three years to pay off that debt."[19]

While Maltese and his colleagues were racing to put together some semblance of a campaign apparatus in New Hampshire, President Nixon was in Peking, announcing the communiqué he had signed with the leaders of Red China. The Conservative Party immediately voiced "shock and dismay" over the contents of the document. Dan Mahoney expressed:

> . . . amazement that President Nixon would predict the withdrawal of our forces from Taiwan in the same statement in which Communist China demanded that withdrawal and reiterated its determination to "liberate" Taiwan. President Nixon's studied refusal to mention our treaty commitments to Nationalist China in the communiqué can only compound the injury done both the Nationalist China and to the credibility of all our nation's alliances in Asia and elsewhere.

"The Conservative Party," Mahoney concluded, "has opposed, from the outset, the Nixon visit to Red China. The diplomatic ineptitude and lack of moral fortitude embodied in the final communiqué have, however, greatly magnified the predictably disastrous consequences of the Peking visit."[20]

Although Bill Buckley and *National Review* publisher William Rusher campaigned in New Hampshire, it had no real effect. Ashbrook received only 10 percent of the vote in the March 7 Republican primary.

The insurgent campaign limped its way to Florida, and Maltese tried once again to organize a grass-roots effort. Recognizing that Ashbrook was being ignored by the media, Dan Mahoney urged that they "provide fair coverage at least to the closing day of the Ashbrook campaign in Florida,"

"Congressman Ashbrook has been a candidate for President for approximately nine weeks," Mahoney stated, "and has been campaigning heavily in Florida, but has gone literally without notice in the national media. Republicans in Florida deserve notice from the media, at least in the closing hours of the Florida primary, that Congressman Ashbrook is affording them an opportunity to vote for the 1968 Republican platform and against President Nixon's wholesale departures from that platform."[21]

Florida Republicans were as indifferent to Ashbrook's message as those in New Hampshire had been, and, again, he received just 10 percent of the vote. Although Ashbrook's name was to appear on the Wisconsin and California primary ballots, the movement had pretty much come to a halt. Maltese packed his bags and returned to New York.

But the Conservative Party did get some satisfaction in Florida. John Lindsay, who finally became a Democrat on August 11, 1971, announced in December that he would seek his new party's nomination for president. He skipped the New Hampshire primary and went straight to Florida, where he believed retired New Yorkers would rally to his side. Instead, the mayor learned a bitter lesson: many ex-New Yorkers had moved to the Sunshine State precisely to escape his inept leadership. Lindsay finished in fifth place in the March 14 primary, receiving only 7 percent of the vote. Thus were his White House aspirations forever dashed.

When it became apparent that the Democratic nomination of the extreme liberal, George McGovern, was inevitable, discussions between Conservative and Republican leaders about a joint endorsement of Nixon began in earnest. The White House made it clear that such an endorsement would be welcome, and this time Governor Rockefeller did not stand in the way.

Although many New York Conservatives were still unhappy about Nixon's support of family assistance programs and with aspects of his foreign policy, they were pleased with Nixon's decision to retain Spiro Agnew as his running-mate. In addition, Conservatives were assured that the Republican platform would have planks favoring the appointment of "strict-constructionist" judges and the employment of a defense policy in which the "U.S. will be second to none."[22]

An August 30 meeting of the Conservative Party's state committee endorsed a slate of electors committed to Nixon and Agnew. The Republican State Committee, meeting that same day, endorsed the identical slate. Bill Buckley signed on. "A vote for Nixon-Agnew on Row C," he wrote, "will be heard loud and clear in Washington as a mandate for conservative policies in the next four years."[23]

At the same Conservative Party meeting that endorsed the Republican presidential ticket, Dan Mahoney also hailed the gains his party had made during its first ten years. Mahoney stated that the party would be fielding Conservative or Conservative-endorsed candidates in 130 assembly, 56 state senate, 37 congressional, and the three statewide court-of-appeals races, as well as innumerable other local races throughout the entire state.

Another portent of the future growth, prestige, and influence of party was the increase in its enrollment from 10,329 in 1963 – the first year of Conservative mobilization – to 129,017 by the end of 1971.

Mahoney concluded his statement by telling the faithful: "We welcome and are gratified by the voters of the other major parties who swell the Conservative Party total and who gave a spectacular victory to Senator James L. Buckley. In addition, we point with pride to the statewide election figures that indicate that on its 10th birthday, our relatively young party has a substantial reservoir of party loyalty as well as a faithful following which is many times our growing enrollment."[24]

In releasing the party's 1972 state legislative rating, Mahoney pointed out that nine assemblymen and one state senator had attained the highest ratings of 100 percent. In the assembly: Rosemary Gunning (C-R, Ridgewood), Charles A. Jerabek (C-R, Bay Shore), Vito P. Battista (R-C, Brooklyn), Alfred A. DelliBovi (R-C, Richmond Hill), John T. Flack (R-C, Glendale), John T. Gallagher (R-C, Bayside), Edward M. Kinsella (R-C, Solvay), Edwyn E. Mason (R-C, Hobart) and the late George E. Van Cott (R-C, Mt. Vernon). And in the senate: Martin J. Knorr (R-C, Ridgewood).

"I am pleased to note," Mahoney said, "that all these distinguished legislators are Conservatives or Conservative-endorsed and I am especially pleased that Assemblyman Jack Gallagher is among these special friends, as he presently is the Conservative-endorsed Republican candidate in the 6th congressional District and I am certain that he will continue to serve our country with the same distinction he has shown here in the state legislature."[25]

In the fall campaign, many New Yorkers saw Richard Nixon as the champion of blue-collar ethnics, whereas they saw George McGovern as "further polariz[ing] society by appearing to become the captive of dissidents and outsiders who were looking to the federal government for special privileges."[26] Even Mario Cuomo conceded that McGovern drove away the blue collar voter, "who felt alienated by a new Democratic Party which he thought neither understood nor related to him."[27]

On Friday, October 13, at the Conservative Party's tenth anniversary dinner, Senator Buckley, Bill Buckley, and special guest Vice President Spiro Agnew reminded the crowd gathered at the New York Hilton's grand ballroom that Conservatives could provide the margin of victory in New York State for the Nixon-Agnew ticket.

To cheers, Jim Buckley told the faithful, "I believe it to be of the utmost importance that each one of us does everything in his power to guarantee the re-election of Nixon and Agnew. The forces which George McGovern represents must be delivered a decisive defeat."

As the campaign came to a close, the party leaders sensed they would have a tremendous victory at the polls. Citing a *New York Times*-Yankelovich voter survey which reported that 38 percent of New Yorkers classified themselves as conservatives, 28 percent as moderate, and 23 percent as liberal,[28] Kieran O'Doherty pointed out that: "A new constituency composed of conservative-minded Republicans, Democrats and independents now constitutes the largest issue-oriented voting bloc in New York State." He went on to proclaim that: "The Conservative Party has played a leading role in forging the new majority in New York State of moderate and conservative-minded voters who will deliver a decisive defeat to the radical left forces represented by the McGovern candidacy. The Conservative Party has set the pace in setting in motion the conservative trend over the last ten years which has changed the political landscape in this state."[29]

On November 7, 1972, New Yorkers shocked the liberal pundits by casting 59 percent of their votes for Richard Nixon. Like 48 other states, New York rejected the forces of the counter-culture that had taken over the Democratic Party.

Reacting to the results, Dan Mahoney said that "the Conservative Party vote statewide for President Nixon and Vice-President Agnew of 366,349 compared very favorably with the Liberal Party vote for Senator McGovern of 180,719. A Conservative Party vote that more than doubled the vote of the long-established Liberal Party must be viewed as a major accomplishment especially in view of the fact that the Liberal vote in 1968 for Senator Humphrey was 311,622, which indicated a sharp decline."

Mahoney pointed out that the Conservative vote had provided the margin of victory for Conservative-endorsed Republicans Judge Domenick I. Gabrielli and Hugh R. Jones in the statewide, hotly contested court-of-appeals races.

In the Congressional races, the Conservatives provided the margin of victory in Westchester's 23rd congressional district for Congressman Peter A. Peyser (R-C), who defeated former Congressman Richard Ottinger (D-L).

The new state senate would have eighteen endorsed state senators, including sixteen Republican-Conservatives, one Democrat-Conservative (James D. Griffin-Buffalo), and one Republican-Conservative-Democrat (John D. Calandra–Bronx).

Three state senators won by their Conservative Party margin: Frank Padavan (Queens), who toppled incumbent Democrat Murray Schwartz, and Senator Martin J. Knorr (Queens), who was successful against Democratic Assemblyman Fred D. Schmidt. Fred J. Eckert (Monroe) defeated incumbent Democrat James Powers.

The picture was similar in the assembly, where forty-seven Conservative-endorsed assemblymen won office. This included Conservative Rosemary R. Gunning (Queens) who was endorsed by the Republican Party, forty-five Republican-Conservatives and one Democrat-Conservative Stephen R. Greco (Buffalo).

Elected by the Conservative margin were Vincent A. Riccio (Brooklyn), Harold K. Grune (Orange-Rockland), Albert J. Hausbeck (Erie), and Alan J. Justin (Erie) who beat incumbent Democrat-Liberal John B. Lis, assembly minority whip.

Had the ban on cross-endorsements not been in effect in Nassau and Suffolk counties, the Conservative Party vote on Line C would have elected three additional Republican-Conservative assemblymen, rather than resulting in one loss in Suffolk and in two assembly seats in Nassau.[30]

The Conservative margin had also resulted in the election victories of numerous local candidates. Particularly significant examples were the countywide victory in Rockland of Raymond Lindemann (R-C) for sheriff, and the countywide victories in Monroe of Michael Telsea (R-C) for surrogate and Culver Barr (R-C) as county judge.

Mahoney, O'Doherty, Maltese, and all the party leaders believed the Conservative victories in 1972 were a major reason why President Nixon began moving back to the center-right politically. More important still was the forging a new political constituency. Reacting to pro-Conservative statements made by the president in a November 9 interview in the *Washington Star-News*, party headquarters stated that the party "heartily endorses and applauds the president's reaffirmation of his commitment to conservative reforms and policies in the second Nixon-Agnew administration. In doing so, President Nixon forthrightly reiterated the policy positions which he and Vice President Agnew steadfastly adhered to during their campaign for re-election. The new majority of moderate and conservative-minded American voters in New York, as across the nation, have given the President and Vice President the mandate they sought for these conservative reforms."[31]

The Biaggi Affair

In the off-year election cycle of 1973, it was the hope of the Conservative Party to have the views of its constituency heard and implemented at local levels, particularly in the City of New York.

The city was exhausted after eight years of John Lindsay. And after his disastrous presidential run, the mayor realized he had no chance of being elected to a third term. The liberal-Republican money people, who had financed him in the past, now deserted him, and the power brokers in his newly adopted party simply didn't trust him.

With the expectation that city voters would turn back to the Democrats, there were numerous candidates who sought the crown: Congressman Ed Koch, former Lindsay Sanitation Commissioner Jerome Kretchemer, Assemblyman Al Blumental,

Congressman Herman Badillo, City Council President Sanford Garelik, Comptroller Abraham Beame, and Congressman Mario Biaggi.

While Nelson Rockefeller was trying to resurrect his pal, former Mayor Bob Wagner, as the fusion candidate of the Republican and Liberal Parties, the Conservatives were taking a serious look at Democrat Mario Biaggi.

During his twenty-three-year career as a member of New York's Finest, Mario Biaggi was wounded eleven times in the line of duty. By the time he retired as a detective-lieutenant, he had received the Police Department's highest award, the Medal of Honor, plus twenty-seven other decorations.

After retirement he practiced law, and in 1968 was elected as a Democrat with Conservative Party endorsement to represent the Bronx in Congress. Biaggi endeared himself to Bronx Conservative leaders Tom Cronin and George McGuinness with his endorsements in 1968 and 1970 of Jim Buckley.

Since it was unlikely that a right-wing Republican could make it to city hall, the Bronx Conservative leaders promoted the idea that the right Democrat with Conservative endorsement could be elected. Many leaders bought into the idea, including Brooklyn Conservative Party Chairman Mike Long. "I liked Biaggi," Long said, "and believed this 'hero cop' could be the law and order candidate who could win. I thought the voters would want someone tough enough to clean up Lindsay's garbage. Clearly Biaggi could be that guy."[32]

William F. Buckley Jr. reported in his syndicated column that before Biaggi was formally nominated at the March convention, "there were rumors floating about that Mr. Biaggi, when questioned by a grand jury a while ago, declined to answer certain questions. The chairman of the Conservative Party, Mr. Daniel Mahoney, had a breakfast meeting with Mr. Biaggi and asked him point-blank whether the rumors were true. Mr. Biaggi answered point-blank that they were not true. Mr. Mahoney is an experienced gentleman and wrote a longhand letter to Mr. Biaggi later that day recapitulating what Mr. Biaggi had said. The Conservative Party then proceeded to nominate Mr. Biaggi."[33]

By April, due to lack of funds, Koch and Garelik had dropped out of the race, and Biaggi was considered the front runner. Also, when Rockefeller's plan to nominate Wagner at the Republican convention failed to materialize and the poorly financed John Marchi was nominated to run a second time, most analysts viewed this as a plus for Biaggi. Finally, the Liberal Party had to pick one of the Democrat wannabes before the primary. Picking the wrong candidate (as they had done with Al Blumenthal) could lead to a race against Biaggi and a weak Republican. The Liberals were worried, but it was a scenario in which Conservative leaders believed their guy would win "in a walk."

In early May, however, reports surfaced in the *Daily News* and the *Times* that Biaggi had indeed invoked the Fifth Amendment when questioned by a federal grand jury in 1961. "Absolutely untrue," Biaggi claimed. "I never evaded a question in my life."

Biaggi, who knew grand-jury minutes could not be released, urged a panel of three federal judges to read the minutes and make public whether he claimed the "Fifth Amendment or any other privileges on my personal finances and assets."

To counter Biaggi, the U.S. attorney for New York's Eastern District, Republican Whitney North Seymour, went to a federal judge and asked for a release of the grand-jury transcript. Biaggi now fought the issue in the courts, and when it began to be clear that he was going to lose, he admitted on TV that after all he had invoked the Fifth. He claimed he had done so in order to protect his "emotionally fragile" daughter when asked about a $7,200 consulting fee she had received. He said he just wanted to avoid a witch-hunt into his daughter's life.

When the transcripts were released, however, they revealed that Biaggi had actually taken the Fifth Amendment on sixteen occasions. He dodged questions on his finances, IRS returns, private immigration bills he introduced in Congress, and on campaign fund raising.

In response to the Biaggi revelations, Dan Mahoney released the following statement on May 14:

> The eight members of the Conservative Party leadership who have been consulting with respect to the Biaggi candidacy remain in disagreement on this matter. Henry Paolucci and four of the county chairmen from New York City believe that the Conservative Party should continue its support of Congressman Biaggi. Messrs. Serphin Maltese, Kieran O'Doherty and I do not, and further believe that the joint county executive committees which originally authorized Congressman Biaggi's designation by the Conservative Party should be reconvened to consider the new information revealed by release of the grand jury transcript.
>
> At a personal level, we feel compassion for Congressman Biaggi's current predicament. Nonetheless, Congressman Biaggi obtained the Conservative Party designation by representing that he had never invoked the privilege against self-incrimination before a grand jury; and we now know that representation was not true. Under the circumstances, we do not believe the Conservative Party should continue its support of the Biaggi candidacy.[34]

Two days later the executive committee of the Conservative Party of Queens County met and passed a motion, 45 to 3, to reconsider the Biaggi nomination. After much discussion, a motion was passed by 36 to 12 calling on the five city leaders to strip Biaggi of the Conservative Party nomination.

Before a meeting of the five county leaders called by Mahoney was convened, Biaggi asked for a meeting. Mike Long recalled that: "Biaggi was very ill and was confined to bed in a room at Manhattan's Roosevelt Hospital. Tom Cronin of the Bronx (who was on Biaggi's payroll), Dan Master of Staten Island and Manhattan's Henry Middendorf, told me that if I stayed with Biaggi they would too." According to Long, Biaggi apologized from his sick bed for being less than truthful, and admitted he could not now win the election for mayor. But to protect his Congressional seat – and to repair his image – he asked for the okay to continue on in the mayoral race anyway. He promised to run as credible a campaign as possible. "Congressman," the sympathetic Long said, "I will stay with you but we don't need any more problems."[35]

With that, the City Conservative leaders, in a 4 to 1 vote, decided to stick with Biaggi. But Dan Mahoney, Kieran O'Doherty, William F. Buckley Jr., Serphin Maltese, and Senator Buckley broke ranks and endorsed State Senator Marchi, the Republican candidate. Maltese recalls that "Dan was very hurt that Biaggi lied to him." Kieran O'Doherty was blunter: "He lied to the party, the press and the public. The honor and integrity of the Conservative Party is at stake."[36]

On the state level, the only significant race was for chief judge of New York's Court of Appeals. Historically, a candidate in this race received bi-party endorsement and was unopposed, but in 1973 for the first time in 57 years, this was not the case. The Republican and Liberal Parties nominated a sitting associate judge, Charles Brietel. An insurgent, Jacob Fuchsberg, won the Democratic primary, and the Conservative Party turned to James Leff, the man whose skills as an election lawyer had helped get the party on the ballot in 1962. In 1968, all four parties had nominated the Harvard-educated lawyer for the New York Supreme Court. Many inside politicos believed that Rockefeller permitted his bi-partisan nomination because the governor was tired of losing election-law cases to Leff, and this was the way to get rid of the skilled adversary once and for all.

On the bench, Leff proved to be a tough "law-and-order" judge, who even carried a gun and had used it to foil an assault attempt. When Leff sentenced convicted mugger Gregory Slowe to fifteen years in prison, a *Daily News* had this to say in an editorial titled "Tell 'Em Your Honor":

> Manhattan Supreme Court Justice James Leff has sentenced convicted mugger Gregory Slowe, 24, to 15 years in prison and, at the same time, worked over some of his colleagues with the rough edge of his tongue.
> What raised Judge Leff's ire was the fact that Slowe had taken four previous falls and received marshmallowy treatment each time from mushheaded jurists.
> Criminals and would-be criminals, said Judge Leff, won't be deterred until they learn the hard way that "vicious crimes bring severe and swift punishment."

Well said, your honor. And if there were more Judge Leffs, we dare say there would be fewer Gregory Slowes around preying on law-abiding citizens.[37]

Back in the New York mayoral race, the Democrats chose Abe Beame and Herman Badillo to face each other in a run-off. Biaggi had come in third. In the run-off, Beame easily won with 65 percent of the vote, and he now faced Republican John Marchi, Liberal Al Blumenthal, and Biaggi, who remained the Conservative candidate. In a lackluster race, Beame (who ran on the slogan "He knows the Buck") became New York's first Jewish mayor.

Candidate		Number	Percent
Beame			
	Democrat	896,265	52.5
	Civil Service	67,277	3.9
	Total	963,542	56.5
Marchi			
	Republican	259,781	15.2
	Integrity	14,271	0.8
	Total	274,052	16.1
Biaggi			
	Conservative	178,967	10.5
	Safe City	8,010	0.5
	Total	186,977	11.0
Blumenthal			
	Liberal	233,265	13.7
	Good Government	29,335	1.7
	Total	262,600	15.4
Other candidates		18,489	1.1
Total		1,705,660	

The Conservative Party's candidate for comptroller, Joseph Perrini, received an impressive 280,000 votes (20 percent) and outpolled the Republican candidate Al Lemishow who received just 231,000 votes. The Republican-Conservative candidate for city council, Tom Galvin, lost to Paul O'Dwyer but received a combined total of 440,000 votes, a 30 percent share.

With a very light voter turnout statewide, Judge Leff received 219 thousand votes, or 5 percent of the total cast.

In 1973, the party also had a contest to select an animal that symbolizes the Conservative Party. New York election law provides for party emblems to distinguish the candidates of the different parties. The Conservative Party emblem is the "Torch of Liberty." Although no provision in election law exists, nevertheless, the party believed that since the Democrats use the jackass and Republicans the elephant, they too should have a symbol. Dan Mahoney announced that "after a close examination of the many entries, the judges have selected the Beaver as the Party symbol." Deputy Fire Chief Clifford H. Goldstein of Jackson Heights won first prize of a $100 U.S. Savings Bond for suggesting the beaver. In his entry form, Goldstein wrote: "I submit the American Beaver, species *Castor canadensis*, as symbol of The Conservative Party. Just as the beaver dam prevents soil erosion and creates an environment of permanent water for fish growth, so do the policies of The Conservative Party prevent social erosion and create the environment for human political progress. While the elephant trumpets and the jackass brays, the beaver works with *quiet* integrity, making noise only when endangered – as does The Conservative Party."[38]

Exit Rockefeller: "Apres Moi le Deluge"

More and more headlines in 1973 were being devoted to the Watergate scandal. The Conservative Party was loyal to Nixon and lauded the firing in October 1973 of Special Prosecutor Archibald Cox. When it came to the issue of the Nixon tapes, the state executive committee also unanimously supported a resolution that read:

> The Conservative Party supports the President's proposed resolution of the tapes matter as constituting a good faith effort to comply with the order of the District of Columbia Court of Appeals, despite his well-founded belief that he is not required to comply by the United States Constitution, in an effort to resolve the constitutional and political crisis that would otherwise be presented.[39]

A great blow to conservatives throughout the country was the October 10 resignation of Vice President Spiro Agnew after he pleaded "no contest" to a felony bribery charge. Five days later at the Conservative Party's eleventh anniversary dinner, keynote speaker Bill Buckley summed up the views of most attendees with these words on the "Terrible Sadness of Spiro Agnew":

> It is a terrible irony that at the moment in history when liberalism is sputtering in confusion, empty of resources, we should be plagued as we are by weak and devious men. The terrible sadness of Spiro Agnew's existence touches everything we do today; our manifestoes, our analysis, our hymns, and our laughter. Through our participation in this adversity we must seek strength, such strength as we derive from knowing that Mr. Agnew was profoundly right about many of the causes of our decline; that though he proved to be a physician who could not heal himself, in his words, as uttered over four years, there were the rocks of truth, and to these truths,

however dazed and saddened, we rededicate ourselves, without hesitation, with faith, with hope, and with charity.[40]

Chairman Mahoney asked the president to chose a successor to Agnew who is "in tune with the 1972 mandate."

Dear Mr. President:

I respectfully urge you, in behalf of the Conservative Party of New York State and conservative voters throughout the nation, to propose to the Congress a successor vice president in tune with the overwhelming mandate delivered by the voters of this nation less one year ago. The designation of a moderate or liberal nominee would alienate the vast majority of your Congressional supporters, and repudiate the constituency that elected you overwhelmingly to your second term.

We understand, of course, that the successor must be a person of unimpeachable probity and integrity, and are certain that this vital objective can be attained consistent with the selection of a conservative successor properly attuned to the 1972 mandate.

Thank you for your consideration of these views.[41]

The biggest political event of 1973, however, was the December 11 resignation of Governor Nelson Rockefeller from the office he had occupied for a record-breaking 14 years, 11 months, 11 days. Proclaiming that "New Yorkers' best interests are affected by problems over which we do not have control in the state," Rocky was stepping down to chair his newly created (and financed) Commission on Critical Choices. This platform, he believed, would permit him to speak out on current issues.[42] There were mixed reactions to his announcement; some believed Rocky sensed that Nixon's Watergate woes would give him another shot at the presidency, while others believed that the governor realized the state was running out of money and the day was rapidly approaching when someone would have to answer for the cumulative consequences of the decisions made during the previous fifteen years. Hearing of the news, Dan Mahoney fired off a telegraph to Lieutenant Governor Malcolm Wilson that read: "Dear Malcolm – what's new?" He also quipped that Rockefeller was leaving the state "locked in a financial half Nelson."[43]

On December 18, 1973, after waiting in the wings for so long, the fifty-nine-year-old Wilson was finally sworn in as the state's fiftieth governor. All agreed that he was uniquely qualified to take on the job. Wilson intimately knew the inner workings of the executive branch and both houses of the state legislature. He also knew that there were dark clouds assembling over the state's fiscal horizon. Within a week after taking office, Wilson had to deal with the monetary hemorrhaging at the Urban Development Corporation (UDC).

Forced down the throat of the state legislature by Rockefeller in the aftermath of the Martin Luther King assassination, UDC had a wide mandate to provide housing, industrial development, and civic improvements throughout the state. Also, the bonds it issued were backed by the *moral obligation* of the State of New York. Designed by municipal finance expert John N. Mitchell (who served as Nixon's attorney general and 1972 campaign manager), "moral-obligation" bonds constituted a financial gimmick to get around bonding limitations of the state constitution and to make questionable building projects more palatable to the bond underwriters in the investment community. When UDC was created, language was added to the incorporating papers providing the "legislative intent" was to supply money to meet principal and interest payments in the event of revenue shortfalls. Since the state had no *legal* obligation to aid the authority, the concept became known as a "moral obligation."[44] In early 1974, with cutbacks in federal grants and a recession settling in, UDC had a cash-flow problem when several of its projects went belly up. Wilson was able to assure the banks by providing necessary cash to meet principal and interest payments on UDC bonds, but this was only the first of Rockefeller's follies that were to turn sour and haunt his successors – but more of that later. Wilson's immediate problems were political: he was frantically attempting to put together a team that could elect him in his own right to a full term as governor.

For years, Wilson had been the Conservative Party's back door to the state's executive branch. Now the governor wanted to take advantage of that relationship to be the first Republican gubernatorial candidate to be cross-endorsed by the Conservatives.

No longer stuck "playing second fiddle in a one-man band," as Albany Mayor Erastus Corning described him, Wilson began to advertise his conservatism. He told journalist Richard Reeves: "This is a conservative state. New York is a conservative city, except for some parts of Manhattan. . . . [P]eople have been going along with programs they didn't really like for a long time. They were only talking their true feelings in the golf club, locker rooms, or on the street – wherever they talk. The conservative feeling broke into the open about June of 1970 – you could almost feel it – people could see what was happening in their own lives."[45] *The New York Times*, in a special report dated January 15, 1974, appeared to be confirming the new governor's position:

> Although New York has the reputation as the most liberal city in America, more city residents today consider themselves conservatives than they do either moderates or liberals.
>
> This ideological swing to the right is reflected in strong attitudes among New Yorkers in favor of the restoration of the death penalty, in giving life sentences without parole to drug pushers, in support of crackdowns on pornography and in opposition to the legalization of marijuana and the busing of children to achieve racial balance in the city's schools.

The survey, which confirmed the beliefs of the Conservative Party's founders, concluded that conservatives are more likely to be found in Brooklyn and Queens; that Catholics and Protestants are more conservative than Jews, 39 percent to 28 percent; and those of Irish descent were the single most conservative group of all those surveyed:[46]

1973 Survey by Borough in percent (figures are rounded)	Manhattan	Brooklyn	Bronx	Queens	Staten Island
Conservative	28	37	31	35	31
Moderate	26	34	24	35	41
Liberal	30	20	34	23	20
Radical	3	3	2	2	2
Not Sure	13	6	9	6	7

To further endear himself to the Conservative Party, Wilson tossed a few patronage plums in its direction. Conservative Hugh McShane of Queens was the first party member to be appointed a judge of the New York State Court of Claims. The governor also nominated conservative Genevieve Sanchez Klein of Bayside, Queens, to the state board of regents that oversees the state's educational system. Mrs. Klein, a professional educator in New York City's public schools for thirty-five years, was a controversial choice due to her outspoken opposition to busing.

On the twentieth anniversary of *Brown v. Board of Education of Topeka, Kansas*, Mrs. Klein delivered these remarks:

> I believe that the effect of compulsory busing to achieve an allegedly better balance of races will harm the very children that it is intended to help. . . .
>
> It is incumbent upon the Regents at this time to assess our 20-year experience with integration. An integrated education where white and black children can learn about each other in a classroom setting remains a desirable goal. It cannot, however, be the exclusive one. The bitter fruits of forced integration have already poisoned race relations despite the intent of the Regents to improve race relations through the instrumentality of the school.
>
> There is no sacrifice of racial pride if blacks go to school with blacks, where the many techniques of bringing about integration have been tried and found wanting. The Regents should, of course, be as determined as ever that no segment of the school population be discriminated against in the apportionment of services. In fact, we must be prepared to extend

additional services where the educational needs of children warrant com-
pensatory programs. The effect of this stance would be to moderate the
heated tempers that flare when children are being used by "social engineers" to establish a racial balance in the schools. . . .

In the more peaceful school environment that will be induced by this
counsel of moderation, we can advance educational objectives that will
help the children and, thereby, the State.[47]

Dan Mahoney publicly commended Klein's statement "against the social engineers, the proponents of forced busing and for the best interests of all our children,
who must no longer be treated solely in terms of their race."

During a spirited debate on the floor of the state legislature, the Queens delegation of Republican-Conservative legislators spearheaded the fight for her confirmation, and they carried the day. Mahoney congratulated them and told the media: "The
Board of Regents needs a strong conservative voice that will resound with the hard
experience of the classroom in recent years. Mrs. Klein is fearless and knowledgeable
about a variety of problems in education that will face the board. This 1-2 combination will stimulate the board and contribute to sound, effective public education."[48]

At the second annual Albany Conservative Party Seminar in 1974, event moderator Anthony Rudmann invited the governor to attend the February 5 reception and
dinner. To the satisfaction of over 100 party leaders, and the delight of all those in
attendance, including police officers, firefighters, veteran's organization leaders, and
over seventy legislators, a governor of New York appeared for the first time at a party
function. Wilson told the press covering the event: "I do not find myself among
strangers."

To a cheering crowd, Wilson said: "The coming into being of this party is the very
best evidence that we could ever offer of the opportunity that is provided for the effective articulation of a point of view."

He went on to tell the audience that he was grateful for their help in electing
Republican majorities to the legislature and for providing a "countervailing force."
Chairman Mahoney cheerfully related to his guests that: "It's a new experience for me
to be able to get the Governor of New York on the telephone whenever I want."[49]

One consequence of the Conservative Party's new status in Albany came later in
the year, after the Republican convention had nominated Wilson and Nassau County
Executive Ralph Caso as his lieutenant-governor running mate: an end to the cross-
endorsement ban on Long Island. Jack O'Leary, Nassau County Conservative chairman
from 1972 to 2000, recalled in 2001 that Wilson intervened with Republican boss Joe
Margiotta to end his policy. On June 10, 1974, Margiotta agreed to change the by-laws
of the Nassau Republican Committee and told the press: "My belief in unity and party
loyalty make subservient my own personal wishes and aspirations to the will of the
majority."[50]

But sudden access to the governor's second-floor office in the state capital did not necessarily mean a Conservative Party endorsement of Wilson was a fait accompli. When Chairman Mahoney called to order the June 15 nomination meeting of the state committee at the LaGuardia Airport Holiday Inn, he knew there were many disgruntled leaders in attendance.

The original plan of those opposing Wilson was to nominate the retired *New York Times* international affairs reporter Herman Dinsmore. But his candidacy did not get off the ground because it turned out that Dinsmore mistakenly thought he was a registered Conservative, whereas he was actually a Republican. Instead, party vice-chairman and Schuylerville apple farmer T. David Bullard (whom earlier in the year Wilson had appointed to the Agricultural Resources Commission) decided to make the run.

Claiming that Wilson's "reputation as a conservative is awfully hollow," the forty-seven-year-old Bullard garnered 40 percent of the convention vote with Wilson receiving 60 percent. Professor Henry Paolucci, who always considered himself the "loyal opposition" in most party affairs, entered the fray as a candidate for lieutenant governor. He too received 40 percent against Wilson's running mate, Ralph Caso.

Under the state election law governing political nominating conventions, the candidate who receives the most votes becomes the official designee of the party. The law, however, permits any other candidate who receives at least 25 percent of the convention vote the right to choose to enter a primary against the designee *without* going through the laborious and expensive statewide petition route.

Shortly after the convention adjourned, Bullard and Paolucci signed the documents declaring they accepted their rights to enter the primary. This of course, created a dilemma for Malcolm Wilson. According to the 1974 state board of elections calendar, if a candidate did not withdraw from the primary fight by Saturday, June 29, 1972, the candidate's name must appear on the primary election day ballot. This gave Wilson exactly two weeks to either convince Bullard to withdraw or to avoid a primary by declining the Conservative nomination.

Either decision could wreck his chances of being elected governor in the fall because appearing on Row C was an important part of the Wilson campaign strategy. Wilson's political consultants realized that their candidate's constituencies were different from Rockefeller's. The former governor always ran well upstate, but – for a Republican – he also did extremely well in liberal New York City, generally garnering over 40 percent of the vote. But the Wilson campaign assumed their candidate would fare poorly in New York City, and that in order to make up those lost votes, they would need the 500,000 that are cast on the Conservative Party's Row C. Without it, they knew Wilson was doomed.

For days after the convention, the phone wires to Bullard's home were burning. Dan Mahoney, Serf Maltese, Senator Buckley, and others tried to convince him to withdraw. In a conversation with Frances Clines of *The New York Times*, Bullard did give an opening: "Agreeing that the Governor needed the Conservative line to win and that a primary fight could box him in too far to the right and cost him moderate support in the November election, Bullard said, 'I think Governor Wilson is over the barrel.' He also said that he would withdraw if the Governor made an outward and visible commitment to Conservative principles within the next few days.'"[51]

To satisfy Bullard's request, the governor issued a June 26 statement describing the actions he'd taken since assuming office that he thought would be viewed favorably by Conservatives:

> In my budget message, I proposed a series of steps to lighten the burden on our taxpayers and to improve the climate for job-producing businesses.
>
> I approved the following tax reduction measures which constitute the first step in reducing tax burdens on the citizens and businesses of this State. The total annual reduction in taxes paid to the State will be $138 million.
> * Repealed for the 1974 tax year the 2½ per cent surcharge on personal income tax liability to increase take-home pay ($85 million).
> * Doubled the investment credit available to New York businesses, to stimulate job production in the State ($10 million).
> * Provided for refund of sales taxes and motor fuel taxes paid by private omnibus carriers on most purchases used in providing local transit service ($3 million).
> * Increased sales tax exemption of goods purchased by exempt corporations ($8 million).
> * Broadened sales and use tax exemption for goods used directly in manufacturing or production ($15 million).[52]

The governor also announced additional actions including welfare fraud investigations that were going to yield savings of $30 million a year and medicaid-program investigation that was reducing program costs by 8 to 10 percent. The Governor stated that these efforts reflected his continuing determination to ensure that the tax dollar is spent in the most efficient possible manner. He also reiterated his determination to establish a favorite Conservative Party proposal, a "Little Hoover Commission" to review all aspects of state government for efficiency and economy.

In addition to this statement, Wilson met privately with Bullard the evening of June 26.

As a result of Wilson's public and private statements the day before the deadline, June 28, 1974, David Bullard made the following statement:

> During this recent fortnight I have discussed with Governor Wilson the

concerns of my Party. I have discovered in this gentleman a sharing of ideas and a practical sympathy with our principles.

Malcolm Wilson perceives that his is an historic opportunity to alter the nature of government to restore the State to its function as the peoples' servant to recreate an atmosphere of enterprise, liberty and order. And he knows how to accomplish these ends better than I.

I have taken the man's measure. He is honest, devoted, skilled. My opponent of a few days past is now my friend.

I withdraw from the Conservative Party primary in favor of Governor Malcolm Wilson.[53]

Believing that an overwhelming majority of the state committee now supported Wilson, Dr. Paolucci also withdrew his candidacy telling party faithful:

I am proud to say that I plan to give my whole-hearted support to the heads of our ticket, Governor Malcolm Wilson, and his Lieutenant Governor candidate, Ralph Caso. God willing, and with strenuous effort, we will get our largest vote ever in a gubernatorial election and have a continuing impact, as Conservatives, in the governance of this state for the next four years.[54]

To the media, the Wilson-Bullard controversy was a big story, and they gleefully devoted plenty of ink describing the infighting within conservative ranks. What they missed at the Convention, however, was the story of the woman who was not only nominated to run against Senator Jacob Javits, but who was to become the sweetheart of the Conservative Party, Barbara A. Keating.

Mrs. Barbara Ann Keating for Senate

When Barbara Ann Keating's husband Major Daniel J. Keating, Jr. USMC, was shipped to Vietnam in August 1967, she and her five children moved to her girlhood town, Mamaroneck, in Westchester County, New York. Disturbed that her children were exposed daily to extreme left-wing public-school teachers (who instead of teaching English, reading, or the sciences, were denouncing our government, denigrating our soldiers, and being disrespectful to the flag), Mrs. Keating wrote a letter of complaint to the *Mamaroneck Daily News*, which chose to publish the letter as an op-ed piece.

June McGloine, wife of local Conservative Party leader John McGloine, contacted Mrs. Keating, and after numerous discussions they formed a group called the Honor America Committee of Westchester County, Inc. It would be the business of the committee to make sure that students recited the Pledge of Allegiance and that Old

Glory was flying over the schools. After Barbara learned that her husband had been killed in action on May 22 in an ambush while on patrol in Hue, she took a more active role in the organization, speaking at American Legion and VFW halls, high schools, and colleges defining the role of our boys serving in Vietnam.

In 1970, Barbara became an enrolled Conservative and was elected a member of Westchester County's Executive Committee. In 1973 Westchester County Chairman Wilson Price decided that the theme of the statewide party's October 15 dinner, which

1974 U.S. Senate candidate Barbara Keating campaigning in Brooklyn. Mike Long is in the back seat, and Tony Spinelli is in the front passenger seat.

he was organizing, would be a salute to America's fighting men, with a special salute to the recently repatriated Vietnam prisoners of war.

Thanks to the efforts of John McGloine, Mrs. Keating spoke at the dinner, and although she was up against such notable speakers as Bill and James Buckley, her comments electrified the crowd. Finding herself inundated with speaking invitations to Conservative Party events throughout the state, she and Jane McGloine took her raw speaking notes and turned them into a formal text. After she spoke at the Rockland County Conservative Party dinner, John McGloine sent Barbara's text to Senator Buckley, who published them in the January 21, 1974, *Congressional Record*.

Here are excerpts:

To the men who were taken prisoner by an enemy which did not heed the Geneva Agreement, what can we say when we face them . . . they leave us in such awe. Day in and day out they survived on rice and cabbage soup dreaming of their return to America and they heroically survived the longest imprisonment of any previous war.

Now what of those of whom no fate is yet known. Their families are still living in the dark nightmare, afraid to hope, afraid to abandon hope. We cannot turn our backs on them. All they want to know is the fate of their loved one. Surely our representatives in the Congress must be continually pressured by all of us not to relinquish attempts at acquiring this information.

And we must not forget those hundreds of disabled young men who must carry the burden of their sacrifice with them for the rest of their lives. Because of improved medical attention, so many more wounded survived with disabilities in their war, as in previous wars where their lives might have been lost. We must show these young men that we are not through thanking them. It was not easy for them to go and face dangers in a far off and unpopular war and it is harder still for many of them to wage that continuing battle of life from a wheel chair.[55]

Serf Maltese, who first introduced Keating to Dan Mahoney, believed, as others did, that she would make a great candidate for U.S. senator in 1974. Looking back recently, she recalled that when they first approached her with the notion, she thought they were joking. But after numerous discussions, she agreed to run, but she insisted on boning up on the issues before her candidacy was made public. Serf Maltese loaned Barbara a decade's worth of bound copies of the conservative news weekly *Human Events*, and she went to work. "I compiled articles and essays on all the current domestic, defense and foreign policy issues," Keating recalled, "and studied them for several weeks."

Shortly before the June 15 convention, Bill Buckley received an unexpected call from Roy Cohn, the noted attorney and former chief counsel to the Senate Permanent Investigations Subcommittee headed by the late Senator Joseph McCarthy in the 1950s. According to Buckley, "he called me and said 'I'd like to make an appointment in your house to meet with Dan Mahoney, just the three of us . . . because I think it's ridiculous that I'm not being nominated for Senator.'"[56] Both Buckley and Mahoney were stunned. They could not understand why Cohn, who loved playing the behind-the-scenes power broker, wanted to run for public office. In their private meeting, Buckley recalled that Cohn said he "figured out that Mahoney, as a courtesy to the Nixon administration, was not putting out a strong person [Keating] who could really keep the Republican from prevailing. Anyway he thought it was a fix, the quid pro quo being a federal job for Mahoney's brother-in-law [Kieran O'Doherty]."[57] Nothing could have been further from the truth, yet Cohn insisted on running.

At the same convention that designated Malcolm Wilson for governor, the names of Barbara Keating and Roy Cohn were placed in nomination for senator. Before the balloting began, Keating remembered that Cohn told the delegates that even though Barbara was a nice young widow with five children, he was better qualified to be the party standard bearer against Jacob Javits. Mrs. Keating, replying, wooed the audience with these words:

> As this campaign would be my first experience in seeking public office, I feel an obligation to cite the reasons that compel me to offer my candidacy for the United Sates Senate.
>
> At a time when the major quality of government is so widely questioned, the professional politicians of both the Republican and Democratic Parties in New York have again based their senatorial nominations on "politics as usual." I say today our destiny has become too important to leave to the politicians. They have again failed to meet their responsibilities and we must again accept the challenge they have avoided. They have again had the gall to thrust two liberal candidates for the U.S. Senate upon the voters of New York. The people of New York rejected that kind of hypocrisy in 1970 and elected Jim Buckley to the U.S. Senate on Row C. I believe they will have even more reason this year to reach the same conclusions.
>
> Frankly, I think it is time for Jacob Javits to give up his seat to a lady. I know conservatives will be only too happy to help him out of his chair – assist him to his feet – perhaps even make him realize what it is to stand up for something worthwhile – in short, help him to rise to the occasion.[58]

When the ballots were counted, Barbara Ann Keating was declared the designee of the party having received 63 percent of the delegate vote to Roy Cohn's 37 percent. In accepting the nomination, Mrs. Keating told the crowd:

> Be assured I am in this race all the way and to win. I would not make the personal sacrifices that this campaign will involve nor ask for your time and effort in support of my candidacy for any other objective.
>
> It has been suggested that the lack of financial resources and the fact that I am not a nationally known figure are liabilities to my candidacy. I can only say to you here today that I am accustomed to overcoming obstacles and I will overcome any this campaign presents. While, as of the present moment, I am only a word in the household – I will be a household

word when I am finished confronting Senator Javits and his liberal Democratic echo.

I know with your help and your prayers New York will overwhelmingly mandate another voice in the U.S. Senate, a voice carrying the banner of conservatism which is the only beacon of hope for America's future.[59]

Annoyed that he was not selected as the party's nominee, Cohn threatened a primary fight and told the press assembled at the convention that "the selection of Mrs. Keating was part of a deal with the Republican Party to put weak candidates on the Conservative ballot."[60] But like David Bullard, Cohn too came to his senses and on June 27, he signed an affidavit that notified the New York secretary of state that he "withdraws his acceptance of, and declines the right to run for the office of United States Senator in the Conservative Party Primary to be held on September 10, 1974."[61]

The Democrats, smelling victory in the air, were also facing a primary battle. Millionaire Howard "Howie the Horse" Samuels, who gained fame as the first president of Off-Track Betting (OTB) was chosen as his party's designee, but a seven-term Congressman from Bay Ridge, Brooklyn, Hugh Carey, received 25 percent of the convention vote, and he was fighting to the finish in the September primary.

Mike Long, looking back, claims that Hugh Carey was indirectly responsible for his becoming the Brooklyn County chairman in 1972. According to Long, in 1972 Congressman Carey was facing a tough re-election battle because his district was dominated by Irish and Italian blue-collars, who were becoming more conservative in thinking and voting. Carey, who was elected in 1960 by the margin of his Liberal Party vote, became friendly over the years with Nelson Rockefeller, particularly when he became a ranking member of the powerful Ways and Means Committee. Carey was a key player in devising the state revenue-sharing plan proposed by President Nixon and enthusiastically supported by Governor Rockefeller. In 1972, he used his friendship with Rocky, to help him get re-elected.

The New York Times reported:

> In the 1972 election, Carey was in trouble in his own district against John Gangemi, who had the Republican nomination for Congress and whose name was already printed on Conservative party nominating petitions. But Gangemi never got the Conservative nomination – somebody named Jones was put on the ballot at the last minute, and Carey was re-elected with 52 percent of the vote.[62]

According to Long, Gangemi had the money, the talent, and the looks to run a serious race against Carey, and at the spring 1972 Kings County Executive Meeting,

Republican Gangemi was named the Conservative Party candidate for the 15th Congressional District. At the next meeting when the minutes were read, Mike Long realized that Gangemi's name was omitted as the party's candidate. Believing it was an error, Long asked for the minutes to be changed before adopted. Upon hearing Long's inquiry, Brooklyn Party Chairman Bill Wells told the executive committee that Gangemi was never nominated. Other members came to Long's defense, and they soon agreed that Wells was deceiving them. As it turned out, Rockefeller leaned on Brooklyn Republican Chairman George Clark to help Carey. Clark, in turn, made a deal with Wells to get him the Republican nomination for a competitive assembly race if he dumped Gangemi. Wells agreed without consulting his County Executive Committee and dropped Gangemi's name out of the minutes of the nominating meeting. Long, who in 1968 had supported Wells for county chairman against James Gay, was livid that Wells had lied to him. But Wells could have been hiding more. According to *The New York Times*:

> William Wells, then the Brooklyn Conservative leader, says his party got "certain promises" from Rockefeller's man Cannon, and from Carey. George Clark, then the local Republican leader and now the county chairman, was publicly backing Gangemi. But he says he agreed to set up a meeting between Carey and Wells, at Carey's request, and: "They met in my real-estate office and I was there. Carey told Wells that he wanted him to pull the Conservative backing of Gangemi . . . 'We can't do that. We can't back a liberal so-and-so like you,' Wells Said. Carey said he didn't want support, just another candidate to cut Gangemi's vote. 'Let's talk absolute specifics,' Carey said, and I knew they were going to talk money and I didn't want to be there. Carey came out smiling later and said Wells was 'reasonable.'... Wells told me later that Carey gave him $10,000."
>
> Wells, [who supported Carey in 1974] says that Clark, who is close to Wilson, is lying. "I didn't get a dime," he said. "Rockefeller and Carey got what they wanted and I just don't want to say anymore." Carey says that it's true that Rockefeller helped him through Cannon and that Wells did ask him for money or for legal advertising for small newspapers Wells owned. "I gave him nothing," Carey said, "I don't handle money in my campaigns."[63]

Long, who made the deal public, claims the incident catapulted his successful candidacy for county chairman in 1972. "If Wells had called me in and said 'listen, there's an opportunity here to gain a conservative assembly seat by making a deal' and (as I learned in later years) that even Dan Mahoney approved of the deal, I would have at least listened. Instead he lied to me and tried to erase his fingerprints."[64] As a result of the cover-up, Wells went down in defeat in his assembly race and Hugh Carey (who was re-elected with 52 percent of the vote), told an aide on that election day that he didn't want to go through another tough congressional race and had to run for something else.

While Hugh Carey and Howard Samuels spent the summer battling for the Democratic nomination, Republicans and Conservatives were beginning to realize that President Nixon's battle to stay in office in the wake of Watergate was hurting their already slim chances for victory in November.

On March 19, 1974, Senator James Buckley was the first major conservative to have the guts to call on Nixon to resign:

> I speak out reluctantly because I know that what I have to say will bring pain and distress to many who are my good friends and who have been good to me, Richard Nixon numbered among them. . . .
>
> History would come to a stop for the duration of the impeachment trial – in the country and throughout the world. The ruler of the mightiest nation on earth would be starred as the prisoner in the dock. . . .
>
> I propose an extraordinary act of statesmanship and courage – an act at once noble and heartbreaking....That act is Richard Nixon's own voluntary resignation as President of the United States. . . .
>
> My proposal reflects no personal judgment on the matter of guilt or innocence, for I have made none. . . .
>
> I do not doubt that, as he sees and judges his own conduct, Richard Nixon has acted throughout this time of troubles for what he believed to be the well-being of his country. I hope and pray he will realize that the greatest and culminating action he can now take for his country is the renunciation of the world's highest office. His countrymen and the historians of the future, I feel sure, would judge that action in terms of the courage, patriotism, and self-sacrifice it would so dramatically display.[65]

Realizing by July that impeachment proceedings were a real possibility, Senator Buckley told his constituents:

> In my own case, I have made no judgment as to either the Constitutional sufficiency of the Articles of Impeachment recommended by the House Judiciary Committee or of the evidence offered in their support. Furthermore, I do not intend to address myself to these important and time-consuming matters unless and until it is my constitutional duty to do so. . . .
>
> The perfect judge or juror may not exist, and all of us have our personal feelings about the events of the past eighteen months. But we can and should strive for objectivity.

> I have, therefore, instructed my staff to withhold from me all mail urg-
> ing either an affirmative or negative vote on the question of the President's
> guilt or innocence. The President deserves an objective hearing based on
> the evidence and should be neither convicted nor acquitted because of
> public pressure.[66]

After Nixon resigned on August 9, 1974 and President Ford pardoned Nixon on
September 9 for any crimes he may have committed while in office, conservatives
gave a big sigh of relief. At the October 18, 1974 annual Conservative Party dinner,
William Buckley described what he believed would be the cost of Mr. Nixon's decep-
tion:

> In the past year we have gone through a terrible ordeal, one that divided
> conservatives – divided them for very good reasons. There were those who
> simply assumed that Richard Nixon was being candid with us when he
> insisted that he had not known of, let along participated in, the cover-up of
> Watergate. Others – some of them relying on instinct, some of them natu-
> rally suspicious – felt that Mr. Nixon was *not* being entirely candid. Indeed
> it turned out that he was not. *His* lack of candor is going to cost the Ameri-
> can people a great deal: it will result almost certainly in a Democratic
> Congress, probably a veto-proof Congress, which will lurch the country
> leftward, precisely in the opposite direction from the one the American
> people expressed themselves as desiring in their vote in 1972. It is of
> course an irrational act, to punish one's conservative congressman or sen-
> ator or governor for the grave deceptions of Richard Nixon. But who ever
> said that democratic justice is orderly?[67]

Nevertheless, Republicans throughout the nation sensed a brewing voter backlash
and in liberal New York there was plenty to fear.

In September, dark horse Hugh Carey, who outspent Samuels eight to one on television, shocked the political world by winning decisively with 61 percent of the vote.

In the fall elections, Malcolm Wilson, who was brilliant behind the scenes, proved
to be a weak and ineffective before the cameras. Hugh Carey, on the other hand, had
the Irish gift – he loved campaigning and could charm everyone in any room.

In the Senate race, Mrs. Keating proved to be an able campaigner against incumbent Senator Javits and the radical left-wing ideologue who won the Democratic primary, former U.S. Attorney General Ramsey Clark.

On the campaign trail, Keating attacked Javits in early October for his "lost weekend in Castro Cuba." Pointing out that *The New York Times* reported that Jacob Javits,
on Saturday, September 28, 1975, went to the island "against the express wishes of the
State Department," she thundered that:

Jacob Javits' lost weekend in Castro Cuba is one of the most disgraceful episodes in the recent history of American foreign policy. Just as his ideological bed-fellow Ramsey Clark was used by North Vietnamese communists for their own propaganda purposes when he foolishly visited Hanoi while Americans were being tortured, Javits was used by Castro in a shameful manner, during the Cuban fiasco. Press reports tell of a vicious anti-American speech made by Castro, of Javits being told to his face that his visit was "a triumph for the revolution," of brainwashing sessions in which Javits and Senator Pell listened dutifully, and without criticism, to Communist propaganda experts telling of the alleged glories of Castro Cuba. And, after such humiliating treatment, after being used as a prop in a series of Castro propaganda stunts, Javits returns with the news that Castro is "interested" in new ties with the United States. Small wonder since Castro now probably has the impression that all Americans are like Jacob Javits. Both Castro and Javits are in for a surprise.[68]

In a 2001 interview, Mrs. Keating described how Serf Maltese ran on the tarmac at Syracuse Airport to successfully stop a plane to New York City they had missed by seconds. "We had to get to CBS Television in New York to appear at the first senatorial debate," she recalled. "Although we were not invited to participate, by just appearing at the studio and after some finger pointing, the embarrassed station allowed me to participate." Keating continued:

"During most of the debate, the moderators ignored me and confined their questions to Javits and Clark. Finally at the very end, they threw me one question on abortion. Agitated by not being included, I said, 'Yes, I am pro-life, but here are my views on other issues.' I never took a breath; I wouldn't let them cut me off and I just kept talking. And I could see and hear Kieran O'Doherty in the back end of the studio yelling, 'Right on!'"[69]

Mrs. Keating was then invited to the final two debates of the campaign and more than held her own. Bill Buckley, watching her, concluded that: "her performance glowed with lucidity and candor."

In late October, Javits complained to the Associated Press that Mrs. Keating was "siphoning votes from his re-election effort" and that "some voters may turn to her in an anti-liberal protest." Mrs. Keating called the senator a "cry-baby" and added:

Of course my candidacy is attracting the growing support of moderate conservative New York voters. Who else can they turn to in this senatorial race? On his certified liberal record, Senator Javits has no more claim to their support than Ramsey Clark has.

Senator Javits is obviously trying to attract moderate to conservative voters by peddling the idea that liberal as he is, he's the lesser of two evils as between himself and Ramsey Clark. From the election results of four years ago in a similar senatorial contest, New Yorkers know they don't have to make that kind of negative choice in this election. They have a positive alternative in my candidacy where they can vote for a candidate who represents their convictions. Senator Javits and Mr. Clark know this race is developing into a genuine three-way contest just as in the 1970 senatorial campaign.[70]

Bill Buckley was quite taken by her candidacy, and in an October 27, 1974, *On the Right* column, he wrote:

The other candidate is something of a revelation. She is a beautiful woman, so that right away she violates a New York taboo, which steadfastly refuses to put beautiful women on the ballot, preferring Bella Abzug. Secondly, she is a functioning housewife, with five children under the age of ten. Third, her husband was killed in the Vietnam War, but she refuses to denounce that war, believing it to have been the high cost – for her, and 50,000 families like her own, the ultimate cost – of a network of treaties and alliances that have kept the world peace. A couple of years ago, Foreign Minister Abba Eban of Israel said that anyone who could automatically denounce America's spoken obligations to Vietnam, could never be trusted to underwrite America's spoken obligations to Israel. By Abba Eban's logic, new Yorkers for Israel could not trust Javits or Clark: but they could trust Barbara Keating.

Toward the end of the campaign, Mrs. Keating arrived late in Rochester due to a breakdown in her rental car and found that her hotel reservation had been lost. Looking around the hotel lobby, she noticed that one of her favorite targets, Ramsey Clark supporter Dr. Benjamin Spock, was also without a room. "Nice that the Liberals aren't organized that well too," she said. "He's one of Ramsey Clark's favorite doctors. I use him in all my speeches. I quote him when he describes a child; it's the perfect description of a liberal."[71]

Mrs. Keating maintained a grueling schedule throughout the fall and concluded her campaign with this double-barreled shot at her opponents:

Senator Javits and Ramsey Clark are cut from the same liberal cloth and they're both contesting for the same liberal vote, the only vote they're entitled to. I'm going after the mainstream Democrats and Republican voters in this state who have had enough, and more than enough of the Javits-Clark formula of ultra-liberal, big spending, welfare state government. I intend to win this election, and with the support of the moderate and conservative voters in this state, I will win this election. One thing is clear right now: Jacob Javits is running scared. Ramsey Clark is running in circles and I'm running to win.[72]

On November 5, 1974, the American people, angered by the Watergate scandals, the Ford pardon of Nixon, and rising inflation, punished Republicans throughout the nation. The Democrats picked up four U.S. Senate seats, forty-three House seats and four governorships.

In New York, Hugh L. Carey trounced Governor Wilson at the polls ending sixteen years of Republican rule:

	Wilson Rep.	Carey Dem.	Wilson Cons.	Carey Lib.
Outside New York City	**1,527,414**	**1,723,208**	**166,532**	**88,559**
Bronx	64,184	174,452	16,288	19,336
Brooklyn	112,745	336,756	25,495	38,532
Manhattan	67,303	231,734	11,166	34,526
Queens	149,189	298,639	40,623	37,092
Staten Island	29,752	42,935	8,976	2,734
Total New York City	423,173	1,084,516	102,548	132,220
Total State	**1,950,587**	**2,807,724**	**269,080**	**220,779**
Percentage	**37.1**	**53.5**	**5.2**	**4.2**

Reviewing the results, political analyst Michael Barone concluded: "Malcolm Wilson was burdened with the unpopularity of the Rockefeller record without the kind of resources – on the order of $10 million – Rockefeller had been accustomed to use every four years to change people's minds about the kind of job he had done."[73]

While Republicans now had to cede Row A to the Democrats, at least the Conservatives would keep Row C for four more years.

The Carey tidal wave cost Republicans their control of the assembly. Democrats made impressive inroads picking up sixteen seats. The assembly Republican majority leader, Jack Kingston of Nassau County, who refused Row C even after the ban was dropped, lost his seat:

Angelo Orazio, Dem.	20,917
John Kingston, Rep.	18,714
Thomas Clark, Cons.	2,731

The Conservative candidate received enough votes to bring Kingston down.

Republicans did manage to maintain their majority in the state senate, but their membership declined from thirty-seven seats to thirty-four seats. They also lost five congressional seats, leaving their delegation with twelve out of a total of thirty nine.

As Conservatives were recovering from their hangovers on Wednesday, November 6, they realized the only good news was Barbara Keating's remarkable showing:

	Javits Rep.	Clark Dem.	Keating Cons.	Javits Lib.
Outside New York City	**1,571,474**	**1,255,486**	**580,776**	**85,354**
Bronx	76,153	117,741	37,150	23,788
Brooklyn	158,818	203,807	64,546	50,904
Manhattan	89,400	185,371	24,939	32,394
Queens	173,655	185,888	92,440	46,474
Staten Island	29,029	25,488	22,733	2,745
Total New York City	**527,055**	**718,295**	**241,808**	**156,305**
Total State	**2,098,529**	**1,973,781**	**822,584**	**241,659**
Percentage	**40.8**	**38.5**	**16.1**	**4.6**

With 822,584 votes, Keating managed to keep Javits at the lowest plurality of his career, 45.4 percent.

In Putnam County she outpolled Ramsey Clark 6,657 to 6,276. Her best county in New York City was Staten Island, where she received 28.5 percent (22,733 votes) versus Javits's 36 percent and Clark's 31 percent.

In other races, Conservative comptroller candidate Bradley J. Hurd received 247,701 votes (5 percent), and attorney general candidate Edward F. Campbell received 232,631 (4.6 percent).

Chapter 10

We Told You So

The Fiscal Follies of 1975 and the Election Ecstasies of 1980

When in the first month of his administration Governor Hugh Carey told the public that the "days of wine and roses are over," no one, not even the new governor himself, knew quite how true his remark really was. When Nelson Rockefeller entered office, his first budget was $2 billion; when he left office, his last budget was $8.7 billion. New Yorkers were the most heavily taxed citizens in the nation, and their state had the highest public debt in the nation. Viewing the financial mess Carey inherited, Rockefeller said, "Poor Hugh. I spent all the money. And it's no fun being Governor of New York if you haven't got the money."[1]

And it wasn't fun. On February 25, 1975, the New York State Urban Development Corporation (UDC) defaulted on $104.5 million in short-term notes when the state legislature refused to appropriate the money. Ignoring the state's "moral obligation" to pay principal and interest due to UDC debt holders was devastating. Said a Wall Street bond trader, "Why should I buy the moral obligations of immoral politicians?"[2]

Suddenly the state, its agencies, as well as local municipalities throughout the state had trouble borrowing. New York City's Mayor Beame and Comptroller Harrison Goldin told the public that the "recent default by the State UDC has created an unwarranted climate of suspicion in the marketplace." The city was forced to pay the extraordinary price of 8.69 percent for one-year borrowing. In order to find purchasers, the State Housing Finance Authority had to issue one-year notes at the record-breaking rate of 9.6 percent. Analyzing the financial disaster he inherited, Carey concluded: "I've seen delicatessens in bankruptcy in better shape than the state of New York."[3]

After four weeks of this, Carey persuaded the legislature to come up with the money they "morally" owed, and the city was advanced $800 million to avoid defaulting to creditors. He hoped to add some sense of stability to the debt market.

Since its inception the Conservative Party had constantly warned that flagrant spending and magical financing would catch up with the government of New York State. Every year party spokesmen went to Albany to caution legislative finance committees that "pinched between the rising costs of inflation on the one hand, and the soaring costs of welfare, education, and state government on the other, the New

York State taxpayer has been pushed closer and closer to the brink of himself having to go on welfare to subsist."[4] Every year the party critiqued the budget and described line-by-line reductions that could easily be made.

The Conservative Party had constantly reminded the legislators that Rockefeller was creating a shadow state government in the form of authorities and agencies that spent money outside the state budget and without the approval or control of either the legislature or the voters. And Hugh Carey agreed: "He's [Rockefeller] constructed a perpetuity. . . . The way he's set up the authorities, boards and commissions with term appointments, it's almost beyond the reach of a governor to effectuate policy because he had these overlapping directorships in so many ways that their policy – which used to be his policy – becomes state policy without the intervention of the public. To call it a dynasty is one thing, but it's feudal."[5]

From the moment Rockefeller introduced legislation in 1968 to create the Urban Development Corporation, the Conservative Party vigorously opposed it. The Conservatives recognized that the UDC's power of eminent domain could be abused by social engineers intent on forcing their agendas on local governments, and the party predicted it would be a financial boondoggle. In 1974, the party supported legislation to drastically cut the powers of UDC. Dan Mahoney told the legislature that "it has long been our position that the 1968 legislation which put UDC in business, went too far in allowing the Urban Development Corporation to act virtually without reference to local governments or local concerns. The state or regional agency should not have the power to override local zoning and building codes." He argued that other legislative approaches could "assure local communities the right to establish reasonable rules and regulations for their own growth and development."

Mahoney concluded by saying that the legislator's should be guided by the truth that "those people who are most closely affected by the actions of UDC will be better represented by making certain that the Urban Development Corporation will have to comply with local rules and follow the wishes of local residents."

When the party sensed in January 1975 that UDC was facing serious financial problems, the party opposed a bailout. "Taxpayers have subsidized the adventurism of the UDC for too many years already," said Conservative Party Executive Director Serphin R. Maltese. "It is time to call a halt to this 'sham' public authority which was created in 1968 primarily to enhance the presidential ambitions of a former governor."[6]

But UDC was not the only crisis Governor Carey had to face, 1975 was also the year in which New York City's fiscal house of cards finally collapsed.

In 1965 mayoral candidate William F. Buckley Jr. had the guts to warn New Yorkers:

> New York City is in dire financial condition, as a result of mismanagement, extravagance, and political cowardice. . . . New York City must

discontinue its present borrowing policies, and learn to live within its income, before it goes bankrupt.[7]

Looking back, one notes that as early as 1941 the Citizens Budget Commission had warned that the city faced "a crisis in its fiscal affairs." Between 1926 and 1941, annual city expenditures, exclusive of emergency unemployment relief, had grown three times more rapidly than the city population, while the debt multiplied five-and-a-half times faster than population growth. Over and above a 210 percent increase in federal and state contributions, city expenditures advanced by more than 40 percent, while gross bonded debt doubled.

Rather than accept this as the price of good intentions and large government, Mayor Fiorello LaGuardia had used every possible fiscal artifice to hide the full cost of his progressive urban policies. During the war, LaGuardia took advantage of the forced savings produced by the war economy (supply shortages prevented some expenditures that had already been approved and budgeted, and the draft pulled a large number of civil servants off the salary rolls) to camouflage growing municipal costs.

Then he continued to overspend. Come year's end, when the city was behind in its receipts, LaGuardia's comptroller would roll over the city's bills to the next year's budget. *Brooklyn Eagle* columnist William Heffernan referred to the camouflaged budget as "the final stage of a municipal rake's progress . . . the gimme philosophy raised to the nth degree, the legacy of a 'government that has spent without discretion and taxed without care.'"

The post-war boom helped lift the city from its fiscal malaise. However, during this period the liberal ideological seeds were planted that eventually destroyed its financial base.

It was Mayor Robert F. Wagner who expressed the political view that prevailed in the 1950s, 1960s, and early 1970s. He stated: "I do not propose to permit our fiscal problems to set the limits of our commitments to meet the essential needs of the people of the city." This philosophy and various federal and state decisions eventually led to the distorted revenue estimates and rollovers that once again closed the financial community's door to the city. It also led to the situation where by 1975, twenty-five types of taxes supported a nineteen municipal hospitals, a network of day-care centers and foster homes, a tuition-free City University system, and over 1 million people on welfare.

November 1961 city-charter revisions granted Mayor Wagner absolute power to estimate general-fund revenues. Recognizing the significance of this change, the Citizen's Budget Commission reported: "When you had a Mayor operating with a Budget Bureau which was creative, the sky was the limit. There were no checks. You had creative budget officials playing the fifth violin, the piccolo and the kettle drum all by themselves."

The sanctioning of budgetary abuses continued throughout the 1960s and 1970s.

In 1964, the New York State Legislature amended Chapter 284, Section 2, of the Local Finance Law, permitting the city to place general-fund expenditures into the capital budget. Additional changes in the finance law (1967) allowed "the costs of codification laws and fees paid to experts, lawyers and consultants, advertising and costs of printing and dissemination" to be included in the capital project funds. The rationale was that they had a three-year period of probable usefulness.

Taking advantage of these loopholes, John V. Lindsay transferred $84 million of the city's general-fund expenditures to the capital budget in 1968. By 1975, that figure proliferated to $835 million – more than half of the capital projects budget.

During this period, the mayor also received the authority to issue revenue-anticipation notes based on his own "guesstimates" and not on the actual receipts of the previous fiscal year. In 1971 the city began issuing budget notes to cover distorted revenue estimates – $300 million were issued in 1971 and $400 million in 1972. There was apparently no intention to ever pay them off; they were just rolled into new borrowings.

Succumbing to the demands of the civil service, unions also contributed to the city's demise. In March 1958, Mayor Wagner signed an executive order that permitted over 100,000 city employees to join unions and to hold collective-bargaining sessions. By 1977, 98 percent of the city's employees belonged to unions. Bureau of the Budget figures reveal that between 1960 and 1975, city-employee wages jumped 31.6 percent. This was substantially greater than both salary gains in the private sector and the inflation rate. Retirement at half pay after twenty years' service, granted to the police in 1957, was granted to almost every municipal union. The Committee for Economic Development observed that between 1960 and 1970, New York State enacted fifty-four city pension bills. Retirement costs, according to the Temporary Commission on City Finances, rose more than 600 percent (from $206 million to $1.48 billion) during the period 1961 to 1976, and unfunded pension liabilities hit $8 billion by 1977.

Budgetary gimmicks, phantom revenues, and the capitalizing of expenses led to a situation wherein by 1975 city expenditures totaled $12.8 billion with revenues of just $10.9 billion. Fifty-six percent of locally raised taxes were appropriated for debt service, pension, and social security payments. In addition, short-term debt, which in 1965 was $536 million (10 percent of total debt), had ballooned to $4.5 billion (36 percent of total debt) by 1975. With 1976 short-term debt needs projected at $7 billion, the financial markets closed their doors to New York City.

In his book *The Bankers,* Martin Mayer wrote:

> On the simplest level, the story of New York's financial collapse is the tale
> of a Ponzi game in municipal paper – the regular and inevitably increasing
> issuance of notes to be paid off not by future taxes or revenue certified to
> be available for that purpose, but by the sale of future notes. Like all chain

letter swindles, Ponzi games self-destruct when the seller runs out of suckers, as New York did in spring 1975.

New York was brought to its knees because of its huge permanent short-term debt. Viewing the mess, journalist Ken Auletta declared, "The rollovers, false revenue estimates and plain lies have robbed the taxpayers of literally billions through excessive borrowings to cover-up excessive fraud."

Gov. Hugh Carey, grasping the magnitude of the situation, forced the city to begin internal reforms. In a September 1975 message to an emergency session of the state legislature, he stated: "[I]n the hope that further drastic reforms of the city's internal financing and management structure would restore the financial community's and the public's confidence in the city, far-reaching steps were taken or agreed to by the city, in close consultation with the state and the recently formed Municipal Assistance Corporation for the City of New York to improve its condition, including:

* the formation of a Management Advisory Committee to assist in streamlining the city's management,

* a ceiling on the size of the city's budget;

* a moratorium on additional taxes;

* the dismissal of thousands of municipal workers, the elimination of thousands of positions from the city's budget, and a freeze on new hiring;

* a suspension of wage increases of city employees;

* an increase in public transit fare;

* a further reduction in the budget of the City University and an increase in student fees that endangers its long-standing free tuition policy;

* a significant reduction of the capital budget;

* appointment of a special mayoral deputy for finance."

These measures were not enough to restore investor confidence, and in November 1975 the city *defaulted* by decree of the state legislature. Moratorium legislation was enacted on $2.6 billion of notes. Holders of the paper were offered ten-year, 8 percent MAC bonds in place of principal payments.

The city went to Washington and exerted tremendous pressure for a federal bailout, but U.S. Treasury Secretary William E. Simon held firm, insisting that the federal government "should offer no help to New York until and unless a powerful commitment was first made to adopt a responsible fiscal program." New York capitulated to Washington's demands, and in December 1975 President Ford signed legislation permitting short-term loans up to $2.3 billion a year.

To regain access to the credit markets, New York City was forced to overhaul its governing institutions. The offices of the mayor and comptroller developed sophisticated accounting, reporting, forecasting, and internal-control systems. In *American Cities and the New York Experience*, Charles Brecher and Raymond Horton commented:

The city has improved its information systems and integrated them into a financial planning process with a long-term perspective. The city that literally did not know how many people it employed in 1975 now projects staffing levels, borrowing, and cash flow for four-year periods, and has a 10-year plan for capital investments. The system . . . is probably one of the best management information systems among large American cities and rivals the practices of well-managed private firms.[8]

Liberal Hugh Carey had no choice but to force on New York City a fiscal conservatism that Bill Buckley and the Conservative Party had been demanding since 1965.

The Fight over ERA

The women's-rights section of the Conservative Party's Legislative Program read:

The Conservative Party is committed to the concept of equal opportunity for all people regardless of sex, race, and religion in all areas of life. Recent legislation has correctly removed barriers to women in employment, education, and credit. We favor elimination of those barriers to women which remain in our society by specific legislation. At the same time we oppose, on both state and federal levels, the so-called Equal Rights Amendment whose adoption would not contribute to the overall welfare of women.

So it was no surprise when the Conservative Party mounted a campaign against proposed Amendment No. 1 that appeared on the November 1975 ballot. The text of the proposed change to New York's constitution read in part:

Equality of rights under the law shall not be denied or abridged by the United States or by any State on account of sex. Congress and the several States shall have power, within their respective jurisdictions, to enforce this article by appropriate legislation. This amendment shall take effect three years after the date of ratification.

Serf Maltese explained the party opposition this way:

Women have played a major role in the New York State Conservative Party since it was formed in 1962. They have been active not only in the Party organization as County Chairmen, County Officers, and State Executive Committee members, but in addition have been Conservative candidates for the New York State Assembly, State Senate, City Council, Congress,

President of the City Council, Borough President and United States Senator. The Conservative Party has elected a woman to the New York State Assembly and as a delegate to the New York State Constitutional Convention. There are at present eight women serving as Conservative County Chairman.

The New York State Conservative Party believes in practicing equality not talking about it.

No one can deny that there is discrimination being practiced against women particularly in certain specific areas. Further, no one can reasonably argue that this discrimination should be ended, wherever it exists.

But the Conservative Party, while it supports Women's Rights and would like to see an end to discrimination against women, cannot support the Equal Rights Amendment (ERA) presently on the November 4 ballot.[9]

The party took the position that the wording of ERA was unclear and legally imprecise. If approved, the voters would effectively place every provision of the law concerning women into an issue to be resolved by the courts at the taxpayers' expense.

For instance, in mandating equality the ERA failed to take into consideration the preferential treatment accorded women under the laws of the United States and the laws of the respective states, e.g., exemption from the draft, privileged treatment under the labor and the domestic-relations laws. The most obvious question was: Will men be given the preferential treatment accorded to women or, will women be deprived of their privileged status under the law and accorded the same treatment as men?[10]

Questions like these were appropriately raised because the wording of the proposed constitutional amendment was so vague. Some Conservatives predicted that the ERA would produce a variety of undesirable results including the legalization of homosexual marriages and prisoners being held in common detention facilities.

In the fall of 1975, Conservative Party member Jack Swan of Flushing and his business partner Joe Bierbauer, decided they would organize opposition to the amendment. Swan and Bierbauer, who ran a small community-relations firm called Institutional Planning and Development Corporation, had contacts around the state they intended to activate in the fight. Their strategy was simple: With proponents of ERA doing almost no campaigning due to overconfidence, Swan and Bierbauer wanted to strike under the opposition's radar the weekend before the Tuesday, November 4 election.

With $11,000 they had raised, they printed a simple "palm card" that listed the possible undesirable results of the Amendment if it were approved. This 3 x 5 flyer was distributed by volunteers outside the state's 1,500 Catholic churches at the end of every mass on Sunday, November 2.

It worked. More than 57 percent of the voters said no to the ERA.

	Yes	No
Outside New York City	1,015,160	1,636,378
Bronx	58,750	47,605
Brooklyn	115,103	89,702
Manhattan	131,993	40,900
Queens	129,800	112,171
Staten Island	19,407	24,237
Total New York City	**455,053**	**314,615**
Total State	**1,470,213**	**1,950,993**

The feminists were shocked and irate. Many claimed that the forces of darkness had spent millions of dollars. Sandra Abramson of the League of Women Voters attributed the Amendment's defeat to "bad timing and the New York City financial crisis."[11]

She also admitted that many voters thought "there would be court controversy over interpretation and [this caused] them to vote no or not at all. It is a lack of trust in the judiciary's ability to resolve controversy."

The Sainted Junior Senator from New York

It was on the floor of the United States Senate when he was commemorating the tenth anniversary of the publication of Barry Goldwater's *The Conscience of a Conservative* that Senator James Buckley described his vision of his role as a Conservative public official:

Americans are hungry for a sense of commitment to an ideal higher than the satisfaction of their appetites. We are there to fill the void with our passionate concern for individual freedom. We bring to the political front a concept of man and of society with which the most idealistic can identify.

Yes, the opportunity is there, the challenge is there. We can build a conservatism relevant to the Seventies that can be translated into political consequence; and I believe profoundly that any political party that forthrightly builds its platform on the bedrock of Conservative principle and insight will be the majority party of the 1980s. I believe with equal strength that if no party so bases itself, if each of the major parties attempts to prevaricate, to straddle, then we will see a continuing erosion of our freedoms and vitality that in time will spell the end of the American nation as we have known and loved it.

We cannot allow ourselves to falter in our work. And above all, we must never lose sight of the fact that central to all our political action must be the Conservative conscience.

Whatever success Conservatives may achieve in this decade – and I am convinced it is going to be enormous – no success is worth the having if we abandon the conscience that has sustained us through these difficult years.[12]

When Jim Buckley entered the Senate in January 1971, he was catapulted to the level of a national Conservative spokesman, and indeed he did serve as a new conscience for the movement. This became obvious in his first days in the Senate, particularly when he insisted on being listed in the *Congressional Directory* as a "Conservative-Republican":

> I chose to be listed as Conservative-Republican to reflect the fact that I was elected to office as the candidate of New York State's Conservative Party while being enrolled in the state and working within the Senate as a Republican. An extraordinary fuss was raised over the insistence on this particular designation, which I believed to be the most accurate way of describing what I was and how I had arrived in the Senate. It provided the meat for at least one Evans and Novak column and one of the arguments in Senator Javits' case for trying to have me excluded from the Senate Republican Caucus until I had had the opportunity to demonstrate my Republicanism.[13]

The senior senator from New York, Jacob Javits, also helped lift Buckley's profile when he unsuccessfully opposed Buckley's request to join the GOP senate caucus. Buckley's public announcement in his first week in office that he was opposed to President Nixon's Family Assistance Plan and to funding for a supersonic transport airplane also enhanced his reputation as the movement's conscience.

In his maiden speech before the Senate, Buckley introduced S-1577, a *revenue-shifting* proposal to provide for sending a percentage of federal income tax collections to the states. His proposal differed from the Nixon's Administration's *revenue-sharing* bill in that the revenue to the states would not be restricted and would provide state and local governments with a new source of unrestricted revenue without imposing additional taxes on an already overburdened public.[14]

Appointed to the Public Works, Aeronautical and Space Sciences, and District of Columbia committees, Buckley proved to be a diligent member. He appointed notable conservative talent to his staff, including Michael Uhlmann, who had served as minority staff director and counsel to the Senate Select Committee on Equal Education Opportunity, and the Hudson Institute's William Schneider.

Although he was shocked at "the enormous demands that [were] made on my time, seven days a week" and at "my loss of anonymity," the freshman Senator did admit that he "would like to serve here for the next 17 years – three terms. . . . I think 66 would be an appropriate age to retire."[15]

In year two, although he was critical of Nixon's wage and price controls and the

China trip, he did not join his brother, Bill, Conservative Party Chairman Dan Mahoney, and other prominent Conservatives when they suspended their support of Nixon and endorsed Congressman John Ashbrook. As early as January 1972, he said Nixon had "remarkable patience and endurance in tackling national problems while facing a Democratically-controlled Congress."[16] In March, he told a Cayuga County Conservative Party reception that: "I have heard Humphrey, McGovern, Kennedy, and there is no question who will further conservative principles – Nixon will." By June, to enhance Nixon's chances of carrying New York, he urged Conservatives and Republicans to put aside any misgivings they might have on Nixon's foreign policy. Buckley told a crowd at the Roosevelt Hotel's Republican Luncheon Forum that "if we Conservatives fail to choose, if we decide to 'sit this one out' we will in effect be helping those whose programs will lead the United States into disaster."[17] His efforts helped convince the Republicans and Conservatives to have for the first time, joint electors, which permitted the Nixon-Agnew ticket to appear on both Row A and Row C. Buckley also boosted the candidacy of Barbara Keating, by endorsing her over his Senate colleague, Jacob Javits.

But this was 1973, and while Buckley was introducing a flurry of bills promoting conservative principles, including a constitutional amendment to ban abortions by defining the fetus as an unborn child, the unfolding Watergate scandal was beginning to distract not only the U.S. Senate, but the entire nation.

On May 9, a *New York Times* op-ed piece by Senator Buckley called on Americans to give the president the "benefit of doubt." But it was beginning to become difficult to back the president. At a reception he hosted on May 23 saluting former Vietnam prisoners of war, the press haunted Senator Buckley on Watergate. He urged Mr. Nixon to appoint a special prosecutor, insisted that all the "cards be placed on the table, face up of course." He also gave a philosophical twist to the growing crisis:

> Watergate shows us the dangers that are inherent when you concentrated as much powers as Congress has concentrated in the President. It's important to begin to dismantle the Federal responsibility, beginning in the social welfare fields, and return authority to local areas.[18]

In the coming months as he watched the Watergate "cancer" grow and the administration "dig in," and Buckley began to have serious misgivings about Nixon's ability to govern. By Christmas 1973, he was consulting with trusted friends, and one close aide said:

> "Nixon has a 25 percent constituency, every one of whom is a hard-core Buckley constituent, and they will end up calling you a traitor." Another probability was that the White House response would be financial punishment, pressure on contributors to withhold campaign funds. Buckley's

conclusion was: "I can't make a decision based on what will happen to me personally."[19]

By February of 1974, Buckley became convinced that a lifeless Nixon White House could not be resurrected, and he began contemplating a call for Nixon's resignation, realizing that such a change in his position regarding the president's fate might destroy his political base in New York.[20] On March 18, Senator Buckley sent a telegram to his brother Bill (who was traveling in Kenya), saying he would call on Nixon to resign the next morning. He signed the telegram, "Saint Sebastian," a reference to the third-century Christian martyr who smiled as archers aimed their arrows at him.[21]

Although some local Republican leaders called Buckley's actions "dumb, dumb, dumb," over the next few months, being the first to call for Nixon to quit established renewed respect for the senator's independence and his political conscience.

Reviewing the reactions of Washington insiders, Jim Buckley himself concluded:

> One thing that astonished me when I got this job was that there are some people here who chronically never take anything at face value. I've become very philosophical about it. This was one of the things that caused it to be such an anguishing decision. I knew it would hurt some people. I knew that some would impute motives to it. And I knew it would give aid and comfort to people who, from less than the highest motivation, have been loading on Watergate.[22]

In the final days of the Nixon presidency, Buckley attempted to keep on working and introduced legislation that would add an inflation index to the tax code, one designed to reflect changes in the cost of living and to eliminate earnings limitations for elderly social-security recipients.

Among other stands he took that were ahead of the times was his condemnation of affirmative action, which he called not "reverse discrimination," but "discrimination period." Testifying before a special subcommittee on Education of the House Labor and Education Committee, he said:

> The absurdity of the exercise ought to be self-evident. But it is worse than absurd. The notion of affirmative action plans designed to achieve precise goals is inherently vicious, inherently discriminatory. It flies in the face of everything that the civil rights movement has sought to achieve – a society in which every human being is judged on his merits as a human being, a society that is truly colorblind, a society that applies a single set of standards for employment and advancement irrespective of the accident of birth.

> This is true whether quotas are applied to universities or businesses or unions. The human soul does not know distinctions or race or sex or ethnic origins. To attempt to catalog human beings by such categories for purposes of employment is to insult their humanity.[23]

In the fall, Buckley helped Republican fundraising and campaigned nationally for conservative candidates. Although the Watergate backlash resulted in serious losses nationally, Jim Buckley's reputation as the conscience of the conservative movement was actually enhanced.

Senator Buckley made it clear early in his term that he would fight to get New York's share of federal dollars. He developed his own no-strings revenue-shifting program that if passed would have been fairer to New York than Nixon's strings-attached, revenue-sharing bill. Recognizing that numerous local New York governments were under fiscal pressure, he still insisted on maintaining fiscal integrity. In August 1972, he made this point in a *New York Times* op-ed essay:

> There is no doubt of the severity of the financial problems which face state and local governments in New York and elsewhere across the nation. But these problems must be solved in a way which will preserve the fiscal integrity of all levels of government without destroying the political integrity of the federal system.[24]

In 1975, Jim Buckley's principles faced their severest test when it became evident that forty years of irresponsible fiscal policies had brought New York City to its knees. Sticking to his beliefs, Buckley announced in September 1975 that his opposition to federal bail-out aid was based on his opposition "to further eroding in our federal system, which is based on independent self-governing bodies."[25] Buckley firmly believed that taxpayers throughout the nation should not be stuck subsidizing New York City's extravagance and mismanagement. Brother Bill came to his defense claiming a "senator demeans his office . . . to wage a form of guerilla warfare against other states in the union." He viewed the senator's views as "living up to the promise he made to the people who elected him: to guard the federal system, to preserve the independence of the state, to speak the truth as he sees it."[26]

But Bill Buckley's voice of defense was a lonely one. Most editorials and pundits throughout the city hammered away at the senator. Claiming his "cold words can only evoke mingled dismay and disbelief," the *New York Post* concluded: "Buckley's statement will deservedly reaffirm his credentials as a faithful spokesman of Conservative Party doctrine. His stand will not be forgotten when he faces the general electorate next year."[27] The *New York Daily News* complained that: "The risks involved in adopting Buckley's casual complacent attitude toward default are very high. . . . Fortunately, his attitude isn't shared by those most concerned with the problem. They are waging a spirited vigorous fight to save the city from disaster."[28]

In November, Buckley proposed a bill that would require a change in the federal bankruptcy law by creating a federal trustee to work with the newly created Emergency Financial Control Board to "devise a plan that would continue all essential services and the payment of interest on all existing bonds and notes."[29] He preferred this approach to the Senate Banking Committee's, which would "impose the equivalent of an occupation government in New York City in the form of a three-man federal board having virtually unlimited power to dictate the most fundamental policies."[30] Even though Buckley's plan was sensible calling for "default now and pay later," it caused liberals to condemn him publicly – daring to mention municipal default was anathema. He was the lone senator in the tri-state area to call for federal-aid to the city only after New York petitioned for bankruptcy.

On November 21, 1975, Senator Buckley endorsed a $2.5 billion loan to ease the city's fiscal crisis. In a sitting room off the Senate floor, he told the press that "all of the conditions that I have envisioned under the default option have been met. The feds would not be running New York City, although the City would be required to balance its budget and the Federal Government would have a first call on the City's tax revenue stream."[31]

The senator did admit, however, that his insistence that default (which is exactly what the city did in November of 1975) would not lead to chaos probably hurt him, "I'm sure it has not helped at this stage," he said. "In New York City and the suburbs, it probably hurt."[32] Looking back, Mike Long said in a 1999 interview: "When New York went broke, Buckley was philosophically correct in his actions but the print media made him look like he committed 'Hari-Kari.' The Senator brought about his own demise by doing the right thing."[33]

As 1975 drew to a close, political sharks in both parties smelled blood and began to circle around the Buckley life raft. To run for a second term in 1976, Buckley planned on having both the Republican and Conservative Lines. For five years, as much as he disliked it, he had managed to make the rounds throughout the state at both Republican and Conservative fund raisers. But his comments on New York City's finances and his statement that "President Ford cannot take [Conservatives] for granted" did nothing to endear him with all elements of the Republican Party. New York's State Chairman Richard Rosenbaum (a Rockefeller stooge who was to prove that without the former governor's money he had no clue how to help Republicans win elections), conceded in September 1975 that Buckley "is our front runner and we'll be behind him as long as he doesn't do anything like oppose Nelson Rockefeller,"[34] by which Rosenbaum referred to the underground campaign to dump Rockefeller from the 1976 Republican national ticket. (Rocky had been tapped by Gerald Ford to be vice president after Mr. Ford took office upon Nixon's resignation.)

Westchester County Republican Congressman Peter Peyser, whose district included Rockefeller's Pocantico Hills estate, started making noises about challenging Buckley in a Republican primary. Fearing to flame conservative opposition to his renomination as vice president, Rockefeller did decline Peyser's requests for a meeting, but the *Daily News* reported that it was no secret that Rocky preferred Peyser. "[B]ut Rockefeller aides said privately that there is no way he can support Peyser without giving Conservatives further incentive to 'take a walk' next year."[35]

To show he was serious about a second term, Buckley announced in February of 1975 that F. Clifton White would run the campaign and chair his fundraising apparatus, Friends of Jim Buckley. Fundraising letters went out signed by prominent Republicans, including Senators Barry Goldwater and Howard Baker. White claimed that Buckley had general appeal because of his independent "let the chips fall" attitude on major issues but that he also had a special appeal to young people because of his "tell it like it is" character.[36]

While friends found Jim Buckley's gentleness, unfailing courtesy, and common-sense attitudes to be strengths, many Democrats viewed these same virtues as weaknesses. As a result, numerous Democrats were considering challenges, including former Mayors Wagner and Lindsay, consumer advocate Bess Myerson, Congressman Mario Biaggi, and Congresswoman Bella Abzug. Yet the September 18, 1975, issue of the *Times* reported that a poll taken by New York Democrats indicated that Buckley would defeat any of these five candidates.[37]

At Manhattan's 43rd Street Town Hall on Monday evening, April 26, 1976, Senator James Buckley, flanked by brother Bill and Senator Barry Goldwater, formally declared his intention to seek a second term. Twenty-one incumbent Republicans in the United States Senate and over fifty Republican Congressmen publicly announced support for their colleague.

On June 18, 1976, the New York State Conservative Party State Committee, which consisted of party leaders from every one of the state's 150 assembly districts, met in Manhattan to unanimously re-nominate Jim Buckley. Among the Conservative leaders at the event were a score of delegates pledged to Ronald Reagan, including three from Queens and fiften from Brooklyn, who broke with the state organization in order to back the former governor of California over the incumbent President Ford. Five days later at the Waldorf-Astoria Hotel, the 345-member New York Republican Party designated James Buckley as its candidate for the U.S. Senate.

Throughout the summer, while Reagan and Ford battled it out for the Republican nomination and Vice President Rockefeller surprised and pleased conservatives by withdrawing from consideration as the No. 2 man on the ticket, James Buckley's name was prominently mentioned for vice president. And when it looked like the Republican National Convention would be deadlocked, newspaper headlines throughout the nation read "Buckley For President?" Rumors abounded that Buckley "was considering offering himself as an alternative presidential choice in case the convention could not decide between the two closely matched front runners."[38] If nothing else, the rumors – which died in forty-eight hours – gave Buckley some decent publicity back in New York.

On the Democratic side, radical left-wingers such as Congresswoman Bella Abzug, former U.S. Attorney General Ramsey Clark, and City Council President Paul O'Dwyer, were campaigning vigorously to win their party's nomination to oppose Buckley. One Democrat, who was making a name for himself as President Ford's United Nation's Ambassador, was being urged by many to enter the primary. But on a *Face the Nation* segment in the previous October, Daniel Patrick Moynihan had seemed to rule out his candidacy saying:

> I would consider it dishonorable to leave this post and run for any office, and I hope it would be understood that if I do, the people – the voters to whom I would present myself in such circumstances – would consider me as having said in advance that I am a man of no personal honor to have done so.[39]

But on June 10, 1976, Moynihan tossed aside honesty, changed his mind and declared that he would seek the Democratic nomination for senator. The Democratic establishment was not thrilled, since Moynihan's core supporters consisted of neo-conservatives Midge Decter and Irving Kristol, Suzanne and Leonard Garment, and Richard Ravitch.

While the Democrats fought a particularly ugly primary, Peyser's whiny challenge to Buckley fell on deaf ears with most of the Republican establishment. On primary day, Tuesday, September 16, Senator Buckley easily defeated Peter Peyser 70.5 percent to 29.5 percent, with Buckley receiving 242,507 votes to Peyser's 101,629. The Democratic "donnybrook," however, was a late nighter with a surprise victor: Ambassador Moynihan, who won by a single percentage point:

	Votes	Percentage
Moynihan	333,697	36.4
Abzug	323,705	35.3
Clark	94,191	10.3
O'Dwyer	92,689	9.0
Hirshfield	82,331	9.0

The Democratic establishment was shocked by the results. Party powerbroker Pamela Harrimann told the *Washington Post* that the victor was a "buffoon" with too much "alcohol in his head."[40] The Buckley camp was also shocked. They planned all summer to have an easy race against the radical, left-wing, loudmouth Bella Abzug, but now they feared a race like the 1974 Wilson vs. Carey: two Irish

Catholics splitting the conservative blue-collar vote. Liberals, of course, would stick with the Democrat.

On the plus side, Jim Buckley had sufficient campaign funds, and he was to appear on both Row A and Row C with President Gerald Ford (there were no Republican objections in 1976 to Conservative-endorsed Ford electors), who was making a remarkable comeback in the polls against Jimmy Carter. The senator's '76 campaign theme was: "A Conscience comes to Washington" and "Integrity hasn't gone out of style." And he had a record he could proudly articulate to New Yorkers.

> He was, for instance, among those who opened up the highway trust fund, thereby providing New York a source of money for public transportation; he has worked to restore the jobs of policemen and firemen and construction workers; he has advocated tax deductions for city apartment dwellers to parallel the deductions home owners get for interest on their mortgages; and he voted against allowing the SST to land at Kennedy. He can also argue, legitimately, that by voting against the first bail-out program he helped prevent massive federal intervention and possibly total federal control over the city.[41]

On the negative side, Moynihan, unlike Buckley, had the Irish gift: he could walk into a room and effortlessly charm hundreds of people. Mike Long recalls that "Jim Buckley was not a backslapper – his shyness and politeness were interpreted by many as snobbishness."

"I remember," Long continued, "when Buckley was a guest at my Brooklyn Conservative Party Dinner, and I offered to take him around the ballroom and make introductions while people were eating. He declined telling me he did not want to intrude while people were enjoying their food. In New York, however, people expect to be disturbed at political functions and they thought his politeness was really a lack of interest in meeting them."[42]

In their first debates, *The New York Times* reported that Buckley and Moynihan "differed on many issues but their differences were couched in gentility, humor and cordiality – befitting candidates from Yale and Harvard who had not come up the hard way in elective politics."[43] But by late October, with the race looking tight, a *Times* headline read "Breeding Gives Way to Brawling."

Buckley warned that a Senator Moynihan would "join the pack of those who feel there is a federal answer to every problem." On the campaign trail and in debates, he reminded voters that Moynihan's support for "public service jobs, health insurance, nationwide welfare benefits and increased spending would cost taxpayers an extra $152 billion a year." The flamboyant and pompous Moynihan, on the other hand, actually had the nerve to accuse Buckley of being "eccentric, uncaring and haughty."[44] Moynihan did, however, cut in to Buckley's support because even though he "[took] the liberal Democratic position on virtually all the major domestic issues of the day, he [presented] a moderate image by his emphasis on family and personal opposition to abortion; his hawkish position on Communism and defense spending, and his tendency toward Roosevelt rather than McGovern liberalism."[45]

On Tuesday, November 2, the man who William F. Buckley Jr. described as the "Sainted Junior Senator from New York" went down to defeat:

	Moynihan Dem.	Buckley Rep.	Buckley Cons.	Moynihan Lib.
Outside New York City	**1,908,625**	**2,018,471**	**219,752**	**86,535**
Bronx	213,857	73,339	13,215	13,187
Brooklyn	395,772	135,923	22,348	25,889
Manhattan	300,223	82,218	11,735	29,536
Queens	368,991	175,709	35,023	26,049
Staten Island	51,043	39,479	9,421	2,887
Total New York City	**1,329,886**	**506,668**	**91,742**	**97,548**
Total State	**3,238,511**	**2,525,139**	**311,494**	**184,083**
Percentage	**51.7**	**40.3**	**5.0**	**2.0**

Looking back on the campaign in the early 1990s, Clif White concluded that Jim Buckley's problem was he was concerned more about good legislation than good politics. White summed up the 1976 Buckley campaign by relating this incident:

> One of the most disheartening moments for me took place in Grand Central Station when I ran into Jim's secretary, Dawn Cina, who later married Tom Winter of *Human Events*. She was almost in tears. "Mr. White, we're going to lose, aren't we?"
>
> "It doesn't look very good, Dawn."
>
> "I said a prayer that if Jim wins, we'll keep our lines of communication open with every county chairman in New York."
>
> The Almighty, however, was not inclined to work miracles in 1976. Jim lost, and the U.S. Senate ended up losing one of its most idealistic and dedicated members because he was not a good enough politician.[46]

The defeat of Senator James Buckley was a serious loss to the Conservative Party. The senator, a hero to conservatives all over the nation, gave the party visibility, a philosophical forum, and aid in raising money.[47] Yet even with the loss of its top salesman, the Conservative Party was still in business.

The state senate that convened in January 1977 had thirty endorsed senators, including twenty-nine Republicans and one Democrat. Senators Owen Johnson of Nassau-Suffolk, John Marchi of Staten Island, and John Calandra of the Bronx won by the margin of their Conservative Party votes. A total of fifty-nine assemblymen were elected with Conservative endorsement: fifty-two Republicans and seven Democrats. Seven assemblymen were elected by their Conservative margins.

One lost assembly seat was that of retiring registered Conservative, Rosemary Gunning. Serf Maltese was unsuccessful in his race to succeed her. In a 2000 interview, Maltese said he lost because "my opponent, Cliff Wilson, took the section of the Party's platform opposing rent control and made sure everyone in the district who lived in a rent-controlled apartment knew about it. They came out in droves and voted against me."

In the congressional races, the party provided the margin of victory in the Twenty-Third Congressional District for Bruce Caputo. Also, Conservative candidate James Young's 15,337 votes in the Twenty-Ninth Congressional District prevented Republican Joe Martino from beating Democrat Edward Patterson.

Conservative Party margins were also instrumental in the election victories of numerous local candidates. Significant examples were the countywide victories in Suffolk of John Finnerty (R-C) for county sheriff and Jean Tuthill (R-C) for county treasurer. In Nassau, the party provided the margin of victory for County Clerk Harold McConnell. Wayne County Sheriff Paul Byork was also elected thanks to Row C. Two enrolled Conservatives were also elected: Robert Doyle was elected Suffolk County judge and Thomas Clark won the race for Oyster Bay councilman.

Dan Mahoney, in his year-end report, thanked the faithful for their dedicated support and reminded them that their "splendid achievements have enabled us in the past to triumph over seemingly insurmountable obstacles and I am certain that with your continued support, our efforts will ultimately be crowned with success."

Liberal Pipe Dreams Go Up in Smoke

At the annual Conservative Party Albany conference in February 1977, Dan Mahoney released the year's legislative program. Although the party was "somewhat encouraged by [Governor Carey's] attempt to slow the rate of expenditure growth and his initial suggestions designed to reduce state mandates," the platform listed $410-million worth of tax and budget cuts essential for the state's economic recovery:

> New Yorkers have long suffered with the highest per capita tax burden in the nation. State taxes alone claim nearly 8 percent of all personal income in New York. . . . the Conservative Party believes that what New Yorkers need most in 1977 is substantial tax relief and it is our position that the Legislature must make sufficient reductions in state expenditures to grant immediate tax relief to overburdened Empire State individual and business taxpayers. We have made these proposals toward that end, in the hope that they will act as a forerunner to not only further cuts in taxes, but also, a reduction in unnecessary and wasteful expenditures.[48]

One issue on which the Conservative Party had major impact in 1977 was the defeat of efforts to ease state laws on marijuana possession.

Republican Senator Douglas Barclay and Democratic Assemblyman Richard Gottfried introduced a bill that would have decriminalized the possession of up to two ounces of marijuana, the transfer of up to half an ounce of marijuana, or the growing of marijuana plants. Under the proposed legislation, these criminal acts would now be classified as "violations," each subject to a maximum penalty of a $100 fine. Additionally, a person alleged to possess more than two ounces and up to eight ounces of marijuana, caught smoking or ingesting marijuana in a public place, or caught selling sale up to one-half ounce of marijuana could not be arrested. Instead the police officer would be limited to issuing an "appearance ticket" (essentially a summons) for an appearance in court at a later date.

For the first time in its fifteen-year history, the party succeeded in having legislation withdrawn from floor action in the legislature.

Serf Maltese vigorously opposed the bill and told legislators:

> We doubt the wisdom of encouraging – as this bill does – the use of an undesirable substance where its effect on human health is at best uncertain. There is no concrete evidence that marijuana does not contribute to birth defects, certain hereditary diseases, lung diseases, lung damage, and brain damage.
>
> As a former Assistant District Attorney, I wish to stress that we view this bill with especial alarm when we consider the opinions of many respected law enforcement experts to the effect that marijuana usage will increase as a result of decriminalization or legalization. In addition, we can expect a greater number of our youth making the progression to heroin, cocaine, L.S.D. or other death dealing substances.
>
> We also object to these proposals since they would further open up the "youth market" to the sellers by reducing the penalties on sales to minors. This provision coupled with the decriminalization of the growing of marijuana would seem to be a prescription for disaster in elementary and secondary schools throughout the state.[49]

Although the bill's sponsors boasted that the "bill will receive swift passage in the Senate and Assembly," the Conservative Party led an effective lobbying effort to kill it in the senate. On May 14, 1977, *The New York Times* published a front-page story with the headline: "Conservatives Peril Albany Bill To Ease Laws On Marijuana." Serf Maltese was quoted as saying, "We have it stopped in the Senate. It's dead." An upset Senator Barclay told the *Times*: "The Conservatives have done a job and are continuing to do a job. . . . It's irritating."

Mahoney and Maltese had focused their efforts on the thirty Senators who were elected with Conservative Party support. Maltese also visited Barclay's district to line up community groups to pressure the senator. Fear of Conservative Party reprisals made the Barclay bill DOA. With the victory, the party demonstrated that it still had plenty of clout . . . and didn't fear using it.

As this battle was going on, the party was also viewing the landscape of the approaching 1977 New York City mayoral race.

Even though the financial disciplines Hugh Carey forced upon the city stopped the monetary hemorrhaging, the city was not yet out of the woods. Fiscal watchdogs projected years of deficits, and it was essential that the mayor be ever vigilant in managing the budget.

Mayor Abe Beame, who four years earlier had run on the slogan, "He Knows the Buck," proved to be inept during the 1975 crisis – a figurehead chief executive with the financial control boards calling the shots. Nevertheless, he insisted on running for another term and was willing to take on all comers, which meant the usual suspects: Bella Abzug, Herman Badillo, Joel Harnett, Percy Sutton, Ed Koch, and Mario Cuomo.

After watching the financial collapse of New York City, one would think the Republicans would have learned a lesson: no more John Lindsays. One would have thought they would have turned in 1977 to a philosophical conservative. This was not to be the case. The Republican organization turned to a Lindsay clone, State Senator Roy Goodman.

Elected to represent Manhattan's "Silk Stocking" District in November 1968, this heir to the Ex-Lax fortune was a classic Harvard-educated Manhattan "Goo-Goo." Before his election to the senate, he had served as Mayor Lindsay's finance administrator. In other words, he had helped Lindsay spend the city into bankruptcy.

Dan Mahoney could only shake his head at this selection. He believed that a suitable Republican with Conservative endorsement might be able to beat Goodman in a primary, and the man he had in mind was the articulate radio talk-show host, Barry Farber. Over the years, Mahoney and Maltese had come to know Farber well through their numerous appearances on his show.

Barry Farber, a noted linguist fluent in a dozen languages, had an interesting career as a journalist. He had led Hungarians across their border after their failed revolution and had reported the repression of Soviet Jews from a Moscow Synagogue as early as 1956. By 1977, he had been host of his own WOR talk show, five nights a week for sixteen years.

In 1970, he had challenged Bella Abzug in Manhattan's very Democratic Nineteenth Congressional District (as the Republican-Liberal candidate) and had actually held her to only 52 percent of the vote.

The campaign theory behind the Farber effort was simple: If he could win the Republican primary and face a Democratic and a Liberal candidate, he might be able to pull off a "Jim Buckley" split victory with just 40 percent of the vote:

In a three-way race, Farber estimates that, assuming he gets the GOP nomination, he can count on a solid 350,000 votes from Conservatives and
Republicans. He would then have to build upon this base by picking up
about one-fourth of the Democratic vote, looking for support to such
groups as the Jews, Eastern Europeans, Italians and Hispanics.[50]

Farber believed he could achieve this because his conservative views on crime, abortion, welfare fraud, and gay rights would appeal to many ethnic blue-collar voters.
According to Farber, "As a Jew running on the Conservative line, I'm more 'Catholic'
to many Catholics than a Catholic running on the Liberal line."[51]

Farber received unanimous Conservative Party support, but his real problem was
getting his name onto the Republican ballot. Conservative Party operatives Mike
Long and Allenn Roth ran the Farber campaign, but enrolled Republicans were needed to circulate Farber petitions door-to-door. While dedicated volunteers throughout
the city managed to
scrape together 18,000
signatures (the mini-
mum requirement was
10,000), the Goodman
forces dragged petitions
through the courts, hop-
ing to expel him from
the ballot or to exhaust
Farber's campaign treas-
ury in legal fees. Or
both.

To avoid the politi-
cal humiliation that
Lindsay had suffered in
1969, the Goodman
operatives resorted to
every trick in the book
to terminate Farber's
Republican candidacy.
They harassed petition

1977 candidate for New York City mayor, Barry Farber.

signers with subpoenas and dragged them into court.

Even before the petitions were filed, the Farber team, led by election lawyer Bob
Clark, had to go into court and successfully obtain a judicial order that forced
Brooklyn Republican leader George Clark (a Goodman supporter and no relation to
Bob) to turn over 2,000 Farber signatures that he had received from a Farber defector.

The court battles took all summer, and even though Farber eventually prevailed in the court of appeals, his supporters didn't know until a week and a half before the September 8 primary that his name would appear on the Republican primary ballot. Mike Long, whom Mahoney had asked to manage the campaign six weeks before primary day, recalls that the campaign ran out of money, and that thousands of envelopes stuffed with Farber brochures never got mailed because the campaign couldn't afford the postage. Out in Flushing, Queens, on Labor Day weekend, Genevieve Klein, who was helping a room full of volunteers stuff envelopes in Conservative Party county headquarters, wrote a personal check to cover the cost of postage so that the work they were doing wouldn't be wasted.

The mailings that did get out contained this message from Bill Buckley:

> When I ran for mayor against John Lindsay, I warned that his policies were a prescription for galloping bankruptcy and disorder. Now Roy Goodman, Lindsay's Finance Administrator, wants to be mayor. Why not bring back Lindsay himself?
>
> I'm supporting Barry Farber for mayor. We need a fresh leader in City Hall. Barry Farber has the courage, the energy and the intelligence to lead us back to municipal sanity.[52]

The Goodman campaign had plenty of money to spend, and its resources were used to obscure its candidate's pro-abortion, pro-gay rights, and anti-death penalty records. The Goodmanites mailed a series of scurrilous last-minute mailings, including one charging that the anti-pornographic candidate, Barry Farber, was actually the "originator and producer of a sex show." Pointing out that it was "a psychodramatic workshop to help people with potentially dangerous sexual compulsion," the Farber campaign contended that Goodman was using "desperate efforts to discredit him with New York City's Republican voters motivated by a fear that Mr. Farber would win the primary."[53]

On Thursday, September 8, 1977, Barry Farber lost the Republican primary:

	Farber	Goodman
Bronx	4,108	4,689
Brooklyn	9,236	10,045
Manhattan	5,442	12,330
Queens	12,084	12,864
Staten Island	3,912	4,739
Total	34,782	44,667
Percentage	43.7	56.3

Allen Roth, a Farber political consultant and future Conservative Party vice chairman, conceded that "lack of funds and the 'Goodman sex mailing' did Barry in."

It was the results of the Democratic battle, however, that changed the dynamics of the full mayoral race. Conservatives believed Farber could have run a credible race because they expected to face the inept incumbent, Mayor Beame, or the radical feminist, Bella Abzug. The Democratic primary voters, however, had different ideas. The top two vote getters were the little known Manhattan Congressman Edward I. Koch and Governor Carey's handpicked candidate, New York Secretary of State Mario Cuomo. Since Koch and Cuomo, who received respectively 20 and 19 percent of the vote, each had polled less than 40 percent, they had to face a primary runoff on September 19. In a bruising battle, Koch managed to prevail, but Cuomo announced he would fight on to November as the Liberal Party candidate.

In the November general election, Farber received only 4 percent of the vote running on Row C. He did that poorly because of the presence of Cuomo in the race. Although he was running on the Liberal line, Cuomo appealed to outer-borough blue-collar ethnics as "one of them." He ran as a neighborhood guy who was "tough, dedicated and competent." He also created an additional ballot line for himself that was called the Neighborhood Preservation Party. Cuomo told his constituency that he was "as angry as you are about crime. . . . We need more cops, more judges, more people going to jail." He also proclaimed that he was dedicated to neighborhood preservation: "If I stand for anything in politics, it is that neighborhoods must live!"[54] His campaign flyer declared in bold print: "**Vote as if your neighborhood depended on it!**"

It is also true that during this period Cuomo was perceived as Pro-Life. During his unsuccessful 1974 primary run for lieutenant-governor, Cuomo, reported *The New York Times*, said in a televised debate that "he would have voted against the 1970 law that relaxed abortion curbs in the state."[55] An August 29, 1974, column in the Brooklyn Catholic diocesan newspaper, *The Tablet*, praised Cuomo, saying, "He deserves the loud and enthusiastic endorsement of Right to Life. . . . Mario Cuomo is, in my personal opinion, qualified and true, through and through." The *Daily News* and the *New York Post* also reported that Cuomo would veto a gay rights bill "that would give homosexual teachers the right to proselytize or advocate their lifestyle . . ."[56]

When the 1.4 million votes cast on election day, Tuesday, November 8, 1977, were tallied, Barry Farber had come in fourth:

Candidate	Number	Percent
Koch	717,376	50.0
Cuomo		
Liberal	522,942	36.4
Neighborhood Preservation	64,971	4.5
Total	587,913	41.0
Goodman	58,606	4.1
Farber	57,437	4.0
Other Candidates	13,822	1.0
Total	1,435,154	100.0

The Conservative Party did poorly because Mario Cuomo had co-opted their message and carried the traditional conservative neighborhoods of Ridgewood, Long Island City, Astoria, Woodside, Middle Village, Richmond Hill, South Ozone Park, Douglaston, Bayside, and Queens Village – all in his home borough, Queens County.

In the long-time Conservative bastion of Staten Island, Cuomo received 61 percent of the vote. In Brooklyn, he carried the ethnic neighborhoods of Greenpoint, Boro Park, Park Slope, Bay Ridge, Bath Beach, Bensonhurst, and Sheepshead Bay. In fact, Cuomo's Neighborhood Preservation Party actually received more votes than were cast on Row B and Row C. Bad as Farber did, however, he nearly outpolled Republican Goodman.

It is interesting to note that Conservative Mike McSherry, the comptroller candidate, received a significantly higher vote total – 70,193 – than did Farber. Mike Long related that the night before the party convention that nominated the 1977 citywide ticket, the five county leaders met with Dan Mahoney until 1 o'clock in the morning trying to come up with a comptroller candidate. When the meeting finally broke up, Long, Staten Island leader Jim Molinaro, George McGuinness of the Bronx, Manhattan's John Denehy, and Serf Maltese were standing on the sidewalk discussing their dilemma.

The name of saloon proprietor Mike McSherry of the Bronx, came up and all agreed he would be a suitable candidate. George McGuinness made the call at 1:15 A.M., and the suddenly awakened McSherry agreed to meet them at 2:00 A.M. at his bar, The Fireside, on 35th Street and Third Avenue. After a few cocktails, McSherry agreed to be their candidate. "Compared to the Farber campaign," Long said, "McSherry spent very little money, but he got the most votes on our ticket that year." All was not bleak in the election aftermath. Farber had come within 2,000 votes of outpolling the Republican candidate, and for the first time a councilman-at-large, Vincent Riccio of Brooklyn, was elected on the Conservative Party line.

The party provided the margin of victory in Patrick Henry's victory over Democratic incumbent Henry O'Brien in the race for Suffolk County district attorney. And in the state's second largest city, Buffalo, State Senator James Griffin was elected mayor on the Conservative line. Griffin, who had been serving as a Democratic-Conservative state senator since 1967, had lost by 1 percent in the September Democratic primary to Assemblyman Arthur O. Eve who, according to *The New York Times*, "sought to be the first black mayor of a major city in New York State."[57]

Senator Griffin, who already had the Conservative nod, decided to make a serious run in the fall election and his efforts paid off:

James Griffin, Cons.	53,365	42.3%
Arthur Eve, Dem.	39,976	31.7%
John Phelan, Rep.	32,634	26.0%

Finally, the state party came out strongly against a $750-million boondoggle economic-action bond proposed by Governor Carey. The bond went down big time with 1,468,128 (60 percent) against to 988,899 (40 percent) in favor.

The 1978 Disaster

As soon as the 1977 election results were tabulated, the Conservatives turned their attention to the upcoming 1978 gubernatorial race.

While it is fair to say that early in his term Hugh Carey had saved the city and the state from financial bankruptcy, by 1978 many voters had come to see him as a facetious and disinterested person, a man who had little time for his job and spent too much time in Upper East Side public houses. Carey's sharp Irish wit was not always appreciated. When he had a chance to review the state's financial condition, for instance, most people didn't appreciate the black humor of his remark: "I'm here to get the hangover. Someone else drank the champagne."[58] When a fire in a Binghamton State Office Building caused carcinogenic PCBs to be released, Carey's offhand reaction, "I'll walk into Binghamton into any part of that building and swallow an entire glass of P.C.B. and walk a mile afterwards," caused the *Binghamton Sun* to run the headline: "Carey's Gone Cracker Dog."[59] The *Albany Times Union* reported in October 1977 that "Governor Carey's close associates are fearful that his flip-flops on issues and failure to stay abreast of events and flippant remarks may lead to his downfall in the heat of his re-election campaign next year."[60]

Dan Mahoney and Serf Maltese had crossed swords frequently with Carey, particularly over his support of state funding of abortions and his opposition to the death penalty. On March 30, 1978, when legislative leaders recommended approval of a nearly $12-billion budget, it was held up by Conservative Party pressure to delete money allocated for abortion funding. Carey, angry that the budget would not reach his desk by the time the new fiscal year began on April 1, blamed the party for "stirring up the abortion and death penalty issues for political purposes."[61] Continuing his assault, he said that "an awful lot of the momentum and steam on the abortion issue was coming from Conservative Party leader Serphin Maltese . . . [who] was threatening legislators' Conservative endorsements to get political mileage."[62] And this, Carey noted, Maltese and the Conservatives were doing "with all the political relish they can muster."[63] Carey said he believed the pressure from the Conservatives was aimed at "total domination of the Republican Party and then of the State of New York."[64]

The budget line item for Medicaid funding of abortions was later voted upon successfully as a separate measure. Nevertheless, Carey's tantrum proved that the party did indeed have clout in Albany.

The party's visibility in these clashes coupled with Carey's vulnerability led Mahoney to believe that the governor could be beaten in 1978. When Congressman Jack Kemp told Erie County Conservative Party Chairman George Vossler (who had started a "Draft Kemp" movement) that he was not interested in seeking the post in 1978, it made inevitable the candidacy of Assembly Minority Leader Perry B. Duryea, Jr.

Duryea had arrived in Albany in 1961 and when the Republicans regained a majority in the assembly in 1969, he was elected speaker.

Duryea, who grew up on eastern Long Island and had made his fortune in the lobster-farming-and-distribution business, was known for his ambition to be governor. Writing in *New York* magazine, Jon Margolis observed that Duryea fit the part: "He has the silvery hair, classic features, and ramrod bearing of an aristocrat. He is at ease with chairmen of boards and presidents of banks."[65] But Margolis also raised an important question that troubled Conservatives: "Does he actually believe in anything else besides winning?"

Duryea tried to get on the tax-cutting bandwagon (particularly after Californians voted overwhelmingly in June 1978 for Proposition 13 that put a cap on property taxes), but the record showed that he had voted for most of the Rockefeller tax increases during the sixties. And it was Duryea who had cast the deciding vote for the 1970 bill that liberalized New York abortions, and he had later flip-flopped on the question of Medicaid funding of abortion. In 1978 he cast a vote opposing cuts in abortion funding, then changed his position in another vote after Maltese pointed out the earlier vote could jeopardize his chances of getting Row C.[66] When the decriminalization of marijuana came up, he skipped most of the debate and voted "no," but several days later when the bill came up for another vote, this time slightly amended, he voted "yes."

Viewing his record, one Republican official said: "It's okay for a guy to be ambitious but toward what end? Self-advancement, yes. Winning, yes. But for most of us there's something else to it. For Perry, I'm not sure there is." When asked bluntly why he should be governor, Duryea gave the old elitist progressive Republican reply of the Dewey years: "I can run a more efficient, effective administration."[67] Duryea also had one other problem as a candidate: he came across as a "cold fish." This was a man who lacked the common touch.

But the Conservative Party thought he was a probable winner, and at their June 17, 1978 convention at the Hotel Roosevelt in Manhattan, Duryea received Conservative endorsement. Nervous though many were, the Conservatives were at least happy that Duryea chose as his running mate the man who had been guest speaker at the party's 1977 annual dinner, Congressman Bruce Caputo of Westchester. Not all Conservatives were pleased of course. To many, Duryea bore responsibility for the 1970 abortion law, and they would not hold their noses and support him the top of their ticket. Looking back on the events of 1978, Mike Long admitted "the only thing the Conservative Party accomplished was to help create the Right to Life Party. . . . We lost large numbers of former Democrats who were pro-life."[68] In fact, when the newly formed Right to Life Party nominated Mary Jane Tobin of Merrick, Long Island, as their gubernatorial candidate, Liberal Party Executive Director James

Notaro observed: "The Right to Life Party has a gubernatorial candidate and if she gets 20,000 to 25,000 votes at the Conservative expense, we got a shot at regaining Row C."[69]

The Duryea campaign never got off the ground. Serf Maltese blames a lot of the problems on the incompetence of the campaign staff. With Rockefeller no longer writing the checks, the Duryea crowd did not know how to raise money. "Also," Serf continued, "Perry never ran outside of his home neighborhood of Montauk and did not know how to run in 'the big leagues.'"[70]

Although there were plenty of inconsistencies to go after in the Carey record, Carey bested Duryea in debates. By the end of the campaign, Carey looked like the big tax cutter, and even though Carey was against the death penalty and Duryea had the endorsement of the NYPD police union, the governor came across as tougher on crime.

Carey started the campaign twenty points behind in the polls, but then hit Duryea hard in their thirteen debates, especially on Duryea's refusal to release his personal income tax records. Accused of using tax shelters and other gimmicks to pay less tax than he actually owed, Duryea denied any wrongdoing but refused to release any returns except the most recent. Even Duryea's campaign consultant, John Deardourff, admitted that "a fundamental mistake was failing to deal with the personal finance issue early on. . . . It's our sermon to all candidates in the post-Watergate era to face up to the personal finances issue early on. I was never listened to on this one."[71] Mike Long agrees: "Duryea lost credibility carrying around a briefcase that contained his taxes. He told everyone they were in the case, but he didn't show them to anyone. It was an important reason why he lost to Carey."[72]

On November 4, 1978, Hugh Carey bucked a national trend and while five Democratic governors lost, he became the first Democratic governor of New York to be re-elected in forty years:

	Carey Dem.	Duryea Rep.	Duryea Cons.	Carey Lib.	Tobin R. to L.
Upstate New York	1,423,036	1,533,770	175,148	53,482	108,150
Bronx	137,934	54,002	9,142	9,595	3,148
Brooklyn	252,725	106,158	18,203	21,540	6,095
Manhattan	204,761	60,609	7,247	20,198	2,296
Queens	251,043	131,162	25,659	16,655	8,368
Staten Island	36,316	27,731	7,573	1,987	2,136
Total New York City	882,779	379,662	67,824	69,975	22,043
Total State	2,305,815	1,913,432	242,972	123,457	130,193

As if the Duryea fiasco wasn't bad enough, the Conservative Party had to swallow the fact that other, disgruntled conservatives, the ones who founded the Right to

Life Party, had managed to break the 50,000 vote mark in their first try. They became a permanent party, outpolled the Liberals, and gained Row D. Mary Jane Tobin outpolled Duryea's Conservative numbers in Albany, Erie, Clinton, Lewis, and Oneida counties.

But there were several pleasant surprises: Erie's County Executive Ned Regan, in his second try for comptroller, beat back Democrat Harrison Goldin. Elected by a slim margin in 1965 as Buffalo's councilman-at-large, Regan, an Irish-Catholic, was tapped by Rockefeller in 1970 to be the sacrificial lamb against Comptroller Arthur Levitt. In 1971, Regan was elected county executive and re-elected in 1975. Although Regan fully expected to run ahead of Duryea, at best he expected only a "moral victory" over his opponent, New York City's comptroller, Harrison Goldin. But Regan was running this time with Conservative Party support. But then, in the campaign's closing days, Regan received help from an unexpected corner: retiring Comptroller Arthur Levitt, for decades the state's fiscal watchdog, endorsed Regan, saying he had "the character and the integrity to be the next comptroller." This move gave numerous Democrats, who disliked the obnoxious Goldin, an excuse to vote for Regan. The Levitt endorsement (which was negotiated by Dan Mahoney) plus the Conservative Party endorsement, made the difference in his second run for comptroller:

	Goldin Dem.	Regan Rep.	Regan Cons.	Goldin Lib.
Outside New York City	**1,191,111**	**1,664,198**	**209,244**	**55,501**
Bronx	128,845	45,006	9,700	9,337
Brooklyn	248,080	84,546	18,484	21,315
Manhattan	182,795	64,083	8,332	19,160
Queens	237,518	119,177	30,161	17,221
Staten Island	35,730	25,168	8,786	2,188
Total New York City	**832,968**	**337,980**	**75,463**	**69,221**
Total State	**2,024,079**	**2,002,178**	**284,707**	**124,722**

In eastern Long Island's First Congressional District, William Carney received 57 percent of the vote and became the first member of the Conservative Party to be elected to the House. Carney, who took over the seat held by Democrat Otis Pike for 18 years, told his constituents, "I will absolutely not change my enrollment. I believe the distinction of being an enrolled Conservative will prove to be an advantage in the long run."

Assemblyman Gerald Solomon (R-C), who took on Congressman Edward Pattison in the upstate Twenty-Ninth Congressional District, learned from the experience of 1976 loser Joseph Martino, who had declined Row C. This dedicated conservative went on to beat the liberal incumbent with 54 percent of the vote.

In Queens, Assemblyman Al Della Bovi, a founder of the influential national alliance of conservative legislators known as ALEC (American Legislative Exchange Council), lost in the race to succeed Congressman James Delancy. His opponent, who spent the then huge sum of $382,000, was Geraldine Ferraro, who got her start in Queens politics by being appointed as assistant district attorney by her cousin, Queens D.A. Nick Ferraro.

Helping to Launch the Reagan Revolution

After five years of statewide setbacks, Dan Mahoney and Serf Maltese decided to get back to basics. In 1979, they began to organize in anticipation of the 1980 presidential and U.S. Senate races. At the party's seventeenth annual dinner in June, Maltese said of his guest speaker, Congressman Jack Kemp, "all we would need to make [the dinner] a political success is for Jack Kemp to announce his candidacy for the U.S. Senate."[73]

A Conservative Party poll of leaders revealed strong support for Ronald Reagan. At its October 23, 1979, state committee meeting, a unanimous resolution was adopted to endorse Reagan and to endorse the participation of Dan Mahoney in appropriate Reagan for President Committees and activities. Dan Mahoney, along with Jack Kemp, Bruce Caputo, William Casey, Gerald Solomon, Guy Molinari, Genevieve Sanchez Klein, and numerous state legislators formed the nucleus of New York's members of the national Reagan for President Committee. During the late sixties and early seventies, Richard Nixon forged the realignment of northern blue-collar ethnics, southern whites, and midwestern farmers. That portion of Franklin Roosevelt's coalition that remained in the Democratic Party – the left-wing element – ran the 1972 convention that had given America George McGovern.

Chairman Mahoney introducing Ronald Reagan. Sitting to Reagan's right, Ned Regan, and to Mahoney's left, Senator Buckley.

Even with the overwhelming 1972 defeat of the so-called counterculture, the Left continued to maintain control of the Democratic Party. These "social engineers" pursued a program that Theodore H. White described as "not equality of opportunity, but equality of result stipulated in goals, quotas, and entitlements, based not on excellence or merit, but on bloodlines."[74] To promote their agenda, they adopted the caucus system, which spawned the Lesbian-Gay Caucus, Asian-Pacific Caucus, Black Caucus, Women's Caucus, and the Liberal-Progressive Caucus. Rejected was the "All-American Caucus," which would have consisted of white males.

The Watergate scandal stalled for four years what Kevin Phillips has called the "Emerging Republican Majority." But when Jimmy Carter, who was perceived as a new kind of centrist Democrat, attempted to blame his shortcomings on "America's malaise," Middle America turned on him. In analyst Michael Barone's view, Carter was rejected in 1980 because "the cultural segment of America which was emotionally most inclined to see Jimmy Carter as its kind of American had decided he was not; its members felt at the least disappointed, and in some cases betrayed."[75]

By running on a platform that pledged to restore America's traditional morals at home and its strength and respect abroad, and that pledged to reject redistributive politics at home, Ronald Reagan cemented Richard Nixon's coalition. Richard Darman best describes the voters that found Reagan appealing. They were, he wrote:

> people who were not poor but who were often lower-middle class or working class. They were people with just enough money to stick their heads up, look around, and feel certain feelings. They were people who always thought someone or something was keeping them from getting ahead, from achieving in some way. They were resentful. It is partly a resentful movement. But they were also hopeful. They believed in America and the American dream; they came from people who packed up in Europe or wherever and took a dangerous journey across the ocean, often alone, in search of a better life. That is not the action of someone who is demoralized or driven into helplessness by circumstances. It is a profoundly hopeful act.[76]

Ronald Reagan, a former Democrat who portrayed himself as the antithesis of cultural liberalism, described the transformation that took place in New York and the national political structure during the sixties and seventies:

> The secret is that when the Left took over the Democratic Party we took over the Republican Party. We made the Republican Party into the Party of the working people, the family, the neighborhood, the defense of freedom, and yes, the American Flag and the Pledge of Allegiance to one Nation under God. So, you see, the Party that so many of us grew up with still exists except that today it's called the Republican Party.[77]

For years Ronald Reagan had been the star for rank-and-file members of the Conservative Party. Reagan was a featured speaker at gatherings from Maine to his home state, California, including the New York Conservative Party's 1975 state dinner, at which he received the party's highest honor, the Charles Edison Memorial Award.

The Conservative Party's Reagan enthusiasts may have been barred from running as delegates, just as they had been for Goldwater in 1964, but that did not stop them from helping elect Republican delegates pledged to Reagan.

In Syracuse, party activists Tom and Viola Hunter, sensing that the local Republican organization was going to go with uncommitted delegates as they had in 1976, called Reagan's California office and were encouraged to assemble Reagan slates.

The Hunters turned their downtown Syracuse office into Reagan headquarters. With the help of Conservative Party volunteers Jim Brewster, Ian Hunter, Glen Holden, Michelle and Bernie Miller, Allison Jarvis, Dick and Clara Carpenter, and Paul and Joan Bertan, they put together Reagan slates in the surrounding congressional districts.

Realizing the Hunter efforts were serious, the twenty-seven-year old political genius, Lee Atwater, arrived in Syracuse and camped out in Hunter's office for the two weeks before primary day. Adam Clymer, of *The New York Times*, interviewed Atwater in Hunter's office and he filed a March 23, 1980, front page story titled: "Delegates Shifting To Reagan Support: Upstate Primary Reflects Decline in Republican Competition." Clymer related:

> Those who were for Mr. Reagan from the beginning included some long-time supporters like Thomas Hunter, a magazine dealer here, and Frank Armani, a lawyer. Disappointed four years ago when Mr. Reagan got only 20 votes from New York's then 153-member delegation and barely lost the nomination, they called the Californian's headquarters when he announced his candidacy last November and offered to put up a slate for him. . . .
>
> They started campaigning early this month with paid telephone canvassers but soon enlisted enough supporters to make the callers all volunteers. In the last few days, Lee Atwater, who ran Mr. Reagan's successful South Carolina campaign, has come up to aid the organization.

Ronald Reagan, following Atwater's advice, flew into Syracuse in March to campaign, and he stayed at the home of Reagan delegate candidate, Dr. Patrick J. Buttarazzi, an Auburn, New York surgeon.

After he won the delegate primary with over 60 percent of the vote, Reagan wrote this note to Tom and Viola Hunter:

> Our victory in the New York State primary was a most gratifying one.

Besides the fact that it is the largest Reagan delegation thus far, the 40 delegates won out of 40 races contested were achieved with long and dedicated hours of work. As an organizer in your area, you gave that extra effort to make it succeed, and I am truly grateful.

I look forward to working with you in the campaign in the fall and repeating our victory in November.

The state race that became the main target of Conservatives in 1980 was for the senate seat held by Jacob Javits. Many believed that the right candidate could knock off the twenty-four-year incumbent in a Republican primary.

In the fall of 1979, Dan Mahoney and Serphin Maltese founded the Committee to Retire Jacob Javits. In a letter to potential supporters, Dan Mahoney reminded them:

> Javits has been the *leading liberal* among Senate Republicans. He has been wrong on all the key issues: taxes and spending, SALT, the Panama Canal, busing, Taiwan, welfare, abortion – you name the issue, Javits votes the liberal line. That's why the Liberal Party of New York has endorsed Javits in his last two Senate races and will endorse him again in 1980. That's why the ultra-liberal Americans for Democratic Action gives his voting record an extremely favorable 75 percent rating, the highest of any Republican Senator, while the American Conservative Union rates him a miserable 9 percent.
>
> This year, we have the chance of a lifetime to stop Javits in his tracks. With Nelson Rockefeller gone, and the New York Republican Party no longer under his strong liberal control, Javits can be challenged in a Republican primary by a candidate backed by the Conservative Party.
>
> Javits is completely vulnerable to this challenge. He has never faced a Republican primary. He will be seventy-six years old next May. He can be taken.[78]

On January 15, 1980, when Ronald Reagan attended a Manhattan Conservative Party fundraiser at Regine's on Park Avenue and 59th Street, most of the chatter among the 200 guests was about the upcoming senate race. Would Senator Javits retire? If not, would a strong candidate have the guts to challenge him in a primary? At this time, four people had a serious interest in taking over the seat: Congressman Jack Kemp, Bruce Caputo of Westchester, investment banker John Loeb, Jr., and the Town of Hempstead's presiding supervisor, Alfonse D'Amato.

Jack Kemp wanted the nomination if Javits didn't run. But Maltese recalls that Kemp did *not* want to upset the Republican establishment by entering a primary. "He wanted," Maltese says, "to be crowned."[79]

The thirty-six-year-old Bruce Caputo, who gave up his congressional seat to run unsuccessfully for lieutenant-governor in 1978, was working the state and was willing to enter a primary. Caputo had lined up the support of Conservative Party county chairmen George McGuinness of the Bronx, Mike Long of Brooklyn, and Leo Kesselring of Monroe County. According to Mike Long, "My good friend George McGuinness asked me to support Caputo, and I agreed. Later on, after I spent time with D'Amato, I realized in my heart I really liked Al, but I stayed with Caputo because I gave my word."[80]

While Kemp was waiting on Javits to decide if he was running again, D'Amato was traveling the state meeting Conservative Party leaders. "More often than not," D'Amato recalled, "this involved informal meetings in restaurants or taverns where we would drink and tell stories until midnight to assure all concerned that I was a regular guy who could be trusted."[81]

Serf Maltese first heard about D'Amato's desire to run from Al's brother, Assemblyman Armand D'Amato. Serf agreed to meet the presiding Supervisor out in Hempstead. "When I arrived, I thought I was at the palace of a potentate. Motorcycle cops greeted me at the gate with a salute." According to Maltese, D'Amato told him that he would be re-elected Town Supervisor that November [1979] by a large margin and that he wanted to be a U.S. Senator. "D'Amato was brash and he gave me chapter and verse on the resources he could get to run."[82] Mike Long also got the potentate treatment in Hempstead, but he recalls being dismissed when he said he had given his word to Caputo and would not break it."[83] But Mike did walk out of the audience liking the tenacious and sometimes obnoxious D'Amato, and he learned in 1980 that D'Amato remembers grudges. "He didn't talk to me his first four years in office," Long laughs.

Maltese set up a dinner for Al to meet Dan and Kathleen Mahoney at an Italian restaurant. D'Amato later recalled that at the end of the evening, Dan took him aside and told him "how he had dreaded coming to meet this eager local politician. He was afraid I was going to bore him to death with war stories. Instead, we told jokes and I played the piano till three o'clock in the morning. We wound up closing the place."[84]

In a 1999 interview, Maltese said that Dan and Kathleen were leaning toward Caputo but after that dinner they took a strong liking for Al.

To have a maximum impact on that 1980 Senate race, Maltese came up with the idea of holding a pre-convention in early March. Mahoney liked the idea, because even though it would be non-binding, it would give everyone the opportunity to speak out for his candidate and afterwards they could all unite around the winner. This was essential if the Conservative Party tail was to wag the Republican Party dog.

On the eve of the pre-convention, Jack Kemp asked Maltese to put off the meeting, since Javits had not yet declared his intentions. The request was rejected, and the March 22, 1980, state committee meeting, held at the run-down Diplomat Hotel in Manhattan, was described as the "most hard fought, well-informed and best attended in memory."[85] After eight hours of parliamentary maneuvering by both sides, D'Amato won the Conservative Party designation by a weighted vote (based on the Conservative Party gubernatorial vote total in 1978 of 242,972):

D'Amato	155,877
Caputo	80,587
Egan	1,048

Shawn Marie Levine, future executive director of the party, recalls how impressed she was when immediately prior to the official announcement of the vote, Caputo's most vocal supporter, Mike Long, graciously switched Brooklyn's 18,000 votes and called for party unity in backing D'Amato. "Mike was a real man in defeat; he didn't go off and sulk," she said.[86]

Chairman Mahoney explained to the media that although the endorsement was three months premature, the party's actions that day were "a moral commitment to reaffirm the endorsement at the official designating meeting in mid-June."[87]

Long Island's *Newsday* viewed the party's actions this way:

> That endorsement of D'Amato is expected to be a major piece of ammu-
> nition in a bid by his Republican supporters, particularly the county lead-
> ers of Nassau and Suffolk, to qualify him to oppose Javits in the GOP's
> Sept. 9 primary. Without question, the Conservative endorsement amounts
> to a major psychological boost. If D'Amato does not get 25 percent of the
> GOP state committee vote in early June, he would be forced to undertake
> the time-consuming and expensive job of collecting the signatures of
> enrolled Republicans on petitions. Now, thanks to the Queens Conserva-
> tives, D'Amato's job, although still difficult, may be within his power.[88]

At the June 6 meeting of the Republican State Committee, D'Amato received 35 percent of the vote, more than enough to get him on the primary ballot.

In the primary battle, D'Amato stressed that Javits did "not represent the main-stream of thinking of the people of this state, let alone Republicans." He also pointed out that at 76, "Javits' age and illness may affect his ability to do his job." On Tuesday, September 6, New York Republicans told the last of the Dewey progressives that he was through.

	D'Amato	Javits
City		
Bronx	4,887	3,492
Brooklyn	11,762	7,548
Manhattan	6,336	14,453
Queens	16,740	10,940
Staten Island	4,208	2,362
City Totals	43,933	38,795

	D'Amato	Javits
Suburbs		
Nassau	71,485	25,485
Rockland	4,220	2,935
Suffolk	30,379	13,508
Westchester	15,852	17,214
Suburban Totals	121,936	59,142
Upstate		
All Others	150,542	148,944
Total	**316,411**	**246,881**

Al D'Amato won the primary with 56.2 percent of the vote.

In the Democratic primary, super-liberal Congresswoman Elizabeth Holtzman of Brooklyn beat media favorites Bess Myerson and John Lindsay. The fall line up had the makings of a 1970 Jim Buckley replay, with Al D'Amato appearing on the Republican, Conservative, and Right-to-Life lines, Holtzman on the Democratic line, and Senator Javits, on the Liberal line. Javits insisted on running, saying he was now seeking a middle-of-the-road coalition.[89]

On Monday, September 15, 1980, in the grand ballroom of Manhattan's Doral Inn, the Conservative Party nominated "a man of compassion, of strength, of conservative traditional values," Ronald Wilson Reagan.[90] Vice-presidential candidate, George Bush, told the party's state committee:

> Our country faces unprecedented danger with the economy out of control here at home and a literally rudderless, directionless foreign policy.
>
> Our job in the remaining days of this campaign is to make certain that Americans are awake to these dangers.
>
> Governor Reagan and I intend to go forward carrying our message to the American people, a message not only of danger but of hope.[91]

After Bill Buckley, Friends of the Conservative Party chairman, William E. Simon, and Al D'Amato had each addressed the convention, the press asked Mr. Bush how he felt about supporting D'Amato over so senior a Republican as Sen. Jacob Javits. Bush said: "D'Amato is the man of our party and I'm a party person. I respect Sen. Javits, but if you're like I am, you have no option."[92]

With liberals fighting for their political lives, the fall campaign was raucous throughout the state with several interesting congressional battles.

In Brooklyn's Fifteenth Congressional District, Brooklyn Chairman Mike Long and his executive committee withdrew the party's endorsement of incumbent Democratic Congressman Leo Zeferetti.

Long explained why:

It would have been easier for us to stand by Mr. Zeferetti, the incumbent. But, after carefully reviewing Mr. Zeferetti's Congressional record and hearing him (Zeferetti appeared before the Executive Committee on January 20, 1980) defend such unsound policies as deficit spending which leads to inflation, we reached the conclusion that it is our civic duty to inform Mr. Zeferetti's constituents that their Congressman has not fulfilled his promises.

Instead of fighting inflation and supporting America's allies, Mr. Zeferetti's record shows that he repeatedly voted contrary to the best interests of his community and his country.[93]

Zeferetti also committed the grievous offense of supporting his surrender of the Panama Canal.

The Fifteenth District, which primarily covers Bay Ridge, Brooklyn, was described by analyst Michael Barone this way:

Bay Ridge is a couple of steps up the ladder for middle-class Brooklynites of Irish and Italian ancestry. It has some impressive housing, but much of it looks like Tony Manero's neighborhood in *Saturday Night Fever*. Bay Ridge is thus not the highest-income neighborhood in Brooklyn, but it is politically the most conservative. People here take their cues from the *Daily News*, not the *Times* nor the *Wall Street Journal*. In most elections, this is the most reliably Republican part of New York City. It is also an area whose mores and cultural attitudes have traditionally been conservative and hostile to Manhattan's. Indeed such attitudes were of cardinal importance throughout the 15th district in the late 1960s and early 1970s and have moved the entire district closer to the Republican column in many elections.[94]

The Conservative Party threw its support behind a thirty-year-old Conservative named Paul Atanasio, a former Marine captain, lawyer, and investment banker who also beat Zeferetti in the Right-to-Life primary. Long lined up strong support for Atanasio both locally and nationally. House Republican Leader John Rhodes, Congressman Jack Kemp, and former Treasury Secretary William E. Simon all endorsed and campaigned for Atanasio.

But Atanasio's campaign was hurt when Zeferetti made an issue of a campaign letter ostensibly signed by Congressman Henry Hyde. Zeferetti complained to postal officials that the signature was bogus. Indeed, Hyde had not actually signed the letter, but Mike Long explained to the media that he had been authorized to sign Hyde's name by a high Republican official. It was true, but the damage was done. Congressman Zeferetti squeaked by, receiving 49,684 votes (50 percent) to Atanasio's 46,467 (47 percent).

In the 17th Congressional District (Staten Island), the Conservative Party provided the margin of victory for Assemblyman Guy Molinari, who beat eighteen-year Democratic incumbent John M. Murphy. And in the Nassau-Queens Sixth Congressional District, twenty-seven-year-old John LeBoutillier raised a half million dollars

Right to left: Serf Maltese, Chairman Mahoney, Lewis Lehrman, Paul Atanasio, Mike Long (1980).

and beat eight-term incumbent Lester Wolf. The 11,299 votes LeBoutillier received on Row C provided his margin of victory. In Suffolk County's Third Congressional District, Gregory Carmen, in his second try for the office, beat incumbent Jerome Ambro in a squeaker, thanks again to the votes he received on Row C.

On election night Conservatives were jubilant. Nationally, Ronald Reagan decisively beat Carter, and thanks to the Conservative endorsement, Reagan managed to carry New York. And Al D'Amato did pull off a "Jim Buckley." In a three-way race he won with 45 percent of the vote.

	Holtzman Dem.	D'Amato Rep.	D'Amato Cons.	D'Amato R. to L.	Javits Lib.
Outside NYC	**1,552,873**	**1,806,816**	**205,505**	**118,373**	**455,813**
Bronx	158,543	62,651	9,236	4,715	25,915
Brooklyn	295,406	127,936	16,979	8,950	51,896
Manhattan	296,815	55,765	6,525	3,395	63,217
Queens	277,469	171,077	27,497	12,681	58,651
Staten Island	37,555	47,837	9,358	4,356	9,052
Total New York City	**1,065,788**	**465,266**	**69,595**	**34,097**	**208,731**
Total State	**2,618,661**	**2,272,082**	**275,100**	**152,470**	**664,544**

Without the conservative vote, split between the Conservative Party and the Right-to-Life Party, D'Amato would not have defeated Miss Holtzman, who was not exactly gracious in defeat. She refused to concede, and for hours held up recognizing

D'Amato's victory while her aides sought a court order impounding all paper ballots used statewide. It wasn't just the narrowest of narrow margins (barely 1 percent) that frustrated Miss Holtzman, it was also her sense of entitlement: She was a liberal; New York is a liberal state; therefore she deserved to win!

The Conservative Party of New York State hailed the election of Governor Ronald Reagan, together with Republican control of the United States Senate, as "marking a historic turn for America."

Daniel Mahoney, also called the election of Alfonse D'Amato to the United States Senate "a major breakthrough for common-sense government in New York that will provide unprecedented New York support in the United States Senate for the incoming Reagan administration."[95]

In other races, of the sixty victorious state senators, twenty-five of the thirty-one Republicans were Conservative Party endorsed and two were Democrat-Conservatives.

The Conservative Party endorsed fifty-five of the sixty-four victorious Republican assemblymen including four who beat Democratic incumbents: Douglas W. Prescott (R-C, 25th A.D.), Thomas P. Morahan (R-C, 96th A.D.), Dale E. Rath (R-C, 133rd A.D.) and Carol A. Siwek (R-C, 142nd A.D). There were four new Republican-Conservatives. Assemblymen who won in seats formerly held by Republicans, and eight winning Democratic-Conservative assemblymen.

Viewing the political landscape, *The New York Times* had to admit: "Stage Set for Shift of G.O.P. Power in New York State." After eighteen years of effort, the Conservatives had finally driven from office the last of the Rockefeller Republicans.

Columnist William Safire explained the results in his post-election column: "Like a great soaking wet, shaggy dog, the Silent Majority – banished from the house during the Watergate storms – romped back into the nation's parlor this week and shook itself vigorously."[96]

Chapter 11

The Wilderness Years
1981–1988

In November 1980, it had become obvious to political analysts that the Republican Party of Tom Dewey and Nelson Rockefeller was a dead volcano – dormant anyway. The D'Amato challenge had proved that old-line Republican insiders, who for generations had considered themselves political wizards, were little more than windbags without Rocky's bankroll. As 1981 began, New York's Republican Party was intellectually and financially bankrupt, and this was most evident in New York City.

For four years, Mayor Ed Koch had charmed his city. His frequent shout – "How'm I doing?" – to citizens on street corners or along parade routes was downright endearing. Elected in 1977, Koch had run on the slogan, "After eight years of Charisma [John Lindsay] and four years of the Clubhouse [Abe Beame], why not try Competence?" He viewed himself as a "liberal with sanity," and a lot of the time he seemed to have his feet pretty firmly on the ground.

Thanks to his gutsy approach in handling government finances and his receptiveness to Reaganomics, the city was operating in the black, and throughout the remainder of the decade it experienced an unprecedented economic boom. Koch was not afraid to confess his past political sins, as when he admitted:

> I have publicly stated and referred to myself as "Mayor Culpa" for having voted for programs in the Congress which added to the city spending. I neither knew nor cared at the time how those wonderful programs would be paid for and by whom. Indeed, I have summed up my responsibility by saying that if I had the power I would punish every member of Congress who participated in those days, and perhaps even today, with some of their mandates imposed on cities, by having them serve one year as mayor.

With the White House and the U.S. Senate in Republican hands and his own standing high among many in both major parties, Mayor Koch decided to be a "fusion" candidate in his bid to win re-election in 1981. In other words, he would seek both the Democratic and Republican Party nominations. With a few exceptions, all the city's Republican leaders were eager to support Koch, since to the victor – and his cronies – belong the spoils, even if that meant a few patronage crumbs.

But there was some dissent among Republicans in Queens. Miffed that the mayor had refused to support a bill restoring the veterans property-tax exemption, Queens Republican Senators Frank Padavan and Martin Knoor, as well as Assemblyman John Flack, expressed opposition to Koch's move on their party, by throwing their support behind Queens Republican-Conservative Assemblyman John Esposito, the Queens Village legislator, who had made headlines in the past year by opposing full value assessment of residential real estate.

Even though most Conservative activists were impressed by the mayor's chutzpah, they could not swallow his views on numerous social and cultural issues, particularly his pro-abortion and pro-homosexual-rights positions. So, when Esposito declared his intention to challenge Koch in the Republican primary, the Conservative Party gave Esposito its endorsement. It was to little avail. Koch crushed Esposito in the primary, receiving 68 percent of the vote. And in November, even though the under-funded Esposito gave it the old college try, he could not come close to stopping the nominee of the two major parties:

Candidate	Number	Percent
Koch		
Democrat	738,288	60.4
Republican	174,334	14.3
Total	912,622	74.6
Barbaro – Unity Party	162,719	13.3
Esposito – Conservative	60,100	4.9
Codd – Liberal	41,718	3.4
Other Candidates	45,489	3.7

The Conservatives licked their wounds and turned their eyes to the 1982 governor's race. With Governor Carey's approval rating at an all time low, they believed a challenge from the Right could prevail.

The Lehrman Campaign

Back in 1977, at a dinner at Gallagher's Steak House, Dan Mahoney, Serf Maltese, Mike Long, and several other key party leaders met with an entrepreneur named Lewis L. Lehrman. A native of Pennsylvania who now lived on Park Avenue, Lehrman told his guests the story of how he had helped build his family company, Rite Aid, into one of the nation's top pharmaceutical retailers, and how, now that he had financial independence, he looked forward to doing something in the political arena. The idea of running for comptroller in 1978 was kicked around, but Lehrman made it clear that, even though he was a political neophyte, he intended to run for governor in 1982. Mike Long recalls that he and Lehrman hit it off that night because: "I was confrontational with him . . . I looked at him and said, 'You mean you're telling us exactly what you are going to do five years from now.' And Lew replied, 'That's exactly what I'm doing.'"[1]

Over the next five years, Lehrman showed up at Conservative Party functions, spoke around the state, and addressed party members at the Albany Conservative-Political Action Conference (C-PAC). On the Republican side, after Lehrman helped the financially strapped party, he was rewarded with the chairmanship of the 1978 platform committee. Lehrman took the job seriously, held hearings all over the state and took advantage of the opportunity to meet as many Republican leaders as possible. Upon reporting the platform to the Republican state committee, he learned an important political lesson. His report was all but ignored, and Lehrman realized, as he put it, that "ideas don't always rule."[2]

After the Perry Duryea disaster, Lehrman spent the next few years staying in touch with Conservative and Republican leaders and bought tickets to and appeared at functions all over the state. And there are a lot of them.

Brooklyn Conservative Party dinner dias (left to right: Frank Taormina, Mike Long, Bill Buckley, Jack Kemp, Jim Gay, Julian Miller (circa 1980).

In late 1981, Lehrman asked then-Brooklyn Chairman and New York City Councilman Mike Long to head up a "Conservatives for Lehrman" committee. "Lew realized that to have real leverage with Republicans, he had to secure Row C," Long said. "He also wanted to head off a Ned Regan candidacy. We assumed correctly that Regan wanted to be crowned. He decided to run for re-election as Comptroller when he realized he'd have to fight for the Governor's nomination."[3]

In early 1982, when Republican State Chairman George Clark tried to steamroll Regan as the choice for governor, the Conservative Party announced that Lehrman was its guy. On January 26, 1982, *The New York Times* reported:

The ingredients of the attempt by "the Conservative tail to wag the Republican dog," as several angry Republican leaders described it in Albany last week, are the total control of the Conservative Party by a handful of leaders, the mutual admiration between the party and Mr. Lehrman, who has been courting its leaders for five years. . . .

The tight control of the party by Mr. Maltese and its state chairman, J. Daniel Mahoney, means that they can get Mr. Lehrman the Conservative nomination while denying any other non-Conservative the chance to challenge Mr. Lehrman in a Conservative primary. Both Conservative leaders said they would not allow Comptroller Regan in their primary.

Under the state's Wilson-Pakula law, party leaders must authorize a nonparty member to enter a primary.

But Republican leaders cannot bar Mr. Lehrman from challenging Mr. Regan in the Republican primary, a primary in which a major issue would almost certainly be Republican charges that the Conservatives are trying to wield undue influence on the Republican party.[4]

Long told the *Times* that over the past five years Lehrman had attended numerous events in Brooklyn and had been a guest speaker at two major party dinners. "Regan was invited to Kings County over the years," Mr. Long said, "but never had the time to be there."[5]

Lew Lehrman was what Republican insiders pejoratively labeled "a true believer." The old-line establishment opposed him because he was devoted to the fundamental principles of conservatism. Sure, his optimistic vision was in tune with Ronald Reagan's – lower taxes and supply-side growth – but New York's Republican hacks saw Lehrman as an outsider, and feared most of all that they would be left out in the cold if he were elected.

At the Republican state convention in 1982, Lehrman became the party's designee, but the old guard managed to muster 25 percent of the delegates for an uninspiring candidate, a former U.S. Attorney named Paul Curran. Curran's convention showing guaranteed him a spot in a Republican primary. The establishment was prepared to go down in flames with Curran rather than risk loss of party control to the likes of Lehrman.

In a series of primary debates, Lehrman and Curran went for each other's jugular veins. In the hottest debate, sponsored by the *Buffalo Courier Express*, Curran attacked Lehrman's character, and Lehrman replied: "When people like Paul Curran talk about character, I think it's time to start counting the silverware."[6] Lehrman criticized Curran's campaign tactics, which had been developed by political consultant, Arthur Finkelstein. Curran's approach, he said, "is designed solely on personal attacks – that's the way Arthur Finkelstein has worked in the past."[7] Pointing to Curran's intellectual bankruptcy, Lehrman said: "There's a time to draw the line when a man is so irresponsible that he'll run for high office of governor without a single idea."[8] Finally, pointing to Curran's "old boy" reputation, Lehrman "accused Curran of having 'two standards of morality' and said 'his principal backer' [Nassau County Republican Chairman Joe Margiotta] is a convicted felon."

It wasn't pretty, but it was effective. On primary day, September 23, 1982, Lehrman flattened his opponent:

Lehrman	464,231	80.6%
Curran	111,814	19.4%

It was another humiliation for the old Rockefeller crowd.

Conservatives also exploited the 25-percent rule. During the Republican convention, Dan Mahoney convinced Lehrman to use his influence with delegates to make sure that the Conservative Party's U.S. Senate candidate, Assemblywoman Florence Sullivan (R-C), got at least 25 percent of the vote so she could enter the Republican Primary. Although it annoyed many establishment Republicans, Lehrman delivered and Florence Sullivan qualified to face Manhattan's Whitney North Seymour and Muriel Siebert.

Sullivan, a lawyer from Bay Ridge, Brooklyn, was elected to the Assembly in 1978. When her seat was eliminated by gerrymandering in 1982, Mike Long and Brooklyn Conservative State Committeemen Allen Roth and Gerard Kassar convinced her to take a shot as the U.S. Senate. In the Republican primary, she faced two liberals: Seymour, a former U.S. attorney who had run for John Lindsay's congressional seat in 1968 and lost to Ed Koch, and Siebert, a former New York State superintendent of banks and the founder of the first women-owned broker-dealer investment company. Mrs. Sullivan was nervous about entering this battle, but campaign managers Roth and Kassar coached her on national issues, and she became confident she could hold her own.

On a shoestring budget (Roth pegs the number at $40,000), Mrs. Sullivan's campaign managed to strike a cord with this simple theme: She was the only Conservative in the race. Allen Roth remembers witnessing a Siebert temper tantrum after she read the Sullivan brochure labeling her as a pro-abortion super-liberal. Florence Sullivan scored a stunning primary victory against her well-financed opponents:

Sullivan	216,486	42.4%
Siebert	157,446	30.8%
Seymour	136,974	26.8%

When Hugh Carey announced in January 1982 that he would not seek a third term, Ed Koch made what he called "an ill-advised and ill-fated decision to enter New York's gubernatorial campaign."[9] In a tough fight, Lieutenant-Governor Mario Cuomo beat Koch 52.3 percent to 47.7 percent. Koch says that Cuomo beat him because many New Yorkers wanted him to continue being their mayor. It didn't help though that Koch had quipped in a *Playboy* interview that "country life," by which he meant life outside the city, was just pickup trucks, women in "gingham dresses," and men in Sears suits. He called the suburbs "sterile" and rural areas a "joke."

The race between Republican-Conservative Lehrman and Democratic-Liberal Cuomo was a classic. Two very bright and intense men who loved to debate, each articulated ideologically opposed visions for New York's fiscal, economic, and cultural future.

The New York Times described Cuomo as an "old liberal committed to using the government to promote, as he likes to put it, 'jobs and justice.' He proclaims such unfashionable words as 'New Deal' and 'Great Society' with pride, for he looks back in his ideals and constituencies not so much to Jimmy Carter as to Hubert Humphrey."[10] Although Cuomo objected to these labels, he preferred to call his approach to government "a kind of government-aided progressive pragmatism," a term first used by political scientists Gerald Benjamin and James Underwood to describe Nelson Rockefeller's approach to governing.[11] In the 1982 campaign, Cuomo opposed capital punishment, supported homosexual rights legislation, and was a proponent of government funding of abortions for the poor.[12]

As lieutenant governor (and later as governor) Cuomo displayed a copy of Holbein's portrait of St. Thomas More (the patron saint of politicians) on his office wall. During the 1982 campaign, the painting came down "because of snide suggestions that the candidate was 'flaunting' his religiosity."[13] Reading about the portrait's removal, the prominent Catholic preacher and scholar, Father George Rutler, had this reaction: "It was not the first time the Saint had his head removed; but while in Tudor times the loss of one's head signaled the end of a career, it has come in these late democratic times to be a requirement for starting one."[14]

Lewis Lehrman, a conservative with libertarian leanings, believed "that the most important issue is establishing the guiding principle that life in New York must be work not welfare."[15] He believed that for the previous decade New York had been losing its economic competitiveness because of high state and local taxes, and he believed that to get New York moving, to create jobs and new business enterprise, an overhaul of the state's tax code was necessary, and he advocated a 40 percent cut in the income tax over the next eight years.

Lehrman was pro-death penalty, pro-tuition tax credits for parochial schools, and against state funding of abortion. To those who accused him of wanting "to turn back the clock," Lehrman answered this way: "It's my critics who want to turn the clock back, who believe the best days are behind us. I'm an optimist. I believe the last three centuries are but a prelude for an American millennium. Mario Cuomo is the true conservative in the race. Better than anybody I know, he represents the politics of the past. . . . If there is a reformer in the campaign, it is I."[16]

The Lehrman campaign was certainly well financed. By election day he had spent $9.6 million versus Cuomo's $4.8 million. Lehrman hired the best talent money could buy, including Reagan pollster Richard Wirthlin and media man Roger Ailes. This team realized that saturating television with the image of Lehrman in his trademark red suspenders was not enough. To win the election they had to persuade blue-collar ethnics, ordinarily conservative voters, to move over to the Lehrman camp. The trouble was these voters viewed Cuomo as "one of us."

Two weeks before election day, when Lehrman was about ten points behind in the polls, his campaign began sending out millions of pieces of direct mail on abortion and the death penalty to neighborhood Catholics. Journalist Ken Auletta recalled, "He [Lehrman] was playing right to the Catholics. . . . I spent the day with Cuomo. He was scared, literally scared that the Lehrman thing would shift the tide and he could lose the race. Clearly it was moving."[17]

Cuomo's October 9, 1982, diary entry reveals that the Lehrman mailings were getting under his skin:

> Apparently the targeted mailing he's sent has gone to all the Irish and Italian surnames in the state. It attacks me – viciously – on "traditional values," crime, abortion and homosexuality. It's especially annoying because I won't have the capacity to answer him pamphlet for pamphlet.[18]

In the final days of the campaign, it appeared that the Lehrman mailings had had the desired effect: the undecided vote had grown to 19 percent by October 26, the rule of thumb being that the undecided vote generally breaks toward the party out of power. The internal tracking polls predicted the election would be a squeaker.

On Election Day, Tuesday, November 2, 1982, voters faced the clearest philosophical choice in recent political history. In the closest election since the 1954 Harriman-Ives race, they chose Mario Cuomo as New York's fifty-second governor.

	Cuomo Dem.	Lehrman Rep.	Lehrman Cons.	Bohner R. to L.	Cuomo Lib.
Upstate New York	1,542,975	1,808,042	171,441	39,105	52,398
Bronx	168,775	51,339	7,351	2,104	7,691
Brooklyn	283,896	118,257	15,085	3,245	12,540
Manhattan	241,478	78,727	6,468	1,898	28,765
Queens	277,732	155,808	22,207	4,456	12,374
Staten Island	44,751	36,568	7,601	1,548	1,838
Total New York City	1,016,632	440,699	58,712	13,251	63,208
Total State	2,559,607	2,248,741	230,153	52,356	115,606
Percentages	49.3%	43.2%	4.4%	1.0%	2.2%

The voter breakdowns revealed some interesting trends. While Cuomo carried the traditional Democratic strongholds of Manhattan, Brooklyn, The Bronx, and Queens, he managed to get 51.1 percent of the vote in the Republican bastion of Staten Island. Italians stuck with Cuomo in that area. But overall, Lehrman's last-minute mailings appeared to pay-off. Statewide he received a majority of the Catholic vote. This was most evident in traditionally Democratic, blue-collar Erie County which Lehrman lost by only 1,200 votes:

Cuomo	178,337	49.8%
Lehrman	177,146	49.5%
Bohner	2,375	0.7%

By contrast, Hugh Carey had received 64 percent of Erie County's vote in 1974 and 52 percent in 1978.

The most interesting results, however, were those in the Republican dominated counties of Nassau and Westchester. Lehrman actually lost Westchester County, with Cuomo receiving 155,393 votes to Lehrman's 148,764. Insiders agree that old-line Westchester Republicans sat on their hands during the election, since they wanted the Cuomo-Del Bello team to win, because if elected Del Bello would have to resign his post as Westchester's county executive, thus clearing the way for Republican Andrew O'Rourke. The Republicans figured they would get more patronage from County Executive O'Rourke than from Governor Lehrman, so they stabbed Lehrman in the back.[19]

Lehrman's poor showing in Nassau County, which boasted the strongest Republican machine in the nation, was even more startling: Lehrman carried the county by a mere 19,000 votes, or 50.8 percent. Why? Well, in 1981, Nassau County's long-time Republican boss, Joseph Margiotta, had been convicted of fraud and extortion. During the campaign, Lehrman had publicly referred to Margiotta as a convicted felon and had refused to appear on the same stage with him at a huge Nassau Republican pep rally. (Margiotta's conviction was appealed and eventually reviewed by the U.S. Supreme Court, which ruled against him. He began a prison sentence in 1983.) Mike Long agrees with other political insiders that word went out to Nassau's Republican County Committee that Lehrman had to be punished for slighting Boss Joe.[20] This becomes even more plausible when you consider that Republican Comptroller Ned Regan carried Nassau with 60.6 percent of the vote.

There was more bad news that election night. Florence Sullivan went down big to incumbent Daniel Moynihan. On a campaign budget of $117 thousand (versus Moynihan's $2.7 million), Sullivan received 1.7 million votes – just 34 percent.

In the New York State Assembly, Republican-Conservative membership continued to decline. In 1973, Conservatives held a majority of eighty; in 1975 it stood at sixty two. And, thanks to re-apportionment, on January 1, 1983, the number of Republican-Conservative legislatures had dwindled to fifty two. In Queens County the entire Republican-Conservative delegation was wiped out in the '82 election:

Doug Prescott, John Esposito, John Flack, and John LoPresto. Florence Sullivan's Brooklyn Assembly seat was eliminated and Assemblyman Guy Velella went down in The Bronx.

The election results of 1982 established the trend for the remainder of the eighties: declining fortunes in the conservative movement.

Serf Maltese failed in his attempt to be elected to the Congressional seat vacated by Geraldine Ferraro after she had been nominated as Walter Mondale's vice-presidential running mate. According to Maltese, he was dining with Al D'Amato when the Ferraro nomination was announced, and the senator talked him into running for the seat. It was believed that Maltese had a good shot at winning until Woodside City Councilman Thomas Manton squeaked through a four-way Democratic Primary. Manton, a former Marine and member of the NYPD, won his council seat with Conservative Party support. He was pro-life, pro-guns, and had voted against the so-called "Gay-Rights Bill."

"Every time we faced one another in debate," said Maltese, "Manton would say 'I can't be that bad, Serf has endorsed me in the past.'" Maltese lost 53 percent to 47 percent.[21]

The only good news in 1984 was that the party helped Ronald Reagan carry New York in his re-election triumph.

Lambs and Lions: Ups and Downs in the Eighties

In 1985, an unknown named Diane McGrath served as the Republican-Conservative sacrificial lamb against Mayor Ed Koch. McGrath received just 8.7 percent of the vote. Liberal Party candidate Carol Bellamy outpolled McGrath with 9.7 percent. But thanks to Conservative Party support, Congressman Guy Molinari's daughter, Susan,

1984 state dinner dias (left to right): William F. Buckley Jr., Vice President George Bush, Daniel Mahoney, Barbara Bush, William Simon, Senator Alfonse D'Amato.

became the first Republican elected to the city council since 1982. In Brooklyn, former councilman-at-large Mike Long lost a hotly contested council race to Democrat incumbent Sal Albanese.

During his first term, President Reagan had appointed former Senator James Buckley to the post of under secretary of state and later moved him into the office of president of Radio Free Europe/Radio Liberty. In October of 1985, it was announced that Buckley would be appointed to the United States Court of Appeals, and many thought at first that he would sit in the New York circuit. He wound up in the District of Columbia instead, because the usual liberal groups began grousing. While both Senators D'Amato and Moynihan agreed that Buckley was right for the job, the liberal New York City Bar Association claimed the former member of the World's Greatest Deliberative Body was, in fact, unqualified. Also, the loud-mouth liberal Republican Senator from Connecticut, Lowell Weicker, joined the chorus, saying that Buckley was not only unqualified, but, as resident of Connecticut, he "had not contributed to building the Republican Party in the state."

Weicker's reasoning was as absurd as it was petty. After Jim Buckley moved back to Connecticut, he had upset the Republican establishment in 1980 by winning a primary race for the United States Senate. Although Buckley lost the race to Chris Dodd, self-righteous liberal Republicans such as Weicker held a grudge against Buckley thereafter.

The U.S. Senate easily approved Jim Buckley for the D.C. Court of Appeals, and the Buckley family later got sweet revenge when Bill led a successful committee to rid Connecticut of Weicker by endorsing the ultimately victorious Democrat, Joe Lieberman.

The 1986 political cycle began on Thursday, January 23, when Vice President George Bush, who was speaking at the Conservative Party's annual dinner, took a shot at comments recently made by Mario Cuomo. *The New York Times*, in a story titled "Bush Accuses Cuomo of Fostering Divisiveness with Bias Compliant," reported that the vice president had "accused Governor Cuomo of 'pitting one American against another' by contending that as an Italian-American, he might be discriminated against as a potential Presidential candidate."[22] Bush was reacting to Cuomo's pained observation that: "If anything could make me change my mind about running for the presidency, it's people talking about 'an Italian can't do it, a Catholic's can't do it.'"[23]

For many in the room, the vice president was trying to look tough because another guest, Congressman Jack Kemp was using the dinner as a forum to hold a rally to boost his 1988 presidential candidacy. Democrat James Griffin (who was re-elected to another term as Buffalo mayor with the support of the Conservative Party) also attended the dinner and was making noises about challenging Cuomo. "Griffin said he would be interested in a statewide campaign against Cuomo if he can gain the backing of the Republican, Conservative and Right to Life parties."[24]

The annual dinner was held early in 1986, because it was the last to be chaired by Dan Mahoney. In late November 1985, President Reagan had nominated the fifty-four-year-old Mahoney for a seat on the U.S. Court of Appeals for the Second Circuit. Dan was to get the seat that Weicker had denied to Jim Buckley earlier in the year.

At the February Conservative Political Action Conference, held in Albany, 150 Party leaders gathered to gossip about the changes that were to take place once Mahoney's nomination was confirmed by the U.S. Senate. Gubernatorial wannabes Jim Griffin and Liberal-Republican Roy Goodman, addressed the faithful, as did Democrat John Dyson. Dyson, the former chairman of the New York Power Authority, was a self-righteous child of privilege known for his obnoxious behavior. He wanted to be state comptroller and was hoping Conservatives would dump incumbent Regan in favor of him. There were rumors circulating around the conference that many party leaders were disgusted that Regan rolled over dead every year for Cuomo by certifying the governor's budget projections. But there were enough Regan loyalists to ensure that Dyson's ambitions were thwarted.

While the Conservatives gathered in Albany may have disagreed over candidates for governor and comptroller in 1986 and for president in 1988, one thing they agreed on was that electing Maltese as state chairman would provide a seamless continuity of leadership.

Maltese, executive director of the party since 1971, was elected chairman of the party in April 1986. He told the media that his main objectives would be to work more closely with the Republican Party and to increase the Conservative Party's visibility in upstate New York. "We've pretty much fulfilled our potential in Long Island," he noted, "and New York City is a tough nut. But upstate, there is great potential for growth and I plan to increase my own visibility up there as well as having state party meetings up there."[25]

To meet these goals, Maltese announced that he was appointing Brooklyn leader Mike Long as executive vice chairman and long-time upstate party activist Anthony Rudmann as executive director to oversee statewide administrative operations.

Tony Rudmann, a graduate of Siena College, became active in the party during its organization in 1962. He formally joined the party in 1963 during its initial legal enrollment period, and he was the first executive director who was never a member of another political party.

Prior to his appointment to the unsalaried position, he served as deputy executive director and regional vice chairman of the party. In his new position, Rudmann continued to serve as a member of the Conservative state executive committee and as a State Committeeman from the Twenty-Third Congressional District.

Locally, Rudmann served as Treasurer of the Albany County Conservative Club. He was a charter member of the club and served as its chairman from June 1981 to January 1986. Originally from Schenectady County, he held a number of positions in the Schenectady Conservative Committee, including city chairman and county first vice chairman. Rudmann and his wife Ann, who were living in Colonie, New York, in 1986, had four boys and two girls ranging in ages from eleven to twenty one.

With Cuomo possessing a re-election war chest of $10 million and voter-approval ratings of 70 percent, the Republicans decided in 1986 to put all their energy into re-electing Al D'Amato and Ned Regan.

Left ro right: Mike Long, Party elder George Vossler, Laura Schreiner, Bill Delmonte, Tony Rudmann.

D'Amato had spent his first term in the U.S. Senate aggressively protecting and promoting New York's interests and establishing a first-class office of constituent relations. He earned the title "Senator Pothole" for his nitty-gritty involvement in local problems. The joke circulating in political circles was, if you want a lecture on immigration go to Moynihan's office, but if you want a green card, call on D'Amato.

On the Democratic side, Mark Green and John Dyson (who had abandoned a run for comptroller) fought it out for the privilege of facing D'Amato in the fall. Cuomo delivered the Liberal Party line to the conservative-leaning Dyson, who went on to spend $6 million in a losing primary bid. Green won decisively, receiving 59 percent of the vote. Al D'Amato best described his fall opponents: "Dyson didn't scare me. Even with his father's millions, he lacked any real gray matter and was no real threat. If it weren't for his father's money, no one would have talked to him."[26] On Mark Green: "[He] attacked me for being Senator Pothole. His tone was elitist and disdainful. . . . Every time Green attacked me for my pothole politics, he lost more votes. . . .

In the end, we buried Mark Green and his negative campaign by 650,000 votes. Even the *New York Times* said: 'If Democrats are unhappy with D'Amato they've kept it well hidden.'"[27]

The Republicans and Conservatives endorsed Westchester's County executive Andrew O'Rourke as the sacrificial lamb against Cuomo. O'Rourke, who had no money to spend, wandered around the state carrying a cardboard likeness of Cuomo demanding debates. O'Rourke's campaign had little effect, except that the governor, who was expected to win a record-breaking victory, came to be perceived publicly and in the media as a "sore winner." Cuomo got a whopping 65 percent of the vote, but political analysts criticized his tactics. Albany reporter Frederick Dicker wrote: "Gov. Cuomo won the battle, but the rough-and-tumble hardball political tactics may have cost him the war as the electoral focus shifts to the 1988 presidential race."[28] In its endorsement of Cuomo, *The New York Times* said Cuomo "acted authoritarian" and showed "a taste for endless intricate contentious argument."[29] Even the very liberal *Village Voice* pointed out the governor was "a 'swaggering pol' whose recent behavior has been 'a disgrace'"[30] Liberal *Daily News* columnist Bill Reel wrote in his October 21, 1986 column: "There is a dark side to Gov. Cuomo that makes him unfit to lead the state. On Election Day in two weeks, voters should take the opportunity to return Cuomo to his old job in Brooklyn: Court St. lawyer. . . . Success ruined Mario Cuomo, a decent guy when he was a Court St. lawyer. Send him back there. Maybe he can redeem himself."[31]

Reviewing Cuomo's campaign behavior, Republican political consultant Roger Ailes said, "This election has shown that Mario Cuomo can't run for national office unless he gets a personality transplant. . . . On his best days Cuomo makes Richard Nixon look like Dale Carnegie."[32]

Comptroller Ned Regan survived the Cuomo landslide, beating Herman Badillo 57 percent to 41 percent. Nassau County Comptroller Peter King lost in his bid to unseat incumbent Attorney General Robert Abrams. King received just 35 percent of the votes cast.

In a 1987 radio interview with SUNY (Potsdam) professor John K. White, Comptroller Ned Regan admitted, "There is no state Republican party – it is dormant. . . . [T]he party has ceded its role as 'loyal opposition.'"[33] This was evident in the 1986 Cuomo race, and the trend continued in 1987 and 1988.

While George Bush was carrying forty states in his successful 1988 bid for the presidency, he lost New York to Michael Dukakis. Mr. Bush, running on both the Republican and Conservatives lines, got just 48 percent of the vote. Republican-Conservative senatorial candidate Robert McMillian, who ran on a paltry budget of $528,000, got creamed by Senator Moynihan, who won with 67 percent of the votes cast. Moynihan managed to carry fifty nine of the state's sixty counties.

One bit of good news in 1988 was the election of Serf Maltese to the state senate seat of the retiring Martin J. Knorr, who had represented the Ridgewood-Glendale-

Middle Village part of Queens for over two decades. The *New York Post* reported that "Democratic voters defected in droves to send Maltese to Albany and [Democratic opponent] Sansivieri back to his teaching job."[34]

Maltese realized he could not simultaneously serve his new constituents and run the Conservative Party, so he decided to step down as state chairman in December 1988. A *New York Times* editorial praised Serf and asked other elected public officials to follow his example.

In late December, the State Executive Committee met at the Backyard Restaurant in Middle Village, Queens and chose Party Executive Vice Chairman Mike Long to succeed Maltese. The *New York Times* described the forty-eight-year-old Long as "more aggressive" and "feisty" and "more inclined to stronger ideological positions than Mr. Maltese." Long told the *Times*, "I tend to lead with my chin."[35]

Chapter 12

True Grit
Mike Long at the Helm

After Mike Long finished his three-year stint in the Marine Corps in 1961, he returned to Brooklyn a fervent anti-Communist, ready to lead the home guard. Mike opened an ice-cream parlor in Cypress Hills – with financial help from his friend John Schmidt – and thought about joining the Knights of Columbus. But that organization was not militant enough for the young Long, and he yearned for a more active role in the life of his neighborhood, his city, his state, and his nation.

By 1962, he had purchased Schmidt's share of the business, and for the next twenty-two years he – and his brother Tom, who joined him as a partner in 1968 – was a leading Cypress Hills entrepreneur. In 1963 he married a neighborhood girl, Eileen Dougherty, and began a family that was to grow to nine children.

Long took his responsibilities as a neighborhood shopkeeper very seriously. He became a community activist and took guff from no one. He would boast in later years that he threw out Tony Danza (later a star of the TV sitcom "Who's the Boss") and other "wiseguys" who disrupted business in the ice-cream parlor. G.K. Chesterton's description of the guardian of the neighborhood in *The Man Who Was Thursday,* fit Mike Long: "He [finds] himself filled with a supernatural courage that came from nowhere. . . . he did not think of himself as the representative of the corps of gentlemen. . . . But he did feel himself as the ambassador of all these common and kindly people in the street."

And Long was an ambassador for the folks in his neighborhood. He went on to become president of the Cypress Hills Businessman's Association, head of the Blessed Sacrament Holy Name Society, a vice president of his parish council, executive secretary of the Cypress Hills Civic Association, an executive member of the Cypress Hills-Woodhaven Association, an officer of the Boy Scouts of America and the Veterans of Foreign Wars, a school-board member, and the chairman of the Committee to Restore Respect, Honor, and Dignity to Policemen.

Mike's activism went beyond mere civic-mindedness. He was downright militant about the safety and security of the citizens of Cypress Hills. In February 1972, after returning from an Irish dance at St. Michael's Parish in East New York, Long learned from his brother Tom that a friend's car, which had been parked in front of their ice-cream parlor, had been sideswiped and damaged by a hit-and-run driver. Long and his brother roamed the neighborhood until he found a smashed car that contained a hunk of the friend's car grill. It happens that the car was parked across from the Crystal Room, a place Long describes as a "mob joint."

Long called the police, but while he was waiting for the cops to arrive a gang came out of the Crystal Room. When Long told them he was waiting for the police, words were exchanged, and a rumble began. After Long punched out one guy, another thug swung around with a revolver and shot Mike at point blank range. He survived the wound, but the thug that shot him was never found. Needless to say, the incident did nothing to diminish Mike's reputation as a protector of the neighborhood.

Long was truly an urban, street-corner conservative who believed the neighborhood is as much a state of mind as it is a dwelling place. In his 1975 book, *Street Corner Conservative,* William Gavin, a former Nixon speechwriter and special assistant to Senator Jim Buckley, describes the Mike Longs of America's cities:

> [U]rban conservatives are, in a way, revolutionaries. They are in an undeclared revolt against the dominant philosophy of liberalism that has shaped the cultural and intellectual directions of life in this country for a generation. Their revolution is peaceful because the one thing they are certain of in an increasingly unsure world – where dotty nuns and deranged priests marry, denounce their country and mirthfully flaunt the law – the one thing they are certain of is that this country is too damned good to be burned down or subverted or destroyed. It is a good country for them and for their kids. And it is precisely because this is a good country that they are revolting against the dominance of liberalism.[1]

Long took notice of Barry Goldwater and began paying attention to political issues. The political epiphany in his life took place when he attended the great Goldwater Rally at Madison Square Garden in 1964. The enthusiasm at the rally was infectious, and Long decided then and there he had to be actively involved in politics.

He registered for the first time – as a Republican – and joined the local GOP club.

He realized very quickly though that the local pols were more interested in playing cards than in working to elect Goldwater.

Disgusted, he decided to re-register as a member of the fledgling Conservative Party and joined the local club chaired by Dennis Kormanik. The entire membership, including Long, would stand on street corners promoting Goldwater and handing out copies of John A. Stormer's *None Dare Call It Treason*, a book that chided America's leaders for coddling Communists at home and abroad. In his shop, Long hung up a huge Goldwater poster, one that bore the campaign slogan: "In Your Heart You Know He's Right." He took great pride in rejecting the advice of local businessmen to take down the sign. He didn't care if it hurt business.

In 1965 he took over as chairman of the Cypress Hills Conservative Club and became an active neighborhood worker in Bill Buckley's mayoral race. Long recalled that "legions of people came out of the woodwork to hand out literature for Buckley." Clubs began to spring up all over Brooklyn, and the membership in Long's club grew dramatically thanks to the Buckley campaign. By 1966 he had over 100 members and a full-time clubhouse.

It was in the 1966 Paul Adams race for governor that Long made his first impression on the party's founders. Long had organized an Adams rally for an October Sunday afternoon to be held in front of the Hamburg Savings Bank on the corner of Fulton and Crescent Streets. The club had gone door-to-door and handed out over 5,000 flyers, so a large crowd was expected. Long also organized a reception for Adams to be held in his apartment, which was over the ice-cream parlor.

At the last minute, the Brooklyn coordinator for Adams, Ken Starret of Bay Ridge, called and told Long to cancel the rally. "Starret told me that Adams did not campaign on Sundays," Long recalls, "and I was pissed off." Long spoke to Dan Mahoney for the first time and told him that the last-minute notification was unacceptable, particularly since he'd also found out that Adams was appearing at a King's County Conservative Party dinner that very night. Realizing he was getting nowhere with Mahoney, Long said he would be attending the Brooklyn dinner and would create a commotion. A frazzled Mahoney turned the phone over to Kieran O'Doherty, to whom Long repeated his position. "The conversation got ugly," Long said, "and we each threatened one another. Finally, I told O'Doherty that if Adams didn't appear in Brooklyn on Sunday, I would hold a press conference denouncing the ticket."

On Sunday morning the Adams-O'Doherty ticket arrived in Cypress Hills, Brooklyn, to greet 500 people who came out to the rally. Both Adams and O'Doherty gave fiery speeches to the assembly and afterwards met 150 people at Long's apartment. "Everyone was happy with the event," said Long, "but I'm sure Mahoney's and O'Doherty's first impression of me was that I was a lunatic."

Long put his name on the Conservative ballot for the local state senate race in 1966 and received 9.5 percent of the vote. In 1970 he ran again as the Republican-Conservative candidate. According to Long, he convinced himself that like all candidates, "I was going to win and like a fool I spent some money intended for a down payment on a house. I lost, receiving 31.8 percent of the vote and when my wife, Eileen, found out what I did, I was in the dog house for a long time."

Long stayed active in the Brooklyn Conservative Party organization, and in 1972 he decided it was the right time to go for the county-chairman spot. After the Hugh Carey–John Gangemi scandal (described in Chapter 9), Long believed incumbent chairman Bill Wells was vulnerable. At a July 7 meeting of the county committee held at the Hotel Bossert in downtown Brooklyn, a raucous meeting was held that ended when the manager of the hotel called on the police to empty out his ballroom. The Long forces believed numerous proxies supporting Wells were forged and filibustered the meeting for ten hours in a challenge to the proxy certificates. According to a court petition filed by Fiftieth Assembly District leader Stephen Marion, "The meeting ended with no motion to adjourn and no announcement of continuance of the meeting." Dr. Marion further stated that, "Mr. Wells held a secret meeting the following day and, with approximately 16 persons in attendance, was re-elected County Chairman."[2] Marion also alleged that proxies Wells intended to use at the meeting were forgeries.

A committee to fight Wells was formed, called "Conservatives for Responsible Government." Members included party activists, Louis Montrone, John Andrew Kay, Stephen and Mabel Marion, James Gay, and Rita Natoli.

At the court hearings, attorney Robert Clark had fifty local county-committee members testify that proxies submitted in their name at the county-committee meeting were forgeries. Also, Robert Martin, a handwriting expert, testified that 96 percent of the proxies he examined were forgeries.

While waiting for Judge Charles Rubin's ruling, the newspapers gave the case plenty of coverage. For instance, the weekly *Flatbush Life* proclaimed in a bold headline: "**CONSERVATIVE LEADER CHARGED WITH FRAUD**," the New York *Daily News* headline read "Testifies Proxy was a Forgery." And the *Brooklyn Courier Life* announced that "Fifty Testify in Fraud Case."

On Friday, August 28, Judge Rubin set aside the Wells vote and ordered a new election. He also stipulated that Conservative Party state headquarters had to supervise the new election. Dan Mahoney was ordered to chair the meeting and directed to appoint an impartial credentials committee.

Mahoney announced that the new, official organizing meeting of the Kings County Conservative Party would be held on Thursday November 30, 1972, at Brooklyn's Prospect Hall. In the ensuing election, Mike Long won going away, receiving 308 votes to just 6 for Bill Wells.

The Rough and Tumble of Politics

As county chairman, Long devoted his energies to rebuilding the Brooklyn organization and to helping elect strong candidates with deep roots in their communities. After Long emerged as a major decision maker during the 1973 Mario Biaggi mayoral race, Dan Mahoney encouraged him to run for vice chairman of the party's state committee. "I beat incumbent Tom Cronin of the Bronx in 1974," Long said in a 1999 interview. "I believe Dan wanted me as Vice Chairman to make sure I stayed on the reservation and not become too independent."

In 1977, Long had his first run-in with Mario Cuomo at a mayoral forum at Fort Hamilton High School in Brooklyn. Candidate Cuomo was boasting that his "Neighborhood Preservation Party" was the only political party in New York to have a platform. Hearing this, Mike Long interjected that Cuomo was wrong, and reminded him that the Conservative Party has a platform. When Cuomo told him he was wrong, Long yelled to him, "You're a liar!" What followed was a scene one would ordinarily expect to see in a schoolyard brawl: a pushing match. Long recalls: "Mario and I sneered at one another and began pushing back and forth. He pushed me through swinging doors and I pulled him along with me. The cops didn't know me but they certainly knew the mayoral candidate, so they broke things up and searched me while Cuomo left in his car."

"Moments later," Long continued, "Cuomo came back in the car and called me over under some trees to chat. He apologized, and when I told him we did have a platform, Cuomo asked for copies. Next day, I had State Headquarters send him a copy of every platform since the Party's inception. Later I received a note from Cuomo conceding that the Conservative Party did indeed have a platform."

Mike Long with his clan after being sworn in as Brooklyn councilman-at-large (June 1981).

Also in 1977, Long help Conservative Vincent Riccio become a Brooklyn councilman-at-large. Over time, Long also helped elect Chris Mega to the state senate and Dominick DiCarlo and Florence Sullivan to the assembly. Gerard Kassar, a young state committeeman in the 1970s and a future Brooklyn County chairman, said that "Long had a charisma that attracted talent and had a commonsense ability to organize winning coalitions in local elections. Most of the Republican-Conservative legislators elected in Brooklyn were loyal to Long and this did not sit well with the Republican establishment – they were jealous."

"Mike Long," said Kassar, "taught me everything I know about day to day operations of neighborhood politics."[3]

In 1981, after Vince Riccio was sentenced to jail for misappropriation of government funds, Mike Long was appointed to complete his term in the city council. At the time, the federal courts were reviewing the constitutionality of New York City's "at-large" seats.

"I was supposed to serve out the remaining six months of Riccio's terms," Long said, "but the feds froze the election clock until the issue was ruled on; so I wound up serving until the at-large seats were eliminated two years later."

During his first day on the city council, Long learned the hard way how easy it was to become unpopular.

"On the day I was sworn in," Long recalled, "I was the only vote against the new city budget. The entire membership was shocked. Apparently once the budget deals were cut everyone was expected to fall in line and vote yes. For two weeks no one said hello to me."

Long believed he was there to promote a philosophy of government and not to bargain for crumbs. So for the next two years, with the help of his chief of staff, Allen Roth, Long fought issues ranging from budget pork to so-called "gay" rights bills.

"I enjoyed the council and when the at-large seat was eliminated, I decided to run for a local seat in my new neighborhood of Bay Ridge. I moved there after my brother and I opened a liquor store in the area."

Long, who ran a well-financed and well-organized campaign, admitted after he lost to Sal Albanese that "I thought my reputation would elect me and I was wrong. I was new to the neighborhood, and the locals stuck with the local guy. I should have known better."

When Serf Maltese was elected state chairman in 1986, he asked Long to take the spot he was vacating, executive vice chairman. And when Maltese stepped down in 1988, the state executive committee unanimously agreed that Long was the guy to lead the party into the nineties.

Upon taking office, Long had no choice but to address party finances, since on December 28, 1988, federal marshals froze what few assets the party possessed. A certain law firm was tired of waiting to be paid for services rendered, so they called in the marshals.

Unable to pay the tab for his party's payroll, Long turned to long-time party supporter Bruce Bent. The inventor of the money-market fund and president and CEO of The Reserve Funds, Bent was an old friend of Dan Mahoney and had been a financial contributor to the party since 1962. Mike asked for a loan of $10,000 and insisted the party was good for it. Bent gave Long the money, but he doubted the loan would ever be repaid.

To economize, Long moved party headquarters from Manhattan to Brooklyn. This made it easier for him to spend more time at the party office, and it saved $35,000 a year.

"I spent most of 1989," Long said, "trying to pay off the debts, and thanks to people like Bruce Bent and Ronald Lauder, I was able to do it. When I sent Bent a check for $10,000, he was so shocked that he actually forgave the loan."

At the annual Albany Conservative Conference in February of 1989, Chairman

Long made it clear to his statewide leaders and to the media that he planned to energize the party.

"Our Party is more than a political party. Our Party is a movement. I want to rejuvenate that movement."[4] Long said that he wanted to make sure that people did not confuse Conservatives with Republicans.

"I'm going to drive a little harder on philosophy . . . I don't want us to be seen as part of the Republican Party."

Long also took his first shots at Governor Cuomo and the state legislature:
"Key to that movement," he said, "is getting legislators to decrease all state and local taxes and to do away with regulations that drive businesses away and create housing shortages."

"People don't leave this state because of earthquakes, tornadoes, bad weather," he said. "In fact some people are moving to some states where they have earthquakes. We're in a non-growth state. We have to re-energize. We have to unleash the housing market, we have to lower taxes, we have to encourage growth."

"Government has to learn what business people have known for a long time," Long said. "When business is stagnant, when business is slow and you run into trouble in a retail shop, you don't raise your prices. You lower your prices to stimulate business. What I'm saying is the state has to lower its prices, lower its taxes."[5]

Long's goals were robust: to build the party, to have an impact on public policy, and to elect a governor. He wasn't sure if these things could be happen in 1990 or 1994 or at all, but his political decisions all centered around achieving these objectives.

The first test came in the 1989 New York City mayoral race. On January 10, Rudolph W. Giuliani had resigned as U.S. attorney for New York's Southern District, a job he had received thanks to Senator D'Amato and during which he had attempted to become the Tom Dewey racketeer-buster of his time. Al D'Amato says that at last minute he recommended Giuliani over John Keenan for the job because:

> Rudy Giuliani came to see me. He wanted to return to the Southern District
> as U.S. Attorney. I thought he was crazy. . . . In fact, Rudy later joked that
> his mother had said just that. But he explained that he was eager to return
> to New York. He had just become engaged to TV reporter Donna Hanover,
> who was moving to New York for a job with WPIX-TV. While Washington-
> New York power couples did exist, he did not consider such a commute a
> scenario for a happy marriage, and I respected that. . . . I considered Rudy's
> request intriguing. My screening committee, however, was stunned. They
> had spent time and effort on their recommendation. Some members warned
> of Giuliani's personal ambition and told me I was making a decision I would
> regret. Ultimately I went ahead and recommended Rudy for the post.[6]

Giuliani was being seriously considered for mayor and Congressman Guy Molinari and Bay Ridge State Senator Chris Mega put together a meeting between Rudy, Mike Long, and the city's five Conservative county leaders. At that meeting, the leaders were impressed with Rudy, particularly when he told them he was pro-life and assured them he would not take the Liberal Party line. But just a week later the Conservative leaders were disturbed to read in the newspapers that Giuliani had stated publicly that he was indeed interested in the Liberal Party nomination . . . and that he was pro-choice.

Meanwhile, there was another Republican interested in being mayor, cosmetics heir Ronald Lauder. The forty-four-year-old Lauder had served as deputy assistant secretary of defense and as ambassador to Austria during the Reagan Administration, and on January 4, 1989, he announced that he would seek the Republican nomination for mayor. Lauder had at least one powerful ally: Al D'Amato. According to the senator:

> In 1989, when Rudy ran for the Republican nomination for mayor of New York City, I did not support him. I gave my support to my friend Ron Lauder, who came to me months before Rudy announced his candidacy. Ron had been one of my earliest supporters when I challenged Jacob Javits in 1980. Ron had stood with me when the odds were long, and I wanted to do the same for him.[7]

In February, Ron Lauder's limousine pulled up to the Tiffany Diner in Bay Ridge, where Mike Long and party Executive Vice Chairman James Molinaro were waiting to interview the candidates. Lauder made it clear he was a serious candidate and that his views on the issues were more conservative than Giuliani's. "Ron Lauder was not completely on the reservation on pro-life issues," Long has said, "but he was better than Rudy; he was against government funding and for parental consent." At the end of the meeting, Long encouraged Lauder to reach out to county leaders.

By the spring of 1989 Giuliani had changed his mind and made it clear he was no longer interested in the Conservative Party's nomination, although he continued to court the Republicans and the Liberals. Another potential candidate, NYU professor Herbert London, dropped out of the race because he lacked the finances to run a credible campaign. Thus Lauder became the unanimous choice at the Conservative Party convention, but like Rudy, he also wanted the Republican nod.

The Republican primary campaign that followed was a rough one. Lauder had ample resources, which he used to expose flaws in Giuliani's record. "Lauder's first ads – which ran in April on radio and TV at a weekly cost of $350,000 – assailed Giuliani for accepting the Liberal endorsement, voting for George McGovern and supporting tax hikes."[8]

Lauder, who with the aid of Conservative Allen Roth, put out numerous white papers that thoughtfully laid out his vision for New York, ran on the theme: "Conservative leadership you can trust." His brochure read, "Ronald Lauder is proud to call himself a Conservative Republican. No apologies. No excuses."

Arthur Finkelstein, who ran the Lauder media campaign, spent millions on commercials that pounded Giuliani. They even bought commercial time on WPIX Nightly News, knowing that anchorwoman Donna Hanover Giuliani would have to sit and watch the ads assaulting her husband. The Lauder campaign reminded the public how Giuliani had employed ruthless tactics as U.S. attorney in order to get media attention and headlines. They also pointed out that during Giuliani's tenure prosecutions and convictions in the Southern District were actually down. The Lauder campaign also received help from the *The Wall Street Journal*, that in an editorial took this shot at Rudy:

> Mr. Giuliani solicited the Liberal Party nomination, he actually *says*, partly because many of his friends and relatives would have been too embarrassed to vote for a Republican. Mr. Giuliani campaigned for Bobby Kennedy and says he voted for George McGovern. His campaign staff includes at least one former Mike Dukakis aide. He told a TV interviewer, "I do not look to see what the catechism of conservatism says about how to solve a problem."[9]

New York Post columnist Ray Kerrison went after Giuliani's flip-flops on social issues:

> A Democratic mayoralty candidate, Comptroller Harrison Goldin, said the other day, "The mayor of this city is a moral leader." If that's true, then moral values are integral to the contest, and voters have a right to know where the candidates stand.
>
> Giuliani is trying to dodge them, and he's confusing everyone. I still can't figure out where he stands on abortion. One day, he says he opposes it on moral grounds but he would do nothing to curtail abortion rights. Next, he says a mayor has little control over abortion – which is not so. Mayor Koch last year used city funds to subsidize 23,000 abortions.
>
> Giuliani has also sent confusing signals on homosexuality. He said he opposes homosexual marriages, conferring family status on them and giving them bereavement leave. This prompted gay activists to boo him and for Koch to call him a "gay-basher." The reality is that anyone who does not support the homosexual agenda across the board will be labeled a homophobe, bigot and gay-basher.
>
> Just when we thought we knew where Giuliani stood, he said he

thought homosexuality was "good and normal," which is sharply at vari-
ance with his church, not to mention the Bible, which describes it as an
"abomination."[10]

During a Sunday, September 3, debate on WNBC's "News Forum," Lauder and
Giuliani went for each other's throat. Lauder opened up by thanking moderator Gabe
Pressman for the opportunity to "discuss my conservative ideas and Mr. Giuliani's lib-
eral ideas." At one point, Giuliani said:

"Ronnie really doesn't understand suffering in this city. He has no idea what it's
like. Suffering to him is the butler taking the night off."

Reacting to Rudy's personal attacks, Lauder said, "I wanted to talk about
Republican issues and what we saw here was Rudy being very liberal and very
mean."[11]

Viewing the battle, the *New York Post* editorial page had this to say:

> It seemed to us that while he had been a first-class federal prosecutor over-
> all, his efforts, on occasion, were animated by an excess of zeal. Still, this
> was a flaw we felt we could life with.
>
> Then came Giuliani's decision to accept the Liberal Party nomination,
> and to run as a fusion candidate in the tradition of John V. Lindsay.
> However wise this strategy may seem politically, it inevitably reduces the
> enthusiasm of those inclined to embrace Giuliani's candidacy for ideolog-
> ical reasons.
>
> We think the Liberal Party and the GOP stand for very different prin-
> ciples. We would have preferred to see a Republican willing to run just as
> a Republican – or as a Republican-Conservative. We do not, moreover,
> share Giuliani's frequently expressed view that ideological questions have
> little to do with municipal governance.
>
> Also dismaying has been the candidate's tendency to flip-flop on
> issues ranging from abortion to commercial rent control.[12]

In spite of all the money he spent, Lauder could not overcome the efforts on
behalf of Giuliani supporter Congressman Guy Molinari of Staten Island. Most of the
city's Republicans lived in that heavily Catholic borough, and Guy delivered it to
Giuliani. On primary day, Tuesday, September 12, Giuliani beat Lauder with 67 percent of the vote: 77,150 to 37,960.

On the Democratic side, three-term incumbent Mayor Ed Koch lost his bid to run
for an unprecedented fourth term to Manhattan Borough President David Dinkins. In
the fall, Giuliani lost to Dinkins in a close and hotly contested election.

Lauder's name still appeared on the Conservative Party line in November, but he
ceased any active campaigning after the primary. This was because he believed if

Dinkins were elected mayor he would not serve the city well. Yet even with a non-campaigning candidate, Long was satisfied with his political decisions in 1989.

"Even though we lost, it was my first opportunity to let the Republicans know I was not going to roll over dead for them. I let them know that principles and policy ideas were driving the party."

This position was to become more evident in the 1990 gubernatorial race.

London v. Cuomo

Since his electrifying keynote speech at the Democratic National Convention in 1984, Mario Cuomo's star was rising nationally, but New York was going down the rathole fiscally. By 1990 the state faced a $1.5-billion budget gap and the governor's primary method of closing it was not dramatic spending cuts, but deferral of scheduled cuts in the state income tax.

Between 1983 and 1989, per capita spending in New York increased 55.9 percent while the national average was 38.2 percent. Viewing New York's deteriorating finances, Standard & Poor's dropped the rating to "A," which left New York the forty-eighth lowest rated state in the nation.

Mike Long believed a bona-fide conservative could make a run at Cuomo in 1990 – maybe even beat him. Long's first choice was Jack Kemp, but as in previous years, the Congressman Kemp couldn't pull the trigger and declined to enter the race. As a result, Long met with Herb London on January 5, 1990, at the Tiffany Diner and asked him if he would be interested in running for governor. Herb said yes.

Although the Republicans were mentioning numerous names for 1990 (including Jonathan Bush, David Rockefeller, and even former Democratic governor, Hugh Carey), Long knew that they really didn't have any serious candidates. He thought, therefore, he might have a shot at selling Herb London to the Republicans.

Herbert I. London, born in Brooklyn in 1939, received his B.A. and M.A. from Columbia University and his Ph.D. from NYU. The 6 foot, 5 inch, scholar played basketball center for Jamaica High School and Columbia, and was also drafted in 1960 by the Syracuse Nationals (now The Philadelphia 76ers) but declined due to a knee injury. Instead, London began teaching high school in Harlem and in Syosset, Long Island, before being hired as an assistant professor of history at the NYU School of Education. In 1972, the university asked him to be the founding director of the Gallatin Division, an adult education program that emphasizes a "Great Books" core curriculum. A prolific author and editor, London served in 1984 and 1985 as a member of President Reagan's Committee for the Next Agenda.

Long arranged for London to speak at the Albany C-Pac in February, really to see if Herb would spark interest with party leaders. And, sure enough, as the conference luncheon guest speaker London managed to energize the audience.

Meanwhile, Long was holding a series of meetings with Republican State Chairman Patrick Barrett. The self-made Syracuse millionaire wanted to combine forces with Long and agreed to place London's name in the Republican hopper, but Long soon sensed that there could not be a marriage. "Herb was viewed as a 'true believer,'" said Long, "who would not fit in their circle." *The New York Times* confirmed Long's gut feeling: "several Republican leaders said that Mr. London lacked statewide stature, was too conservative even for many Republicans and did not have any financial resources. Barrett said 'London doesn't bring any money to the table.'"[13]

Left to right: Ronald Lauder, Herbert London, Lew Lehrman, U.S. Senator Connie Mack.

The state's Republican Party, which was over a half million dollars in debt, began what became an embarrassing search. As the May 29 convention was approaching, a *Times* headline read: "GOP Short of Time and a Candidate." Liberal-Republican Roy Goodman, a member of the search committee, and his friend, investment banker Laurence Leeds, frantically combed their address books and under "R" came across the name of economic consultant Pierre Rinfret. They telephoned him and after a brief conversation, Rinfret agreed to be the candidate, and he said he would put up $500,000 in "earnest" money.[14]

That was that. One phone call had decided the Republican nomination. A Rinfret campaign team was quickly assembled that included political consultant Eddie Mahe, Jr., conservative writer Bill Tucker, and Columbia County Assemblyman John Faso, who was named campaign manager.

Mike Long and Jim Molinaro met Rinfret at Brooklyn party headquarters shortly before the Republican Convention. After listening to Rinfret contradict himself again and again for over an hour, Long and Molinaro agreed that Rinfret would be the Republican Party's "worst nightmare," an arrogant and bombastic man with no political skills.[15] That same night, over dinner with Republican chairman Barrett, Long stated flatly that Rinfret was not "ready for prime time, had no knowledge of state issues, and would not fly with the Conservative Party."

To the press, Long gave this explanation: "The post-Rockefeller years of Republicans and Conservatives working in tandem are clearly over, and we are back to fighting one another. It's almost as if the campaigns of [former GOP Senator] Jim Buckley, [1982 gubernatorial nominee] Lew Lehrman, and Ronald Reagan – all of which were joint Republican-Conservative efforts – had never happened." Long urged Barrett to take another look at London. The answer was *No*, because Goodman and his associates insisted their candidate had to be pro-abortion.[16]

The day after the Republican Convention adjourned, Mike Long announced that his party's convention would be held on Saturday, June 2, and added:

> I will recommend that members of the Conservative Party's state commit-tee endorse Herb London for Governor. I reached this decision after inter-viewing all candidates who sought our Party's endorsement. My endorse-ment is based on Dean London's qualifications, his in-depth knowledge of the issues confronting this state, his philosophical commitment to the free market, anti-crime, family oriented principles of the Conservative Party, and his considerable communications abilities. . . .
>
> In the past the Conservative Party has changed the politics of New York by being instrumental in the elections of Jim Buckley and Alphonse D'Amato. We are equally proud of having supported Bill Buckley and Lew Lehrman. And now we are fortunate to have the opportunity to endorse a superior candidate in the person of Herb London.[17]

Herb London was the unanimous choice of the party.

By early June, Republicans were beginning to recognize that Long had been prophetic: Pierre Rinfret was a nightmare. Old-time Nixon people refuted Rinfret's boast that he had been a major adviser to the president. *The New York Times* claimed Rinfret's use of the title "Doctor" was fraudulent. In fact it was proven that Rinfret, who swore he was a Republican, was actually a registered Independent. Worst of all, Rinfret was not coming up with the money he'd promised.

All in all, he was the loosest of loose cannons. To wit:

* He called incumbent Republican Comptroller Ned Regan an idiot and endorsed his opponent, Democrat-Liberal Carol Bellamy;
* he called the man who discovered him, Senator Roy Goodman, "one of the most destructive people in this state";

* he said Republican State Chairman Patrick Barrett "hasn't been a leader," and that he should resign;
* he called Jack Kemp a traitor to the party and "a lackey" for Governor Cuomo;
* he told a female reporter to come to his inaugural and to leave her husband home;
* he referred to African-Americans who live in Harlem as "those people" and insisted they prefer to live outdoors in the streets.

Columnists Rowland Evans and Robert Novak said Rinfret "has turned out to be a worse candidate than even his critics feared." Kevin Phillips called the candidate a "near joke," and Nassau County's comptroller, Republican Peter King, referred to Rinfret as "the brainless wonder." Republican insiders called him a "bozo," a "buffoon," and other things unprintable.

Watching the Rinfret circus, Herb London said: "I've never seen a man so unprepared for public life." And Mike Long concluded that the "Republican Party has lost its way. Our Party is running the only bona fide Republican in the race."

Thanks to "Club for Economic Growth" members like investment banker Dusty Rhodes (president of *National Review*), entrepreneur Bruce Bent, and financier Richard Gilder, Long was able to put together about $200,000 for upstate advertising and travel for the London campaign. In headquarters, Mary Roth was in charge of operations, while Nelson Warfield and Mike Gannon served as political consultants.

On the road, London was garnering reams of favorable press for his vivid descriptions of his vision for New York. Newspapers proclaimed:

> "LONDON opposes New York State reliance on borrowing, short-term or long-term, to balance the state budget."

> "LONDON favors decentralization of control over public schools and proposes State vouchers for up to $2500 per student to allow parents to shop for the best schools for their children – public or private."

> "LONDON opposes AFFIRMATIVE ACTION – "It 'fuels the fires of racism.'"

> "LONDON favors the DEATH PENALTY – ' . . . even if it doesn't deter crime, because it is just retribution against criminals.'"

Herb London addressed the problems New Yorkers faced with a mixture of sweet reason and good humor. "New York is awash in debt and taxation," he told them.

This is how bad it is: If you combine the state personal income tax with local taxes passed on by the state, every New Yorker pays $164 of every $1,000 earned in state taxes. That's an astonishing number.

Money is being squandered at a huge rate in New York, but because we don't have "sunshine" laws [that would force more detailed disclosure of government expenditures] the people can't find out where it's all going. Cuomo says the general budget has increased only 2–3 percent, but what he doesn't tell you is that he takes items out of the general budget and puts them in something called the Special Revenue Budget – which has gone up 404 percent in the last eight years.[18]

By September, Republicans were jumping off the sinking Rinfret ship in droves and endorsing the Conservative candidate. The group included Henrietta Town Supervisor James Breese, former Rye Mayor Mary Ann Ilse, Yonkers Mayor Hank Spillone, Orange County Legislator David Russell, Cayuga County Legislative Majority Leader Sam Derosa, as well as seven Monroe County legislators, and scores of Republican state committeemen and women, clubs, and organizations.

On October 6, 1990, at the *National Review* thirty-fifth anniversary dinner, the political world shook when Housing Secretary Jack Kemp enthusiastically proclaimed: "I endorse Herb London for governor of New York State." Reacting to the endorsement, Mike Long noted that "Jack Kemp has sent a very clear message: Herb London is the only alternative to Mario Cuomo's destructive liberal policies."[19]

Several days later, another shoe dropped when former Republican gubernatorial candidate Lewis Lehrman also endorsed London:

As a New York Republican, I am proud to join with Secretary of Housing and Urban Development, Jack Kemp, and the scores of elected Republican officials who have endorsed Herb London for Governor. . . .

During the course of his campaign, Herb London has set out a sound economic policy that will rescue New York. Herb London understands that working people and businesses insist on limiting government spending and reducing tax rates in order to spur economic growth.

Herb London has identified specific ways New York can save billions of dollars. In short, Herb London is a champion of true Republican principles that lead to more jobs and economic growth.[20]

Ronald Lauder also came out strongly for London, saying in part that Herb "supported the Republican principles that I'm convinced would turn New York around."

In his syndicated column, Bill Buckley also gave London a thumbs-up:

Herbert London is a proud and principled man, an eloquent spokesman of civilized conservatism. Mario Cuomo will win big and, as things stand, might just as well be running unopposed by any Republican. But alert voters have a fine opportunity both to applaud the work of Herbert London on the Conservative line and to instruct the GOP.[21]

About $121,000 worth of Conservative Party television ads blanketed upstate New York. The first were ten-second spots linking together Cuomo and Rinfret as two Liberal politicians, "Tweedledee and Tweedledumber."

Another thirty-second spot cast Cuomo and Rinfret together in a similarly humorous vein. After an announcer's voice explained that both are "liberals running for governor," who support abortion, high spending, and attacks on Republicans, the faces of Cuomo and Rinfret burst out of a video pea pod to the slogan: "Two peas in a liberal pod." The ad then featured London with headlines detailing his endorsements by Kemp and Lehrman along with his opposition to abortion, support for the death penalty, and commitment "to end Cuomo's tax-and-spend economics."[22]

Polling began to show that the Conservative Party was making deep inroads into the Republican voting base, and there was a possibility that London would outpoll Rinfret. As Mike Long explained:

"Even if one accepts that the re-election of Mario Cuomo is a certainty, the scenario of Herb London getting more votes than Rinfret is a distinct possibility. And if that happens, the Conservatives would hold Row B [the second line on the state ballot] instead of the Republicans for the next four years."[23]

"If conservatives held a higher ballot position than Republicans in New York," Long predicted to *Human Events*, "GOP legislators and other office-holders would have to come to us for endorsement, at which point we would make our positions opposing abortion and tax increases very clear to them."[24]

In the final weeks of the campaign, the Republicans panicked. Deserting their gubernatorial candidate, their entire effort was focused on preserving their Row B ballot position and the Republican majority in the state senate. Mailings went out to registered Republicans, urging them to help the party survive. They put the fear of God in all the local poll watchers and anyone who had a patronage job by telling them they would lose their livelihoods if the party lost Row B on election day.

The incumbent could hardly believe his luck. With a war chest of $8 million, Cuomo was able to sit back and watch the Republicans self-destruct. He spent his money to promote a very positive image of himself. He did face his opponents in two debates, although they were oddly scheduled: one during the World Series and the other the morning of the New York City Marathon. Columnist Ray Kerrison, reviewing the substance of the debates, labeled Cuomo as the "Artful Dodger of the Year."

The governor's attempt to palm himself off as a prudent fiscal manager is so patently fraudulent it snaps the breath right out of you. Herbert London, the Conservative Party candidate, deftly dissected the Cuomo record, which shows that in virtually every spending category, New York is in the top tier. That's why New York has the 48th worst credit rating among the 50 states. . . .

It was a disastrous hour for Cuomo. The challengers put so much fiscal heat on him that he was defensive and, in trying to transfer responsibility for the financial crisis to the Republicans, totally unbelievable. Not exactly a profile in courage.[25]

London ended the campaign reminding voters what the election was all about:

This election is about trying to give a voice to those forgotten New Yorkers who pay their taxes, care about their kids, respect their families, respect their God and are not out on the streets demonstrating. In New York, they don't have a voice. They are disenfranchised. We have substantial numbers of people who are going to flee New York. We have already lost 280,000 under Mr. Cuomo's stewardship. Those people were taxpayers.[26]

On election day, Tuesday, November 6, the political world was shocked by the results:

	Cuomo Dem.	Rinfret Rep.	London Cons.	Wein R. to L.	Cuomo Lib.
Total Upstate	**1,339,627**	**747,901**	**692,864**	**116,401**	**41,516**
Bronx	113,644	12,962	15,071	2,778	3,410
Brooklyn	210,274	28,302	35,209	4,838	6,889
Manhattan	191,744	22,779	21,261	2,584	10,562
Queens	184,771	40,175	46,686	6,974	6,950
Staten Island	46,010	13,829	16,523	4,229	1,690
Total New York City	**746,443**	**118,047**	**134,750**	**21,403**	**29,501**
Total State	**2,086,070**	**865,948**	**827,614**	**137,804**	**71,017**

The Conservative Party had come within 38,334 votes of outpolling the Republicans. London carried outright five counties and outpolled Rinfret in nineteen other counties. "This is a wake-up call for the Republicans," London told the press. Rinfret received the lowest vote percentage of any GOP candidate in the twentieth century.

The results were also bad for a Cuomo presidential run; he barely mustered 53 percent of the vote, down 12 percent from four years earlier. Back in September, viewing the hopeless Rinfret, *New York Observer* columnist Rick Brookhiser had concluded, "If Mario Cuomo can't get 60 percent of the vote running against this guy, he should be put out to stud." And for the twenty-four hours after election day, Cuomo's career seemed destined for the pasture. The *New York Times* analysis, headlined

"Cuomo, Omnipotence Blunted," stated that, "Mr. Cuomo, who under better circumstances rarely misses an opportunity to meet the press, was uncharacteristically silent yesterday on the subject of the election. . . . In his own race, Mr. Cuomo showed unexpected weakness . . . against opponents who early on in the race had been dismissed as sure losers."[27]

It actually took two full days for Cuomo to come out of seclusion. On Thursday, November 8, he admitted that New Yorkers had sent him "more of a message than a mandate and he said that New Yorkers no longer trust their government." Cuomo told the press that, "The signals that did go out, as regrettable as they are – the defeat of the bond issue and Carol [Bellamy], the fact that we didn't get the margins we wanted, we didn't get the exultant shout that we wanted from the people – that can be instructive to us."[28] The *Times* reported that "the Governor pledged to heed the electorate's warning to cut spending and keep a lid on taxes."[29]

As expected, Cuomo's coattails were short, and he failed to carry any Democrats into the state senate. The $1.975-billion environmental bond proposal, for which he had campaigned extensively, went down in flames.

In his toughest race to date, Comptroller Ned Regan managed to squeak by, thanks to the Conservative Party's endorsement:

	Bellamy Dem.	Regan Rep.	Regan Cons.	Kearney R. to L.	Bellamy Lib.
Total Upstate	**1,137,173**	**1,290,321**	**308,006**	**99,130**	**50,829**
Bronx	95,504	26,484	9,914	2,514	3,187
Brooklyn	178,467	64,748	21,106	4,024	6,841
Manhattan	161,475	60,302	11,431	2,361	10,169
Queens	154,922	80,288	29,718	5,460	7,042
Staten Island	34,469	29,025	11,568	3,254	1,748
Total New York City	**624,837**	**260,847**	**83,737**	**17,613**	**28,987**
Total State	**1,762,010**	**1,551,168**	**391,743**	**116,743**	**79,816**

In the fifties, sixties, and seventies, for a Republican to have a chance to win statewide, it had been essential that he pick up over 40 percent of the New York City vote. In 1990, Ned Regan managed to win by garnering only 33 percent of the city vote. This decreased dependency on the Big Apple vote may be attributed to changing voter demographics.

As a result of liberalized immigration rules, New York City experienced a tremendous influx of Latinos and Asians. While its overall population remained at about 8 million, the voting population began to drop, and this was reflected in turnouts on election day. This phenomenon was a plus for Republicans, because their upstate base became a larger percentage of the overall voting population. The importance of this voting shift will become evident later in this book.

Mike Long was delighted with the 1990 results. The Rinfret disaster proved the decrepit condition of the state GOP, and it also proved that Conservative issues and endorsements remained essential parts of any Republican victory formula. In a post-election press conference, Long said: "The Republican Party has a lot of grass roots growing to do. They have to really take a deep look at themselves. They have to understand where they want to go philosophically." And he hoped that the GOP leaders had learned that they should "never again select a candidate without discussing the issues with" Conservative Party leaders.[30]

Reflecting on the results in a 2000 interview, Long admitted that the party was better off not outpolling the Republicans in 1990. "A second place finish would have meant replacing thousands of Republicans in the sixty-two county election boards. And I'm sure the GOP would not quietly let go of the spoils. They would have had hundreds of Republicans re-register as Conservatives, and they would have taken over the Party in counties all over the state. They would have put us out of business."

"No," Long concluded, "we were better off remaining on Row C because the party is more a philosophical movement than a patronage mill. We were better off continuing our mission, which is to force the major parties to deal with issues."

Long made a public announcement in early December that he intended to sit down with Senate Majority Leader Ralph Marino, Assembly Minority Leader Clarence Rappleyea, and Comptroller Ned Regan "to ask some questions, lay out an agenda, and put a little fire in their bellies."[31]

Long made it perfectly clear that "we are not going to compromise our relationship with the Republicans; it's up to them. We know where we are. I don't think they know where they are. If there is no coalition, we will go on." Long reminded the GOP that Reagan and D'Amato won twice in New York when carrying the banner of conservatism. "If you stick to principles, hard working, law abiding, disaffected Democrats and Independents will flock to you."[32]

Long also met privately with Senator D'Amato in December 1990. D'Amato agreed to take an active role in rebuilding the state's Republican Party. Agreeing that Cuomo would be beatable if he decided to run for a fourth term, Long and D'Amato made a pact to stay in touch and to help avoid another Rinfret-like debacle. In the spirit of such a cooperative effort, Long agreed not to endorse a candidate early in the election cycle. "In return," Long said, "I demanded that Herb London be seriously considered as the next Republican nominee. D'Amato agreed and we shook hands."

Herb London and Mike Long also sat down shortly after the election, and Herb made it clear he wanted another shot at the executive mansion. Long agreed that Herb had earned the right to be a serious contender, but when London asked him to endorse him now, four years before the conventions, Long had to decline. "I know Herb was not happy with my answer," Long said later, "but I told him he had to prove he could raise money and win support within the Republican ranks."

Chapter 13

Change New York, Save Our City

Nineteen ninety one was an off-year in terms of election cycles, but from an organizational perspective it had the makings of a very good year.

The February 1991 Annual Albany Conservative Conference had a record-breaking crowd. Chairman Mike Long was happy to announce that party registration had jumped up 5 percent in the past year. But Long was as combative as ever and warned legislators that the "legislative process in this State, certainly over the past two decades, has failed to serve the people of the state ... when legislators come back each year . . . [they only] reach into the pockets of the working taxpayers."[1] Long even threatened to take away the Conservative endorsement from Senate Majority Leader Ralph Marino if he failed to pay attention to the Conservative agenda.[2]

At the main luncheon, Long introduced keynote speaker Herbert London as "an asset and a treasure." After a standing ovation, London told the crowd that New York "is changing. . . . It's no longer the Empire State. I would describe it as a vampire state. And Mario Cuomo is sucking the blood of working people who are trying so hard to learn a living."

While activists were still excited over the party's achievements, Long spent the first half of 1991 traveling all over the state meeting with his leaders, speaking at their fund raisers, and encouraging them to energize their grassroots efforts.

In May, Long suspended his efforts long enough to help lead the mourning for party co-founder Kieran O'Doherty, who died at the age of 64. O'Doherty, who for several years had been semi-retired and living in eastern Long Island's Hampton Bays, died at University Hospital in Salt Lake City of complications following a heart transplant. Long reminded his membership that O'Doherty and his brother-in-law, Judge Daniel Mahoney, "had the guts, the fortitude and the principles to be the prime movers in a cause that was now championed by hundreds of thousands throughout New York State."[3]

Long was also reaching out to numerous Republican activists who were disenchanted with the GOP. The "Club for Growth" members – that now included Dusty Rhodes, Bruce Bent, Richard and Virginia Gilder, former Ambassador Alfred Klingon, and economist Larry Kudlow – were taking active roles in the plan to take over the state house.

A number of them announced in June 1991 the formation of a new think tank, The Empire Foundation, whose mandate was to get the state's fiscal house in order by studying state issues and developing policies designed to stimulate economic growth and jobs in New York.

The Albany-based 501(c)(3) was chaired by Thomas "Dusty" Rhodes, then a partner of Goldman, Sachs and Co. Advisory board members included Richard Gilder, Kudlow, Walter Wriston, former head of Citibank, and neo-conservative journalist Irving Kristol. Tom Carroll, who was to serve as president and CEO of the new think tank, was also to run Change-NY, a statewide grassroots organization that actively critiqued Cuomo and the state legislature. Reacting to the group's formation, Long said, "I think Change-NY is the best thing that has happened in New York since the [1962] founding of the Conservative Party."[4]

Because Change-NY went after the Republican-controlled senate for approving a $1-billion tax package, the Republican establishment did not welcome the new advocacy group with open arms. The new Republican state chairman, William Powers, defended Senator Marino and the Republican majority with a feeble reply to Change-NY's proposals: "If these people have a problem, they ought to direct their concerns at those who have controlled the state for the past 16 years, the Democrats. . . . We're a minority party in the State and we control only one house of the Legislature. I *salute* Ralph Marino for what he has been able to do."[5]

Tom Carroll replied that senate Republicans "live a double life. . . . In their newsletters they talk about controlling spending. Then they come up here to Albany and cut a deal. For the first time in history, we're telling people what really happens."[6]

In November, former Conservative Party mayoral candidate Ronald Lauder went on the offensive in a full-page open letter to Governor Cuomo and the state legislature that appeared in *The New York Times* and other papers throughout the state. The letter described New York's fiscal and economic plight and urged the implementation of the findings of the New York State Advisory Commission on Privatization that he chaired. The privatization opportunities, Lauder wrote, "can save and raise billions in revenues without raising taxes."[7]

And the Conservative appraisal of political failures was not limited to policies coming out of Albany. Mike Long was increasingly unhappy with the administration of George Bush.

"They say 'Read my lips – no new taxes,' and we get taxes. They say 'No quotas,' and we get a quota bill," Long complained,[8] and to show his displeasure, Long set up a meeting and rally for Sunday, December 15, in support of Pat Buchanan, who was threatening to run against Bush.

"With Buchanan in the race," Long told the media, "it's going to be a wide-open ball game. We're not going to be so fast to move into an endorsement position of the president."[9]

But at the last minute (just two hours before the rally), Buchanan called to tell

Long he would be a no-show. According to *Newsday*: ". . . Buchanan explained he had decided to stay away from the nation's media capital and the inevitable avalanche of questions about columnist William F. Buckley Jr.'s assertion that he had been guilty of anti-Semitism."[10]

Long was livid. Never one to mince words, he said of Buchanan: "If he didn't have the courage to face his critics in New York, how could he withstand the pressures of a national campaign?"[11]

Disappointed as he was, Long did not miss the opportunity to put President Bush on notice: "It is very clear," Long said, "that Bush's retention of the Party line in 1992 is in jeopardy. If Buchanan does well in New Hampshire's notoriously quirky primary, you could be witnessing a one-term president."[12]

The 1992 Elections

At the top of the Conservative Party's 1992 agenda was the re-election of Senator Al D'Amato. Most political pundits agreed that in his bid for a third term, Senator "Pothole" was vulnerable. After being cleared on August 2, 1991, by the Senate Ethics Committee of allegations that he used senatorial influence and pressure to enrich friends and contributors, the senator turned his attention to mending political fences in New York. D'Amato took the Conservative Party very seriously, appearing at party functions all over the state.

Left to right: Tony Rudmann, Sen. D'Amato, Vice President Dan Quayle, James Molinaro, Mike Long (1992).

D'Amato was popular among Republicans, but he did have a challenger from within the GOP, political ne'er-do-well Laurence Rockefeller, the nephew of Nelson. In envisioning his candidacy, Mr. Rockefeller obviously failed to conjure Republican elections results over the past few years. He claimed that "significant majorities of Republicans were unlike [D'Amato]", by which he meant that they are "pro-choice and pro-environment and dismayed at the never ending parade of scandals associated with his name."[13] Apparently Mr. Rockefeller spent too much time jawing with his cronies in Manhattan, and thus overlooked the fact that statewide Republican winners in recent years, including Ronald Reagan and D'Amato, were articulately pro-life.

Even *The New York Times* (March 3, 1992) knew enough to report:

> The Republican Party is a suburban, blue-collar party now," one long-time party strategist, who insisted on anonymity, said. "The high WASPs have moved left. They're Democrats now. We used to be a progressive Protestant party. Now we're a conservative Catholic party. There's no better manifestation of this change than Al D'Amato.

A Marist Poll confirmed this sentiment: 52 percent of New York Republicans are Roman Catholic and just 36.4 percent are Protestant.

In any case, the Rockefeller threat was short-lived. The state Republican Party ridiculed his candidacy and revealed Federal Election Commission filings that showed how Larry Rockefeller and his wife, Wendy, contributed mostly to Democratic presidential and senatorial candidates. His lackluster candidacy died in late summer when the courts knocked out his petitions.

But there is an interesting footnote to the Rockefeller candidacy. Rudy Giuliani, who was mulling another run for city Hall in 1993, made a revealing comment about Rockefeller to *The New York Times*. He represents Giuliani said, "a tradition in the Republican Party I've worked hard to re-kindle – the Rockefeller, Javits, Lefkovitz tradition." Giuliani said he considered Rockefeller's senate candidacy "a healthy development."[14]

On the Democratic side, New York City Comptroller Elizabeth Holtzman, New York Attorney General Robert Abrams, former vice-presidential candidate Geraldine Ferraro, and "community activist" Rev. Al Sharpton lit up the political stage with a vicious free-for-all primary fight. In September, Robert Abrams took the prize, topping second place Ferraro by 11,000 votes. Most analysts figured Abrams would beat D'Amato in a walk, but then most analysts are Democrats.

When it was apparent Bill Clinton was to be the Democratic standard bearer in the '92 presidential race, the Conservative Party Executive Committee recommended that the state committee support the Bush-Quayle ticket in the November election. Mike Long commented:

> After much debate, the Executive Committee has chosen to commit itself to re-electing George Bush and Dan Quayle. During our deliberations we took into account the Bush Administration's record and compared it to those of Perot and Clinton. While we've had our disagreements with the President he looks good in comparison to his primary rivals.

The Conservative Party's support is largely based on the Administration's commitment to conservative social policies, educations choice, privatization and a substantive role for the party in the conduct of the campaign and the next four years. We feel from our recent discussions with the Bush Administration that they are learning from their mistakes and building on their strengths. We are encouraged by the President's recent performance in Rio where he placed American interests ahead of the agenda promoted by radical environmentalists.

We firmly believe that if the Bush Administration continues to address the issues of family values by focusing attention on the failures of liberalism, George Bush will lead this country out of its doldrums and engineer his own re-election. We are confident he will do so, and with the Conservative Party support New York will be in the winners column this November 3.[15]

On September 21, 1992, Marilyn Quayle, wife of the vice president, accepted the Conservative endorsement on behalf of the Republican ticket. In a rousing speech, Long told the party faithful:

George Bush has admitted that he made a mistake in joining with the Democratic Congress to raise taxes, but Bill Clinton and Mario Cuomo are unrepentant in their advocacy of higher taxes. Bill Clinton claims that he only wants to increase taxes on the wealthy; unfortunately his definition of wealthy will include the bulk of the middle class.

Following the lead of Mario Cuomo, Bill Clinton is an advocate of all things big in government. His prescription for reforming the health care system will impose higher costs to consumers, through higher taxes and the rationing of essential services. In New York we have the nation's most extensive public health system. Once you've experienced it you know why your chances of improving your health are far greater if you use private sector facilities. Only Mario Cuomo and Bill Clinton still believe in the superiority of public health care.

Recently, President Bush outlined an economic program that will rejuvenate America. It calls for lower, not higher, taxes. It advocates reducing government interference into our lives, not increasing it. And it opposes hiring quotas.

The Bush plan is in sharp contrast to the liberal policies of Bill Clinton and it is a primary reason why the Conservative Party is endorsing Bush/Quayle.[16]

In the fall campaign, Al D'Amato derided Robert Abrams as "hopelessly liberal."

When Abrams called the Senator a fascist and refused to apologize for seven days, the D'Amato campaign attacked back in a TV ad that included a photo of Mussolini.

George Bush did poorly in New York, receiving only 34 percent of the vote, but D'Amato overcame a 20-point gap in the polls to pull off the upset of the year and squeaked by with a margin of 80 thousand votes:

	Abrams Dem.	D'Amato Rep.	D'Amato Cons.	D'Amato R. to L.	Abrams Lib
Outside New York City	**1,787,794**	**2,020,112**	**223,865**	**181,904**	**95,681**
Bronx	177,078	73,169	8,072	5,974	7,541
Brooklyn	304,530	181,716	17,287	11,640	11,179
Manhattan	367,571	98,089	6,715	5,219	15,306
Queens	264,761	202,130	22,919	13,358	10,976
Staten Island	41,267	77,606	10,400	6,819	2,516
Total New York City	**1,155,207**	**632,710**	**65,393**	**43,010**	**47,518**
Total State	**2,943,001**	**2,652,822**	**289,258**	**224,914**	**143,199**

The Conservative and Right to Life parties provided D'Amato with his margin of victory.

In another notable race, Peekskill Assemblyman George Pataki beat long-time liberal-Republican incumbent State Senator Mary B. Goodhue in the September primary, thanks to the support of the Conservative Party, Change-NY, Ronald Lauder, and Bruce Bent. In the November general election, the forty-seven-year-old Pataki romped over his Democratic opponent:

Vote in 1992 General Election
George E. Pataki Rep. 57,765 Cons. 10,128	67,893
Marshall S. Belkin, Dem.	34,263
James J. Hamilton, R. to L.	4,378
Mary B. Goodhue, ITP	17,889

By late November, the media began pestering Mike Long on his thoughts concerning the 1993 New York City mayoral race and the looming shadow of Rudy Giuliani: "Every year's a new year," Long said. "I don't know if he [Giuliani] wants to talk about the mayoral election or what. My thoughts? I'm open."[17] Long was open all right; he was open to waging a battle to uphold party principles.

It's Our City, Fight Back!

In the late 1960s New York City's cultural elites faced a grave dilemma on the issue of school decentralization. There was, on the one hand, the lingering spirit of the "Great Society" calling for "maximum feasible participation" of minorities and local communities in their schools; on the other hand, there was the liberals' historic distrust of citizens actually participating in the making of public-policy decisions. If Manhattan's elites openly opposed decentralization and community action, they would appear racist and insensitive; yet if they approved, they might lose control to the neighborhood "louts."

Legislation that would have allowed parents a greater say in their children's education had remained in limbo for several years, bouncing back and forth between New York's city council and the legislature in Albany. But the stalling became too embarrassing, and a system was finally agreed upon that made principals, teachers, and administrators accountable to minorities and neighborhood activists. Or so it was alleged. Here's the background:

The hero of Manhattan's enlightened salons, Mayor John V. Lindsay, had announced the dawn of a new municipal era in 1970: New York City would thereafter have thirty-two elected school boards. In addition, the board of education was to be revamped: two members were to be appointed by the mayor, and the five borough presidents were each to appoint one member, for a total of seven. Although education bureaucrats and union leaders had to put on their happy faces at Lindsay's press conference, it soon became apparent that they had no intention of permitting local political, civic, and religious activists to decide the fate of their own children's education.

New York University sociologist David Rogers observed that the board of education headquarters at 110 Livingston Street in Brooklyn (which houses over 5,000 bureaucrats) "never really dedicated itself to implementing the law and supporting the districts . . . and continued to overregulate the districts and schools, limiting their flexibility, while at the same time failing to set standards for performance and monitor compliance." For example, the first chancellor of the new system, Dr. Harvey Scribner, was hounded from the job after only two years, precisely because he was an enthusiastic supporter of decentralization.

For the next twenty years the entrenched bureaucracy bullied the school boards, while the seven appointees of the board of education served as a rubber stamp for the liberal chancellors who, as the apex of the central bureaucracy, ran the city's schools. Increasingly, the educational system became a target of social-engineering experiments that were brewing in Manhattan's intellectual labs.

In the 1970s, New York's elites began to press a political and educational agenda that would eradicate the influence of Judaeo-Christian principles on public policy. By 1986, for example, a so-called Homosexual Rights Sexual Orientation bill was passed that bestowed minority status – and privileges – based on sexual proclivity. The homosexuals' historic plea for privacy in the bedroom was discarded in favor of a radical program of public acceptance and celebration of homosexual culture, most especially in the city's classrooms.

For years the Conservative Party had opposed the so-called "gay rights" bill and had helped defeat it no fewer than twelve times. Conservative Party member Jack

Swan, working with neighborhood activists, parents, educators, and religious leaders throughout the city, had put together winning coalitions. Then–councilman-at-large Mike Long, City Council Majority Leader Tom Cuite, and General Welfare Committee chairman, Councilwoman Aileen Ryan of the Bronx, controlled the votes in committee and on the floor of the council and succeeded in defeating the bill.

While he was executive director and party chairman during the 1970's and 1980's, Serf Maltese had testified regularly against the bill, his reasoning simple, yet compelling:

> The Conservative Party is committed to the concept of equal opportunity for all people regardless of sex, race and religion in all areas of life.
>
> We reaffirm and continue to support traditional civil rights protection for all and continue to oppose discrimination, reverse discrimination, quotas and the creation of preferential classes. Thus, we most certainly oppose this bill which would have the effect of creating a new protected class of homosexuals, who given the interpretive propensities of certain of our eminent jurists, would eventually acquire and require affirmative action programs, preferential status in hiring, housing and other benefits under this expanded definition of civil rights.[18]

Throughout the 1980s the political clout of the homosexual movement grew. In 1986, when Tom Cuite retired from the city council, Peter Vallone agreed to permit the "gay rights" bill to pass in order to secure the votes necessary for him to become the new majority leader. And so it was that in 1989 the mayor of New York declared that marriage is no longer a requirement for a family: David Dinkins signed the "domestic-partnership" order, which meant that homosexual couples and unmarried couples who were city employees were recognized as the legal equals of married families. And not only were married couples beginning to lose their legal pre-eminence; they were also about to lose their rights as parents.

AIDS expert Dr. Mathilde Krim testified at a public meeting of the board of education that "parents are not qualified to decide whether their teenagers should have access to condoms and that parents should not really have a say if schools should hand them out." Mayor Dinkins and Education Chancellor Joseph Fernandez concurred and agreed to a condom-distribution program in which students would be given condoms over their parents' objections, with no counseling required.

The ultimate assault on parents' rights, however, was the 1992 unveiling of the revised kindergarten to sixth grade "HIV/AIDS Curriculum" and the "Children of the Rainbow Curriculum." The K-6 HIV/AIDs curriculum is a New York City supplement to a New York state-mandated program. It informs elementary students how to have safe sex. In the fourth and fifth grades, kids get lectures on oral, anal, and vaginal sex, and children are also taught how to use condoms, dental dams, contraceptive gels, and lubricants. (In-class demonstrations of proper condom techniques led to the nickname by which these lectures became known: the *Cucumber Curriculum*.) A glossary was provided that defines such terms as bisexuality, homosexuality, lesbianism, body fluids, and barrier method.

Fourth-grade students were introduced to counseling agencies, including Planned Parenthood, the Gay Men's Health Crisis, and ACT-UP, the group that has regularly demonstrated at St. Patrick's Cathedral and enthusiastically desecrated the Communion Host.

But the social engineering didn't end there; the K-6 HIV/AIDS was only the sex-education component of the controversial curriculum. There was also the *multicultural* program, the Rainbow Curriculum, which describes homosexuals as a normal cultural group but has nothing to say about Judaeo-Christian cultural norms.

The curriculum's bibliography includes the now-famous books *Heather Has Two Mommies*, *Daddy's Roommate*, *Gloria Goes to Gay Pride*, and *Rapunzel's Revenge: Fairytales for Feminists*.

After fifteen years on her local school board, Conservative Party activist Mary Cummins thought she had seen everything, but on the February day in 1992 when she perused the package that arrived from 110 Livingston Street, the president of Queens School Board 24 realized the bureaucrats had outdone themselves.

"I cannot compromise with evil," she told a friend. And her board agreed – they rejected the Rainbow curriculum in April by a vote of nine to zero. Before long, half the city's school boards had followed her lead by rejecting all or part of the program.

Chancellor Fernandez was livid, and in early September he demanded that rebel District 24 produce an acceptable alternative by the end of October. Cummins struck back by organizing, with Jack Swan's help, a massive protest. "We're taking this right to the chancellor's front door," she said. "He and the mayor will know that they are on a hot seat. The clergy at the rally will represent congregations of tens of thousands. That translates into a lot of votes, especially when you add in tens of thousands of parents."

On October 6, 1992, over 2,000 concerned parents marched on Board of Education headquarters. The Reverend Michael Faulkner, associate pastor at Manhattan's Calvary Baptist Church, expressed the crowd's sentiment with these words: "A change is coming. We will no longer tolerate those destructive ideas that are destroying our families. . . . Our children should not be treated like animals. Abstinence is not a dirty word."

The controversy did not end with the demonstration. In a letter dated November 12, 1992, Mary Cummins answered Fernandez's ultimatum:

> As we always have in the past, we are going to continue to teach our students to appreciate the wide variety of religious traditions and racial and ethnic cultures represented in contemporary American society. We are also

going to continue to teach our students to love their country, to obey its laws, and to foster unity and harmony by behaving fairly and decently toward everyone they encounter.

However, we are not going to teach our children to treat all types of human behavior as equally safe, wholesome or acceptable. On the contrary, we are going to teach them that they should never engage in conduct that would cause harm to others or themselves. . . . Accordingly, we are going to make any use of your teaching guide entitled *Children of the Rainbow-first Grade* because it is shot through with dangerously misleading propaganda.

On November 16, another letter was sent that defined the Queens district's own multicultural program, "Reaching Out":

In reply to your letter dated November 16, 1992, please be advised that this district is convinced that our multicultural education is in full compliance with Board of Education policy, and we, therefore, reject your suggestion that it needs to be expanded to include material aimed at promoting acceptance of sodomy.

Because Cummins and her colleagues boycotted a December 1 conference at 110 Livingston Street, Fernandez suspended the nine duly elected representatives of Community School Board 24 the next day. Fernandez then seized control of the district, appointed his own trustees (all board of ed bureaucrats), and ordered them to implement the Rainbow Curriculum.

Fernandez appeared triumphant for the moment, but many observers sensed a change in the political climate. A December 6 *New York Times* article admitted that the curriculum, "like all those approved by the chancellor's office is merely an advisory document and local boards can use it or ignore it as they like." This comment seemed out of character for a paper whose editorial three days earlier was entitled, "Chancellor Fernandez Stands Tall." Similarly, a front-page *Newsday* investigative report revealed that the curriculum (two years in preparation) was hastily pasted together and that Fernandez had never read its entire 430 pages.

At the December 9 meeting of the board of education, a motion to reinstate Mary Cummins's District 24 School Board was approved six to zero with one abstention. The affirmative votes included Mayor David Dinkins's two appointees, H. Carl McCall and Dr. Westina L. Matthews.

One month later, the re-instated Cummins faxed a letter to the seven-member board of education:

The proverbial twelve days of Christmas have now passed and we still have no reply to the letter we faxed Chancellor Fernandez on December 23 offering him a choice of two alternative ways to mediate our dispute.... Under the circumstances we can only conclude that he has no genuine interest in mediation. Indeed, it is becoming increasingly obvious that the only thing he is interested in is a face-saving statement – no mediation, no retraction of *Children of the Rainbow,* and no legal showdown in which he would have to defend it.

An unrepentant Mary Cummins, representing the ordinary parents in her district, had faced down the central bureaucrats and foiled their efforts to indoctrinate New York's children.[19] For her courage, the Conservative Party in 1992 bestowed on Cummins their highest honor, the Charles Edison Memorial Award.

The Making of the Mayor, 1993

Now my own personal story with the Conservative Party became a part of its history. Throughout 1991 and 1992, I had worked closely with Mary Cummins and my old friend Jack Swan to help defeat the Rainbow Curriculum and its sister outrage, mandatory condom distribution. I regularly testified at board of education hearings on these matters and joined in various protests. I was also reporting on these battles and analyzing the mores and voting potential of New York's blue-collar neighborhoods for various periodicals.

Living in borough neighborhoods most of my life, I knew first-hand the damage incurred over the decades by the "urban renewal" projects of elitist social engineers.

I had watched as thousands of lower- and middle-class homes were bulldozed and replaced with "projects." I had watched the bureaucrats create a welfare system that, in the words of Daniel Patrick Moynihan, resulted in the formation of a "permanent dependent class." I had watched many an erstwhile neighborhood collapse into something called "the community," with its permanent underclass, rampant racism, runaway crime, and all the myriad social programs that dreamers dreamed could solve the problems they had created. And those programs became a beast with an insatiable appetite for tax dollars.

In August of 1992, I re-read Bill Buckley's memoir of his 1965 mayoral campaign, *The Unmaking of a Mayor,* and realized that the Lindsay-Buckley battle had significant parallels to the upcoming Giuliani-Dinkins race. Rudy Giuliani, like John Lindsay, wanted to run under the smoke screen of a "fusion" candidacy, which meant – among other things – running on the Liberal Party line, not just the Republican line. And Dave Dinkins was as liberal a liberal as there was anywhere, which meant he wanted to feed the beast with the insatiable appetite.

The Giuliani strategy was essentially the same as Lindsay's: hold on to the traditional Republican base and co-op enough liberal Jewish votes to bag the election.

Giuliani's strategists also realized they had one advantage Lindsay had not. As an Italian-American, Giuliani could also appeal to neighborhood ethnics as "one of them." They would clone Cuomo's 1977 strategy and run Rudy as a "neighborhood preservationist." They believed they could have their cake and eat it too: They could be as liberal as they had to be to attract Manhattan Democrats, because ethnic voters, who had come to loathe Mayor Dinkins, had nowhere else to go.

This "anybody-but-Dinkins" strategy annoyed me, because I believed it was a big con. Rudolph Giuliani, whose family moved out of Brooklyn when he was seven, grew up in the high-rent district of Garden City in Nassau County. He was not a neighborhood kid, and he was certainly not a "street-corner conservative," and yet his handlers were prepared to con traditionalists in New York's neighborhoods into supporting the liberal Giuliani.

I had spent hours throughout 1992 studying the city's voting demographics and had concluded that in 1993 a Conservative Party mayoral candidate could implement a strategy similar to Buckley's in 1965 and maybe – just maybe – upset the Republican-Liberal establishment. And after hours of discussion with my pal, Jack Swan, I decided I wouldn't mind being that candidate.

In late September 1992, I had dinner with Mike Long at the Hotel Gregory in Bay Ridge and discussed my position. Long and I had first met in 1975 when I was executive director of the Former Police Officers Association that represented laid-off cops during New York City's financial crisis. Long made it clear that a decision had not been made for 1993, but it was obvious to me that Mike was hardly thrilled with the prospect of endorsing Giuliani, given Rudy's views on various social issues. Besides, if Giuliani took the Liberal line, the party's door would be closed to him. I gave Long a copy of the book I had written about municipal bonds and pointed out that with eighteen years of experience in the municipal finance industry – plus the fact that I was the son and grandson of New York City cops and still lived in an old-fashioned neighborhood – I could be a credible candidate. After a couple of cognacs, Mike and I agreed to stay in touch.

In early October, I was guest speaker at a Women's National Republican Club luncheon in Manhattan that Mike Long attended. The topic of my speech to this bastion of Rockefeller Republicans was "The Republican Party and Family values." Journalist Richard Brookhiser covered the event and in his *New York Observer* column reported:

> Mr. Marlin began with a look at his own neighborhood, Ridgewood, Queens: white, ethnic, working-middle class. For eons, neighborhoods like Ridgewood were dependably Democratic, but in the 60's something changed. Ridgewood cast 30 percent of its vote for William F. Buckley Jr. in the 1965 Mayor's race. In 1970, it gave 66 percent to James Buckley for Senate. In 1972, Richard Nixon got over 80 percent of the Ridgewood

vote. In 1988, the only New York City campaign stop made by George Bush was at Christ the King high school in Ridgewood. (I remember it: I covered it for this newspaper.) "The heirs of Al Smith's common man and F.D.R.'s forgotten man became members of Richard Nixon's silent majority and Ronald Reagan's moral majority," Mr. Marlin said.

How? A national political realignment, symbolized by Ridgewood, occurred, Mr. Marlin argued, "because the Democratic Party rejected middle-class values." Following Michael Barone, Mr. Marlin identified Adlai Stevenson as the turning point – the elitist from central casting, the first Democratic presidential candidate to be a "critic, not a celebrator" of the great mass of Americans and the way they lived and thought. The Republicans caught the Democrats bathing and stole their polyesters, and so the GOP has won seven out of the last 10 Presidential elections.[20]

My conclusion on that day was this: If the Republican deserted traditional values, they risked destroying the Reagan election coalition and losing the presidency (as they did a month later). My words fell on deaf ears, but Long told me afterwards that he wanted me to meet with several of his leaders.

In early January 1993, in a private dining room in the Union League Club, Mike Long introduced me to four of the party's county leaders: Brooklyn's Gerry Kassar, Manhattan's Michael Berns, Tom Long from Queens, and William Newmark from the Bronx. For several hours they grilled me with questions about my views on issues and political strategy. One thing became obvious to me that evening: the four county leaders were looking for an excuse not to support Rudy Giuliani.

Long asked me that night to be a guest speaker at his February C-Pac conference. "Give them your family values speech," he said, "and let's see how they react."

It was at this conference that moderator Tony Rudmann made the first public reference to me as a possible candidate.

During the balance of February, I met with local Conservative leaders throughout the city, and I received generally good receptions in every county . . . except Staten Island. Residents of Staten Island have always believed that they were the "bastard children" of the rest of the city, and that as long as Democrats ruled city hall they would never be "legitimate." Thus the borough's Conservatives were bitterly opposed to four more years of Dinkins. In my meeting with Staten Island leaders and Conservative Party Executive Vice Chairman Jim Molinaro (who also served as Staten Island's deputy borough president), it was made crystal clear to me that although they liked my views on social issues, the local party would side with Giuliani to stop Dinkins. Obviously my Conservative colleagues didn't see me as a winner.

On Friday, February 26 (which was the day of the '93 World Trade Center bombing), Mr. Giuliani and I were slated to be speakers at the Manhattan Conservative Party's annual dinner, until, that is, Giuliani heard that he was to share the dais with me and cancelled his appearance. Giuliani's snub not only annoyed Conservative leaders, but it became news. *The New York Times* ran a three-column story, complete with my photo, titled, "Conservative Foe Challenges Giuliani." And *Newsday* reported: "Conservatives Dub Rudy No Show a Snub." Manhattan Leader Mike Berns, in a sidebar to the *Newsday* article, was quoted as saying, "There's a serious question about why he didn't want to address us. The feeling right now on the committee is very strong that they will not vote to endorse Mr. Giuliani." The March 15 edition of *The New York Observer* ran a huge front-page article called, "Giuliani Nibbles at Line, But Conservative Party is Reeling in a Marlin." Author Terry Golway wrote:

> Instead of taking up Mr. Giuliani on his offer to have a share in the governance of the city, the Conservatives seem eager to exploit the potentially explosive cultural cleavage laid bare in the struggle that ended the tenure of Mr. Fernandez. They currently appear to be rallying behind a political unknown named George Marlin, who, not coincidentally, lives in the same Queens school district that gave birth to the revolt against Mr. Fernandez and the Rainbow Curriculum. . . .
>
> Though Mr. Marlin lacks the feisty body language of the three former Presidential candidates, he doesn't shy away from spirited language. "If you are tired of liberal crackpots, join me in the crusade to take back our city," he told the assembled Conservatives. "We must love God, family, neighborhood and country. Only by revitalizing these values can we revitalize our government and economy . . ."
>
> If Mr. Marlin's quixotic campaign does win the Conservative nod at the party's convention next month, the mayoral campaign will have taken another unexpected turn well before the candidates begin their hawking in earnest. The Queens investment banker is nothing if not eager for the contest, although he has never run for office before.[21]

Later on in March, in a *Newsday* op-ed piece called, "With Right on Our Side," I explained why a registered Republican, like me, could enter the political fray as a Conservative Party candidate:

> I believe the Conservative Party is essential to a conservative victory in the upcoming battle for the soul of the New York GOP.
> The Conservative Party's electoral strength must be the key to overtaking the Republican Party's old guard. That strength not only can ensure the visibility of conservative candidates who might otherwise be silenced, it can also spark a revival of the Republican Party as a true party of principle.
> Although Republican pragmatists have given us 20 years of defeat in

New York, they still manage to hang on. Even after their last gubernatorial disaster, Pierre Rinfret, they refused to die of embarrassment. The only way to end the reign of these political bankrupts is for conservative Republicans to ally themselves with the Conservative Party and re-construct the Reagan coalition.

On May 11, 1993, surrounded by my wife Barbara, my father John, and my brother Steven, as well as by friends and supporters, I declared my candidacy on the steps of New York's city hall. I told the assembled press:

> Another part of New York City died today. Another hard-working taxpayer gave up on the crime and the taxes and the moral decay. Another honest citizen fled. Another family left. And unless we take a stand today, another part of New York City will die tomorrow. That's why I've come here today to declare my candidacy for the nomination of the Conservative Party and Right to Life Party for Mayor of the City of New York. I'm running to give voters a choice.

Noting that Dinkins and Giuliani agreed on support for abortion, condom distribution in schools, gay rights, opposition to educational vouchers, and their "groveling at the boots of Ray Harding's Liberal Party," I concluded that the only difference between this perfectly matched pair of Liberals, "is the way they part their hair."

Prior to the May 26 party convention, Giuliani had a two-hour meeting with Mike Long at party headquarters in Brooklyn. I remember calling Long's executive assistant Laura Schreiner every half-hour and being shocked to learn they were talking so long. I couldn't help wondering if Giuliani might be softening up Long. Long later told me that he and Rudy had "wrestled with the social issues and while Rudy inferred he would like the party's nomination, he never asked for it."

"I also made it clear," Long said, "that if he ran again with the Liberal Party, the Conservatives, in good conscience, couldn't support him."

At the party's convention, held at Manhattan's Warwick Hotel on Wednesday, May 27, Bronx County Chairman Bill Newmark nominated me and urged the delegates to stick by their principles. I looked to be a shoe-in. But in a last-minute turnaround, Giuliani decided he wanted the Conservative line after all, and, in a letter to Queens County leader Tom Long, he asked for an open primary. "This year's election," Giuliani wrote, "should not be a referendum on ideology, but on the management and future of New York City."[22]

The Douglaston, Queens, Conservative leader William Lewis, nominated Giuliani. "Principles are fine," Lewis told the delegates, "but you have to be elected first."

Given the events of September 11, 2001, and their aftermath, it may stretch credulity, but I actually beat Rudy Giuliani on the first ballot, receiving over 70 percent of the delegate vote. I lost Staten Island and a few delegates from Queens. Mayor Giuliani's performance under the extreme pressures following the terrorist attacks on New York have understandably swallowed up the fact that he was about as much a Republican as was Mario Cuomo, whom, by the way, he would endorse for re-election in 1994 – over Cuomo's Republican opponent, George Pataki. To say that a lot can change in eight years is to ignore the fact that the world can change in a single day.

In my acceptance speech, I said I was running to give voters a "conservative" choice between "four more years of Mayor Dinkins's failed liberal policies or four years of Rudy Giuliani's failed liberal policies." My toughest comments were reserved for what I called "fifty years of liberal social engineering" that were responsible for creating a "permanent underclass in our city: Welfare abuses that have allowed an entire generation to live off the labor of hard working taxpayers. Well, the free ride is over," I said, "because it's our City and it's time we fought back!"

Also nominated at the Convention were Howard Lim for comptroller and Ron Reale for public advocate. Lim, who was Manhattan's Conservative party leader for over a decade before stepping down in 1992, ran Senator D'Amato's New York City office for six years. In 1978, he ran on the Conservative line for Congress against Bill Green and Bella Abzug. Reale was president of the Transit Police Benevolent Association and was also running for public advocate in the Democratic primary.

Mike Long had extensive meetings with Club for Growth members Bruce Bent, Dusty Rhodes, Dick and Virginia Gilder, and others to promote my candidacy. His argument went this way: By supporting Marlin, we are making a statement to the Republican gubernatorial wannabes that if we did not sell out our principles in the current race against an inept mayor who is destroying our city, then we are not going to sell out to them. In a 2000 interview, Long said to me: "If we would have given Giuliani a pass on the Liberal Party, taxes, abortion, gay rights and the other social issues, in 1994 the Republicans would have expected us to give them a pass and we would have wound up with an empty suit candidate."

The Club for Growth accepted Long's reasoning and contributed generously to the campaign. They raised about half of the $500,000 the party spent. This infusion of cash permitted the campaign to hire a full-time campaign manager, Mike's daughter,

Eileen Long, a recent graduate of St. Francis College, where the 5 ft. 10 in. Eileen had a full scholarship for basketball. Weaned on politics, Eileen was anxious to take on the eighteen-hour workdays demanded in a campaign. As the only full-time employee, she organized the campaign with the help of Mike Long's executive assistant Laura Schreiner and part-time workers, Maureen and Debbie Long and Debbie Schreiner. It was a family affair to say the least.

Eileen, who grew up surrounded by seven brothers, was a good choice, because she was tough enough to put up with my antics as well as those of my friends, Pat

Foye, Jack Swan, and Jim Kelly, who were often with me on the campaign trail. Foye, a partner in the prestigious law firm of Skadden Arps, was then heading up his firm's European offices and spent most of his time in Moscow, Budapest, and Brussels. But whenever he flew into New York, he found the time to hand out flyers with me at bus stops, subway stations, and shopping areas. Swan, who was then 67 years old and hobbling on a cane, was constantly with me, and *Newsday* described him as the "elderly volunteer who wore a three-piece black suit and carried a pocket watch and cane." Political consultants Mike Gannon and Nelson Warfield (who would be Bob Dole's press spokesman during the 1996 presidential campaign) also joined us and designed brochures and TV and radio commercials. Tony Fabrizio and John McLaughlin also served as pollsters. Conservative Party Vice Chairman Allen Roth was the principal author of a ten-page report called, "Marlin Fiscal and Economic Plan for New York City." It was a terrific "supply-side economic" document, and we unveiled it on July 29. We told New Yorkers that their city was drowning in a tide of wasteful spending, high taxes, and onerous regulations, and that under Dinkins the city had lost 351,000 jobs. The plan called for a cut in taxes, a reduction in spending, and the privatization of city services.

Left to right: Pat Foye, Nelson Warfield, Jim Kelly, the author, Mike Long (1994).

I promised that as mayor, I would immediately eliminate:

* The Unincorporated Business Tax
* The Commercial Rent Tax
* The Corporate Income Tax
* The Hotel Occupancy Tax
* The Income Tax Surcharge

Our plan also included over $7-Billion in potential savings and assets sales including:

* Selling Kennedy and LaGuardia Airports
* Mandating competitive bidding for city contracts
* Eliminating provisional employees
* Eliminating rent control and selling public housing to its tenants
*Privatizing city buses and privatizing the Health and Hospitals Corporation.

Our plan represented a radical restructuring of the way New York City would govern itself, and it was based on proven supply-side measures and plain common sense.

I also endorsed Ron Lauder's campaign to get a term-limits referendum on the ballot, and I was the only mayoral candidate who signed the term-limits petition. Indeed, ours was the only campaign that publicly took a stand on the referendum.

I sent a letter to Jack Kemp, blasting him for his endorsement of Giuliani and for saying that "Rudy [Giuliani] is the only candidate in the race who understands that the tax base requires lower tax rates."[23] I reminded Kemp that the Conservative Party was the only party supporting Kemp's supply-side vision of tax cuts, and that the Liberal Party candidate, Rudy Giuliani, had said publicly that he would not rule out raising taxes. Kemp sent me a hand-written letter of apology.

In addition to his financial support, Dusty Rhodes served as co-chairman with Virginia Gilder of Republicans for Marlin. Rhodes also helped secure the endorsement of numerous national Republicans, including former Reagan secretary of education and chairman of the Republican National Committee, Bill Bennett, Governor Pierre DuPont of Delaware, former U.S. attorney general Edward Meese (Giuliani's old boss), and former Vice President Dan Quayle's chief of staff, William Kristol.

When Bennett endorsed me on the steps of city hall on September 22 and most of the media ignored it, a livid *Wall Street Journal* ran an editorial titled, "New York's Marlin Blackout."

> The real news is man-bites-dog, as when a dignitary opposes his party's nominee. All the more so since Mr. Bennett was a prominent speaker at the Houston Republican convention, where 15,000 reporters were straining to find every drop of discord in the GOP, above all over its divisions on cultural issues like schools, gay rights and so on. So you would think that the media capital of the world might stop to take notice of Mr. Bennett and Mr. Marlin.
>
> George Marlin is a media black hole, and when Mr. Bennett enters to endorse him no light can escape to be detected. Come to think of it, Mr. Giuliani is also running as the invisible man, trying at all costs to avoid saying anything; discussing an issue would blur the point that he is not David Dinkins.

It was often frustrating to be ignored by the media, but we did manage to score a few hits: Both *New York* magazine and *Insight* magazine did six-page feature articles. *The New York Times*, *Newsday*, and *The New York Observer* each did three major stories. Richard Brookhiser wrote essays in *National Review* and the *Observer*, and Ray Kerrison devoted a *Post* column to our campaign in which he described me as the "real alternative," as the only one in the race with the "convictions of Reagan." George Will, Pat Buchanan, and Bill Buckley wrote columns promoting my candidacy, and Buckley also hosted a fundraiser and press conference endorsing me.

The attention our campaign received from national Republican and Conservative leaders managed to hit a nerve. At a press conference in Washington, Republican National Chairman Haley Barbour took a shot at our campaign. He told reporters "that it was 'possible but not likely' that Marlin could siphon away enough votes to sink Giuliani in his close race for mayor. 'It would be a tragedy for New York City and for conservatives if the Conservative Party re-elects David Dinkins.'"[24]

When asked why Conservatives and Republicans should support Giuliani, who is pro-abortion, pro-gay rights, and against school choice, Barbour replied, "Life is a series of choices. As I have said before, we shouldn't let the pursuit of the perfect kill off the good."

By July, Giuliani had abandoned his quest to force his way into a Conservative Party primary, and his strategists now took the tact of simply ignoring the Conservative challenge. Giuliani would not appear on the same platform with me and announced that he would not participate in any debate to which I was invited. He went so far as to cancel any speaking engagement, whether to civic or church groups, if I were invited to speak separately to the same group. As the *Wall Street Journal* observed, "Giuliani is refusing to appear on the same platform or even the same zip code [with Marlin]."[25]

After the campaign, Giuliani's media guru pointed out what may have been the real reason for avoiding me:

> If we had gotten into a debate with Marlin, I think that would have been fatal for us. All Marlin had to do was stand up and say: "My name is George Marlin. I'm an educated, intelligent man. I went to a very good school, and I think both of these guys [Dinkins and Giuliani] are full of baloney." He would have gotten three points, four points.[26]

Giuliani's handlers realized their candidate took criticism poorly and had trouble laughing at himself. He had a short fuse, and they feared a wisecrack from me (and I had plenty of them stored up) might set him off. Even Giuliani admitted to columnist Murray Kempton: "Marlin might get under my skin and make me angry."[27]

To further enrage Giuliani, our campaign accepted speaking engagements from very liberal Manhattan groups. After all, we knew that where we went, he would cancel. Although we knew that I would never get a vote from any of these organizations, we figure Giuliani would lose votes, since many were livid that he refused to appear before them.

On September 9, I had a private meeting with Governor Mario Cuomo at his World Trade Center office. It may seem strange, but Cuomo and I hit it off. We both grew up in Queens and had common friends and acquaintances. In fact, the guy who introduced me into Queens politics, former Republican-Conservative Assemblyman Jack Gallagher, was Cuomo's St. John's Law School classmate and the governor's appointee to New York's Court of Claims. We had a photograph taken together in front of his copy of Holbein's portrait of St. Thomas More (referred to earlier in this book).

As I told the *Daily News* afterward, "We agreed to disagree about everything except Rudolph Giuliani."[28]

The one thing I did make clear to the governor was that Dinkins could not back down from his stance that I be included in debates. Cuomo told me that he did not expect Dinkins to retreat.

There were two debates during the campaign. The first was n Thursday, October 14, was sponsored by St. Francis College, and was televised live on New York 1, a Manhattan cable channel. The *Times* reported that my "rapid fire style seemed to throw Mr. Dinkins off balance at times." What I said was that the mayor's smoke-and-mirrors policies were destroying the financial bases of the city. As for Mr. Giuliani, I said he was a political fraud, just another liberal wrapped in Republican clothing. What's more, I said he was not "man enough" to debate me.[29] How else was I supposed to smoke him out of his tactical retreat? During the ninety-minute match, I was surprised to find how unprepared Dave Dinkins really was. He had 5 x 7 cards to read from, which was odd, but you figured they contained hard-to-remember data. In fact, there were times when he answered a reporter's question by actually reading from the cards, sometimes the *wrong* card. At one point, I felt sorry for him and even came close to pulling my punches. But I didn't.

The second and final debate was on Gabe Pressman's News 4 program on Sunday, October 17. Giuliani declined the initial invitation, so Pressman offered to have two debates back to back: the first half-hour between Dinkins and me, and the second half-hour between Dinkins and Giuliani. On the day of the debate, no one was sure if Giuliani was going to show up, so NBC had cameramen strategically located at their Rockefeller Center doorways in case he appeared late and tried to make a dramatic entrance. What Pressman didn't know was that if Giuliani had showed up at the end of the first half-hour, I wasn't planning on leaving the studio. The show was live, and the mayor of New York, Mr. Dinkins, was not going to order my arrest. If Giuliani walked off he would have looked like he had chickened out.

As it turned out, Giuliani was a no-show, but during the half-hour session I did manage to portray Rudy as a chicken. The night before, after an exhausting day of campaigning around the city, I had arrived at Brooklyn headquarters to find a livid Eileen Long. It seems that earlier that day Giuliani had held a rally in front of Mike Long's liquor store on Fifth Avenue in Bay Ridge. As the crowd moved down the block, some of Giuliani's goons began to harass Eileen and several volunteers when they were walking out of Conservative headquarters.

I was sympathetic with what had happened to Eileen, but I was very busy. I was trying to prep for the next day's debate with coaches Nelson Warfield and Mike Gannon. But Eileen was fuming. She came into the room where we were working, threw a rubber chicken on the table, and shouted: "You're not a man if you don't pull out this chicken in tomorrow's debate."

Although I was adamantly opposed to using a prop, I also did not relish giving Eileen a reason to torture me for the remainder of my life. On the following day while dressing for the debate, I realized I couldn't hide the chicken on my person. So my wife, Barbara, trimmed the bird's rubber belly – its gizzards? – and it rolled up to fit nicely in my back pocket.

The debate went well, and as we were nearing the conclusion, I realized I'd forgotten to pull out the chicken! While I was watching the clock and hoping for the right opportunity, Mayor Dinkins said, "I don't know if Giuliani is Republican, Conservative or Liberal." Here was my opening.

"Your honor," I said, "I'll tell you . . . this is what Rudy Giuliani is." And I pulled out the scrawny, yellow bird.

In a three-column story the next day, *The New York Times* showed a picture of a uneasy Gabe Pressman, an amused Dinkins, and a stage manager trying to snatch the chicken from the table. According to *Newsday,* Mayor Dinkins, "recognizing political gold, immediately asked for a fowl return. 'George, you should join me in the protest' the Mayor joked."[30]

Giuliani was not amused. "We've gotten the comedy routine with Marlin out of the way," Giuliani told *Newsday*. "Very funny, but now it's time to start debating the issues that affect New York."[31]

Of course that's what we'd been doing for months. The Conservative Party had put out thoughtful policy papers defining programs to fight crime, to address welfare, and to solve a range of other social ills, but each had been ignored. One might have thought the media lacked seriousness. But after the debate, members of the media showed themselves to be positively puerile. The chicken stunt got more ink and air time than we'd ever received before. The clip ran over and over again on all the local stations. It hit national news broadcasts and every paper in the region. This led the pundits to whine that there was not enough substantive discussion of the issues. We humbly asked God to give us strength.

Although the campaign had spent half-a-million bucks, had run some pretty good television and radio ads, and had carried on the campaign full-time from Labor Day right through to election day, we never scored higher than 2 percent in the polls. Even the hardcore Irish Catholic voters in the Rockaways and in Breezy Point were tilting toward Giuliani.

I had an epiphany of sorts on election day, Tuesday, November 2.

Election day is always the longest day for any candidate, and to get out of headquarters for a while, Pat Foye and I strolled down to Shore Road in Bay Ridge and looked up at the Verrazano Bridge. As we were walking back, a station wagon full of kids pulled up along side us, and a young, Irish-looking mother jumped out of the car and asked, "Aren't you George Marlin?"

"Yes."

She looked straight at me and said:

"I owe you an apology."

"What did you do," I inquired.

She hesitated and replied:

"You were the person I should have voted for, because I agree with your views on family, but I voted for Giuliani because I wanted to stop . . ."

She hesitated. I held up a hand of assurance, told her not to be concerned, and said it would all be for the best. I knew where she was going with her comments.

In the final weekend of the race, an unsigned (and illegal) flyer was distributed throughout all the conservative, blue-collar city neighborhoods. It read: "A vote for the Conservative Party candidate is a vote for Dinkins."

The race card was played. People were encouraged to fear that a vote for me would give them four more years of an incompetent mayor – a black mayor – intent on destroying their way of life. Without going into specifics, I'll say simply that the flyer's sentiments were not those of some lunatic fringe, but the frank opinions of some well-known intellectuals, people we thought were on our side. That's politics.

On election day, the voters gave Dinkins his walking papers by a margin of 71,598 votes and elected Rudolph Giuliani as New York's 107th mayor. I came in third, receiving 1 percent of the vote.

At the Warwick Hotel Ball Room, Mike Long told the hundreds in attendance:

> We are gathered here tonight because of a common belief. That you never waste your vote when you vote for what you believe in. All of us and tens of thousands of honest taxpaying New Yorkers stood up for what they believed in today at the polls and refused to vote for the lesser of two evils. Many of you know I have a storefront business in Brooklyn. And if there was one comment during this campaign I heard once, I heard it a thousand times. "I know Marlin's right." "I believe in everything he says." "But we have to get rid of Dinkins." We'll never know how many voters throughout

the City cast their ballots with that in mind. But we do know that it can never be said: The Conservative Party didn't offer what it has always offered: a choice.

The author, election night 1993 with (from left to right) Bruce Bent, MIke Long, Dusty Rhodes, Barbara Marlin.

In my concession statement, I reminded our supporters that what we had wanted most to do was fight the good fight:

> You all know this campaign was about more than a rubber chicken. It was about the very future of our neighborhoods and our city. Ours was not a campaign of personalities and race. Ours was a campaign of issues and ideas. . . .
>
> Throughout this campaign, we took our conservative message to every community in every borough. Our message was straightforward – New York City is on a cultural and economic treadmill to oblivion. And if we don't change things today, there may not be a New York left to save tomorrow. . . .
>
> Now we may not have won this battle. But there are many more to come. And the odds may be just as steep. But every time I stopped and questioned whether it was all worth it, I was reminded of my school board

president, Mary Cummins. I told myself that if a 70-year old grandmother from Queens could take on Joe Fernandez and win, there is no limit to what we can do with right on our side.

The words I spoke in this very hotel five months ago upon receiving the Conservative Party's nomination for mayor are still true tonight. "Never before has one political party been so clearly in the right."

Ladies and Gentlemen, it's our city, let's keep on fighting back!

The one piece of good news that evening was the passage of the New York City Term Limits Referendum. Desperate incumbents dragged the measure through the courts hoping to derail it. But, thanks in part to Ron Lauder's financial support, referendum advocates beat back the court challenges. Even though there were only a few weeks left to promote the measure once the courts cleared the way, New York City voters overwhelmingly supported term limits. Incumbents who spent years on the city payroll awoke to the reality that the day of reckoning was approaching. Soon they would have to seek employment in the real world.

After recovering from our hangovers, Mike Long and I analyzed the past year and asked ourselves if all the work, all the political pressure, and all the abuse had been worth it. I had to agree with Mike's conclusion:

"By standing up for our principles, by being the moral compass and by rejecting the mounting pressure to join a Conservative-Liberal fusion to save the City, we proved to the Republicans running to unseat Cuomo that they just can't assume we'll go along for the ride. They know they will have to earn our support by promoting ideas based on the principles of conservatism."

Chapter 14

The Margin of Victory
The Conservative Party Elects a Governor

By January of 1994 it had become evident to most analysts that New York State was hemorrhaging both fiscally and economically. On the fiscal side, the state's accumulated deficit had grown during the Cuomo years from $2.9 billion in 1982 to $6.3 billion in 1991. Spending had ballooned 126 percent, while inflation was up 50 percent.

State taxes and fees had increased $9.2 billion between 1988 and 1993. The number of Fortune 500 companies headquartered in New York had declined from eighty eight in 1982 to forty three in 1993, and 500,000 private-sector jobs had been lost just during Cuomo's third term – all this while jobs nationwide had increased by 2.1 million during the same period.[1]

New Yorkers, who bore the highest state and local tax burden in the continental United States, were financing a $62.6-billion state budget and funding a bureaucracy of 240,000 state employees. This budget was "balanced" with one-shot revenues and fiscal gimmicks.

And during Governor Cuomo's dozen years in office, welfare roles were 24 percent higher than the national average. That was bad, but what was worse was the state's crime rate: It had risen to a level 48 percent higher than the American average.[2]

The governor became an easy and frequent target of outraged New Yorkers. Lewis Lehrman, who some thought was toying with the idea of another gubernatorial run, blasted the entire political establishment during his keynote address to the annual Conservative Party C-PAC. Lehrman accused Cuomo of running a "caretaker government."

"Governor Cuomo has been a disappointment," Lehrman said. "But the Republican Party in Albany . . . has been a bigger disappointment. . . . New York is a one party government . . . Let us call them the *incumbrocrats*."[3]

Other gubernatorial wannabes attending the conference included Herb London, Oppenheimer Mutual Fund boss Jon Fossel, former Republican chairman and CEO of the Avis rental-car company, Patrick Barrett, Assembly Republican leader Clarence Rappleyea, and Ronald Lauder. A notable no-show was GOP Chairman Richard Rosenbaum of Rochester, Rockefeller's last remaining hatchet man.

Pat Barrett of Syracuse, under the aegis of a non-profit, 501(c)(3) foundation called The Right Way for New York, Inc., started running TV spots to boost his candidacy in February 1993. Barrett said the purpose of the ads (paid for out of his pocket) "was to give those citizens and taxpayers who wish to join me a vehicle to educate our fellow citizens about the waste and abuse that goes into state government."[4]

Throughout 1993, Conservative Party Chairman Mike Long met with most of the candidates and encouraged them to work the state. He urged Herb London, who for most of the past two years had traveled the state massaging Conservative leaders, to spend his time seeking Republican support and raising money. Long also stayed in touch with Senator Al D'Amato, who was stepping up his efforts to find a suitable candidate. New names cropped up (particularly if they had money) including First Boston's CEO John M. Hennessey and former energy czar and Smith Barney chief, Frank Zarb. Hennessey even contributed $10,000 to the Conservative Party.

The wannabes marched up to Albany to attend Long's 1994 C-PAC. Some Republicans, seeing no strong candidate on the horizon, were voicing concern that the GOP was blowing its chances to topple Cuomo. Congressman Gerald Solomon said: "Someone needs to hit all these people with a two-by-four and wake them up."

Staten Island Borough President Guy Molinari also preached pending doom.

"I'm hearing from a lot of Republicans. . . . There's growing concern that we're not getting our act together. As each day passes, I grow more concerned about our ability to win the race."[5]

A major roadblock in the efforts to end Cuomo's reign was the Republican Senate Majority Leader Ralph Marino of Oyster Bay, Long Island. Arguably the state's most powerful Republican office holder, Marino was in no rush to defer to a Republican governor. He was a classic example of those Lehrman had called "incumbrocrats." Marino had grown accustomed to trading approval of Cuomo's budgets for patronage and pork barrel, never hesitating to go along with the governor's spending excesses and tax increases. Observing the annual sell-out, Mike Long said:

"The Senate Republicans don't have the courage of their convictions. All they want to do is keep dealing with pork-barrel projects, more spending, higher taxes, and I think the people of this state are being ripped off."[6]

At the 1994 Albany C-PAC, supporters of Herb London tried to get the state executive committee to endorse him then and there. Even though there were veiled threats to dump him as chairman when his term was up, Long resisted. He argued successfully that it was too early in the process to close the door on other candidates. Although he knew his leadership was at stake, he remembered his handshake with D'Amato after the Rinfret disaster, and he still hoped for a meeting of the minds between the Conservative and Republican parties. He also believed that competition was healthy, and he began holding "beauty contests" all over the state. This gave the party faithful lots of opportunities to meet and greet candidates before making up their minds.

The Rise of George Pataki

Then in March, former Peekskill mayor and current state senator, George Pataki, announced his candidacy. He said flatly that he intended to end the "twelve year night-mare of Cuomo's reign." This unknown and under-financed candidate had up till then an interesting and auspicious political career. The son of a Hungarian mailman, who also ran his own working farm, George Pataki had graduated from Yale and Columbia University School of Law. After a short stint with the Wall Street firm Dewey, Ballantine, he had returned to Peekskill to practice law, and in 1981 had been elected mayor of the largely Democratic city. In November 1984, he beat incumbent Democratic William Ryan for his district's seat in the state assembly. By 1992, bored being in the assembly minority, he set his sights on the state senate seat held by Mary Goodhue, whose campaign he had once managed. Pataki called on Mike Long in early 1992 and described his plans for entering a primary against the only Republican woman in the state senate – a woman who had enjoyed the endorsement of the Conservative Party. Pataki viewed his decision this way:

> She didn't have the commitment. She liked being a state Senator – as opposed to making policy.
>
> I worked 365 days in the Assembly, with extremely limited power, with a clear view and an agenda. And I saw people with enormous power, with no agenda, allowing the opportunities that their power gave them to slip by. And finally I said, "this is it: Either I go back to the real world and make money and practice law and do the farm, or I have an impact." I didn't want to just hang around.[7]

Long looked upon Pataki as a bright, ambitious guy who had a good voting record."He voted against taxes and (even though his people hate when I bring this up) he had a perfect Right to Life voting record."[8]

Long thought Pataki was a more than decent candidate and he looked upon Mary Goodhue as a relic of the Rockefeller era. Since this particular senatorial district crossed the counties of Westchester and Putnam, the state executive committee had the ultimate power to chose the candidate, and Long promised to do all he could to persuade them to dump Goodhue and support Pataki.

Long delivered, and with the financial support of Ronald Lauder and the Change-NY crowd, Pataki beat Goodhue in the primary and went on to win the general election.

In the senate, Pataki quickly earned the wrath of Majority Leader Marino. He voted against tax measures and was the lone Republican to vote against the budget deal in both 1993 and 1994. Marino was livid, because once he'd cut the budget dealt, he expected every one of his Republicans to fall in line.

Based in large measure on his independent legislative record, Pataki announced his candidacy for governor. The fact that not one of his thirty-three fellow Republican senators joined him at his announcement certainly proved his loner status.

Back in September 1993 Pataki had first asked for D'Amato's support and was rebuffed, but by April 1994 the senator, having carefully scrutinized the prospective candidates, began to have second thoughts. When real-estate mogul Donald Trump, entrepreneur David Cornstein, Frank Zarb, and Jack Hennessey all declined to be considered, D'Amato knew the clock was running down. Weak as he may have become, Cuomo was still strong enough to withstand an even weaker challenge, so the senator took a second, serious look at Pataki. Even though Ralph Marino and other Republican leaders were opposed to the Pataki candidacy, D'Amato decided to go with him anyway. And now he used all his power, influence, and muscle to make Pataki the one-and-only nominee, thus avoiding a divisive and damaging primary battle.

For four long years Herb London had traveled the length of the state addressing conservative groups. Conservative leaders such as Steve Miller of Oswego County, Tom and Viola Hunter of Onondaga County, Jim Brewster of Cayuga County, Nassau's Jack O'Leary – as well as numerous others – had worked hard for the London candidacy. While Herb was definitely the favorite son of the Conservative Party's rank and file, he was simply not making inroads among the Republican establishment. And he had failed to raise any serious money. D'Amato rejected London because he believed that in a "London-Cuomo race, London would become the issue and Mario would face an easy race."[9]

Looking back on it some years later, Mike Long couldn't understand why London didn't work harder to court the Republicans, particularly in 1991 and 1992 when he pretty much had the whole stage to himself.

"Perhaps," Long said, "he was just more comfortable with the Conservatives, whom he knew and [who] always gave him a good reception."

But, according to Long, London was getting annoyed because he "could not get me to hold the Conservative Convention before the Republicans met." Long stifled London's strategy of the "tail wagging the dog." Even when Monroe County Leader Tom Cook threatened to lead a revolt against Long, Mike never lost sight of his goal, which was to beat Cuomo. This could happen in 1994 only by avoiding a three-way split.

Meanwhile, Patrick Barrett was still waiting in the wings. Although he did plenty of talking about running and had a campaign staff and TV commercials, he never actually got around to announcing.

"I met with Barrett numerous times," Long recalls, "and every time I left him I thought he was ready to declare, but it never happened."

Long remembers that just weeks before the conventions, Barrett asked for his endorsement. Long declined, giving Barrett the same reason he'd given to London. That was that, since "Barrett wanted to declare only after I endorsed him."

In late April, Senator D'Amato called me to ask my opinion on how a three-way split – Republican vs. Democrat vs. Conservative – could be avoided in the fall. The answer seemed simple to me: "Senator," I said, "at the Republican Convention your candidate must get over 75 percent of the vote. If London gets 25 percent and is eligible to enter the primary, I'm convinced Long will lose control of his convention and it will swing joyfully to London."

I'm pretty sure the senator had already figured this out for himself, but in any case it appears to have been the strategy as the Republicans convened their convention at New York City's Sheraton Hotel in May.

In his quest to secure 25 percent of the Republican delegate vote, London started cozying up with D'Amato's two main foes, Mayor Giuliani and State Senator Marino.

Insiders believed that Marino, who wanted to maintain his status in Albany, and Mayor Giuliani, who wanted to see D'Amato fail, began covertly to help London. They believed that London, who lacked money and organization, would be a weak candidate if nominated and would almost surely lose to Cuomo, and in any case would divide the Republican Party in a primary battle even if he didn't win. From their point of view this was a good thing. In his biography of Rudy Giuliani, Wayne Barrett describes the convention maneuverings this way:

> Giuliani was Cuomo's covert ally at the convention, quietly working to get 25 percent of the delegates to vote for Herb London, the 1990 Conservative Party candidate for governor who was positioning himself to challenge George Pataki in an upcoming Republican primary. Pataki, then a little-known state senator handpicked by Al D'Amato to run against Cuomo, was engaged in an all-out war to block the 25 percent and avoid a primary with London. Yet the officially neutral Giuliani got much of the Queens delegation to vote for London during the nail-biting, three-hour roll-call vote.
>
> Peter Powers called delegates the weekend before the convention, looking for London votes though the anti-abortion and pro-gun professor was to the right of pro-choice Pataki. London had little chance of defeating Cuomo, who'd routed him in 1990, and the attempts to get him on the ballot by Giuliani and Senate Republican leader Ralph Marino were widely seen as indirectly benefiting Cuomo. London narrowly missed the qualifying threshold, thwarted by Pataki's top backer and Rudy's longtime nemesis, D'Amato.[10]

At the convention, D'Amato was able to deliver three-quarters of the delegates to Pataki. But there was a singular mystery: the no-show of the Niagara County delegation. Committed to London, this delegation could have helped London reach 25 percent, but somehow they managed to be lost for twenty-four hours before finally finding the Sheraton Hotel.

In defeat, London realized that he did not have the financial or organizational wherewithal to go the primary-petition route. He also knew that if he procured the Conservative Party nomination, there would be another three-way race that would only benefit Mario Cuomo. Nevertheless, a disgruntled London made it public that he would press on. He stuck with his belief that the "simple truth is George Pataki has not earned his place in this campaign."[11]

The evening after the convention adjourned, Conservatives Mike Long, Tony Rudmann, and Jim Molinaro met with Senator D'Amato, state Republican Chairman Bill Powers, and Pataki chief fundraiser, former Ambassador Charles Gargano, to discuss the London dilemma. Long was asked a simple question: What do you need to avert a London-Pataki Conservative Party primary?

Long told them he needed a spot on the ticket for the Conservatives. He asked them to offer the comptroller spot to Herb London or, if he turned it down, to George Marlin.

My Brief Stint as a Comptroller Candidate

After my mayoral run, I had set my sights on the '94 comptroller's race. When long-time Republican-Conservative Comptroller Ned Regan had resigned in 1993 to head up a foundation, Governor Cuomo appointed H. Carl McCall, a former state senator and president of the New York City Board of Education – those wonder folks who gave us the Rainbow Curriculum. In a potentially strong year for Republicans, most pundits considered McCall vulnerable.

Columbia County Assemblyman John Faso had been working the Republicans for over a year to secure the Republican nomination for comptroller, and he certainly had a vast majority of the delegates supporting him. In the Conservative Party, Brooklyn Chairman Gerry Kassar was leading the charge for Faso.

After my speech at the February 1994 C-PAC, many Conservatives urged me to make the run. A number of county chairmen endorsed me. Regional Vice Chairmen Steve Miller, Viola Hunter, and Al Hollands endorsed me, and others wrote letters to 400-plus party leaders, urging my nomination.

Although I never formally announced my candidacy, I drove 11,000 miles around the state during weekends in April and May, accompanied by Conservative activists Jack Swan, Jim Kelly of Marine Park, Brooklyn, and Jim Gay, the state party treasurer. We called on Conservative and Republican leaders all over the state, and I was a guest speaker at numerous Conservative Party dinners.

My strategy was the classic "tail-wag-the-dog" employed by D'Amato in 1980. I gambled that if I secured the Conservative Party nomination with 76 percent of the vote, Assemblyman Faso would not risk giving up his safe legislative seat to run in a three-way comptroller's race that he would surely lose. I also thought that if the Republicans had to throw a bone to the Conservatives to ensure unity, I might be the guy catching the bone.

I also had several other things going for me. The New York State comptroller is the sole trustee of the state's pension funds (which then stood at approximately $60 billion), and he oversees the issuance of state tax-exempt bonded debt. I could tell potential supporters that I had over eighteen years of experience as a municipal-credit analyst, municipal-bond underwriter, and fiscal adviser to municipalities. I was an author of a book on the subject. I also had over ten years of experience with fiduciary-trust powers as portfolio manager of billions of dollars worth of investments held by banks, mutual funds, individuals, and municipalities.

After spending $5,000 of my own money during our six-week trek to promote my unofficial candidacy, I didn't expect to be the nominee, but I thought that by covering all the bases, I'd be in the best position to take the hit if lightning struck.

In the post-convention m7eeting, it was agreed that London should be offered the comptroller's nomination. Long made the offer. London declined.

At 2:00 in the morning on Tuesday, May 24, Long awakened me with a phone call to tell me that I was to be chosen as the Republican Party's designated candidate. He was standing next to D'Amato, he said, and he assured me it was a done deal. I had a about a day's worth of pleasure from the prospect of running against McCall.

Later on that day, Nelson Warfield, Mike Gannon, Allen Roth, Jack Swan, James Kelly, and Jim Gay met at my house to prepare folders with biographical material for distribution to delegates on Wednesday, and we also worked on my acceptance speech.

On Wednesday, we gathered at the Sheraton Hotel suite reserved by Ronald Lauder to await announcement of the day's schedule of convention events. It was there that Long reached me by phone and informed me that he had received two calls the previous night: one at about 11:00 P.M. Tuesday from the London camp requesting a breakfast meeting in Greenwich Village with Herb. The other call was at about 4:00 in the morning on Wednesday from Pataki political consultant, Kieran Mahoney (son of Conservative Party founder Dan Mahoney), saying that even though they gave their word that the nomination would go to me without a primary, Faso had refused to get out of the race. Mahoney said they would get me 25 percent of the delegate vote and thus qualify me to enter a primary. This changed the picture somewhat, but my advisors and I decided to sit tight and see how events unfolded.

Later on that morning, Long called me again and broke the news that London had changed his mind and decided he wanted to run for comptroller after all. My candidacy ended at that moment.

About a half-an-hour later Herb London called to tell me of his decision. After a moment London paused and then remarked that he had expected me to react angrily. I somewhat stoically told him I had no control over events as they had transpired, and that he could depend on my support in the fall.

The convention, which had been slated to convene at one, was delayed until four o'clock while the Republicans got their act together. George Pataki reports in his autobiography that he made a personal appeal to Faso to withdraw for the sake of party unity. This Faso did (gracefully, under the circumstances), and London was nominated. The next day *The New York Times* reported erroneously that it had been a Giuliani protest that had ended my candidacy:

> At City Hall Mr. Giuliani warned, "If they consider Marlin, what the Republican Party is saying is that it is no longer a Republican Party, that you can run against the party, you can try to destroy the chance to have a Republican mayor, that you can run a largely negative, nasty campaign and then the party is going to reward you by either giving you a nomination or a part of a nomination."[12]

I must say the mayor's comments are hypocritical, given that in just a short time he would desert his party to endorse Cuomo.

In accepting the nomination for comptroller London told the media: "If I ran on the Conservative line [for governor] and it generated even a half a million votes, it would have insured Mario Cuomo's re-election. . . . [I decided] to put my ego aside to do what's best for the party."[13] Candidate Pataki reacted to the political events saying:

> "The Conservatives should be very happy with the ticket they got." He quoted Michael Long, the Conservative Party state chairman, as saying the party's goal last year in fielding a candidate against Mayor Rudolph W. Giuliani "was to make a philosophical statement – this year it's to defeat Cuomo."[14]

Conservative Dissention and an Independent Challenge

As Mike Long was driving up to Albany on Friday, June 3, he knew that he would face some discontented Conservatives at his convention the following day. Hard-core London supporters were angry and believed that the Republicans had cheated Herb London out of the gubernatorial nomination. Monroe County Chairman Thomas D. Cook led the charge to give the convention an alternative to Pataki. Their first choice was Pat Barrett. He toyed with the idea but then dropped out. Party leader Steve Miller of Oswego County was also approached, but after a discussion with Mike Long he too decided against running.

The dissidents did place in nomination Jefferson County Chairman Robert Relph for Governor. Relph, a pro-life activist and insurance agent who lived in the city of Watertown, managed to get 28 percent of the delegate vote and vowed to stay in the primary.

When the name of the Republican candidate for the United States Senate,

Bernadette Castro (of the Castro Convertible furniture company), was placed into nomination, she too was opposed, but here the opposition was more serious: right-to-life activist Henry Hewes received 59 percent of the vote and became the Conservative Party's nominee. Even Mike Long voted for Hewes over the pro-abortion Castro. Since neither Hewes nor Castro was a registered Conservative and had to seek the approval of the party executive committee to enter a primary, Long concluded that it would be healthy to have a primary. There was going to be one for governor anyway, and the executive committee agreed.

The convention was also the party's first exposure to Pataki's running mate, Elizabeth (Betsey) McCaughey. McCaughey, a fellow at the conservative think tank, the Manhattan Institute, received major attention when a critique she authored on President Clinton's plan to transform American health care appeared in the *New Republic* and was rebutted by President Clinton.

At the Republican Convention, Pataki consultant Kieran Mahoney had sworn to Allen Roth that Miss McCaughey was a "movement Conservative." Roth, who was associated with the Manhattan Institute in the 1980s, knew better and told this to Mahoney. Roth recalls that when he met with her before the Conservative convention, she conned him into believing she was pro-life. After the party unanimously nominated her, she made it clear to the media outside the convention hall that she was "definitely pro-abortion."

Attorney-general candidate Dennis Vacco, who was also unanimously nominated, made his debut at the party convention as well. A lifelong resident of the Buffalo area, Vacco had served as an Erie County assistant district attorney and was the U.S. attorney for western New York during the Reagan and Bush Administrations.

In accepting the Party's nomination for governor, George Pataki told the faithful: "This is not about winning a primary, not even about winning the general election. . . . It's about bringing true change to this state and getting rid of Mario Cuomo."[15]

The party's favorite son, comptroller candidate Herb London, gave a rousing speech in which he said in part: "This is our moment, the moment we've been waiting for, the moment when Mario Cuomo is finally ousted. . . . History calls to us. Let's not keep it waiting."[16] Reporting on the London speech, the *Times* pointed out that in his "fiery acceptance speech," London had not mentioned Pataki by name.

Reviewing his tumultuous convention with the press, Long said: "I'd rather not have had a primary but in the end, it could help George get his name out and create some excitement. . . . I have no doubt [Pataki] will win."

Sensing inexperience and incompetence in Pataki Headquarters, D'Amato sent over battle-seasoned professionals to oversee the September primary and fall elections.

Arthur Finkelstein was to manage polling and the media campaign, and D'Amato's hard-nosed press secretary, Zenia Mucha, left his office to take over Pataki's communications operation. Mike Long's daughter, Eileen (who had run my mayoral campaign), was brought in to manage Pataki's Conservative Party primary campaign.

With almost no money, the Relph campaign could not withstand the Pataki freight train. On primary day, September 13, Pataki flattened Relph, receiving 78 percent of the vote. With a 15 percent turnout of registered Conservatives, Pataki received 17,450 votes to Relph's 4,996. Pataki also beat Richard Rosenbaum in the Republican primary. To this day, no one really understands why Rosenbaum went the petition route to enter the primary, since no one really cared about his candidacy. (It is interesting to note, however, that Laurence, Mary, and David Rockefeller contributed $33,500 to his campaign. Jonathan Bush gave $500, and Mary Goodhue, who lost her state senate seat to Pataki, gave $1,000.)

In the Conservative primary for Senate, Bernadette Castro easily beat Henry Hewes, receiving 63 percent of the votes cast.

To help the Pataki ticket and to maximize the vote on the Conservative line, Long decided to run an independent media campaign. As early as July, he ran a statewide radio ad featuring Jack Kemp assaulting Cuomo's record. The ad blamed Cuomo's "liberal economic policies" for New York's "record high taxes, runaway spending and countless lost jobs." An 800 number was given so listeners could call to get a free study entitled, "The Real Cuomo Record." The four-page research report detailed Cuomo's financial gimmicks, tax increases, spending increases, as well as welfare and crime statistics.

Pataki unveiled his economic and fiscal plan before a meeting of the Citizens Budget Commission in late September, calling for a 25 percent cut in the state income tax rate. Long publicly endorsed the plan saying, "Pataki proved himself a visionary and a leader . . . by committing to reduce personal income taxes by 25 percent with the middle-class getting the bulk of the cuts." Tom Carroll of Change-NY praised the plan in a *Newsday* op-ed essay:

> The main reason for New York's disproportionate jobs loss is obvious. High taxes have choked the life out of what should be, but isn't, one of the most vibrant economies in the nation, if not the world.
>
> State Sen. George Pataki, Mario Cuomo's chief rival, has seized the initiative by unveiling a bold plan that would cut income taxes across the board by 25 percent over four years, at a savings to taxpayers of $5.6 billion annually when fully effective. The centerpiece of the plan is a drop in the top tax rate from 7.875 percent to a maximum of 5.9 percent. Middle-class taxpayers would get an even larger tax cut, in most cases exceeding 40 percent.[17]

While Long was promoting the Pataki ticket throughout the state, there was trouble brewing that could dash his dream of electing a governor.

After the primary was over, the Independent Party, created for the 1992 Ross Perot race, nominated Rochester multi-millionaire Tom Golisano. Golisano was spending millions to promote his candidacy, and his increased visibility was cutting into Pataki support. Pataki was basically running an "A.B.C." campaign ("Anybody but Cuomo"), although his handlers were also spotlighting his anti-tax and pro-death penalty proposals. But other than that, they were saying little else. Given the high anti-Cuomo sentiment in the state, they figured they didn't need to say more. Such a strategy was fine when it was a two-man race, but when the third candidate appeared, some portion of that A.B.C. sentiment began switch to him. Polls, particularly upstate, reflected growing support for Golisano.

To counter this situation, Long pointed out that "public-spirited" Mr. Golisano had not voted in an election until 1992, and that he had called for legalized prostitution and decriminalized drug use.

The Mayor's Apostasy

This was an obvious problem for the Pataki campaign, but there was another hidden danger, and that was all the disgruntled Republicans who feared that a Pataki triumph would endanger their power bases. At a September city-hall press conference during which Rudy Giuliani endorsed both Herb London and Dennis Vacco, a reporter asked the mayor if he intended to endorse Pataki.

"Most likely that is what I will do," he replied.[18]

But on another occasion he said: "George Pataki doesn't take positions that tell me what he's going to do as governor of New York. . . . The candidate has elected to have a campaign strategy that is to be non-specific."[19]

Even after Liberal Party Chairman Ray Harding told Rudy that Cuomo's own wish was that the mayor stay "aggressively neutral," the Republican Giuliani decided on October 24 to endorse Democrat Cuomo for a fourth term as governor. To a shocked electorate, he said:

> From my point of view as the mayor of New York City, the question that I have to ask is, "Who has the best chance in the next four years of successfully fighting for our interest? Who understands them, and who will make the best case for it?" Our future, our destiny is not a matter of chance. It's a matter of choice.
>
> My choice is Mario Cuomo.
>
> I've come to the conclusion that it is George Pataki who best personifies the status quo of New York politics – a candidate taking as few positions as possible, all of them as general as possible, taking no risk and being guided, scripted, and directed by others.
>
> Senator Pataki has almost uniformly voted against the interests of the city and often the metropolitan region. . . . Mario Cuomo is his own man. I prefer dealing with someone who is his own man.
>
> The sense that I've gotten from George Pataki is that it is very much

a campaign out of a political consultant's playbook. There are clichés, there are slogans, there's the right sound bite, there's the right position. You become specific only for as long as you have to, and then you become general again.[20]

No one reacted more strongly to Giuliani's betrayal than Mike Long:

Once again, Rudolph Giuliani has demonstrated that liberalism is the foundation of his political philosophy. While Giuliani sold a bill of goods to trusting Republicans and Reagan Democrats that he had abandoned his roots as a McGovern Democrat, in his endorsement of Mario Cuomo, Mr. Liberal himself, he has shown his true colors. Giuliani's argument that Cuomo will be better for the city has a hollow ring to it. Perhaps Rudy wants a governor who will sign over a blank check to constantly bail out the city from its fiscal problems. Giuliani knows, as do all New Yorkers, that Cuomo's liberal policies have been an economic disaster for our city and state.

But Rudy doesn't care. He has proven he will do anything to stop the election of a conservative Republican – but he won't succeed.[21]

On CNN's *Crossfire* the next night, Long said:

[Q]uite frankly, you have to understand the fact that Rudy Giuliani was a McGovern Democrat, he was endorsed by the Liberal Party when he ran for Mayor. In his heart, he's a Democrat. He's paraded all over this country with Bill Clinton and, in fact, he's very comfortable with Mario Cuomo. But what Rudy Giuliani wants is to be bailed out in the city, in the mess he's in, and everybody understands very clearly in politics that they struck a deal, that Mario's going to continue to be the big spender, save Rudy the options of raising taxes by pouring money statewide into the City of New York and bailing it out. Quite frankly, I predict that he will join the Democratic Party.[22]

Long also pointed out that Giuliani put out an order to his city-hall employees that "they cannot work for Pataki, they must rally around the mayor, and they [the city employees] must work for Mario Cuomo."

Most political analysts agreed that Rudy's endorsement of Cuomo was based on his belief that if Pataki lost, D'Amato's power would be on the wane and that he could pick up the pieces and be the top Republican in the state. If Pataki won, however, there would be little downside for the mayor, since after all D'Amato could not hate him any more than he already did.

But there's more to the Giuliani endorsement: Mike Long believes there was a Republican cabal to bring down the ticket. The members: Senate Majority Leader Marino, Nassau County Executive Tomas Gulotta, Giuliani, and Herb London.

Although Marino gave a tepid endorsement to Pataki six days before the Republican primary, it was well known that he preferred the status quo, which meant he himself was the top Republican in Albany. Tom Gulotta, who ran Nassau County to the edge of fiscal bankruptcy by the end of the decade, fancied himself gubernatorial material and knew a Pataki victory would close those doors for four or eight or even twelve years. Both Marino and Gulotta made a point right after the Giuliani endorsement to have an "all-smiles" photo opportunity with Cuomo in the Republican bastion of Nassau County.

Finally there was Herb London, an unhappy man who believed the gubernatorial nomination had been snatched from him. In September, he pummeled Pataki for not announcing a detailed tax-cutting plan, and three days after the Giuliani announcement, "he issued a blistering news release . . . accusing Pataki of dragging down the ticket and calling for him to 'lead or get out of the way!'"[23]

Staten Island Borough President Guy Molinari, who was a key supporter of Giuliani during the mayoral race, now referred to the mayor as "Judas" Giuliani. He demanded that he become a Democrat and told *The New York Times* that he had:

> . . . reluctantly endorsed the Republican candidate for Comptroller, Herbert London, only because Mr. Giuliani had implored him to, and he complained that Mr. Giuliani was now conspiring with Mr. London to "sabotage Pataki."[24]

The day after London's "leadership" comments appeared in the papers, Long chatted with Herb at the wedding reception of a mutual friend's daughter. Long recalls:

"I told him that I knew he wanted to be governor and that he couldn't bring himself to be part of the team. But I said, If Pataki goes down you're going down with him."

London told Long he was wrong and that Pataki was going to lose and he, Herb, was going to be the only Republican winner.[25]

"And when London told me that Giuliani was the only political figure helping him," Long said, "that comment confirmed to me that there was a cabal. The timing of the Giuliani endorsement, the Marino-Gulotta-Cuomo photo, and Herb's attacks – this was not a coincidence but a plan."

As has often been his habit, Giuliani overplayed his hand. Instead of campaigning for Cuomo in New York City and the surrounding suburban counties where he was popular, he decided to do an upstate tour. Hitting all the major upstate cities (where

New York City mayors have never been popular), he was a complete flop. He was greeted at every stop with boos and signs saying, "Traitor" and "Let's make a Deal," referring to accusations that Cuomo, to get the mayor's endorsement, was going to take away aid to upstate cities and give it to Giuliani. Even Cuomo realized the trip was a mistake: "I spoke to [political consultant David] Garth on the phone. I said this is not a good thing for him to do. I said Rudy would be seen as the Mayor of New York. They would think I was going to give all the money to him."[26]

Although Pataki experienced an initial free-fall in the polls, upstate voters were taking the accusation of a Cuomo-Giuliani deal seriously, and Pataki's polling numbers began to stabilize. By the end of the campaign, the Giuliani endorsement had backfired:

> Rudy was riding so high after the endorsement. . . . He also began trying to build an anti-Pataki Republican alliance, effectively recruiting the predisposed London and going out to Nassau County to try to woo Tom Gulotta, the county executive.
>
> This strategy, too, boomeranged when Bernadette Castro of convertible-couch fame, the GOP candidate for U.S. Senate, said Giuliani had invited her for a Sunday schmooze on a Gracie Mansion couch, where he asked her to abandon Pataki and endorse Cuomo. "I have to take George out," Castro said Rudy told her. Giuliani said he wanted Pataki defeated, according to Castro, "because he feels that if George is elected, he [the mayor] will be destroyed," ostensibly by a Pataki/D'Amato cabal. The maneuvering with Castro and the alliance with London – who issued a stinging statement demanding that Pataki "lead or get out of the way" – cheapened the Giuliani endorsement.
>
> Originally presented as a matter of principle, it quickly took on the appearance of a power grab. Giuliani started predicting a "realignment" within the GOP after the election that would obviously revolve around him: "I don't by any means intend to play the only role. I don't think any one person should control a political party. I think that's part of the mistake that was made here," he said, taunting D'Amato.[27]

In the final days of the campaign, Long continued upstate promotion of the party's message about Cuomo's failures and the need to cut taxes and spending. The desperation of the Cuomo campaign became evident when Long revealed that state bureaucrats had tried to muzzle a Conservative TV ad:

> The charge stems from a threat the Conservative Party received today from a lawyer in the New York State Department of Economic Development.

The state lawyer, Leslie Webster, threatened to sue the Conservative Party unless the Party pulled an ad the Party had produced calling for voters to support Pataki on the Conservative Party line.

The ad, entitled "The Conservative Next Door" features a man seated at a kitchen table explaining why he is supporting Pataki. It includes the line: "After 12 years of Mario Cuomo, sure I'm voting for George Pataki. But I'm doing it on the Conservative Line where it means more." On the table in front of the man is a coffee mug with a portion of the "I love NY" logo visible. The state bureaucrat claims this constitutes copyright infringement and threatened legal action unless the ad was pulled immediately.

"This is political harassment of the worst kind," Long said, adding: "Clearly Mario Cuomo barked and his pack bureaucrats responded with this ridiculous threat. With that logo on everything from coffee cups to trash bags, it's clear that this sudden concern for copyrights is very selective. We're keeping the ad up. And we're ready to go to court to countersue over this harassment and this clear violation of our civil rights if need be."

"But there is a sense of poetic justice in this threat," Long added: "This ad has been on the air for weeks. But under Cuomo the bureaucracy has grown so bloated that it couldn't even do his bidding to censor the Conservative Party until just a day before the election. Better luck next time, Mario!"[28]

In the November 8 election, Mario Cuomo was defeated in his bid for a fourth term. Mike Long's dream had come true: the Conservative Party provided the margin of victory to elect George Pataki New York's fifty-third governor:

	Cuomo Dem.	Pataki Rep.	Pataki Cons.	Walsh R. to L.	Cuomo Lib.	Pataki TCN	Galisano Ind.
Total Upstate	1,265,156	1,787,269	285,624	57,807	39,685	42,802	200,974
Bronx	153,477	40,401	4,757	1,499	6,323	1,656	1,937
Brooklyn	285,62	100,703	10,945	2,433	13,510	3,248	3,976
Manhattan	282,299	58,775	4,354	1,492	17,611	1,906	3,742
Queens	237,732	123,496	15,060	3,239	12,564	3,474	5,314
Staten Island	48,614	45,413	7,865	1,280	2,308	954	1,547
Total NYC	**1,007,747**	**368,788**	**42,981**	**9,943**	**52,316**	**11,238**	**16,516**
Total State	**2,272,903**	**2,156,057**	**328,605**	**67,750**	**92,001**	**54,040**	**217,490**

Long had this reaction to the results:

The Conservative Party provided the Pataki candidacy with more than 300,000 votes. Given the fact that Pataki won by less than 200,000 votes the Conservative Party is proud to have delivered the votes that put both Pataki and Vacco over the top.

In contrast, the anemic vote produced by the Liberal Party is indicative of a sea change in voting behavior in New York State. Voters want less government, lower taxes and a criminal justice system that punishes rather than coddles criminals.

The Conservative Party's vote is the largest it has ever produced when cross-endorsing a candidate for Governor.[29]

In upstate New York there was a record-breaking voter turnout; in many areas over 75 percent of registered voters cast ballots. Pataki carried every county north of New York City, except for Albany, the county of Cuomo bureaucrats. He was the first Republican gubernatorial candidate in twenty-four years to carry Erie County. In Eastern Long Island's Suffolk County, a conservative bastion, there was a record turnout and Pataki received 58 percent of the vote.

Pataki managed to win statewide even though he received only 28 percent of the vote in New York City, an all-time low for a victorious Republican. Cuomo, on the other hand, received only 32 percent of the upstate vote and 43 percent of the suburban vote. Pataki received 52 percent of the Catholic vote, 54 percent of the Protestant vote, and 37 percent of the Jewish vote. Registered Independents also cast 51 percent for the governor-elect.[30]

Left to right: Governor George Pataki, Stuart Avrick, Lt. Governor Betsey McCaughey, Attorney General Dennis Vacco.

While the defeated incumbent told the press that he prayed that the Lord would "let me understand the outcome and deal with it," Mayor Giuliani, who had called the governor-elect to congratulate him but did not receive a return call, quipped that George Pataki "has lots of people he wants to thank. I'm sure I'm not one of them."[31]

Dennis Vacco was a surprise victor over Democrat-Liberal Karen Burstein. Vacco squeaked by with 51.4 percent and beat Burstein by 88,340 votes. The 305,961 votes he received on the Conservative line clearly provided his margin of victory. Unlike Burstein, Vacco was pro-death penalty and anti-abortion and ran on a strong anti-crime platform. But one issue that dominated the race was Burstein's sexual orientation, particularly after her campaign put out an official brochure on pink paper listing the various gay and lesbian groups that had endorsed her. "As our next Attorney General," the brochure read, "Judge Karen Burstein will help lead the fight for lesbians and gay men in New York and across America. . . . Help Karen Make History."

Republican Guy Molinari went on the attack. At a Columbus Day reception, the Staten Island borough president made this headline-producing comment: "The next attorney general should not be an admitted lesbian."

In an October 24, *New York Post* op-ed essay, Molinari answered the storm of criticism that followed his remarks:

> If I read my critics correctly, they believe I am wrong to raise sexual orientation as a campaign issue. . . .
>
> Why is it homophobic when I say sexual orientation matters, while when Burstein says the same thing it is called campaign literature? Is this "gay-bashing" or "Guy-bashing?". . . .
>
> In context, my remark is not bigoted, but politically relevant. As a radical lesbian, Burstein's views veer from the mainstream of American politics. Does Burstein support same-sex marriages? I believe most New Yorkers do not. What is her view on what constitutes obscenity? Why was she one of only two state senators to vote against increasing criminal penalties for child pornography? As attorney general, she'll be called upon to give legal opinions for legalization. To what extent will her gay agenda be reflected in office priorities and enforcement patterns?
>
> The facts are clear. It was Karen Burstein who first stated that sexual orientation matters.[32]

And then there was Herb London. He turned out to be the only statewide Republican-Conservative who lost. Carl McCall became the first African-American to be elected to a statewide office.

	McCall Dem.	London Rep.	London Cons.	London R. to L.	McCall Lib.
Total Upstate	**1,378,451**	**1,461,450**	**242,835**	**107,476**	**60,416**
Bronx	138,179	27,934	4,371	2,435	5,308
Brooklyn	259,721	75,314	9,743	4,157	11,301
Manhattan	263,304	52,320	4,505	2,284	15,635
Queens	218,104	93,802	13,971	5,205	10,547
Staten Island	41,368	37,594	7,497	2,866	2,070
Total New York City	**920,676**	**286,964**	**40,087**	**16,947**	**44,861**
Total State	**2,299,127**	**1,748,414**	**282,922**	**124,423**	**105,277**

As Peter Salins, a Manhattan Institute fellow, puts it: "London snatched defeat from the jaws of victory." He continued: "The natural tide would have lifted anyone of the challengers against any incumbent. I think London's stridency and the charge of racial divisiveness cost him the election."[33] Most analysts and political insiders agree that London's attacks on Pataki, the alliance with Giuliani, and his poorly run campaign (and especially his awful campaign ads) cost him the election. Even in Republican strongholds London ran behind Pataki and Vacco:

	Pataki	Vacco	London
Staten Island	54,232	57,062	47,957
Suffolk	233,799	215,883	209,444
Nassau	234,383	226,769	219,840

Of course McCall did outspend London about 4 to 1, and he even managed to outpoll Cuomo in almost every county, just as London lagged behind Pataki in every county. *The New York Times* summed up the race this way:

> But Mr. London, in the eyes of many in his own party, did not help himself either: His own advertising had been condemned as racially inflammatory by Mr. McCall and his supporters, a charge he denied, but it still may have worked against him. Even worse, Mr. London attacked Mr. Pataki on two occasions, gaining himself free publicity, but earning the enmity of several prominent Republicans, like Borough President Guy V. Molinari of Staten Island.[34]

Overall, Long was delighted with the results. The party had provided the margin of victory in most statewide races, and Long expected to leverage this influence in the development of public policy in the new state administration. He saw to it that Conservatives served on Pataki transition teams. Patrick Foye, Paul Atanasio, James Molinari, Allen Roth, and I all served on various committees.

Conservatives were also appointed to various posts in the new administration. Allen Roth was to serve as executive director of the governor's privatization council, Paul Atanasio on the School Construction Authority, Pat Foye as a board member of the Long Island Power Authority, Party Executive Director Tony Rudmann was appointed deputy commissioner of administration in the Office of General Services, and in January, I was nominated for the post of executive director of the Port Authority of New York and New Jersey. Rosemary Braatz, the Putnum County Conservative chairman, became the executive director of intergovernmental affairs, Pat Quinn of Brooklyn became an assistant to Lieutenant-Governor McCaughey, and Eileen Long became the governor's deputy press secretary.

In early December, Long held a fundraiser at Manhattan's Columbus Club, and the packed house gave one the sense that real changes were coming to the Empire State. Even old-line liberal Democrat Herman Badillo (a law partner of Liberal Party Chairman Ray Harding) showed up. Hearing the Columbus Club's manager express concern that the mob scene might be a fire hazard, long-time supporter Bruce Bent quipped: "A Conservative Party fundraiser violating fire department occupancy codes is oxymoronic."

Chapter 15

Great Expectations

In his January 1, 1995, inaugural address, Governor Pataki reaffirmed his pledges: to fight crime, to sign into law a death-penalty bill, to cut taxes, spending, and regulations, and to pursue privatization initiatives.

During his first six months in office, the new governor signed into law a death-penalty measure that had been vetoed for eighteen consecutive years by his two Democratic predecessors. He also implemented stiffer criminal penalties and "no-parole" policy for violent offenders.

On the fiscal side, the governor signed a hiring freeze and a freeze on regulations during his very first day in office, thus actually cutting expenditures for the first time since 1943. What's more, he cut personal income-tax rates by 25 percent.

Because Conservative Party Executive Director Tony Rudmann had joined the Pataki Administration, Mike Long turned to Shaun Marie Levine to fill this important position. A long-time party activist from Albany County, she was the right person to cover party issues in the state capitol. When the old Democratic machine, led by the legendary boss Dan O'Connell, had sent in goons in an attempt to re-register Conservative Party members and thus seize control of the Albany wing of the party, Shaun had been one of the key opponents. For twenty years she had fought against these former Democrats, and thanks to her efforts the bulk of the party structure was back in the hands of bona-fide conservatives by the end of the nineties.

Despite the role the party had played in electing George Pataki and despite the governor's early initiatives, Mike Long understood that promotion of the Conservative public-policy agenda was not always going to be the first order of business within the governor's inner sanctum. There were still plenty of liberal Republicans and Democrats in Albany with whom the governor was going to have to get along.

"As a minor party," says Long, "you are not in the business to appeal to and please the entire population. You have a role to play, and you must be flexible. But you must stand very firmly by your platform and beliefs on which the party was formed."[1]

A Conservative Agenda for the Nineties

Long decided the best route to take was a two-pronged approach: independent promotion of Pataki policies that the party favored on the one hand, and independent promotion of policies important to the party – policies that were not high on the governor's wish list – on the other hand.

This did not always please the governor's gatekeepers, but as Long once said: "We're a splinter party, and splinter's hurt."[2]

At the February 1995 annual Albany C-PAC, Long told the media: The Conserva-tive Party's unprece-dented electoral victo-ries in 1994 are in large

Mrs. Daniel Quayle with Shaun Marie Levine (1992).

part going to determine the Conservative Party's activities this year.

To date, Governor Pataki has formally adopted legislative initiatives on welfare and fiscal policy that mirrors proposals made by the Conservative Party.

Now that we have a Conservative Governor, it is the Party's responsibility to help get his initiatives enacted. Towards this end, the Party will launch a grassroots effort to gain legislative votes for Pataki's plans to reduce state spending and state taxes. The Party feels that Governor Pataki's budget proposals coupled with his proposals for mandate relief ought to become law.

The Conservative Party will also promote the death penalty, term limits and ini-tiative and referendum.

In the Governor's race, the Conservative Party provided Pataki with his margin of victory; in the legislative process we intend to do the same.[3]

He also announced the Party's legislative agenda that included:

*   Elimination of Medicaid funding of abortions.
*   Parental notification prior to an abortion.
*   Prohibition of the distribution of condoms in public schools.
*   Rejection of efforts to establish bias-related crimes.
*   Elimination of parole for violent felony offenders.
*   Elimination of prison perks.

* Re-establishment of the free market in housing through a phase out of rent control and rent stabilization.
* Adoption of a crime victims' "Bill of Rights" to insure the victims of criminal activity receive protection and justice.
* Establishment of a legal definition of "family" along traditional lines.
* Encouragement of educational-choice programs through establishment of a system of personal income tax credits or deductions and/or vouchers in payment to parents or school districts for expenses incurred in elementary or secondary education.[4]

Not every one of these items was on the governor's top-ten list. Indeed, the Pataki administration's preference was to ignore social issues for as long as possible, which was predictable.

In February, Long ran a 30-second radio commercial to promote a "Contract with New York," rather like the "Contract with America" that had helped Republicans win big nationally in the 1994 mid-term elections. It was a ten-point blueprint that included the following terms:

A tax cut for the middle-class and the requirement of a "supermajority" vote for any future tax hikes.

* An across-the-board reduction in state spending.
* A time limit for welfare payments made to able-bodied recipients.
* The imposition of term limits for statewide officers.
* The right of New Yorkers to employ citizen initiatives and referendums.
* The decontrol of rent regulations when apartments become vacant.
* The requirement of cost-benefit analysis and risk-assessment studies for major regulations.
* The implementation of a program of school vouchers.
* An end all racial-preference policies.
* An end to un-funded state mandates to local governments.

Long urged legislators to sign the "contract" and warned them that it would be the standard by which the party would evaluate their performances.

Long began to focus his criticism on Assembly Speaker Sheldon Silver, now the most powerful Democrat in the state. When Silver tried to stall passage of the death-penalty bill, Long called him the "front man for all those liberals who have denied New York State the right to put heinous murderers to death."[5]

The party also began a grassroots campaign to gain passage of Governor Pataki's budget proposals. Long went on the road, attacking Silver for dragging his feet on budget negotiations.

By the fall, it appeared that the party's efforts were paying off. When Long released the party's legislative ratings, in September he was able to boast that "the overall rating of 52.7 percent is a substantial increase over last year's 43.3 percent conservative rating. This is remarkable given the ultra-liberal agenda of Assembly Speaker Sheldon Silver."[6]

In the fall off-year elections, the Conservative Party took on most of the Albany establishment, including Silver, but also including the governor himself. Long announced that the party was spearheading a statewide campaign to defeat the so-called Debt-Reform Act (a.k.a Proposition 3) that in effect would have taken away the constitutional right of New Yorkers to vote on any proposals to increase state debt.

"Currently New Yorkers have the right to vote whenever the Albany politicians decide they want to borrow us deeper into debt" Long said.

> If this constitutional amendment is approved on November 7, it will take away this right to vote. The politicians will be able to run wild, borrowing up to $25 billion at their whim.
>
> New York State residents simply cannot afford an additional $25 billion in debt.
>
> This year reminds me of Mario Cuomo's 1990 attempt to ram a huge bond issue down our throats. At that time the Conservative Party took on the Albany and Wall Street establishments and defeated that measure.
>
> In 1995, we will do the same. We will be taking to the streets and the mailboxes with materials that will educate voters on why they must vote against Proposition Three.
>
> We know we are the underdogs going into this campaign, but we believe that when voters understand the magnitude of this power grab by Albany they will support us at the polls.[7]

Radio ads began airing that urged New Yorkers to vote against the Debt-Reform Act on the November 7 ballot. The sixty-second radio spot resurrected the ghost of Cuomo:

> If you thought the days of Mario Cuomo's big spending and high taxes were over, think again. They call it the Debt Reform Act, but this so-called reform will allow Albany politicians to borrow up to $25 billion, all without the approval of New York taxpayers. That means more welfare for New York City and higher taxes for us.
>
> This is nothing more than a power grab by Albany to end-run the taxpayers and keep spending just like they did during the Cuomo days. That's wrong. We simply can't afford to let this proposal pass.
>
> On Tuesday, November 7, vote to end Mario Cuomo's tax and spend

policies for good. Vote no on Proposition Three and protect our right to say no to more spending and higher taxes.[8]

The ads worked, and Proposition Three went down in flames. Thanks largely to the Conservative Party's efforts, 1,024,492 voted against the measure, as opposed to 656,871 who voted for.

"The Conservative Party and all overburdened New York State taxpayers are gratified by the voters' rejection of Proposition Three," Long said. "Today's rejection of Proposition Three should be a starting point for true debt reform which requires a significant reduction in the size and cost of state government followed by tax decreases to energize the state's economy. We look forward to continuing to work with Governor Pataki to implement his agenda to downsize state government."

The Tyranny of the Status Quo

For anyone active in New York's conservative movement, the most difficult realization is that many in government have little interest in implementing sound reform policies, preferring instead to hold on to power for its own sake. You can take my word on it.

As I mentioned in the last chapter, the governor named me to the post of executive director of the bi-state agency, the Port Authority of New York and New Jersey. At that time, the Port Authority, which was founded in 1921, managed over thirty-five facilities in the metropolitan area, including the World Trade Center, the major local airports – Kennedy, LaGuardia, and Newark – the PATH Subway line, many of the piers in and around the area's waterways, the Port Authority Bus Terminal in Midtown Manhattan, and the four bridges and two tunnels that connect New York to New Jersey.

The actual announcement of my appointment was delayed until mid-January, because Staten Island's Borough President Guy Molinari, who had promoted his own name, believed he would be publicly embarrassed if he were not offered the position.

I was told that after Molinari was publicly offered the job and then publicly declined the honor, I would be named.

But *Newsday* leaked my name, and a great onslaught began. As a pro-life conservative, the liberal media pounced on me. Although I had two decades of experience in municipal finance and had written extensively on municipal and government-agency fiscal issues, the media concluded my résumé was irrelevant. What mattered was my stand on abortion. In news articles, editorials, and op-ed columns, *Newsday* and the *Times* pounded me for weeks. These same papers, that had praised my devotion to principle in the 1993 mayoral race, now condemned me for holding those same beliefs. The difference was that then they'd given me no chance of winning, whereas now I was actually going to have a very visible, powerful job. Joyce Purnick of the *Times* was apoplectic over my pro-life views, and the *Times*'s editorial page became so irrational that even former Governor Cuomo called me to say the paper had gone overboard. He even thought the *Times*'s editorialists had shot themselves in the foot. Cardinal John J. O'Connor called me in for a breakfast meeting during which he voiced his anger that the media rendered me unqualified to run a transportation agency because I was pro-life.

To actually receive the job, any candidate must be approved by a board that consists of six New Jersey and six New York members. I began calling on these members, who were mostly Cuomo appointees in New York, and (believe it or not) a few leftovers from the Rockefeller years. For the most part, the Cuomo people understood that the new governor was entitled to his choice, but the Republican holdovers, including former Governor Rockefeller's brother-in-law, were the sort of self-righteous, progressive Republicans who had been complicit with the agency's twenty years of overspending and who looked upon me as the enemy. I'm sure part of their opposition to me – I'm no Goo-Goo – and part was based on the mandate the governor had given me to clean up the mess the old-timers had created.

In New Jersey, I met privately with Christine Todd Whitman at the governor's mansion in Princeton. Peter Verniero, at that time her chief counsel, grilled me about my views on abortion and gay rights – as if such matters had anything at all to do with running the Port Authority.

In the end, though, what got me over the top was the intervention of Senator D'Amato. Here's *Time* magazine's take:

> Last winter New Jersey Governor Christine Todd Whitman, who was being mentioned as a possible Republican vice-presidential candidate, clashed with D'Amato and his protégé, New York Governor George Pataki, over their bid to nominate a political ally as head of the Port Authority of New York and New Jersey. Pataki announced the choice without consulting Whitman, whose staff then spread word that the nomination was dead. But in mid-January a GOP fundraiser with ties to both camps phoned a top Whitman aide. "Here's what's going to happen," the fundraiser said. "Al's going to call Christie. He'll remind her that he's the kingmaker – she needs his help to get on the ticket. If she blocks this deal, she can forget about it." Whitman changed her mind and backed the nominee.[9]

Although I was able to achieve considerable success in reorganizing the Port Authority, I was also unable to completely overcome what economist Milton Friedman has called the "tyranny of the status quo." It will probably come as no surprise to most readers to learn that very few bureaucrats care much about philosophical concepts, or that most of them care only about preserving their power, their perks, and their pensions. When I set about to privatize some of the Port Authority's functions, to downsize the agency's massive staff, and to emphasize the importance of individual responsibility and accountability, I was met with raging hostility (occasionally open but more often concealed), and it became clear early on that reform was anathema. (I have always admired G.K. Chesterton's definition of reform as "a metaphor for reasonable and determined men: it means that we see a certain thing out of shape and we mean to put it into shape. And we know what shape.") The truth is that many, if not most, bureaucrats actually prefer the murky mazes of big government because the labyrinths of rules and regulations conceal their waste and inefficiency and shield them from the scrutiny of "meddling interlopers," which is how they refer to the people's elected officials and their appointed representatives.

What also struck me is that even though we had a chance to make serious changes, some board appointees often stifled those changes. Some of them lived by a simple rule: If you make a decision you may be criticized, so avoid making decisions.

I would sit through countless board meetings where projects and decisions were put off because a lone member would voice a disagreement on some minor issue. There was never-ending finger pointing. There were leaks to newspapers of sensitive material. There was sheer political cowardice by board members who were fearful of rocking the bureaucratic boat. New York State's brilliant budget director, Patricia Woodworth (who cleaned up Michigan's fiscal mess), visited my office on several occasions, and warned me that we were ridiculed in political inner sanctums as "true believers" and were an embarrassment in the eyes of many insiders.

Sometimes you learn that being in the winner's circle is not all it is cracked up to be.

Mid-Decade Challenges

In 1996 and 1997, Mike Long stuck to his strategy and called his shots on issues where he believed he could have the greatest impact. He ran radio ads in late January 1996 that urged voters to promote the "Contract with New York" by letting "Assembly Speaker Sheldon Silver and the liberals know we demand change now." The purpose of the ads was to begin what he called "a truly grassroots citizen revolution for change in New York."

By late February, the party began attacking legislators who wanted to cancel the second phase of tax cuts enacted in 1995. Long pointed out that New Yorkers work until May 23 each year to pay federal, state, and local taxes.

"That's too much. The fact is New Yorkers pay 36 percent more in state and local taxes than the national average. Delaying or scaling back our tax cut not only will hurt hardworking families, but it will send the message to businesses that New York has lost the fight against the big spending special interests. That means few jobs and less growth."[10]

Long went so far as to threaten Democrats elected with Conservative Party endorsements that they would lose the endorsement in the future if they stood shoulder to shoulder with Speaker Silver.

On October 26, 1996, Long, William F. Buckley Jr., and Judge James Buckley led mourners at the requiem mass at Park Avenue's St. Ignatius Church for Party co-founder J. Daniel Mahoney. The sixty-five-year-old Judge Mahoney had died three days earlier of a massive stroke. At the time of his death, he was serving on the United States Court of Appeals for the Second Circuit, covering New York, Connecticut, and Vermont. After the mass, both Bill Buckley, Mike Long, and Charles Rice reminded those in the church of the enduring importance of Mahoney's vision: to give New Yorkers a vehicle for sending a clear message to public servants to limit the powers of "Big Brother."

The Pataki administration's third year brought its share of successes and disappointments.

The party was not pleased with increased spending, and it led the charge against a proposed $2.4-billion education bond act, calling it a waste of taxpayer dollars that would not improve education in New York. This school construction act, which was supported by both Pataki and former governor Mario Cuomo, was anathema to the Conservatives. As Mike Long said:

> The Conservative Party vigorously opposes this bond act. Along with lacking faith in the Albany pols to do the right thing, we believe New York State cannot afford to create more debt for our citizens. We are already one of the most heavily indebted states in the Union. The per capita debt in New York is $6,850 per each resident.
>
> We also have good reason to believe that voters are not being told where the money will be spent because an overwhelming amount of funds will be going to the inept School Construction Authority, based in New York City. Even Democrat Comptroller Carl McCall has been highly critical of the way the Authority wastes money. . . .
>
> We urge all New Yorkers to vote NO on the bond act. New York voters have the power to send a message to the Albany pols that we are not going to blindly turn over $2.4 billion. We support quality education, but this bond act will not improve public education in New York.

The Party also ran a series of TV ads, including this one:

> The most important election this year has no speeches, debates, or candidates.
>
> It's an election about money, your money, neatly wrapped in a package called the School Health and Safety Bond Act.
>
> But this Act has very little to do with our children's health or safety.
>
> In Fact, the New York City politicians who came up with this proposal refuse to tell us how or where they will spend a single dime of the $2.4 billion dollars they want.
>
> No additional teachers. No new computers. Not even a book.

So it comes as no surprise that New York City's School Construction authority is licking its chops at the prospect of billions in extra tax dollars.

And these are the same people who spent 300 grand to build a wheel-chair ramp under a basketball hoop.

On Tuesday, November 4, say NO to wasteful spending, vote NO on Proposal Three.[11]

Even though 71 percent of New York City voters said yes, the School Bond Act went down with a total of 52 percent of state voters saying no. A jubilant Long told the media:

"Tell Assembly Speaker Sheldon Silver the gravy train has been derailed. You can't sell a New Yorker the Brooklyn Bridge, but that's exactly what Silver and the liberal power elite tried to do. Asking for almost two and a half billion dollars without telling us how or where they intended to spend money was an insult to the intelligence of every taxpayer in this state. Slapping the word 'school' on this act just wasn't good enough."[12]

Ray Kerrison, writing in the *New York Post*, said:

In New York, the bastion of Northeast liberalism, there is every sign that voters are becoming increasingly disillusioned with big-tax/big-spend Democrats.

The defeat of the school-bond act was a perfect illustration. It dealt a sharp blow to liberals, but a devastating hit to their Albany leader, Assembly Speaker Sheldon Silver, who invested everything in its passage. Silver is about as relevant to today's policies as the Model T. . . .

So [Mike] Long and the Conservative Party have helped save the tax-payers $2 million every week for the next 30 years. If that's not a service to the state, what is?

There were other victories in 1997: 62 percent of the voters said no to an old Cuomo favorite, a Constitutional Convention. If passed, the Convention might have re-written the entire document, including voter approval of bonded debt. On December 18, in the wee hours of the morning, the legislature passed a Charter School Law. Supported by Governor Pataki, and heavily pushed by the Conservative Party, the bill contained:

* A blanket waiver of all bureaucratic rules, regulations, and laws applicable to public schools, except for health, safety, and civil rights.
* Total freedom from state tenure laws and pre-existing collective bargaining agreements.
* Total freedom from bureaucratic certification requirements for non-instructional personnel, including principals.

* Total freedom for a charter school to design its own curriculum, decide its own school-uniform policy, and set the length of the school day and school year.
* Complete financial and administrative autonomy from local school districts and flexibility in teacher certification rules.
* Specific authorization for single-sex charter schools.
* Unrestricted participation of private-sector partners and private educational firms.
* Freedom from mandated union representation for 10 charters regardless of school size, and for 90 others if a school's enrollment remains under 250 children for the first year of operation.

The biggest disappointment in 1997 was the extension of the rent-control law. Established during the Second World War as a temporary measure, for half a century Albany politicians have been afraid to abolish the law. Abuses have included rentals by celebrities for huge Park Avenue apartments – flats that would rent in a free market for thousands of dollars – for as little as a few hundred dollars. There is not doubt among housing experts that rent control stifles the construction of new housing.

The Conservative Party lobbied hard for the legislature to let the law expire. Mike Long issued the following statement about the party's grassroots campaign to end rent control:

> The Conservative Party has asked voters in all parts of the State if they support changing the rent control laws. The answer has been a resounding YES.
>
> New Yorkers understand what many elected officials fail to see: our rent control laws are counter-productive and have to be changed. Even a diehard rent control advocate like former Mayor Ed Koch has called on the Assembly Speaker to stop scaring people and to start negotiating changes in the rent control law.
>
> As it is presently constituted, the rent control law benefits many wealthy people at the expense of denying much needed housing to low and middle class New Yorkers. This has got to change.
>
> I urge all members of the Legislature to protect the truly needy as they reform the antiquated rent laws. Let's put aside the often shrill accusations being made in this debate and let's get down to work. The people of New York want and need change in this area.

At one point during this battle, Governor Pataki visited Conservative Party headquarters to chat with Chairman Long. Long walked away with the clear impression that Pataki was not going to fold on the issue regardless of how much pressure was put on him.[13]

Yet just several days later Pataki caved in to pressure from his political consultants, who cited a huge drop in the Governor's New York City popularity, and signed the rent-control extension bill. Long and scores of Conservatives were both angered and flabbergasted. What could the governor be thinking? It wasn't as if the city residents who opposed elimination of rent control were not going to vote for Pataki under any circumstances, so why surrender? It is very hard at times to fathom the Svengali-like influence of political consultants.

Although the party refused to endorse Rudy Giuliani's bid for a second term in city hall, it did announce that for the first time ever it would not field a Conservative candidate. Long explained the party's position this way:

> This year the Conservative Party faced a difficult decision. Do we endorse a candidate who has improved the quality of life in our city, but who we continue to have serious philosophical differences with?
>
> We've chosen the third way, to allow the people of New York to decide on their own without guidance from us.
>
> From the perspective of crime and economic expansion Mayor Giuliani has come a long way toward turning our city around. As a resident of Brooklyn, I am thankful for his great success in restoring law and order to our streets, our communities and our schools....
>
> While we welcome these changes we continue to have sharp differences with the Mayor on several important issues. Currently, we are on opposite sides of the rent control debate and the continued debate over abortions.
>
> These important differences pose a dilemma for the Conservative Party. Rather than fielding a candidate that would take away votes from Mayor Giuliani to the benefit of an ultra-liberal like Ruth Messinger or Sal Albanese, the Conservative Party has decided not to stand in opposition to a Mayor who has done much good and who we hope will earn our endorsement in the future by adopting our free market position on housing and our defense of the most innocent of human beings.[14]

Although Long was more-or-less satisfied with George Pataki's achievements, not all conservatives were happy with the governor's performance. Change-NY President Tom Carroll gave him a low grade:

> The governor's overall performance this year was disappointing not just because he is capable of more (as seen in his first two years), but because

the times demand much more. New York still lags the nation in job creation. Our credit rating is among the very lowest of any state. Our personal income tax rates remain sky high, government spending is out of line in virtually every area, and the state's long-term budget picture is very precarious.

This year, the governor needed to build on his successes in addressing these problems. Instead, in a political conversion that would make even most politicians blush, the governor has embarked on a Cuomoesque spending and debt spree that betrays his campaign promises and squanders the historic opportunity he was handed in November 1994.[15]

Although Carroll made some valid points, Long reminded party members that they were a minority party, and that their share of victories outweighed the losses.

Snatching Defeat from the Jaws of Victory

As the 1998 political cycle began, Conservative Party leaders concluded that George Pataki had kept at least two of his most significant promises: He had reduced taxes, and he had taken steps to reduce crime. For the first time in ten years, Standard and Poor's increased the state's bond rating to "A," and the Justice Department's released figures that showed violent crime had plunged by 25 percent since Pataki had taken office. The governor had also cut the state's work force by 20,000 and had enacted workmen's compensation reform.

Yet just as it looked as though 1998 would be a good year for Conservatives, problems began to surface. Al D'Amato was beginning his eighteenth year in the United States Senate, and he was looking forward to running for a fourth term. Even though he had managed to annoy Conservatives on numerous occasions – What elected official does not? – it was expected that he would receive party endorsement again in 1998. Conservatives had forgiven (or forgotten) his support of gays in the military, although back in January of 1993 an angry Long had made these comments on behalf of the Party:

We would have hoped that Sen. D'Amato would have consulted us before he made himself Bill Clinton's favorite Republican. Because if he had he would have found out that no one is advocating witch hunts against homosexuals, but that a majority of his constituents oppose government certification of their lifestyle.

I know that Sen. D'Amato would have found further opposition to his stated position from the men and women we employ to defend our nation. The Joint Chiefs have unequivocally presented a case why Clinton's policies would seriously undermine our military organization.

Today my telephone is ringing off the hook with calls from

Conservative leaders who are bewildered by Sen. D'Amato's actions. I'm saddened to report that we find ourselves on the side of the working men and women of New York while Sen. D'Amato has sought to embrace the radical liberal position on this important issue.[16]

But if Senator D'Amato continued to have the grudging support of Conservatives, he faced more serious problems with the Right to Life Party, which threatened to rescind its endorsement and even to put up another candidate. D'Amato called me on this matter, and I agreed to help him.

During my race for mayor in 1993, I had been proud to also have the Right to Life nomination and had become friendly with State Chairman Lena Harknett and her husband, Doug. From them I learned that there were numerous disgruntled party members who believed that D'Amato sold them out; that he no longer publicly articulated strong pro-life views. I pointed out that to be pro-life in New York was not an easy task; that you can't expect elected officials to stand on street corners beating tambourines for the pro-life cause. Nonetheless, I argued that among the senator's many flaws, deserting his pro-life principles was not one of them. In eighteen years in the senate, he had not cast one bad vote on life issues.

But for some that wasn't good enough.

On May 30, I accompanied Allen Roth and Jim Kelly to a Right to Life convention where we hoped to lobby delegates on behalf of Senator D'Amato. The senator, himself, spoke to the delegates, but his perfect voting record wasn't enough for the 28 percent who voted to nominate Thomas Droleskey for the Senate. D'Amato received 73 percent of the vote and was the Right to Life Party's designee, but now he had to face a primary fight.

In another closely watched race, Dennis Vacco was up for re-election as the state's attorney general. Vacco, who had won by a whisker in 1994 and who had spent four years building a decent record, had endeared himself to pro-life forces when he argued successfully before the U.S. Supreme Court the assisted suicide case, *Vacco v. Quill.*

In *Vacco v. Quill* the Court ruled unanimously that New York's statutes prohibiting assisted suicide did not infringe on any fundamental rights, and sustained Vacco's reasoning that there was a distinction between refusing medical treatment and assisting a suicide. The Court also held that New York's statutes had rational public interest in mind, namely to avoid intentional killing, to maintain the physician's role as a healer, and to protect people from financial and psychological pressure.

Chief Justice Rehnquist, who delivered the opinion for the Court, pointed out that the New York statues comply with the Fourteenth Amendment's equal-protection clause.

On their faces, neither New York's ban on assisting suicide nor its statues permitting patients to refuse medical treatment treat anyone differently than anyone else or draw any distinctions between persons. *Everyone*, regardless of physical condition, is entitled, if competent, to refuse unwanted lifesaving medical treatment; *no one* is permitted to assist a suicide. Generally speaking, laws that apply evenhandedly to all "unquestionably comply" with the Equal Protection Clause.[17]

So in 1998 Vacco was the unanimous choice of the Conservative Party and was also offered the Right-to-Life nomination. Unlike D'Amato, who was willing to fight to keep that nomination, Vacco permitted his political consultants to talk him into declining the Right-to-Life endorsement. Long and other Conservative leaders tried to talk sense to him, pointing out that his Democratic opponent, Eliot Spitzer, was expected to run a tough, well-financed campaign; that in a close race the votes on the Right-to-Life line could make all the difference. But Vacco insisted in declining the nomination.

At the June 6 Conservative Party convention at Albany's Omni Hotel, Pataki, D'Amato, and Vacco were all unanimously re-nominated, and the majority leader of the Nassau County legislature, Bruce Blakeman, was tapped for comptroller. There was one significant change from four years earlier: Lieutenant Governor Betsey McCaughey, who had proved to be a political nightmare (as Allen Roth and others had predicted in 1994) was dumped from the Republican and Conservative tickets. Mary Donahue, a Rensselaer County judge, a former district attorney, and the mother of two, replaced McCaughey.

But Ms. McCaughey did not leave quietly. She became a Democrat and entered her new party's primary for governor. Liberal Party boss Ray Harding, knowing he needed 50,000 votes in November to keep his party's ballot line, gave her his party's gubernatorial nomination.

All in all, 1998 was shaping up to be a bizarre political year.

While Democrats Peter Vallone (speaker of the New York City Council) and Betsey McCaughey were slugging it out in the Democratic primary, Pataki had amassed a $20-million campaign chest.

When the primary dust settled, D'Amato had handily won the Right to Life nomination, and now had to face an unexpected Democratic opponent, Congressman Charles Schumer, in the general election. The Brooklyn-Queens representative had decisively defeated Geraldine Ferraro and Mark Green in the Democratic primary. He was known to be a tenacious candidate. Some political insiders even called him the Jewish Al D'Amato.

In the fall campaign, the well-financed Pataki machine held a huge lead over Democrat Peter Vallone's lackluster campaign. The governor said as little as possible, avoided debating Vallone, and simply coasted on his lead.

Mike Long, however, was not sitting on his hands and ran an independent campaign to help re-elect the governor. The Conservative Party message was simple: A vote for Pataki on the Conservative line helped to give the party leverage to keep the governor honest on the issues. Long also hoped that his modest campaign budget ($400,000) and his targeted message to upstate conservative-Republicans would increase vote totals to offset any gains made by the Ross Perot's Independent Party. In 1994, they had received 217,490 votes versus the Conservative Party's 328,605. Once again their candidate was Thomas Golisano, who was spending $10 million of his own money in the hope the Independents would edge out the Conservatives to gain Row C.

Running on the slogan: "New York is a better place because George Pataki is our Governor," the governor was re-elected to a second term:

	Vallone Dem.	Pataki Rep.	Pataki Cons.	Galisano Ind.	McCaughey Lib.	Reynolds R to L	Lewis Green	Vallone Working Families
Total Upstate	**713,820**	**1,819,492**	**288,405**	**329,324**	**52,109**	**48,986**	**39,992**	**20,837**
Bronx	133,443	37,171	6,784	3,612	2,553	1,182	926	2,322
Brooklyn	231,610	106,133	16,008	8,696	6,331	1,805	3,944	10,353
Manhattan	219,559	89,205	7,389	11,473	10,195	1,294	4,472	13,276
Queens	194,900	120,402	20,314	8,522	5,405	2,468	2,575	3,793
Staten Island	25,660	50,861	9,827	2,321	1,322	948	624	744
Total NYC	**805,172**	**403,772**	**60,322**	**34,624**	**25,806**	**7,697**	**12,541**	**30,488**
Total State	**1,518,992**	**2,223,264**	**348,727**	**363,948**	**77,915**	**56,683**	**52,533**	**51,325**

Pataki won, but he received only 53 percent of the vote. His New York City percentage went up to 33 percent, which was good, but there were some warning signs too. Golisano received 13 percent in the Republican-Conservative regions upstate. Analysts attributed this to the governor's failure to create a vision for a second term.

The really big disappointment, however, was in the Conservative vote. Although the party had run its own campaign for Pataki and the total votes cast for him on Row C had surpassed the 1994 total by 20,000, the party faced squarely the power of Golisano's $10-million spending spree: the Independent Party outpolled the Conservatives by 16,000 votes. This meant that after thirty-two years on Row C, the Conservative Party would now have to move to Row D. Long's only satisfaction was that the Liberal Party came within 27,000 votes of going out of business altogether. Their candidate, the erratic Ms. McCaughey, received a pitiful 77,915 votes.

But if that was bad, the Senate race was a complete disaster. Throughout the campaign, there were times when it seemed that D'Amato had forgotten his roots. He actively sought and received the endorsement of a national gay organization. At one point he attacked Schumer for "being soft on the Holocaust." (Schumer had missed a vote that permitted a Holocaust ceremony to be held in the Capitol rotunda.)[18] If his consultants thought D'Amato's base vote – suburban and inner-city neighborhood ethnic Catholics – had "no place to go," they were wrong. Many stayed home; some voted for Schumer.

	Schumer Dem.	D'Amato Rep.	D'Amato Cons.	Schumer Ind.	Schumer Lib.	D'Amato R. to L.
Total Upstate	**1,385,420**	**1,385,592**	**228,443**	**87,306**	**33,164**	**90,424**
Bronx	150,843	26,220	5,019	2,819	2,768	1,794
Brooklyn	288,356	82,026	12,302	6,271	6,248	3,532
Manhattan	288,342	53,851	4,981	5,845	7,531	1,793
Queens	237,905	90,229	15,303	5,649	5,048	4,557
Staten Island	35,448	42,285	8,172	1,137	965	2,465
Total NYC	**1,000,894**	**294,611**	**45,777**	**21,721**	**22,560**	**14,141**
Total State	**2,386,314**	**1,680,203**	**274,220**	**109,027**	**55,724**	**104,565**

D'Amato even lost Senator Serf Maltese's district, the most conservative part of Queens. And while D'Amato did carry hardcore Italian neighborhood's in Staten Island and Brooklyn, his margins were dramatically smaller than Giuliani's had been in his 1997 re-election campaign. And D'Amato's margins in Orthodox Jewish neighborhoods of Brooklyn (where there was support for D'Amato's pro-life views) dropped by 50 percent. Even in his home county of Nassau, D'Amato only received 52.9 percent of the vote.

Long had done all he could for D'Amato. He had come out swinging against Schumer's liberalism. He had slammed Schumer for "abandoning principle in the Gulf War and for voting against President Bush's successful effort to turn back Iraqi aggression." That vote, Long said, "puts Schumer out on the far-left Ted Kennedy-wing of the national Democratic Party."

"I'm from the Borough of Brooklyn," Long said on another occasion, "and Chuck Schumer is from the Borough of Brooklyn, but that's the only way we're alike."

Long said Schumer "should stop pretending he's anything other than a Brooklyn liberal," and he ripped Schumer for his comments to the New York *Daily News* on September 17 in which he had said that "Al D'Amato makes us ashamed as Americans." Long charged that "these are some outrageous words from a politician who voted three times against a Constitutional Amendment to ban flag burning and who didn't even bother to show up for a vote two weeks ago to increase health care benefits to our nation's veterans."

As if theses disasters weren't enough, there was the Vacco race. As expected, Elliot Spitzer had run a superb, if nasty, race. He'd hit the all-time low when he said Vacco was "responsible for creating the climate that led to the assassination of Buffalo [abortion] doctor, Barnett Slepian."

It was several weeks before the outcome was official, but Vacco lost by 25,186 votes. Oh, and the Right to Life candidate received 66,357 votes. Vacco's political consultants had talked him out of accepting the Right-to-Life line, arguing that it might hurt him in future elections. They forgot that you have to win the present election before you can win future elections. The under-financed Republican-

Conservative comptroller candidate, Bruce Blakeman, went down big, and Carl McCall was re-elected in a landslide.

	Spitzer Dem.	Vacco Rep.	Vacco Cons.	Spitzer Lib.	Dapelo R. to L.	Moore Green
Total Upstate	**1,119,319**	**1,496,803**	**255,252**	**59,047**	**41,170**	**52,110**
Bronx	133,805	24,040	5,253	2,367	2,941	1,257
Brooklyn	258,568	66,845	12,057	6,005	6,771	1,952
Manhattan	264,830	49,486	5,068	8,054	8,463	1,175
Queens	210,397	81,095	15,891	4,828	5,789	2,721
Staten Island	31,672	39,270	8,702	1,138	1,223	1,184
Total NYC	**899,272**	**260,736**	**46,971**	**22,392**	**25,187**	**8,289**
Total State	**2,018,591**	**1,757,539**	**302,223**	**81,439**	**66,357**	**60,399**

Throughout the 1998 election cycle, Long had preached over and over again that to energize the Party's traditional voter base, Conservative candidates must proudly promote their Conservative credentials as well as a vision for the future. His words fell on deaf ears. Too many candidates listened to political consultants instead. "Hide your conservatism," the pundits insisted. "And say as little as possible."

The consultants may have won the attention of their candidates, but on November 3, 1998, they failed to win the support of voters.

Chapter 16

Fighting the Good Fight for Life
1996–2001

For the founders of the Conservative Party and their heirs, the cornerstone of America's republican democracy is the concept of the person: of his dignity, his inalienable rights, his duties, and his freedoms.

The Conservative Party is guided by the counsel of Thomas Jefferson: "Can the liberties of a nation be secure when we have removed the conviction that these liberties are the gift of God?" The first of all rights, which is the inalienable right to life itself, cannot justly be taken from the innocent by the state, since it is not a right granted by the state in the first place. God, the author of human nature, grants a person's inalienable rights, and those rights are *natural* for precisely this reason.

To promote this end the Conservative Party adopted in 1969 "a policy of advocating protection of the civil right to life of the child in the womb when New York State first considered legislation prior to the U.S. Supreme Court decision that made abortion the law of the land."[1] Ever since then, the party's platform has strongly affirmed its pro-life position for the unborn, the elderly, and the infirm.

One issue the Conservative Party has fought for during the Pataki years – and fought for without regard for the political consequences or the financial costs – is the ban on partial-birth abortion in New York State.

The Conservative Party has always opposed abortion and has called for the overturning of *Roe v. Wade* from the beginning, but the emergence in recent years of partial-birth abortion has given new life to the party's pro-life commitment. Although George Pataki had angered many conservatives in early 1996 when he had pledged, "to help lead the fight to remove the 'pro-life' plank from the GOP platform at the party's August convention in San Diego,"[2] Mike Long did manage to get a promise from the governor to sign into law a ban on partial-birth abortions. Pataki had said: "I am pro-choice . . . but there's a difference when you perform a partial birth abortion. . . . I think that is a horrendous procedure which should only be used to save the life of a mother."[3]

Not everyone liked his approach, but what was most important was his pledge to sign the ban if and when the measure reached his desk.

On April 30, 1996, the state senate passed a bill, sponsored by Serf Maltese, that provided such a ban. Majority leader Joe Bruno said that this "issue is on the Senate floor not as a pro-life issue, not as an anti-choice issue, but as an issue of what is right and wrong." The Maltese bill made it a felony for any physician to perform an abortion by "partially vaginally delivering a living fetus before killing the fetus and completing the delivery."[4] A doctor convicted under the law could receive up to three years in prison, but the legislation prohibited criminal charges being brought against "a woman or girl upon whom a partial birth abortion is performed."[5]

Mike Long hailed the Maltese bill:

> This action is an important step in putting to an end the killing of babies who are in the late stages of pregnancy. Anyone who is familiar with this procedure knows it is a barbaric act. . . . [B]anning this procedure should not be a Democrat or Republican issue. It should not separate Conservatives or Liberals. We are talking here about protecting innocent human lives. I call upon Shelly Silver, a religious man, to follow the dictates of his heart and support this legislation. I hope he does not politicize this matter. The Assembly should join the Senate in outlawing infanticide.[6]

The next task was to get Speaker Silver, an Orthodox Jew but also a mainstream liberal, to bring up the bill for a vote in the assembly, which he did not want to do, since he was afraid there just might be a majority supporting passage. His strategy was simple: keep the bill bottled up in committee. Publicly he justified his opposition this way: A bill "denying the full range of health care options," he said, "is not something we support."[7]

Many people, including some liberals, were shocked to hear partial-birth abortion categorized as merely a health-care option. Both Senator Moynihan and former Mayor Koch had called the procedure a form of infanticide. Governor Pataki's hard-nosed pro-abortion communications director, Zenia Mucha, blasted Silver:

> It's unfortunate that the Speaker is unable to distinguish between politics and policy positions. The overwhelming majority of New Yorkers who are pro-choice, like the Governor, agree this is an abhorrent procedure and in no way, shape or form does it tie in to whether or not you are pro-choice, and it's unfortunate people would use the issue as a partisan, political tool.[8]

To pressure Silver, Mike Long began a statewide petition drive to demand a full assembly vote on the issue. The party mailed tens of thousands of letters to voters asking them to sign this petition:

PETITION TO SHELDON SILVER
TO STOP PARTIAL BIRTH ABORTIONS

WHEREAS, "partial birth abortion" is a heinous procedure that kills a nearly-born fetus, and people on both sides of the pro-life/pro-choice debate support a BAN on partial birth abortions, and

WHEREAS, the New York State Senate has passed S.6901, supported by the Conservative Party, and Governor Pataki has promised to sign it, and

WHEREAS, the citizens of New York have the right to know where each member of the State Assembly stands on this issue,

BE IT THEREFORE RESOLVED, we the undersigned demand Assembly Speaker Sheldon Silver end his scheme of prohibiting a vote on the Partial Birth Abortion Ban, and schedule an "on the record" vote immediately.

SIGNED:_____

The response was incredible, often breaking 10 percent, a huge number for mailing houses accustomed to 1 or 2 percent returns.

The Conservative Party also began airing a 60-second radio commercial on May 28, 1996:

I know abortion is a controversial issue, but now, they've just gone too far.
Partial birth abortions clearly cross the line.
It's cruel, barbaric, and simply unnecessary.
Unfortunately, Sheldon Silver doesn't see it this way.
Silver's the radical Assembly Speaker who's refusing to allow a vote on partial birth abortions.
That's why I called 1-900-896-VOTE to force Silver to allow my legislator to vote on this issue.
The call cost just fifty cents, charged directly to my phone bill.
I called because when I look at my Jason and Julie, I know this isn't about abortion, it's about right and wrong.
Pro-Choice or Pro-Life, we all agree partial birth abortions go too far.
Please call 1-900-896-VOTE today to help give your legislator the chance to end partial birth abortions.

"Shelly Silver's refusal to allow the Assembly to vote on partial birth abortion," Long told the media, "shows who the real extremists are on the issue. . . . [Our ads are] going to let people know that [although] . . . Mario Cuomo's gone, radical liberals like Sheldon Silver are still in power."[9]

Long's strategy in the assembly was to get a Democrat who was elected with Conservative endorsement to attach the anti-abortion measure to a social-service or welfare bill. In 1996 there were eight Democrats who had earned the Conservative Party's banner: Dov Hikind, Eric Vitaliano, Stephen Kaufman, Ronald Tocci, Alexander Gromack, Joseph Rabach, Paul Tokasz, and Frances Pordum.

The party kept the heat on these members of the assembly, barraging them with memos, letters, phone calls, and various appeals to conscience.

In July, the cause suffered a major setback when Vitaliano, the Democratic-Conservative from Staten Island, reneged on his pledge to pursue a vote on the partial-birth bill before the summer recess. His excuse was that he had agreed to put off any action after Speaker Silver had assured him he could bring up the issue later in the year.

Mike Long was livid:

> I don't know how Assemblyman Vitaliano can look at himself in the mirror. In the week before the end of the New York State's legislative session, Staten Island Assemblyman Eric Vitaliano repeatedly promised me and others that he would offer an amendment that would end the barbaric procedure of partial birth abortions. Mr. Vitaliano told us he would do the "right thing." But in the end he broke his word. He put the desires of Manhattan liberal Assembly Speaker Shelly Silver before the lives of innocent children.
>
> Whether or not you support banning partial birth abortions, voters have a right to know that their elected representatives tell the truth. Well the people of the 60th Assembly District should know that Mr. Vitaliano's word cannot be trusted.
>
> I can personally attest to the fact that Eric Vitaliano promised he would make the motion to end the procedure that involves crushing the heads of little babies. He seemed to have the courage to make the Assembly vote on this important issue. But in the end he abandoned the babies and his word.[10]

Since the petitions for ballot endorsements for the upcoming elections had already been filed, it was too late to stop Vitaliano from getting the party's nomination, but that did not stop Staten Island's Deputy Borough President and Party Executive Vice Chairman James Molinaro from publicly condemning the assemblyman.

"If a man makes a commitment to do something," Molinaro said, "he's got to do it. He didn't do it because Silver told him to back off and he backed off."[11]

The betrayal did not stop Long from pursuing a vote on the measure. He applied all the heat he could, and finally, in the waning hours of the legislative year (specifically at four in the morning on December 18), the "shell-shocked" Vitaliano attached the partial-birth ban to a bill pertaining to election-law reform. Silver, who had promised the Catholic hierarchy he would permit a debate, ruled that Vitaliano's motion was out of order. When a vote was taken on the Speaker's ruling, he was upheld by a vote of 77 to 62. This procedural vote effectively killed the late-term abortion bill for 1996.[12]

The Conservative Party brushed off this setback, and when the legislature convened in early 1997, a new plan of action was unveiled. Eighty thousand pieces of mail were sent to the constituents of eleven assemblyman on a hit list drawn up by Mike Long. "Their constituents will get a letter signed by me," Long said. "It will tell them what happened December 19 at 3:30 in the morning – what . . . [their representatives] did, how they voted. It will explain partial birth abortion and what the procedure is like."[13]

The eleven legislators on Long's list were: Democrat Peter Abbate, Brooklyn; Democratic Majority Leader Michael Bragman, Onondaga County; Republican Clifford Crouch, Delaware County; Democrat Audrey Hochberg, Westchester County; Democrat William Parment, Chautauqua County; Democrat Audrey Pheffer, Queens; Democrat Joseph Pillittere, Niagara County; Democrat William Magee, Madison County; Republican Willis Stephens Jr., Putnam County; Republican Frances Sullivan, Oswego County; and Democrat Sandra Galef, Westchester County.

Long said his plan in 1997 was to push for a direct vote on an abortion-ban bill sponsored by Democratic-Conservative Assemblyman Anthony Seminario of Ridgewood, Queens. It was a plan that was to unfold in stages. First he was spending $35,000 on the mailing to the voters in the districts of eleven legislators, and then, after dumping the signed petition cards on the desks of each of the eleven legislators, he was going to go after another fifteen of them. It was his hope to stir the pot enough to get Silver to schedule a vote.

Long also received help from an unexpected source, former Mayor Ed Koch. Bumping into one another at a function, Koch asked Long if he would support a vote of conscience on the proposed "gay right's bill" in the state senate. In response, Long asked Koch why he should support such a vote as long as Silver refused to permit a vote on a partial-birth abortion ban. Koch, hearing this, made a counter-proposal: If he could get Silver to support a conscience vote on the abortion ban, would Long support a similar vote on "gay rights" in the senate? Long said yes, and the men shook hands on it.

To his credit, Koch wrote the speaker on several occasions urging Silver to bring both issues to the floor. In a letter dated February 26, 1997, Koch stated:

> You are a decent, honest and religious person. I believe that you want to do what is right. Is there any question that there should be a vote of conscience permitted in the State Legislature to prohibit partial birth abortion except in cases where a doctor believes it is the sole medical procedure

available to save the woman's life? Even if you, for whatever reasons, cannot vote to abolish the procedure, shouldn't you allow a conscience vote to be cast by the other members?

But even this plea fell on deaf ears.

In February 1997, Ron Fitzsimmons, executive director of the National Coalition of Abortion Providers, whose previous statements had made the case for partial-birth abortion, made a startling admission, namely, that he had lied ("through my teeth") when he said that partial-birth abortion was rarely used and then only to save a mother's life. He said his lies made him "physically ill."[14] He now admitted that the procedure was used often, and that "in the vast majority of cases, the procedure is performed on a healthy mother with a healthy fetus that is 20 weeks or more along."[15]

This revelation re-energized the Conservative Party's efforts in Albany. In March, the senate once again passed the Maltese bill, this time by a vote of 40 to 19. But over in the assembly, where Silver engineered passage of a so-called state "gay-rights" bill, the partial-birth abortion ban remained stuck in a bottleneck.

When Long heard that both the governor and Attorney General Vacco now supported the "gay rights legislation," he blasted them.

"I'm greatly disappointed in both of them," Long said. "Quite frankly, I think they are both out of step with the people who elected them and are now in lock step with Cuomo and Karen Burstein. . . . Those were their opponents and that is not what people of this state voted for. If they wanted this type of legislation, they would have voted for Cuomo and Burstein."[16]

Fred Dicker of the *New York Post* reported that the governor's political consultants were pushing Pataki further to the left on this issue in hopes of increasing his voter base. The sheer arrogance of the consultants was reflected in their reaction to the Conservative Party's anger:

> We love the Conservatives, but we want to win the election. If Conservatives don't like some of the governor's political positions, what are they going to do, vote for Chuck Schumer?" said the strategist, referring to the aggressively liberal Brooklyn Democratic congressman who is eyeing a run for governor.[17]

Long did, however, have the last say: he made sure the "gay-rights" bill died in the state senate.

In early April, the party flooded the offices of targeted assemblymen with postcards, signed by their constituents, that demanded an end to the barbaric partial-birth procedure. Later in the month Long mailed more than a quarter-of-a-million letters to voters, and he sent a personal letter to every member of the assembly urging each and every one to push for a vote on the issue.

By June, the mailings totaled 450,000 and another radio commercial hit the air-waves. Still, by December there was no action in the assembly. Over in New Jersey the legislature had sent a partial-birth abortion bill to its governor's desk, and a frustrated Long issued this statement:

> Congratulations to the Members of the New Jersey State Senate for having the courage of their convictions to end this barbaric procedure in New Jersey.
>
> I can only hope that the New York Legislature, particularly the Democratic controlled Assembly will find the moral fortitude to follow the footsteps of the New Jersey Legislature.[18]

In the following year, the Conservatives were leading the charge once again, even declaring that the ban was the party's no. 1 priority.

At the annual C-PAC, former presidential candidate Steve Forbes warned the faithful:

"You should not underestimate the importance of this partial birth abortion debate. . . . [Success will be] the first step in putting abortion on the road to extinction in America."

In early 1998, Mike Long attended an Albany meeting of select pro-lifers called by New York State Catholic Conference president John Kerry. There were several arguments made at this gathering about the wisdom of continuing to fight for a vote in the assembly to outlaw partial-birth abortion. Some said the effort should be abandoned because the ban was at least seventy votes short of what was needed to discharge the bill from committee. Others reasoned that a continued pursuit of a hopeless cause might anger Speaker Silver to a point at which aid to Catholic hospitals could be jeopardized. Long angrily made it clear that the Catholic Conference and others were free to do whatever they chose, but that the Conservative Party would continue the fight – alone if necessary – to force a discharge vote. In the end Long prevailed, and the big push proceeded.

The Conservative Party continued to pressure legislators through grassroots mailings and by direct pleas from Long. And it began to appear that progress was being made: numerous legislators were agreeing that it was fair to at least permit the bill to come to the floor and let members vote their consciences.

Finally, late in the night of April 8, 1998, the procedural maneuver known as a "motion to discharge" was implemented. Speaker Silver used all the means at his disposal to blunt this move. Political insiders say that Democratic members were threatened with punishment if they betrayed the speaker. And as a desperate eleventh-hour tactic to quell a revolt, Silver announced that he personally would introduce a partial-birth abortion bill, weaker than the Maltese version, that would ban the procedure after twenty-four weeks. Finally a discharge vote was taken: 71 in favor, 73 against.

The result was heartbreaking, but it proved again that hard work and grassroots activism can have an impact. Only a few weeks earlier, the more timid in the pro-life movement were ready to throw in the towel, believing the task was insurmountable or dangerously offensive to the power brokers. Yet within the month, Speaker Silver had succumbed to pressure and agreed to permit debate and a vote on his scaled-down version. *The New York Times* reported:

> The bill would have prohibited the procedure, called partial birth abortions by opponents, only after 24 weeks of pregnancy, instead of at any stage. It was clearly intended mostly to appease Assembly members who generally support abortion rights. Indeed, even Mr. Silver's aides conceded that the bill's only intent was to allow Democrats from more conservative districts to return home saying that they had voted for a ban.[19]

That was a pretty smug sort of cynicism even for Silver and the *Times*, but apparently no good deed goes unpunished. The compromise itself infuriated pro-abortion advocates, who always object to any law that would restrict abortion in any manner, even including as barbaric a practice as partial-birth abortions that many pro-abortionists privately cringe to imagine. They fear that if any restriction is codified, particularly if it recognizes the fetus as human, their fundamental rationale might collapse like a house of cards.

"Even if the bill had no legal effect, there was still a deep symbolic effect," said Kelli Conlin, director of the New York chapter of the National Abortion and Reproductive Rights Action League. "The Speaker apparently realized this was not a wise move for a state that has a history of standing firm on abortion rights."[20]

Needless to say, pro-life activists dislike the Silver compromise, since studies show that most partial-birth abortions are performed before twenty-four weeks.

Interestingly, Speaker Silver ended up opposing his own compromise bill.

"It looks like he realized this was a bad tactical error," Mike Long told the *Times*. "He was playing a game to give some members cover and ended up alienating everyone."[21]

Another year had passed without a partial-birth abortion ban, but Long and the Conservative Party were as determined as ever to get one.

In March Long made another appeal to Speaker Silver and the entire assembly delegation to once and for all allow a vote on a partial-birth abortion bill. He told them that he was "making the appeal because I want to save lives, and because we cannot respect ourselves as human beings if we allow infanticide to continue."[22] Long also continued placing full page ads in Catholic Diocesan newspapers throughout the state, reminding their readers that "Nothing is more precious than Life: So why are Sheldon Silver and some Assembly members still blocking a vote on partial birth abortion?" The advertisement also urged readers to contact local legislators listed their names and phone numbers.

In late March when the state Senate once again supported the Maltese Bill, a Republican-Conservative legislator, Nicholas Spano of Westchester, decided to jump the fence and oppose the bill.

When Spano called Long to tell him that he was breaking his promise to vote for the ban, an angry chairman put out a tense statement saying the senator (who also served as Westchester Republican County chairman) was "an individual who cannot be counted on when he gives his word. . . . Clearly Spano joins the ranks of Bill Clinton in his support of this heinous act, partial birth abortion. And he also joins with Clinton in his inability to tell the truth."

Long had actually shaken hands with Spano just a month earlier, symbolically sealing the deal to pass the ban. Now he felt betrayed, so much so that he told a reporter that Spano has proven he "doesn't really stand for anything" that "to us he doesn't exist anymore." Long also dropped a mailing on Spano's district denouncing his stance and urging constituents to send postcards to Spano condemning him. Conservative County leader Vince Natrella also said he wouldn't support Spano. "I'm with Mike Long one hundred percent on this issue," Natrella said. "I can't speak for every Conservative, but if Nicky doesn't change his position, I'll work against him."[23] *The New York Times* detailed Long's anger:

> "I intend for the next two years to do every possible thing to inform as many people in Westchester about this vote" and that he reneged on a promise, "because if he can get away with it it means every elected official can come to an interview and tell the Conservative Party that they're going to vote to cut taxes or that they are for charter schools, and then when they vote they fold."

In 2000, Vince Natrella tried but failed to strip the Conservative nomination from Spano. Numerous Republicans and union members re-registered as Conservatives, infiltrated the county's executive committee, and voted Natrella down.

On April 12, 1999, Speaker Silver once again killed a motion to discharge the partial-birth abortion ban. Through parliamentary slight of hand, Assemblyman Clarence Norman, temporarily holding the speaker's chair, discarded the rules and refused to acknowledge Assemblyman Patrick Manning's motion to discharge. Instead, the chair substituted another motion that the sponsor had not requested. Assembly minority leader, John Faso, outraged by Silver's latest Machiavellian maneuvering, told the *Albany Times Union*: "The issue is not dead." He vowed that the bill would reappear on the assembly calendar before law makers adjourned for the year.[24]

True to his word, Faso directed Republican-Conservative assemblyman Manning to attach the partial-birth-abortion ban as an amendment to a bill that was on the floor on June 30, 1999. Assemblyman Norman ruled that the amendment was not germane to the bill being debated, and Manning appealed. The appeal vote (which, if successful, would have permitted a vote on a partial-birth ban in amendment form) went down 67 to 61, with twenty-two members mysteriously absent from the assembly floor. In the past the assembly has entertained bills making it a felony to "murder" cats and other pets and has voted 148 to 0 to outlaw the use of certain poisonous substances to eliminate pigeons, but on this day it was barely able to muster a quorum to vote on the fate of innocent babies.

Still the party fought on, opposing medical funding of abortion, abortion-clinic-access bills, pro-gay "bias-crime" legislation, and other, so-called, "progressive" social issues. In September 1999, Conservatives marched in protest against anti-Catholic art displayed at the Brooklyn Museum of Art. Led by Republican-Conservative Congressman Vito Fossella of Staten Island, party members rallied against tax dollars being spent to exhibit a painting that depicted the Virgin Mary splattered with elephant dung.

After the U.S. Supreme Court ruled on June 28 that Boy Scout Troops have a right to set their own guidelines for choosing leaders, the Conservative Party vigorously opposed U.S. Attorney General Janet Reno's decision to investigate whether governmental ties to the Boy Scouts violated President Clinton's executive order of June 23, 1999, banning discrimination based on sexual orientation. Long sent a letter to each elected official in New York State, including congressional sponsors of HR 4892 that sought to revoke Boy Scout Charters, and asked if they really intended to stand idly by as the Boy Scouts were attacked by certain members of Congress as well as certain large corporations.

Long asked each elected official what kind of message we are sending to our youth when we close the doors of a public school to an organization that promotes leadership and values while we incorporate a curriculum that teaches students that *Heather Has Two Mommies*?

"With all the emphasis on campaign finance reform lately, maybe each elected official should return any donations made to their campaigns from Levi-Strauss, Chase Manhattan, Merrill Lynch, Wells Fargo, and Knight Ridder, who have threatened to withdraw funding from the Boy Scouts," stated Long.

Long called upon all elected officials to reaffirm the Boy Scouts of America Charter and their right to choose their leaders as upheld by the Supreme Court. He urged that "all political and corporate leaders in New York and throughout America denounce the efforts to force acceptance of avowed homosexuals as leaders."

"What is next?" he asked "Charles Manson as a Boy Scout Leader?"

In 2000, the party went after the gay "bias-crime" bill. The bill had come to the state senate after flyers handed out by gay-activists at Long Island railroad stations caused Senate Majority Leader Joe Bruno and five Republican members from the county to panic and agree to pass the legislation.

The Conservative Party has historically supported increased penalties for most crimes, but, recognizing that state law already makes it is a crime to assault *any* person, the party questioned why it should be a greater crime to assault a homosexual person. The party's position was very simple: A crime is a crime. All assaults and/or harassments are criminal and should be treated in a manner consistent with current law. A person, for instance, caught desecrating a statue at a place of worship should be penalized for the offense of malicious destruction of property, not for maliciously offending religious sensibilities.

Unfortunately, the party's logic failed to convince enough legislators, and on Wednesday, June 7 the state senate caved: twenty Republicans with Conservative endorsements and three Democrats with the party label voted for Senator Roy Goodman's Hate Crime Bill, S4691. Only Serf Maltese and three other members had the guts to vote no.

Writing in the *New York Post*, editorial columnist Eric Fettmann had this reaction:

> Indeed, it's appropriate that the Legislature is enacting this law out of political calculation – for hate-crime laws are entirely political: Rather than address a real criminal-justice need, they're meant to make a point.
>
> It's also ironic that Bruno's switch came about just as a California judge ruled that the white supremacist who shot up a Jewish day school last year in a widely publicized hate crime could face a death sentence if convicted. If the threat of a date with the gas chamber didn't deter him, what would a possible five-year sentence for committing a hate crime do?
>
> And that's the point: These bills don't criminalize anything that isn't already against the law. Assaulting a gay person is illegal and punishable by a hefty jail sentence. Invading a Jewish school with an automatic weapon and opening fire is illegal.

Similar to Senator Goodman's bias-crime bill is his gay rights bill, which the Conservative Party has faced every year for over a decade and kept bottled up in senate committee. In April 2001, however, the bill was going to make it to the floor for a vote. As described earlier in this book, the Conservative Party has consistently opposed legislation that calls for the creation of special classes of citizens. While the Goodman bill states that its objective is to end discrimination based on sexual orientation, the party believes that, if enacted, the proposed law would in fact require special treatment based on sexual preference. To add a specific category to existing law discriminates against every other person not in that category.

As he has so often done, Mike Long personally called every legislator with Conservative Party endorsement and reminded them of the party's stand on the issue. He cautioned them that if they had any respect for the Conservative endorsement they freely accept, they should think twice before supporting the Goodman bill.

The legislation died quietly in the 2001 session of the New York State legislature.

Throughout its forty-year history, the Conservative Party and its leadership have promoted the belief that there is a higher standard by which all man-made rules must be measured. In dealing with legislative bodies throughout New York, the Conservative Party has never deserted its first principles and was often the lone voice protecting the inherent dignity of every human person against a culture of death that would have us abandon the unborn, the unwell, the unyoung.

Chapter 17

The Race of the Century

When Robert Torricelli, then the junior Senator from New Jersey, suggested on a national television program that First Lady Hillary Rodham Clinton would be the perfect choice to run for retiring New York Senator Moynihan's seat, most American conservatives were amused. Torricelli was just evoking the sainted memory of Bobby Kennedy and his "Carpetbagger" victory of 1964. But the proposal hung in the air; it did not dissipate the way people were sure it would, and before long the Right was getting nervous. Mrs. Clinton may have been the poster-girl of conservative opposition to nineties liberalism, particularly after she tried to blame the L'Affaire Lewinsky on the "vast right-wing conspiracy" against her poor husband, but she was also the liberal opponent many feared most. Bill Clinton was merely a man of little character, one who would take any position or do whatever tap dance was required in order to get people to love him. But Hillary, on the other hand, was viewed as a genuinely intelligent and committed ideologue, who – although she might occasionally exhibit a political "tin ear" – had a record of unfettered determination to implement a radical left-wing agenda. Even her Wellesley College senior thesis, which analyzed the techniques of the extreme radical political organizer Saul Alinsky and how his approach could apply to poverty programs, promoted her ideological vision. Yes, for Conservatives, Mrs. Clinton was a charter member of what P.J. O'Rourke calls "the perpetually indignant left."

When Mike Long heard of Torricelli's pronouncement, he realized that what he thought was going to be a relatively mild political cycle had just come to a screeching halt. He also realized that if Clinton did jump in the race, he would probably find himself on the political hot seat.

No Republican had been elected statewide without the Conservative endorsement since Senator Javits's last successful run in 1974. Long knew that to stop Hillary, conservatives in New York and the nation would argue that he must nominate someone – anyone – with the money and name to stop her – regardless of that candidate's political principles. He dreaded attending the upcoming Washington C-PAC and the next board meeting of the American Conservative Union (on which he served) because he knew the name that would be on everybody's lips: Rudy Giuliani.

The Marriage that Never Was

Although Long respected the progress Mayor Giuliani had made in straightening up the city, he still had serious problems with the man's beliefs, particularly on social issues. And a United States Senator deals with just those kinds of issues, the ones that help shape the very character of the nation, certainly more than any mayor, even the mayor of American's largest city. In early 1999, Long hoped that a Clinton senatorial candidacy was only the pipe dream of the First Family's groupies and that "this too shall pass."

For the next few months, the gossip columns of New York's tabloids chronicled daily both Mrs. Clinton's very public contemplation of her candidacy and the melodrama of the Republican Party's consideration of Giuliani.

Although Long's phones were constantly ringing, he knew that most of Governor Pataki's inner circle disliked Giuliani. And why not? They had not forgiven him for the 1994 Cuomo endorsement, and they dreaded the prospect of "Senator" Giuliani – of the power Rudy might yield from Washington. They were comforted somewhat by the knowledge New York City's mayors have never been well liked upstate. It was "not for nothing" that no city mayor in the twentieth century had ever advanced politically. Robert Wagner, John Lindsay, and Ed Koch had all tried and failed. Also, a young, four-term congressman named Rick Lazio was waiting in the wings. Many analysts thought that Lazio, who was chomping at the bit to make the run, had the better political profile. Unlike Rudy, he represented a district on eastern Long Island, and so was free of the odor of New York City politics. Like Rudy he was Italian and Roman Catholic, but he also had a decent conservative record. On most of the social issues he record was decent: he opposed partial-birth abortion and Medicaid funding for abortions, was in favor of requiring parental consent before a girl could undergo an abortion. However, he did do the Cuomo-Pataki shuffle: although he was personally against abortion, he still considered himself "pro-choice." He wasn't the ideal Conservative Party candidate, but he did manage to meet the requirements necessary to be an acceptable alternative, especially to Hillary Clinton.

In April, Long and Party Executive Vice Chairman Jim Molinaro were invited to dine with Mayor Giuliani and his inner circle at a Manhattan restaurant. According to journalist Michael Tomasky:

> Giuliani and [political aide Bruce] Teitelbaum understood that having the [Conservative] party in the Mayor's corner would be more important in a statewide race than it had been in Giuliani's previous citywide campaigns. The Mayor wanted the Conservative endorsement, but he wanted it on his terms, and he didn't want to do much work to get it.[1]

After an hour of chitchat, Long got to the point. I guess we're here tonight, he said in effect, because you're running for U.S. Senator. The mayor replied that he had not yet made up his mind. After a few minutes of awkward silence, Long spoke again.

"I assume we're having dinner so that in case you do decide to run for the Senate, you want to know what the Party's doing."[2]

The mayor did say he was interested in hearing about the party's frame of mind.

Long made it clear that at that at the moment Lazio was the Party's favorite; that if the convention were held the next day, the congressman would run off with the nomination. But Long also conceded that it was very early in the political cycle and that things could change. Long went on to make it perfectly clear that whomever the party ultimately supported that candidate would have to satisfy two requirements: First, he could not accept the Liberal Party endorsement, and, second, he had to be opposed to partial-birth abortion. Long told the mayor that if he would agree to those matters, he had a good shot at getting the nomination. As Long later told the conservative newsweekly *Human Events*:

"I told him, Mr. Mayor, you've done a great job for the city and we have an open door policy for candidates to come to the Conservative Party and make a case for our support. We would certainly entertain the thought. But I also said that a dual endorsement seemed almost out of the question because the [Conservatives and Liberals] come from such different philosophical directions and that candidates backed by one of the parties should be beholden to one."[3]

In late June, columnist and television commentator George Will came up to New York and had breakfast with Long at the Waldorf Astoria Hotel. In a July 5 *Newsweek* column, Will described Mrs. Clinton as "well-known not for any achievements, but only for her well-knownness. She personifies the politics of celebrity." Will described Long's position this way:

> Mike Long, wary of Giuliani's versatility of allegiance that resulted in the endorsement of Cuomo, wonders: Suppose in October 2000 Al Gore is well ahead of George W. Bush in New York and Giuliani is a few points behind Hillary. Might Giuliani endorse Gore? Besides, will Giuliani even ask for the Conservative endorsement? "He's not," says Long dryly, "the asking type." And, Long adds, Giuliani probably knows he would hate being 1 percent of the Senate, so maybe he will skip the Senate race, finish as mayor in 2001 and run for what he really craves, the governorship.[4]

Meanwhile, Lazio, who attended the party's February C-PAC conference and did his best to meet and inspire the crowd, was calling Long every week, giving updates, seeking advice, and making it clear he wanted the Conservative endorsement. He would enter a primary if necessary.

The Second Listening Tour and the Deaf Man

In July Mrs. Clinton chose the grounds of Senator Moynihan's farm as the place to announce that she would begin a "listening tour" to help determine if she would become a candidate. From then on the heat on Mike Long was turned up. Nearly everybody was urging him to go along with the strongest Republican – no matter what. In an interview with the *Boston Globe,* Long made it clear that the Conservative Party did not wish to play the role of spoiler in the coming election.

"If Hillary Clinton is the candidate," he said, "my game plan is to beat her."

But he added: "The bottom line is we are a party of values. We draw a line."[5]

And on the Republican side the pressure was definitely on forming ranks around Giuliani. State Senator Joe Bruno and New York Republican Party Chairman Bill Powers went on record for Rudy, and many Republicans, local and national, were strongly urging Governor Pataki to dump Lazio and jump on the Rudy bandwagon.

Then on a quiet Friday afternoon in the dog days of August, the governor made this announcement:

"The party must unify behind one strong candidate," he said, "and I believe that Rudy Giuliani has earned the right to be that candidate. . . . I will support him and do everything I can to help him get elected. . . . I don't think a primary will be in the best interests of the Party."[6]

Long was floored. He had received notice of the governor's remarks barely two hours before Mr. Pataki made them. He frankly told the press that he "would have liked to at least have had a discussion" about the governor's decision and pointed out that Mr. Pataki and the Republican Party had just broken a nine-year pact whereby no endorsement of a statewide candidate would be made without the leaders of the two parties being consulted. Long called Pataki's move "a mistake" and the "wrong strategy."[7] And he also made it clear that the Conservative Party was not going to "fix the race by quickly following suit." And by fix, Mike did not mean repair.

"I want to beat [Clinton] with a candidate who will in fact not go to Washington, D.C., and embarrass the conservative movement.[8] . . . Let me say it one more time: The governor does not speak for the Conservative Party. We will continue to look for a candidate who will fulfill the Conservative agenda. A candidate who wants our endorsement has to earn it."[9]

Lazio, who had believed he had Pataki's blessing, was blindsided and now under tremendous political pressure to abandon his candidacy. Instead he followed Long's advice and temporarily suspended his candidacy. Long believed that Rudy wouldn't make it to the starting gate.

The political world and the media now looked upon Long and the Conservative Party as the only roadblock to a Giuliani coronation. The Long story became major news, and he had the national media pounding at his door. He appeared on CNN,

MSNBC, CNBC, the major networks and their talk shows: Chris Matthews, Bill O'Reilly, Brit Hume, Hannity and Colmes, the hosts of *Crossfire* all grilled him. There were also plenty of print media profiles and headlines:

> "BUCKING THE BANDWAGON: Conservative boss isn't jumping to back Rudy for Senate."[10]

> "No Conservative 'Fix' for Senate Race"[11]

> "The Power to Make the Mayor Miserable"[12]

> "Now Giuliani needs 'right' help from a 'Long' shot."[13]

> "N.Y. Conservative Party has big leverage: Refusal to endorse could sink Giuliani"[14]

Mike Long, his liquor store, and his autographed "Goldwater for President" poster appeared in numerous photos in plenty of papers throughout the state and the nation.

Adding fat to the fire, Giuliani made it clear to all that he would take his sweet time deciding whether or not to run, and that no one could force a deadline on him.

And then on August 17, the mayor's office let it be known that "Rudy stays firm on late-term abortions."[15]

"The Mayor is not rethinking his position," said spokesman Sunny Mindel,[16] which meant Rudy was opposed to any ban.

This was hardly the gesture of a candidate seeking the support of the Conservative Party.

Despite this there was still pressure on Long coming from national conservatives to accept Rudy, because he was famous and because he wasn't Hillary. At a board meeting of the American Conservative Union, Long told the other members that he would not be responsible for sending someone to the Senate who might cast the deciding vote to continue partial-birth abortions in the United States. He also told them that they would be the first to point fingers if a candidate his party had supported ended up voting against, say, a Judge Scalia.[17]

Anti-Hillary pragmatism was spinning out of control. Eric Fettmann of the *New York Post* resurrected the familiar, tired arguments against splinter parties when one disagrees with their decisions: "The only purpose that [Liberal Party Chairman] Ray Harding and Mike Long serve in this state is to toss a monkey wrench into the political process. . . . Do all these machinations help the voters? No way – it's time for another good-government movement to come forward and put these anachronisms out of business."[18]

Long was not, however, completely alone. While the editorial page of the *New York Times* was praising the mayor's stubborn streak as "well deployed" and urging the Conservative Party to meet with Giuliani "and respect either his principled stand [on partial-birth abortion] or, at least, the political realities,"[19] Msgr. James Lisante in the *Long Island Catholic* weekly newspaper had this to say:

> [Giuliani] is a bright and talented manager. But he's also a skillful compromiser and some principles simply cannot be negotiated away. Clearly, Rudy thinks Catholics can be convinced to see him as their logical candidate. After all, he supports the concept behind school vouchers. And, impressively, he's taken the lead in condemning anti-Catholicism. His stand over the Brooklyn Museum exhibit would, to many Catholics, make him seem to be "our guy." But Mr. Giuliani is, I suspect, playing a dangerous game. Because while he'll support private schools and decry antireligious art, he parts company on an issue about which there can be no compromise, no negotiation. Rudolph Giuliani not only supports the right to choose an abortion, he also supports the right to perform partial birth. He would defend the right to slaughter a fully-formed and healthy nine month old pre-born on the day it's being born.
>
> To support such butchery negates opposition to dung-covered art or a positive disposition to our schools. If you're willing, Mr. Mayor, to sell out the lives of innocent and defenseless children, then you're really not terribly different from Mrs. Clinton. And that, by the way, is no compliment.[20]

But the mayor was undaunted by such criticism. In October he said on the Evans and Novak talk show: "I've had to deal with [partial-birth abortion] as the mayor of New York and I supported it, and I don't see any reason to change that position."[21]

Candidate George Bush, who met with Conservative Party leaders at a Sheraton Hotel private breakfast that I attended on October 6, 1999, learned there were problems with Giuliani. At that session, attended by about seventy-five people, Governor Bush, after citing his conservative views, asked the party for its nomination. During a question-and-answer session, one brave leader got up and asked Mr. Bush to explain why he had come and asked for the Conservative nomination but Giuliani had not. I thought Mr. Bush gave an incredible answer:

"Perhaps," he said, "I'm just more comfortable with all of you."

Long, who had not heard a word from Giuliani since their dinner in February, told the media at his annual fall fundraiser that he hadn't invited the mayor "because I don't know what his intentions are. He hasn't spoken to me." Insisting that he wasn't snubbing the mayor, Long continued:

> The word going around town is that he is going to run for the United States Senate while he hasn't announced or confirmed that yet . . . he also hasn't announced or confirmed whether he would seek the Conservative Party endorsement. . . . I have made it clear that the door is open. I am willing

to sit down and talk about the possibilities. So the call is really his. . . . If we were in the midst of negotiations or he had indicated to me that he wanted to seek the Conservative Party endorsement, quite frankly he would have been invited tonight. But I don't need to embarrass him and I don't need to embarrass myself.[22]

In late November, Giuliani attended an Austin, Texas fundraiser at which he received the support of presidential frontrunner, Governor George W. Bush. Pointing out that he was seeking the Conservative Party nomination in his run for the White House, Bush added: "And if they support me, I hope I can convince them to support the mayor as well."[23]

At a private breakfast, George W. Bush asks Party leaders for their nomination (October 6, 1999).

Reacting to the Texas governor's comments, Long made it obvious he wasn't impressed: "That's fine, he can call me. But you know what? If Ronald Reagan called me, he couldn't get me to change my mind at this point."[24] Long thought it funny that here was a man from Texas asking the party to endorse a New Yorker when the New Yorker hadn't asked for himself.

"He's got everyone else doing it for him," Long said. "When I was young and had a lot more hair, if I wanted to go on a date, I would talk to the girl. Well, if the Mayor can't talk to me, fine. I really haven't heard anything since last March. . . . Frankly if that's the way he wants to play it, okay by me."[25]

The Giuliani juggernaut was beginning to slow as it seemed to hit one brick wall after another. In early December, Staten Island's Conservative Party leaders insisted that Giuliani must revise his position on partial-birth abortion if he expected to receive their support. Staten Islander Jim Molinaro, party executive vice chairman, said: "[Giuliani] doesn't get it. Absolutely not. No question about it. . . . He keeps putting off a discussion about it, and he asks other people to speak on his behalf. . . . Give me a break. Bush is not going to get Mike [Long] to change his mind. No way will the Conservative Party yield on the issue."[26]

Another Conservative Party leader in Staten Island, Mary Lou Shanahan, was adamant that even if the mayor changed some of his views "that just gives him a ticket to the dance. . . . That means he can come to speak with us."[27]

This kind of reaction, in the county in which Giuliani enjoyed his highest support, spelled serious trouble for his candidacy.

As 1999 came to a close, the Conservative Party still dominated the headlines:

> "Despite size, Conservative Party is a Force to Reckon With: Moderates like Giuliani ignore the Conservative Party at their peril."[28]

> "For N.Y. Mayor, a Minor Problem: Giuliani, Conservative Party Still Apart"[29]

> "CONSERVATIVE PARTY WON'T SEND IT'S LOVE TO PRO-CHOICE RUDY: Don't Expect Roses or a Box of Chocolates from Michael Long."[30]

> "Conservatives to Rudy: Change Abortion Stand."[31]

> "Conservatives: Giuliani Must Oppose Partial Birth Abortion."[32]

> "For Giuliani Bush's Hand Might Not Help: Appeal to Conservative Snags on Abortion Issues."[33]

The Democrats even stuck their nose into the squabble. New York State Democratic Party Chairwoman Judith Hope, who generally condemned Conservatives as close-minded Neanderthals told the *Times*: "There's something almost refreshing about it, though I profoundly disagree with [Long]. It's rare to see what appears to be a principled stand from a party."[34] (One can only conclude that with this backhanded compliment she indirectly smacks her own Party as never standing for principles.)

Instead of sitting down with Long, Giuliani now tried the backdoor technique: his people approached dissident Party leaders and tried to get factions to endorse the mayor. On December 24, Monroe County Conservative Party leader Tom Cook announced the formation of "Conservatives for Giuliani." Claiming the Giuliani people had no knowledge of his efforts, Cook said he was registering with the Federal Election Commission, would begin fundraising, and would mail a letter to Conservative leaders statewide on January 1.[35]

Publicly, Republican leaders were stating that Giuliani would "aggressively reach out to Long in early 2000." They were also spinning stories that Conservatives might allow Giuliani to enter a primary, so Conservative Party members could choose for themselves.[36]

Long found these tactics – and the whispering campaigns that went with them – to be amazing.

"I've never dealt with anyone like this in my entire life," he said.[37]

While Long continued to agree that Giuliani would probably be the strongest candidate against Clinton, he stuck to his guns:

"I think the Mayor has lately become a convenient Conservative. If I am going to support a convenient Conservative who has been quite liberal on a lot of issues, I want to announce to the world if we do endorse him, that we know what we're endorsing, [and] we have the following commitments from him. We're not just about winning elections."[38]

And After All That . . .

In early 2000, it became evident that Cook's challenge was falling flat. Conservative leaders all over the state had begun their own letter-writing campaign to urge their friends and colleagues not to surrender their principles.

John Andrew Kay of Suffolk County wrote this to Cook:

> I respected the fact in 1994 that you supported a candidate against [Pataki] because the Governor was not pro-life. How can you now ask us to all abandon the fight to ban partial birth abortion and declare support for a person for U.S. Senate who himself has not even declared he is running?

Bronx County leader Bill Newmark told his fellow county chairmen that on January 19 his executive committee had "overwhelmingly rejected liberal Rudolph Giuliani's bid for the United States Senate." Newmark continued:

> For Conservatives to seriously consider endorsing Giuliani, the most liberal Republican major officeholder since Senator Jacob Javits and Governor Nelson Rockefeller, would be to *destroy* the very reason for the existence of the Conservative Party. . . .
>
> We, in the Bronx Conservative Party interviewed Mayor Giuliani in 1993 during his mayoral campaign. On issue after issue, from his total

support of the radical homosexual agenda including marching in the "Gay Pride" parade, support of stronger gun control laws, *running as the Liberal Party candidate* IN EVERY ELECTION, not the Conservative Party, his support of domestic partnership, affirmative action programs, minimum wage increases, agency shop, further Federal Government involvement in our lives and opposition to Right to Work laws are among just a small group of issues too lengthy to list in one letter that show his strong Liberalism.

In early January, Republican Party sources were telling *New York Post* reporter Fred Dicker that "the most awaited call in New York politics – Mayor Giuliani to Conservative Party leader Mike Long – will be made 'within the next week.'"[39] For his part Long was not sitting idly staring at his phone. When long-time conservative activist and fundraiser Richard Viguerie took on Giuliani as a client, Long wrote to tell him he was making a mistake:

> Both of us got involved in politics because of Barry Goldwater. We both believe in Conservative principles. . . . That is why I am writing this letter today.
>
> I hate to admit that I agree with Hillary Clinton, but I too was "appalled" by your recent letter, a letter you mailed to conservatives around the country. In that letter, you portrayed Rudy Giuliani as a conservative . . . this could not be farther from the truth. I understand that you're based in Virginia and I'm based in New York. So, let me explain to you, as Chairman of the Conservative Party of New York State, a party which represents nearly 200,000 individuals. In very simple terms, I know Rudy Giuliani. He's not a conservative. . . .
>
> Richard, we have fought the good fight. We've stood up for principle. . . . In good conscience, I'm asking you to drop Rudy Giuliani as a client. If you believe in the conservative principles of Barry Goldwater and Ronald Reagan, and believe in the message you and I have championed for nearly four decades, I trust you will agree with me that the best way to stop Hillary Clinton is to support a true conservative for Senator in New York State.

The political clock continued to tick, and Giuliani's behavior began to slide into wackiness. On February 7, he said he could win the election without Conservative support.

"I haven't given up getting anyone's endorsement, but the reality is that I don't think endorsements really matter, particularly in my case."[40]

Then the next day in a radio interview, the mayor said he would now be willing to enter a Conservative primary.

"I don't really think [Long] can stop me from running."[41]

Disgusted with Giuliani's games and his erratic statements, Long told the *Times*: "I think I would rather that he didn't run."[42]

When George Bush realized that his speech at Bob Jones University, known for anti-Catholic prejudices, was turning into a political disaster, his campaign operatives turned to Mike Long in New York. It was Long who helped the future president get a letter of apology to the ailing Archbishop of New York, John Cardinal O'Connor. And the Bush campaign needed the help. Catholics make up 50 percent of New York's registered Republicans, and the Bush campaign couldn't afford to give its leading opponent, Senator McCain, fodder to use in the Empire State's primary. The letter of apology to O'Connor quelled the issue, but the Bush operatives quickly forgot that Long played an instrumental role in bailing them out.

One week after Long mailed out 12,000 annual-dinner invitations with the announcement that Governor Bush would be the party's guest of honor, the Bush campaign told Long they had scheduling problems. When Long said he would be happy to re-schedule and send out new invitations, Bush operatives tap-danced. It appeared they had succumbed to pressure from the Republican state organization to punish Long for dragging his heels on a Giuliani endorsement.

By late April the promised phone call from Rudy still had not come, and Long began seriously looking for another candidate. He knew Lazio was still available. As late as April 3, Lazio told the media that it looked like state Republicans were "potentially blowing" the race, and he said: "I am ready to run,"[43] which meant as a Conservative. Maybe, Long thought, but since it meant the party would have to go it alone, he looked around at other choices he had.

Virginia Gilder, a wealthy Manhattanite, after meeting with Long, agreed to seriously consider seeking the party's nomination. Mrs. Gilder had excellent conservative credentials, was a good friend of *National Review* president, Dusty Rhodes, and in the 1993 mayor's race she had chaired "Republicans For Marlin."

"If she [ran] she would be completely serious – it would never be for vanity," said William Kristol, editor of the conservative journal, *The Weekly Standard*. "She's really an attractive and interesting person who might compare really well with Mrs. Clinton and Giuliani. In that respect she might pose a problem for the Mayor because she might win some votes that are not ideological votes. She could be the Jesse Ventura of 2000."[44]

Then on April 27, Rudy Giuliani, who was raising millions nationally by direct mail (even though he was not a candidate), announced that he had been diagnosed with prostate cancer. The cancer was found in its early stage and was treatable, yet it added an air of uncertainty over Giuliani's campaign.

To add to this, just two weeks later, while leaving Cardinal O'Connor's wake at St. Patrick's Cathedral, Mrs. Giuliani, news anchor and television personality Donna

Hanover, told the press she hoped to save her marriage even though it was now public that the mayor had "a very good friend," a woman named Judith Nathan.

While the mayor's cancer scare and marriage woes were being played out, soap-opera style, in the nation's tabloids, former Congressman Joseph J. DioGuardi of Westchester announced on April 30, that he would seek the Conservative Party and Right to Life Party nominations for U.S. Senator.

A graduate of Fordham University, DioGuardi, a C.P.A., was a former partner of Arthur Anderson, a company for whom he had worked twenty-two years. As a two-term congressman, he was an orthodox conservative, and had lost his seat in 1990 due to gerrymandering.

At a press conference, DioGuardi said: "When it comes to all social issues, Hillary Clinton and Rudy Giuliani are the same."

When asked if he would be a spoiler, he replied, "No, I'm in this race to win. That might spoil someone's day."[45]

The Giuliani's campaign reacted by announcing that Giuliani might just enter the Conservative primary as a write-in if DioGuardi were nominated.

"I'd be pretty confident that I'd win a Conservative Party primary," Giuliani said.[46]

Reacting to the mayor's latest pronouncement, Mike Long said: "I think he'd be making a big mistake. . . . The Mayor is not a Conservative; he is a Liberal. He's seeking the Liberal Party's support. I think Conservative voters will reject him."[47]

And then, on Friday, May 19, 2000, all the blithering and bitterness turned out to be for naught. Giuliani rocked the political world by announcing he would not run for the U.S. Senate after all.

"This is not the right time for me to run for office. . . . I used to think the core of me was in politics. It isn't."[48]

Rick Lazio officially jumped into the race the next day, and he had a clear road to the Republican nomination. Joe DioGuardi cleared the way with the Conservative Party after he gracefully bowed out.

On Saturday, June 3, at the Albany Omni Hotel, Rick Lazio was unanimously nominated at the Conservative Party Convention. In his acceptance speech, he told the crowd that, "There is no place in our society for the gruesome procedure partial birth abortion." And he added: "I was able to jump into this race without a listening tour because I've been listening to New York all my life."[49]

Looking back on the machinations leading up to the Republican-Conservative senatorial designation, Mike Long is of the strong opinion that Rudy Giuliani never intended to run in the first place; that his posturing was all a very expensive game. There were Giuliani insiders who later told Long that if push had come to shove, Cardinal O'Connor would have called the chairman and asked that he put aside his reservations with Rudy and endorse him. But Long believes this is absurd. In any case, it's easy to say what a dead man might do since it can't be refuted. Still, if the Cardinal had called, Long would have told him what he'd told everyone else: "Thank you Your Eminence for the call, but the Conservative Party is not selling out."[50]

With Lazio now the candidate, the hatchet was buried with the Republicans and Governor Bush came to New York to be with Rick Lazio at a Conservative Party luncheon. Introducing the guests, Long said: "I admit sometimes when I hear people argue about the horrible foreign menace that has suddenly appeared in New York, I don't know if they're talking about the West Nile virus or Hillary Clinton."[51]

The Conservative Party moved aggressively to help Rick Lazio's candidacy. In August, Long went on the offensive when he discovered the Clinton campaign had accepted a contribution from Dr. Martin Haskell, creator of the partial-birth abortion procedure. In an August 17 letter, which Long released to the press, he wrote:

> Dear Mrs. Clinton:
>
> Last week's newspaper reporting revealed you accepted a political contribution from the inventor of the ghastly partial birth procedure, Dr. Martin Haskell.
>
> Like countless other New Yorkers, I was appalled.
>
> Still, I held out hope that it was a mistake. Perhaps your campaign accidentally deposited some of Dr. Haskell's profits from the over 700 partial birth abortions he has committed. Maybe you would set things right, I hoped.
>
> Sadly, your silence is deafening. You seem intent keeping this blood money.
>
> That's wrong.
>
> There is a broad consensus in New York against partial birth abortion. Even Democrats like Ed Koch condemn it, but not you. When it comes to partial birth abortion, a real New Yorker like Pat Moynihan says "infanticide." An artificial New Yorker like you just says, "Where's the check?"
>
> If I am wrong, prove it.
>
> I call upon you to return Dr. Haskell's blood money. If you are too timid to offend your liberal friends in the abortion industry, then you can direct a contribution in the same amount to any of the fine crisis pregnancy centers in New York that help both mothers and children.
>
> It's just $250. Is that too high a price for simple decency, Mrs. Clinton?

The party aired a commercial in September that hit Clinton on health care. "If you trust Hillary Clinton, maybe you should see your doctor while you can."

Radio and television ads and mailings were utilized to display the Clinton record and to push up her negatives, particularly in upstate New York.

When Lazio and Clinton agreed to ban soft-money spending, the Conservative

Party turned its guns on the $3.8 billion bond transportation act. Long told New Yorkers that the state currently carries outstanding debt of $63 billion.

"Every man, woman and child in New York State is responsible for $255,000 of debt," he said. "Quite a burden on each of us. By rejecting this Bond Act, we can increase our credit rating, thereby lowering the costs for future capital projects. New Yorkers must insist that elected officials adopt a 'pay as you go' plan and stop asking voters for a blank check every time they want to 'bring home the bacon' for their pet projects."

The U.S. Senate race in New York broke records as the most expensive in the nation's history: over $80 million was spent. It was also one of the hardest fought, but by the end of the campaign, one could hear the death rattle in the Lazio camp. There was griping from campaign consultants to the press, and there was bickering among campaign aides. To many it seemed as though chief consultant Michael Murphy was still running the McCain presidential campaign from which he had come after the Arizona Senator has conceded the race to Mr. Bush. It was a consensus view that Murphy wanted to prove his approach in the McCain race had been viable and so it became the Lazio strategy. Many complained that too many weeks were wasted on "inside baseball" issues. Six weeks spent debating the use of soft money may have satisfied *New York Times* editorial writers, but it meant nothing to the average New Yorker, especially not with regard to drawing a sharp distinction between Lazio and Mrs. Clinton.

But there were scapegoats aplenty. In the final hours of the campaign, Libby Pataki, the governor's wife, took a shot at Giuliani, complaining that the mayor's inability to decide whether or not to run had wasted valuable months in which Lazio might have been able to get his message out. On Albany's WROW-AM radio, Mrs. Pataki said Giuliani had "hung around way too long. . . . He was just jerking people. It was terribly unfair."[52]

On election day, as Al Gore was carrying New York with 60 percent of the vote, Mrs. Clinton was elected to the Senate Seat once held by James L. Buckley. And she won in a landslide:

	Lazio Rep.	Clinton Dem.	Graham Ind.	Lazio Cons.	Clinton Lib.	Adefope R. to L	Dunau Green	Clinton Wkg. Fam.
Upstate	2,210,763	2,042,623	37,829	156,507	53,418	18,210	27,222	46,320
Bronx	40,363	251,563	651	3,715	4,131	541	899	5,684
Brooklyn	131,990	438,081	1,384	8,798	8,061	739	3,839	21,557
Manhattan	115,112	407,587	1,608	4,151	8,157	538	5,848	17,855
Queens	150,828	367,622	1,331	11,919	7,942	974	2,588	8,893
Staten Island	75,533	54,939	378	6,051	1,092	437	595	1,785
Total NYC	**513,826**	**1,519,792**	**5,352**	**34,634**	**29,383**	**3,229**	**13,769**	**55,774**
Total State	**2,724,589**	**3,562,415**	**43,181**	**191,141**	**82,801**	**21,439**	**40,991**	**102,094**

The turnout in New York City was incredible. While Lazio received 43 percent of the city's Jewish vote (actually two points higher than D'Amato's totals), it wasn't nearly enough to offset the increased turnouts within other minority communities. Mrs. Clinton carried an amazing 85 percent of the Hispanic vote and a whopping 90 percent of the black vote. While Lazio carried Long Island, Clinton cut into what should have been substantial margins.

The Clinton campaign's decision to devote serious time to upstate Republican bastions paid off. Overall Mrs. Clinton managed to rack up 47 percent of the upstate vote, whereas the average Democrat gets about 35 percent. She carried Westchester County and the Republican stronghold of Onondaga County (Syracuse). She carried the female vote by more than 20 points and, with the support of "Giuliani Democrats," she won a surprising 51 percent of the Catholic vote.

For all the finger-pointing in Republican circles, it was impossible to avoid the obvious conclusion: Mrs. Clinton ran a focused, disciplined campaign. She made her share of gaffes, but they were mostly in 1999 and were long forgotten by November 2000. She did her homework and mastered the issues confronting the state. No doubt her "celebrity" status helped, but it is not enough to explain her victory.

And then were the issues. The Republican candidate and his consultants pretty much forgot about them.

But after they analyzed their string of defeats (D'Amato, Vacco, Lazio) Conservatives hoped the Republicans would realize they must get back to first principles. In the 1980s and again in 1994, Ronald Reagan, Al D'Amato, and then George Pataki won elections because they stood tall on platforms built with solid materials: the principles of conservatism. Attempting to be all things to all people, walking the fine line on issues, deserting principles for focus group reports just doesn't cut it with the voters.

Afterword
Subsidiarity in the Twenty-First Century

In the aftermath of Hillary Clinton's senatorial victory, Conservatives did not sit around feeling sorry for themselves. They went back on the offensive.

In Staten Island, for instance, the Conservative Party's executive vice chairman, James Molinaro, took on the Republican establishment in the race to succeed retiring borough president Guy Molinari. With the blessing of the Conservative Party, Jim entered the Republican primary and decisively defeated Republican Assemblyman Robert Straniere. In the fall, Molinaro went on to become the first *registered* Conservative to be elected in New York City as a borough president.

And in Nassau County, long-time party supporter Bruce Bent used the "tail-wags-the-dog" strategy to secure the Conservative endorsement for Nassau County executive and then leveraged Row D into the Republican nomination as well. After he and other brave Conservatives broke ranks with Republican chairman Joe Mondello's creaking machine, Bent succeeded in frightening Republican incumbent Thomas Gulotta from seeking another term. (Gullota had been responsible for driving the county to the brink of bankruptcy.) Unable to find a candidate to stand up against Bent in a primary, the Republican machine capitulated, and Bent was unanimously nominated at their county convention. Although he lost in November, Bent and the Conservative Party had the guts to blow the whistle on twenty years of Republican misrule and incompetence in Nassau County.

Not mesmerized by the liberal Democrat turned Republican, Michael Bloomberg, New York City Conservatives nominated lawyer Terrance Gray in the race to succeed Mayor Rudy Giuliani, who was unable to run again because of term limits. Early on in the campaign, when voters were focused on education and crime, polls revealed that Gray's conservative message would attract six to eight percent of the vote. All of this changed, however, on the morning of September 11.

Recovering from the cowardly act of terrorism that brought down the Twin Towers and destroyed the lives of over 3,000 civilians, New Yorkers found they had a dramatically different view of the type of person who should be their next mayor. If they could not have four more years of Giuliani, they decided they wanted someone with business experience to oversee the city's fiscal and economic recovery.

But before the Bloomberg campaign had begun in earnest (but after he had secured the Republican nomination), there was talk of somehow overturning New York's term-limit rules so Rudy could run for re-election. As if to prove Shakespeare's quip (in *The Tempest*) that "misery acquaints a man with strange bedfellows," Mike Long – with Terry Gray's blessing – sat down with Mayor Giuliani at the Palm Steak House on Manhattan's West Side and actually discussed the possibility of giving Rudy the Conservative Party line on the November ballot.

But New York's Democrats believed that their candidate, the city's public advocate, Mark Green, was a likely winner against Bloomberg, so Assembly Speaker Shelly Silver and the Democratic gang in Albany killed any possibility of a Giuliani third term.

In any case, Giuliani had decided not to pursue any sort of legal change, legislative or judicial, and the mayoral race went on as expected, except that Bloomberg was the upset winner.

Although Gray received less than 1 percent of the vote on Tuesday, November 6, it is worth noting that his running mates, comptroller candidate John D'Emic and public-advocate candidate Joe Dubowski, each received 6 percent of the vote. While grief-stricken New Yorker's turned to a businessman for mayor, many still returned to the Conservative line to send the politicians a message.

The New Face of Conservatism

When the Conservative Party was founded in 1962, its core supporters were inner city, blue-collar ethnics, many of whom were World War II and Korean War veterans. They believed in the American Dream, and held to a few basic beliefs: loving God, county, and neighborhood.

In the sixties and seventies, people turned to the Conservative Party because they were repulsed by the reformists in the Democratic Party and by the flower children rioting in the streets and on college campuses. They abhorred the radicals call for a "new freedom," by which they meant the license to do whatever pleased them.

The neighborhood folks who supported the efforts of the Conservative Party were angered that the traditional values they cherished were disregarded in the universities, the churches, and in the media in favor of moral "neutrality" and "tolerance."

These intuitive conservatives reacted against a social order in which rights are merely the weapons of self-interest and in which responsibility based on a moral hierarchy is anathema.

They were disgusted by the liberal vanguard that dominated New York for decades and whose monument to progress is the South Bronx, once a glorious city of broad, tree-line avenues that thanks to the Goo-Goos became a municipal desert.

These street-corner conservatives instinctively understood the concept of subsidiarity, and they fought the crypto-totalitarians who deny the intrinsic value of man and define liberty as obedience to their own uncertain wills.

Today, many pollsters and political consultants harangue Mike Long and the leaders of the Conservative Party with the claim that the constituency that has sustained the party for decades is no longer a political factor in New York. The residents of the old neighborhoods are aging, dying, or moving to retirement communities in warmer climates. New Yorkers today may be more fiscally conservative than in the past, the pundits claim, but they have little interest in the views articulated by the Conservative Party when it comes to social issues. The sons and daughters and grand-children of the street-corner conservatives have left the ghetto neighborhoods, have achieved upper-middle class status, and are embarrassed by the moral beliefs of their forefathers.

It is true that the face of New York is changing. But as Edmund Burke wrote more than two hundred years ago, a nation – and this applies to states and cities and villages and neighborhoods – "without the means to change is without the means of its conservation." Surely these younger New Yorkers are aware that as a result of three decades of various social "revolutions," the state has witnessed a 400-percent increase in illegitimate births, an almost 50-percent failure in its marriages, tens of thousands of abortions performed annually, and educational systems in inner cities that tolerate illiteracy. And that is a measured, temperate catalog of New York's failures.

Despite the many inroads made by New York's Conservative Party since 1962, it is obvious that its work is not near to completion. The party cannot abandon its historic mission of fighting liberal social and fiscal experiments. The party has often stood alone in its unwavering commitment to the defense of human dignity and in its advocacy of limited government, but lonely or not, the work must continue. As G.K. Chesterton wrote: "Right is right, even if nobody does it. Wrong is wrong, even if everybody is wrong about it."

As the political power brokers were urging the Conservative Party to ignore Giuliani's views on social issues and endorse him in the 2000 Senate race, Msgr. James Lisante wrote this appeal to the Party:

> You were founded out of a conviction that the Republican Party was heading into a wrong path. You've built a powerful means for challenging the Republican Party when it heads in the wrong direction. If you decide to endorse a candidate who agrees with partial birth abortion you compromise one of the essential principles of your platform. Your party has almost single-handedly kept the battle against this child slaughter alive in our state.
>
> Please don't give away your very reason for existing: to be a distinctive voice for moral values sometimes ignored by the two major parties.

But just because the Conservative Party will not abandon its commitment to the principles upon which it was founded, it does not follow that the party can't make changes in its political strategy and in its outreach to potential supporters.

And make no mistake; the party will go in new directions, because throughout the urban deserts of the state's inner cities there are patches of green. You pass by block upon blasted block of slums, only to come across a stretch of tidy, well-kept row houses. These are oases populated by new immigrants and civic-minded minority citizens committed to family, education, self-discipline, and hard work.

Even as some people head to the Sun Belt, others are moving back into urban New York and rebuilding desolate neighborhoods. The Left scoffs, pejoratively referring to the trend as *gentrification*. To them the entrepreneurial spirit is uglier than the burned-out neighborhoods ever were, and the new community builders buying up and renovating brownstones are nothing more than a new class of urban snobs or yuppies or buppies or whatever the chic term of the moment is. But data refutes these charges and confirms that this wave of pioneers is "slowly and steadily replenishing deficits in the value structure of urban areas."[1]

The new immigrants – Koreans, Hispanics, Chinese, Indians, and Pakistanis – are strengthening the quality of urban areas. They are repopulating abandoned communities, fixing rundown schools, and using under-utilized transit systems. They are rebuilding deserted homes and are reintroducing neighborhood shops and ethnic restaurants.

Many of these new immigrants work in the financial and economic centers of their cities, but at the end of the day, they go home to their ethnic neighborhoods and maintain ways of life consistent with their cultural heritage and American tradition.

These are often densely populated areas, and yet they do not add to government bureaucracy; in fact they promote the opposite. The residents of these neighborhoods are parochial and very protective of their turf. To prevent their ways of life from being thwarted and homogenized by statists, they hound their civic and property-owners associations, attend meetings of planning and school boards, and keep pressure on local legislators.

"The ethnic neighborhood," writes Andrew Greeley, "as a strong powerful unit of urban society is a postulate of the principle of subsidiarity function; if you believe in 'no bigger than necessary,' you have got to believe in the neighborhood."

If the Conservative Party is to prosper, and if it is to fulfill its mission, the next generation of leadership must reach out to these new constituencies who exhibit "an ethic of work and family that shrinks the hallowed Protestant ethic to apathy."[2]

The party must become an integral part of their political lives and must serve as the vehicle to promote their beliefs and interests at city hall and in county governments, as well as in Albany. The party must prove once again the words of Michael Novak that a "politics based on family and neighborhood is far stronger socially and psychologically than a politics based on bureaucracy."

The implementation of this strategy will take considerable time and effort, probably including time in the political wilderness. But we've been there before, and Conservatives do not expect or value instant gratification. We've proven before that we have patience and fortitude. After all, it took thirty-two years to win a governor's race.

I am confident that the members of the Conservative Party will live up to the words of President Ronald Reagan: "The Conservative Party has established itself as a pre-eminent force in New York Politics and an important part of our political history."

I am sure that like their forebears, New York's twenty-first century conservatives will be able to look back and say: "We've kept the faith, we've fought the good fight."

Appendix

Conservative Party Awards and Recipients

The Charles Edison Memorial Award

The man for whom the Conservative Party's highest award is named was a man of many passions and pursuits. As the son of the famous inventor, Thomas Alva Edison, much was expected of him. During the New Deal, he held a number of different posts, including Secretary of the Navy. Although he worked for President Franklin Roosevelt, he considered himself an Al Smith Democrat, and he began to see that big government was not the solution to every problem. As a reform-minded governor of New Jersey, he exposed waste, excess, and corruption. He went on to become a successful businessman, a man of letters, and one of the founders of the Conservative Party. Poet, statesman, philanthropist, and entrepreneur, Charles Edison embodied the spirit and ideals of the American conservative movement.

Honorees

Paul L. Adams	Leo J. Kesselring	Russell E. Norris, Jr.
Bruce Bent	Jeanne J. Kirkpatrick	James E. O'Doherty
Thomas A. Bolan	Ronald S. Lauder	Kieran O'Doherty
James L. Buckley	James J. Leff	John J. O'Leary
William F. Buckley Jr.	Lewis Lehrman	Henry Paolucci
Mary Cummins	Herbert London	George E. Pataki
Thaddeus S. Dabrowski	Michael R. Long	Clarence "Rapp" Rappleyea
Alfonse M. D'Amato	J. Daniel Mahoney	Ronald Reagan
Steve Forbes	Serphin R. Maltese	Thomas L. Rhodes
Rosemary R. Gunning	George J. Marlin	Allen H. Roth
Jesse A. Helms	Michael S. McSherry	Anthony M. Rudmann
Kenneth C. Jones	Frank S. Meyer	William Rusher
Barbara A. Keating	Guy V. Molinari	Nicholas A. Schnurr
David Keene	James P. Molinaro	William E. Simon
Jack Kemp	Lyn Nofzinger	George A. Vossler

J. Daniel Mahoney Award

This award, established in 1990, is named after Conservative Party co-founder and long time state chairman, J. Daniel Mahoney. It is presented annually at the party's Albany reception to select individuals in grateful appreciation of their many years of untiring and effective dedication to the Conservative Party, its principles and its goals.

Honorees

A. Terry Anderson	Al C. Hollands	Stephen C. Miller
James D. Brewster	Viola J. Hunter	Thomas Moore
Thomas D. Cook	Marcia Jacobs	John J. O'Leary
Pat Curcio	Gerard Kassar	James F. Quinn, Jr.
Lew Deppner	Shaun Marie Levine	Clifford M. Riccio
Daniel F. Donovan, Jr.	Howard Lim, Jr.	Robert Roe
James M. Gay	Mary G. Loeffler	Nicholas Schnurr
Thomas Griffith	Thomas M. Long	Frances Vella-Marone
Bonnie Hewitt	Nicholas A. Longo	George A. Vossler

Kieran O'Doherty Award

Established in 1992, this award is named after Conservative Party co-founder and first chairman Kieran O'Doherty. It is presented to an enrolled Conservative who has distinguished himself or herself for service to the Party. The award is presented at a Reception after a two-step balloting process by the Conservative State Executive Committee. It is a recognition by peers of hard work and commitment to advancing the ideals of the Conservative Party.

Honorees

James M. Gay	John Andrew Kay	Laura A. Schreiner
Professor Henry Paolucci	Anthony M. Rudmann	John Zimmermann
	Shaun Marie Levine	

Notes

Abbreviations

C.P.P.   Conservative Party Papers

P.R.   Press Release

CHAPTER 1

1 Interview with Judge John T. Gallagher, former Rep.-Cons. Member of the N.Y.S. Assembly (March 20, 1992).
2 Kramer and Roberts, *I Never Wanted to Be Vice President of Anything* (1976), p. 64.
3 Jordon H. Thomson, *The Politics of Birth Control* (1968), p. 131.
4 Robert Wesser, *A Response to Progressivism* (1986), pp. 9–10.
5 Herbert S. Parmet, *Nixon and His America* (1990), pp. 36–37.
6 Daniel J. Kelves, *In the Name of Eugenics* (1985), p. 61.
7 Mark Haller, *Eugenics* (1984), p. 55.
8 Milton Viorst, *Fall from Grace* (1968), p. 131.
9 *Ibid.*, p. 147.
10 Kramer and Roberts, p. 46.
11 William Rusher, *The Rise of the Right* (1984), p. 17.
12 Russell Kirk, *The Political Principles of Robert A. Taft* (1967), p. 3.
13 Michael Novak, *The Spirit of Democratic Capitalism* (1982), p. 132.
14 Herbert S. Parmet, *The Democrats* (1976), p. 43.
15 Gerald Benjamin, *Rocky in Retrospect* (1984), p. 17.
16 Ellis, et al., *History of New York State* (1967), p. 512.
17 See *History of New York State* for a detailed description of the state in the late fifties and early sixties.
18 James F. Underwood, *Gov. Rockefeller in New York: The Apex of Pragmatic Liberalism in New York* (1982), p. 44.
19 Robert A. Caro, *The Power Broker* (1975), p. 463.
20 *Ibid.*, p. 405.
21 *Ibid.*, p. 407.
22 *Ibid.*
23 Richard Norton Smith, *Thomas E. Dewey and His Times* (1982), p. 217.
24 The definitive biography on La Guardia is Thomas Kessner's *La Guardia and the Making of Modern New York* (1989). Citations on La Guardia can be found on pp. xvi, 509, 555–56.
25 Warren Moscow, *The Empire State* (1948), p. 75.
26 F. Clifton White, *Politics as a Noble Calling* (1994), p. 75.
27 Moscow, p. 32.

28 Robert Connery, *Rockefeller of New York* (1979), p. 29.

29 Nico Rae, *Decline and Fall of the Liberal Republicans* (1989), p. 33.

30 Michael Barone, *The Mid-Atlantic States of America*, (1977), p. 276.

31 Connery, pp. 16–170, and Underwood, p. 4.

32 *Ibid.*

33 Rae, p. 33.

34 *Ibid.*, p. 222.

35 Ellis, p. 430.

36 *Ibid.*, pp. 422–40.

37 Smith, p. 361.

38 Ellis, p. 462.

39 Smith, p. 547.

40 *Policy Review* (Fall 1991), p. 18.

41 Robert Kelly, *The Cultural Pattern in American Politics* (1979), p. 7.

42 Michael Barone, *Our Country* (1990), p. ii.

43 *Ibid.*, p. 30.

44 Jeffrey Bell, *Populism and Elitism* (1992), p. 26.

45 Andrew Greeley, *Neighborhoods* (1977), p. 119.

46 See M. Novak, *The Unmeltable Ethics* (1972), and D.P. Moynihan, *Beyond the Melting Pot* (1963).

47 George Reedy, *From the Ward to the White House* (1991), p. 47.

48 *New York Times*, April 12, 1923.

49 Joan Weiss, *Charles Francis Murphy* (1968), p. 75.

50 See James Q. Wilson, *The Amateur Democrats* (1962); Edward Banfield and James Q. Wilson, *City Politics* (1963); and D.P. Moynihan, *Beyond the Melting Pot* (1963).

51 Barone, p. 12.

52 Daniel Patrick Moynihan, *Coping* (1970), p. 54.

53 Barone, p. 254.

54 Jack Newfield and Wayne Barrett, *City for Sale: Ed Koch and the Betrayal of New York* (1988), p. 107.

55 Moynihan, p. 60.

56 For a detailed description of the 1958 New York State Democratic Convention in Buffalo, see Rudy Abramson's, *Spanning the Century: W. Averill Harriman* (1992).

57 Collier and Horowitz, *The Rockefellers* (1976), p. 175.

58 Gary Reich, *The Life of Nelson Rockefeller* (1996), p. 731.

59 Underwood, p. 52.

60 Reich, p. 757.

CHAPTER 2

1 Kirk, p. 21.

2 *Ibid.*

3 Samuel Lubell, *The Future of American Politics*, p. 13

4 Barone, p. 218.

5 George H. Nash, *The Conservative Intellectual Movement in American – Since 1945* (1976) p. 3.

6 *Ibid.*, p. 15.

7   *Ibid.*, p. 65.
8   Brad Miner, *The Concise Conservative Encyclopedia* (1996), p. 136.
9   Nash, p. 56
10 *Ibid.*, p. 135.
11 William Rusher, *The Rise of the Right* (1984), p. 44.
12 Howard A. Scarrow, *Parties, Elections & Representation in the State of New York* (1983), p. 56.
13 Peter W. Colby and John K. White, *New York State Today*, (1989), p. 80.
14 Scarrow, p. 68.

CHAPTER 3

1   Connery and Benjamin, *Rockefeller of New York* (1979), p. 418.
2   William Rodgers, *Rockefeller's Follies* (1966), p. 40.
3   Kramer and Roberts, p. 215.
4   Underwood, p. 181.
5   *Ibid.*, p. 153.
6   Kramer and Roberts, p. 146.
7   Connery, p. 190.
8   Kramer and Roberts, p. 146.
9   *Ibid.*, p. 92.
10 *Ibid.*, p. 213.
11 Rockefeller, *Future of Federalism* (1962), pp. 13–14.
12 Collier, p. 341.
13 *Ibid.*, p. 339.
14 Kramer and Roberts, p. 5.
15 Robert Goldberg, *Barry Goldwater* (1995), p. 145.
16 J. Daniel Mahoney, *Actions Speak Louder: The Story of the New York Conservative Party* (1971), p. 15.
17 *Ibid.*
18 *Ibid.*, p. 19.
19 William F. Buckley Jr., *The Unmaking of a Mayor* (1966), p. 52.
20 Biographical data is in the N.Y.S. Conservative Party Prospectus.
21 Kramer and Roberts, p. 240.
22 Mahoney, p. 37.
23 *Ibid.*, p. 52.
24 *Ibid.*, p. 62.
25 *Syracuse Post Standard*, July 14, 1962.
26 *New York Times*, July 27, 1962.
27 *Newsday*, July 27, 1962.
28 Mahoney, pp. 75–76.
29 C.P.P., P.R., September 22, 1962.
30 Mahoney, p. 84.
31 C.P.P., P.R., October 1, 1962.
32 C.P.P., P.R., September 21, 1962.
33 C.P.P., P.R., October 8, 1962.
34 C.P.P., P.R., October 10, 1962.

35 C.P.P., P.R., October 13, 1962.

36 C.P.P., P.R., transcript, October 14, 1962.

37 C.P.P., P.R., October 16, 1962.

38 *Ibid.*

39 *Ibid.*

40 Mahoney, p. 104.

41 C.P.P., October 22, 1962.

42 Mahoney, p. 109.

43 C.P.P. transcript, October 1962.

44 C.P.P., October 26 and October 27, 1962.

45 C.P.P., October 30, 1962.

CHAPTER 4

1   C.P.P., memo, November 14, 1962.

2   C.P.P., memo, November 23, 1962.

3   Mahoney, p. 125.

4   C.P.P., transcript of Jaquith testimony, February 1963.

5   C.P.P., school prayer position paper.

6   Mahoney, p. 160.

7   *Ibid.*, p. 16.

8   *Ibid.*, pp. 176–77

9   *Syracuse Post Standard*, July 21, 1963.

10 *Ibid.*

11 Mahoney, p. 168.

12 *Ibid.*, p. 169.

13 C.P.P., Syracuse C.P. newsletter, September 1963.

14 C.P.P. Primary Manual.

15 Mahoney, pp. 242–43.

16 *New York Times*, April 23, 1964.

17 C.P.P., P.R., April 29, 1964.

18 *Congressional Record*, May 19, 1964, p. 2652.

19 *New York Herald Tribune*, September 28, 1964.

20 C.B.S. Newsmakers transcript, September 6, 1964.

CHAPTER 5

1   James Q. Wilson, *The Amateur Democrats* (1962), p. 18.

2   Moynihan, *Coping*, p. 58.

3   Peter Brown, *Minority Party* (1992), p. 82.

4   Thomas and Mary Edsall, *Chain Reaction* (1969), p. 5

5   Wilson, p. 288.

6   Brown, p. 82.

7   *Ibid.,* p. 85.

8   *Ibid.*

9   Thomas McNickle, *To Be Mayor of New York: Ethnic Politics in the City* (1993), p. 175.

10 *Ibid.,* p. 175.

11 Kevin Phillips, *The Emerging Republican Majority* (1969), p. 166.
12 David Burner, *The Politics of Provincialism* (1967), pp. 234–36.
13 Phillips, p. 161.
14 *Ibid.,* p. 167.
15 *Ibid.,* p. 181.
16 William F. Buckley Jr., *The Unmaking of a Mayor* (1966), p. 65.
17 Buckley, p. 10.
18 McNickle, p. 197.
19 Vincent Cannato, *The Ungovernable City* (2001), p. 48.
20 Buckley, pp. 18–21.
21 *New York Daily News*, April 7, 1965.
22 *Ibid.*
23 *Ibid.*
24 Buckley, p. 20.
25 John Judis, *William F. Buckley Jr.* (1988), p. 238.
26 C.P.P., June 24, 1965, announcement statement.
27 Mahoney, pp. 276–77.
28 Judis, p. 290.
29 Mahoney, p. 288.
30 *Ibid.,* p. 285.
31 *Ibid.,* p. 286.
32 Judis, p. 249.
33 Mahoney, p. 289.
34 C.P.P., House testimony
35 Charles Markmann, *The Buckleys* (1971) p. 240, and Buckley, p. 149.
36 *Ibid.,* p. 240.
37 Buckley, p. 157.
38 C.P.P., text of complaint, October 20, 1965.
39 Mahoney, p. 295.
40 Judis, p. 249.
41 Mahoney, p. 296.
42 Cannato, p. 53.
43 Judis, p. 256.
44 Cannato, p. 69.
45 Mahoney, p. 304.
46 Buckley, p. 330.
47 *National Review* 10th anniversary issue, November 31, 1965.

CHAPTER 6

1 C.P.P., Mahoney statement, May 5, 1965.
2 See Alan Hevisi, *Legislative Politics In New York State* (1975), pp. 171–75.
3 *Ibid.*
4 C.P.P., medicaid research report, 1965.
5 *Ibid.*
6 Hevisi, pp. 99–102.
7 *Ibid.*

8   Kramer and Roberts, pp. 307– 8.
9   *New York Times Magazine*, January 16, 1966.
10 Buckley, *On the Right*, April 1966.
11 Cannato, p. 168.
12 *Ibid.,* p. 173.
13 *Ibid.*
14 C.P.P., P.R., April 27, 1966.
15 Cannato, p. 168.
16 C.P.P., September 29, 1966, Mahoney statement.
17 C.P.P., Adams policy statement.
18 *New York Daily News*, September 24, 1966.
19 Cannato, p. 161.
20 *Ibid.,* p. 178.
21 Kramer and Roberts, pp. 315–16.
22 *World Journal Tribune*, November 9, 1966.
23 Cannato, p. 183.
24 *Syracuse Herald Journal*, January 29, 1967.
25 Constitutional organization and rules booklet.
26 C.P.P., constitutional revision research paper.
27 T. White, *The Making of the President* (1968), from the jacket cover.
28 Herbert S. Parmet, *Nixon and His America* (1990), p. viii.
29 Fred Siegel, *Troubled Journey* (1984), p. 201.
30 Stephen Lesher, *Wallace* (1994), p. xi.
31 Maltese interview.
32 Markmann, p. 291.
33 *Ibid.*
34 C.P.P., Buckley acceptance speech, April 3, 1968.
35 C.P.P., Conservative Party newsletter.
36 C.P.P., Buckley remarks at Suffolk County dinner, June 28, 1968.
37 WCBS-TV Newsmakers transcript, June 18, 1968.
38 Conservative Party Action Manual, 5A.
39 Interview with Mike Long.
40 James Buckley, *If Men were Angels* (1975), p. 17.
41 C.P.P., J. Buckley, September 19, 1968, transcript.
42 *Ibid.*
43 C.P.P., September 19, 1968 press statement.
44 J. Buckley, *If Men Were Angels,* p. 17.
45 WABC, Page 1, transcript, October 13, 1968
46 C.P.P., Conservative Party newsletter, November 1968.
47 C.P.P., text of speeches, October 1968.
48 C.P.P., P.R., November 7, 1966.

CHAPTER 7

1   Cannato, p. 391.
2   *Ibid.,* p. 190.
3   *Ibid.,* p. 391.

4   *Ibid.*, p. 197.
5   *Ibid.*, p. 195.
6   Kramer and Roberts, p. 298
7   Cannato, p. 265.
8   Harold Saltzman, *Race War in High School* (1972), p. 92.
9   *Ibid.*, p. 107.
10 Interview with Mike Long.
11 Cannato, p. 261.
12 *Ibid.*, p. 262.
13 *Ibid.*, p. 396.
14 *New York Daily News*, February 13, 1969.
15 Cannato, p. 398.
16   *National Review*, June 1969.
17 *Ibid.*
18 *Firing Line* transcript (1969).
19 Long and Maltese interviews.
20 McKinkle, p. 225.
21 Cannato, p. 409.
22 *Firing Line* transcript.
23 *New York Times Magazine*, October 1969.
24 *Ibid.*
25 Cannato, p. 409
26 Marchi campaign literature.

CHAPTER 8

1   Phillips, p. 172.
2   *Ibid.*, p. 173.
3   *Ibid.*, p. 171.
4   *Ibid.*, p. 181.
5   Siegel, p. 220.
6   *Ibid.*, p. 221.
7   Rusher, p. 235.
8   J. Buckley, *If Men Were Angels*, p. 20.
9   *Ibid.*, p. 21.
10 *New York Times Magazine*, October 1970.
11 *New York Times*, April 9, 2000.
12 *Ibid.*
13 *Ibid.*
14 Maltese interview.
15 Kramer and Roberts, p. 334.
16   *Ibid.*, p. 346.
17 C.P.P., Buckley statement on Vietnam, June 1970.
18 C.P.P., Fish statement, July 1970.
19 J. Buckley, p. 23.
20 Richard Reeves, *President Nixon* (2001), p. 245.
21 *National Review*, November 3, 1970.

22 *Ibid.*

23 August 28, 1970.

24 C.P.P., statement by C. White, September 1, 1970.

25 *National Review*, November 3, 1970.

26 C.P.P., transcript of Buckley speech, September 25 1970.

27 Wm. F. Buckley Jr., *Let Us Talk of Many Things: The Collected Speeches* (2000), p. 163.

28 Maltese interview.

29 C.P.P., O'Doherty statement, October 1970.

30 *New York Times Magazine*, October 1970.

31 *Ibid.*

32 J. Buckley, p. 24.

33 C.P.P., P.R., list of Buckley positions, October 28, 1970.

34 J. Buckley, p. 24.

35 Reeves, pp. 271–72.

36 *New York Post*, November 4, 1970.

37 *Time*, November 16, 1970

38 *New York Post*, November 4, 1970.

39 *Ibid.*

40 Markmann, p. 300.

41 Barone, *The Almanac of American Politics* (1972), p. 526.

CHAPTER 9

1 *U.S. News and World Report*, November 16, 1970.

2 Interview with Maltese.

3 *Ibid.*

4 C.P.P., P.R., January 22, 1971.

5 C.P.P., transcript of Leonard statement.

6 Cannato, p. 508.

7 C.P.P., transcript of Dabrowski statement.

8 *Newsday*, December 1, 1971.

9 N.Y.S. Legislative Manual, 1972.

10 C.P.P., P.R., 1971.

11 C.P.P., P.R., 1971.

12 C.P.P., P.R., June 22, 1971.

13 C.P.P., P.R., July 16, 1971.

14 Rusher, pp. 239–40.

15 C.P.P., P.R., December 9, 1971.

16 WCBS-TV transcript.

17 *Wall Street Journal*, December 29, 1971.

18 C.P.P., P.R., January 25, 1971.

19 Maltese interview.

20 C.P.P., P.R., March 1, 1972.

21 C.P.P., P.R., March 13, 1972.

22 *New York Daily News*, July 28, 1972.

23 Quotes appeared on C.P. brochure to re-elect Nixon-Agnew.

24 C.P.P., P.R., August 29, 1972.

25 C.P.P., P.R., July 30, 1972.

26 Barone, *Our Country* (1990), p. 450.

27 J.K White, *The New Politics of Old Values* (1988), p. 83.

28 *New York Times*, September 29, 1972.

29 C.P.P., P.R., November 6, 1972.

30 C.P.P., P.R., November 1972.

31 C.P.P., P.R., November 10, 1972.

32 Long interview.

33 Buckley, *On the Right*, May 2, 1973.

34 C.P.P., P.R., May 14, 1973.

35 Long interview.

36 *Human Events*, May 26, 1973.

37 *New York Daily News*, March 20, 1973.

38 C.P.P., P.R., 1973.

39 C.P.P., P.R., October 1973 resolution.

40 Wm. F. Buckley Jr., *Let Us Talk of Many Things* (2000), p. 208.

41 C.P.P., Mahoney letter, October 1973.

42 Kramer, p. 362.

43 *Buffalo Courier Express*, December 14, 1973.

44 Most of this is taken from my previous book, *The Guidebook to Municipal Bonds* (1991).

45 *New York Times Magazine*, October 1974.

46 *New York Times*, January 15, 1974.

47 C.P.P., transcript of Klein speech.

48 C.P.P., P.R., 1974.

49 *Albany Times Union*, February 6, 1974.

50 *Long Island Press*, June 11, 1974.

51 *New York Times*, June 25, 1974.

52 Office of the Governor, press release, June 26, 1974.

53 C.P.P., transcript of Bullard statement.

54 C.P.P., transcript of Paolucci statement.

55 *Congressional Record*, January 21, 1974.

56 Nicholas Von Hoffman, *Citizen Cohn* (1988), p. 361.

57 *Ibid.*

58 C.P.P., transcript of Keating statements, June 15, 1974.

59 *Ibid.*

60 *Newsday*, June 16, 1974.

61 C.P.P., signed Cohn affidavit.

62 *New York Times Magazine*, October 1974.

63 *Ibid.*

64 Long interview.

65 *National Review*, April 12, 1974.

66 C.P.P., transcript of J. Buckley statement, July 1974.

67 Buckley, *Let Us Talk of Many Things*, p. 211.

68 C.P.P., P.R., September 1974.

69 Keating interview.

70 C.P.P., P.R., October 1974.

71 *Newsday*, October 29, 1974.

72 C.P.P., P.R., November 1974.

73 Barone, *The Almanac of American Politics* (1976), p. 550.

CHAPTER 10

1   Joseph Persico, *The Imperial Rockefeller* (1982), p. 215.

2   *New York* Magazine, October 27, 1975.

3   Kramer and Roberts, p. 13.

4   C.P.P., finance position paper, 1970.

5   Kramer and Roberts, p. 145.

6   C.P.P., P.R., January 1975.

7   *New York* Magazine, October 27, 1975.

8   This succinct description of New York City's fiscal collapse is excerpted from my previous book, *The Guidebook to Municipal Bonds* (1991).

9   C.P.P., P.R., October 29, 1975.

10 C.P.P., position paper, 1975.

11 *Birmingham Press*, October 11, 1975.

12 *Congressional Record*, January 28, 1974.

13 J. Buckley, *If Men Were Angels*, p. 27.

14 Senator Buckley newsletter, April – May 1971.

15 *Rochester Democrat*, December 19, 1971.

16 *Syracuse Herald Journal*, March 6, 1972.

17 *New York Daily News,* June 8, 1972.

18 *New York Times*, May 24, 1973.

19 *New York Post*, March 23, 1974.

20 See J.Buckley, *If Men Were Angels* , pp. 55–63.

21 *New York Times*, April 18, 1974.

22 *New York Post*, March 23, 1974.

23 C.P.P., transcript of Buckley testimony, September 17, 1974.

24 *New York Times*, August 30, 1974.

25 *New York Post*, September 24, 1975.

26 *Newsday*, September 24, 1975.

27 *New York Post*, September 24, 1975.

28 *New York Daily News*, September 25, 1975.

29 *New York Daily News,* November 1, 1975.

30 *Ibid.*

31 *New York Times*, November 21, 1975.

32 *Ibid.*

33 Long interview.

34 *Empire State Report*, September 1975.

35 *New York Daily News*, March 18, 1975.

36 *Syracuse Post Standard*, February 9, 1975.

37 *New York Times*, September 18, 1975.

38 Rusher, p. 285.

39 *National Review*, October 29, 1976.

40 *Ibid.*

41 *Ibid.*
42 Long interview.
43 *New York Times*, October 29, 1976.
44 *Ibid.*
45 *Ibid.*
46 White, *Memoirs*, p. 198.
47 *New York Times*, November 1976.
48 C.P.P., P.R., February 17, 1977.
49 C.P.P., legislative memo, Assembly Bill 10A.
50 *Human Events*, July 16, 1977.
51 *Ibid.*
52 Farber mayoral brochure.
53 *New York Times*, August 26, 1977.
54 From Cuomo 1977 mayoral brochure.
55 *New York Times*, August 24, 1974.
56 *New York Post*, November 9, 1977, and *New York Daily News*, November 1, 1977.
57 *New York Times*, November 9, 1977.
58 Gerald Benjamin, *Making Experience Count* (1985), p. 239.
59 *Ibid.*
60 *Albany Times Union*, October 24, 1977.
61 *Newsday*, March 31, 1978.
62 *New York Times*, March, 31, 1978.
63 *New York Daily News*, March 31, 1978.
64 *Ibid.*
65 *New York* Magazine, June 12, 1978.
66 *Ibid.*
67 *Ibid.*
68 Long interview.
69 *Buffalo Courier*, October 20, 1978.
70 Maltese interview.
71 *New York Post*, November 8, 1978.
72 Long interview.
73 *New York Daily News*, June 25, 1979.
74 T. White, *America in Search of Itself* (1981), p. 35.
75 Barone, *Our Country*, p. 577.
76 J.K. White, p. 60.
77 *Ibid.*, p. 147.
78 C.P.P., copy of Mahoney letter.
79 Maltese interview.
80 Long interview.
81 D'Amato, *Pasta, Power and Politics* (1995), pp. 83–84.
82 Maltese interview.
83 Long interview.
84 D'Amato, p. 84.
85 C.P.P., March 24, 1980.
86 Levine interview.

87 *New York Times*, March 23, 1980.

88 *Newsday*, March 23, 1980.

89 *New York Times*, September 11, 1980.

90 *New York Times*, September 16, 1980.

91 *Ibid.*

92 *Syracuse Herald Journal*, September 16, 1980

93 C.P.P., Long press release, January 31, 1980.

94 Barone, *The Almanac of American Politics*, (1980), p. 760.

95 C.P.P., P.R., November 1980.

96 *New York Times*, November 1980.

CHAPTER 11

1 Long interview.

2 *New York Times Magazine*, October 31, 1982.

3 Long interview.

4 *New York Times*, January 26, 1982.

5 *Ibid.*

6 *Buffalo Courier*, August 20, 1982.

7 *Newsday*, August 20, 1982.

8 *New York Times*, August 20, 1982.

9 Edward Koch, *Citizen Koch* (1992), p. 200.

10 *New York Times Magazine*, October 31, 1982.

11 See James Underwood, *Gov. Rockefeller on New York: The Apex of Pragmatic Liberalism in the United States* (1982), pp. 10–11.

12 *New York Times Magazine*, October 31, 1982.

13 *Ibid.*

14 George W. Rutler, *Beyond Modernity* (1987), pp. 89–90.

15 *New York Times Magazine*, October 31, 1982.

16 *Ibid.*

17 *Atlantic Monthly*, July 1988.

18 Mario Cuomo, *Diaries of Mario Cuomo* (1984), p. 327.

19 Long interview.

20 *Ibid.*

21 Maltese interview.

22 *New York Times*, January 24, 1986.

23 *Ibid.*

24 *Buffalo News*, January 24, 1986.

25 *Changing Faces*, February 24, 1986.

26 D'Amato, pp. 126–37.

27 *Ibid.*, p. 138.

28 *New York Post*, November 5, 1986.

29 *Ibid.*

30 *Ibid.*

31 *New York Daily News*, October 21, 1986.

32 *New York Post*, November 5, 1986.

33 Peter W. Colby, *New York State Today* (1989), p. 112.

34 *New York Post*, November 9, 1988.

35 *New York Times*, December 28, 1988.

CHAPTER 12

1   William Gavin, *The Street Corner Conservative* (1975), pp. 46–47

2   *Flatbush Life*, July 27, 1972.

3   G. Kassar interview, 2001.

4   *Albany Times Union*, February 2, 1989.

5   *Albany Times Union.*, February 14, 1989.

6   D'Amato, *Power, Pasta and Politics* (1995), p. 276.

7   *Ibid.*

8   Wayne Barrett, *Rudy Giuliani* (2000), p. 203.

9   *Wall Street Journal*, August 1, 1989.

10 *New York Post*, July 18, 1989.

11 *Newsday*, September 4, 1989.

12 *New York Post*, September 6, 1989.

13 *New York Times*, May 4, 1990.

14 *Wall Street Journal*, June 20, 1990.

15 Long interview.

16 *Human Events*, June 1990.

17 C.P.P., P.R., June 1990.

18 *New York Post*, September 26, 1990.

19 *New York Times*, October 7, 1990.

20 C.P.P., P.R., October 1990.

21 *On the Right*, October 1990.

22 C.P.P., transcript of T.V. ads.

23 *Human Events*, July 4, 1990.

24 *Ibid.*

25 *New York Post*, October 1990.

26 C.P.P., P.R., October 1990.

27 *New York Times*, November 8, 1990.

28 *New York Times*, November 9, 1990.

29 *Ibid.*

30 *New York City Tribune*, November 16, 1990.

31 *New York Post*, December 12, 1990.

32 *Ibid.*

CHAPTER 13

1   *Albany Times Union*, February 12, 1991.

2   *Ibid.*

3   Long interview, 2000.

4   *New York Post*, June 3, 1991.

5   *New York Post*, April 15, 1991.

6   *Newsday*, June 8, 1992.

7   *New York Times*, November 24, 1991.

8   *Newsday*, December 17, 1991.

9   *Syracuse Herald Tribune*, December 6, 1991.

10 *Newsday*, December 17, 1991.

11 Long interview, 2000.

12 *Newsday*, December 12, 1991.

13 Leonard Lurie, *Senator Pothole* (1994), p. 464.

14 *New York Times*, July 8, 1992.

15 C.P.P., September 1992.

16 C.P.P., September 1992.

17 *Newsday*, November 23, 1991.

18 C.C.P. papers.

19 A significant part of the Mary Cummins story is from an article I authored that appeared in *Crisis* magazine, February, 1993.

20 *New York Observer*, September, 1992.

21 *New York Observer*, March 15, 1993.

22 *New York Daily News*, May 27, 1993.

23 *New York Daily News*, June, 1993.

24 *Staten Island Advance*, June 22, 1993.

25 *Wall Street Journal*, September 29, 1993.

26 *Newsday*, November 11, 1993.

27 *Ibid.*, October 31, 1993.

28 *New York Daily News*, September 17, 1993.

29 *Ibid.*, October 5, 1993.

30 *Newsday*, October 18, 1993.

31 *Ibid.*

CHAPTER 14

1   Tom Carroll, "The Status Cuomo," *Policy Review* (Spring 1994).

2   *Ibid.*

3   *Cortland Standard*, February 9, 1993.

4   *Syracuse Herald Journal*, February 2, 1993.

5   *Albany Times Union*, January 6, 1994.

6   C.P.P., P.R., February 1994.

7   *New York Times Magazine*, March 6, 1997.

8   Long interview, 2001.

9   D'Amato, p. 272.

10 Barrett, pp. 299–300.

11 *New York Times*, May 24, 1994.

12 *Ibid.*

13 *Ibid.*

14 *Ibid.*

15 *New York Times.*, June 5, 1994.

16 *Ibid.*

17 *Newsday*, October 13, 1994.

18 Barrett, p. 300.

19 Andrew Kirtzman, *Rudy* (2000), p. 130.

20 *Ibid.*, pp. 133–34.

21 C.P.P., P.R., October 25, 1994.

22 *Crossfire* transcript.

23 See Barrett, pp. 300–305, for the complete story.

24 *New York Times*, October 30, 1994.

25 Long interview, 2001.

26 Barrett, p. 302.

27 *Ibid.*

28 C.P.P., P.R., November 1994.

29 *Ibid.*

30 *New York Times* survey, November 10, 1994.

31 *New York Daily News*, November 10, 1994.

32 *New York Post*, October 24, 1994.

33 *Newsday*, November 10, 1994.

34 *New York Times*, November 10, 1994.

CHAPTER 15

1 *Empire State Report*, October 1989.

2 *Ibid.*

3 C.P.P., P.R., Long interview, February 13, 1995.

4 C.P. newsletter, January 1995.

5 C.P.P., P.R., February 28, 1995.

6 C.P.P., P.R., September 14, 1995.

7 C.P.P., P.R., October 12, 1995.

8 C.P.P. transcript of radio ad, October 1995.

9 *Time*, September 11, 1995.

10 C.P.P., P.R., February 28, 1996.

11 C.P.P. transcript, October 1996.

12 C.P.P., P.R., November 5, 1997.

13 Long interview, 2001.

14 C.P.P., P.R., May 19, 1997.

15 *New York Daily News*, August 24, 1997.

16 C.P.P., P.R., January 1993.

17 George J. Marlin, *The Politician's Guide to Assisted Suicide, Cloning and Other Current Controversies* (1998), pp. 109–10.

18 *The Empire Report*, November 2, 1998.

CHAPTER 16

1 C.P. platform, 2001.

2 *New York Post*, April 25, 1996.

3 *Ibid.*

4 *New York Post*, May 1, 1996.

5 *Ibid.*

6 C.P.P., P.R., May 1996.

7 *Albany Times Union*, May 1, 1996.

8 *Ibid.*

9 C.P.P., P.R., May 28, 1996.

10 C.P.P., P.R., July 1996.

11 *Staten Island Advance*, July 14, 1996.

12 *New York Post*, December 19, 1996.

13 *Albany Times Union*, February 13, 1997.

14 *New York Times*, February 25, 1997.

15 *Ibid.*

16 *New York Post*, February 17, 1997.

17 *Ibid.*

18 C.P.P. letter, December 15, 1997.

19 *New York Times*, May 21, 1998

20 *Ibid.*

21 *Ibid.*

22 C.P.P., Long letter, March 8, 1999.

23 *The Journal News*, May 27, 1999.

24 *Albany Times Union*, April 14, 1999.

CHAPTER 17

1 Mike Tomasky, *Hillary's Turn* (2001), p. 110.

2 *Ibid.*

3 *Human Events*, May 7, 1999.

4 *Newsweek*, July 5, 1999.

5 *Boston Globe*, August 3, 1999.

6 Tomasky, p. 72.

7 *New York Daily News*, August 19, 1999.

8 *Newsday*, August 19, 1999.

9 *New York* Magazine, August 16, 1999.

10 *New York Daily News*, August 19, 1999.

11 *Newsday*, August 9, 1999.

12 *New York Times*, August 19, 1999.

13 *New York Post*, August 8, 1999.

14 *Washington Times*, November 2, 1999.

15 *New York Daily News*, August 18, 1999.

16 *Ibid.*

17 Long interview, 2001.

18 *New York Post*, August 25, 1999.

19 *New York Times*, December 1, 1999.

20 *Long Island Catholic*, November 24, 1999.

21 *New York Post*, October 9, 1999.

22 *New York Times*, November 17, 1999.

23 *New York Post*, November 30, 1999.

24 *New York Times*, November 30, 1999.

25 *New York Post*, November 30, 1999.

26 *Staten Island Advance*, December 1, 1999.

27 *Ibid.*

28 *New York Times*, November 13, 1999.

29 *The Washington Post*, December 5, 1999.

30 *New York Observer*, December 6, 1999.

31 *Staten Island Advance*, December 1, 1999.

32 *Human Events*, December 1999.

33 *New York Times*, November 30, 1999.

34 *New York Times*, December 13, 1999.

35 *New York Post*, December 24, 1999.

36 *New York Post*, December 6, 1999.

37 *Ibid.*

38 *New York Times*, December 13, 1999.

39 *New York Post*, January 3, 2000.

40 *New York Post*, February 8, 2000.

41 *New York Post*, February 9, 2000.

42 *New York Times*, February 8, 2000.

43 *New York Post*, April 8, 2000.

44 *New York Observer*, April 24, 2000.

45 *New York Times*, May 1, 2000.

46 *New York Post*, May 2, 2000.

47 *Ibid.*

48 *New York Post*, May 20, 2000.

49 *New York Times*, June 4, 2000.

50 Long interview, 2001.

51 *New York Times*, July 15, 2000.

52 *New York Times*, November 8, 2000.

AFTERWORD

1 See Louis Winnick's excellent study, *New People in Old Neighborhoods*, published in 1990 by the Russell Sage Foundation.

2 Winnick, p. 34.

Select Bibliography

Banfield, Edward, and James Q. Wilson, *City Politics* (1963)

Barone, Michael, *The Almanac of American Politics, 1972–2002 Editions*

Barone, Michael, *The Mid-Atlantic States of America* (1977)

Barone, Michael, *Our Country* (1990)

Barrett, Wayne, *Rudy Giuliani* (2000)

Bell, Jeffrey, *Populism and Elitism* (1992)

Benjamin, Gerald, *Making Experience Count: Managing Modern New York in the Carey Era* (1985)

Benjamin, Gerald, *Rocky in Retrospect* (1984)

Buckley, James L., *If Men Were Angels* (1975)

Buckley, William F., *The Unmaking of A Mayor* (1966)

Buckley, William. F., *Let Us Talk of Many Things* (2000)

Buchanan, Patrick J., *The New Majority* (1993)

Burner, David, *The Politics of Provincialism* (1967)

Cannato, Vincent, *The Ungovernable City* (2001)

Colby, Peter W., and John K. White, *New York State Today* (1989)

Caro, Robert A., *The Power Broker* (1975)

Collier, Peter, and Peter Horowitz, *The Rockefellers* (1976)

Connery, Robert, *Rockefeller of New York* (1979)

D'Amato, Alfonse, *Pasta, Power and Politics* (1995)

Dawson, Christopher, *Dynamics of World History* (1956)

Edsall, Thomas, and Mary Edsall, *Chain Reaction* (1969)

Ellis, David, *History of New York State* (1967)

Gavin, William, *The Street Corner Conservative* (1975)

Goldberg, Robert, *Barry Goldwater* (1995)

Greeley, Andrew, *Neighborhoods* (1977)

Greenfield, Jeff, *The Real Campaign* (1982)

Haller, Mark, *Eugenics* (1984)

Hevisi, Alan, *Legislative Politics in New York State* (1975)

Hodgson, Godfrey, *The Gentleman from New York: Daniel Patrick Moynihan* (2000)

Judis, John, *William F. Buckley Jr.* (1988)

Kelly, Robert, *The Cultural Pattern in American Politics* (1979)

Kelves, Daniel J., *In the Name of Eugenics* (1985)

Kirk, Russell, and James McClellan, *The Political Principles of Robert A. Taft* (1967)

Koch, Edward, *Citizen Koch* (1992)

Kramer, Michael, and Sam Roberts, *I Never Wanted to Be Vice President of Anything: Nelson Rockefeller* (1976)

Lesher, Stephen, *Wallace* (1994)

Lurie, Leonard, *Senator Pothole* (1994)

Markmann, Charles, *The Buckleys* (1971)

Marlin, George J., *The Politician's Guide to Assisted Suicide, Cloning and Other Current Controversies* (1998)

McNickle, Thomas, *To Be Mayor of New York: Ethnic Politics in the City* (1993)

Joyce, Milton, *The First Partner: Hillary Rodham Clinton* (1999)

Miner, Brad, *The Concise Conservative Encyclopedia* (1996)

Moscow, Warren, *The Empire State* (1948)

Moynihan, D.P., *Beyond the Melting Pot* (1963).

Nash, George H., *The Conservative Intellectual Movement in American – Since 1945* (1976)

Newfield, Jack, and Wayne Barrett, *City for Sale: Ed Koch and the Betrayal of New York* (1988)

Novak, Michael, *The Spirit of Democratic Capitalism* (1982)

Novak, Michael, *The Unmeltable Ethics* (1972)

Parmet, Herbert S., *The Democrats* (1976)

Parmet, Herbert S., *Nixon and His America* (1990)

Pataki, George, *An Autobiography* (1998)

Persico, Joseph, *The Imperial Rockefeller* (1982)

Phillips, Kevin, *The Emerging Republican Majority* (1969)

Rae, Nico, *Decline and Fall of the Liberal Republicans* (1989)

Reedy, George E., *From the Ward to the White House* (1991)

Reeves, Richard, *President Nixon* (2001)

Reich, Gary, *The Life of Nelson Rockefeller* (1996)

Rockefeller, Nelson A., *Future of Federalism* (1962)

Rodgers, William, *Rockefeller's Follies* (1966)

Rusher, William A., *The Rise of the Right* (1984)

Rutler, George W., *Beyond Modernity* (1987)

Smith, Richard Norton, *Thomas E. Dewey and His Times* (1982)

Saltzman, Harold, *Race War in High School* (1972)

Scarrow, Howard A., *Parties, Elections & Representation in the State of New York* (1983)

Siegel, Fred, *Troubled Journey* (1984)

Taylor, Paul, *See How They Run* (1990)

Thomson, Jordon H., *The Politics of Birth Control* (1968)

Tomasky, Michael, *Hillary's Turn* (2001)

Underwood, James F., *Gov. Rockefeller in New York: The Apex of Pragmatic Liberalism in New York* (1982)

Viorst, Milton, *Fall from Grace* (1968)

Von Hoffman, Nicholas, *Citizen Cohn* (1988)

Ware, Alan, *The Breakdown of the Democratic Party Organization (1940–1980)* (1988)

Weiss, Joan, *Charles Francis Murphy* (1968)

White, F. Clifton, *Politics as a Noble Calling* (1994)

White, J.K., *The New Politics of Old Values* (1988)

White, Theodore H., *The Making of the President* (1968)

White, Theodore H., *America in Search of Itself* (1981)

Wilson, James Q., *The Amateur Democrats* (1962)

Winnick, Louis, *New People in Old Neighborhoods* (1990)

Index

About the Author

George J. Marlin is Chairman and C.O.O. of The Philadelphia Trust Company. He served two terms as Executive Director and C.E.O. of the Port Authority of New York and New Jersey. In that capacity he managed thirty-five facilities including the World Trade Center, La Guardia, JFK, and Newark Airports, PATH Subway and the four bridges and two tunnels that connect New York and New Jersey. In 1993, Mr. Marlin was the Conservative Party nominee for mayor of the City of New York, and in 1994 he served on Governor-elect Pataki's transition team. Mr. Marlin is the author of *The Politician's Guide to Assisted Suicide Cloning and Other Current Controversies* and co-authored with Joe Mysak, *The Guidebook to Municipal Bonds*. He is the editor of *The Quotable Chesterton, More Quotable Chesterton, Quotable Fulton Sheen, Quotable Paul Johnson*, and *Quotable Ronald Knox*. Mr. Marlin also serves as general editor of *The Collected Works of G.K. Chesterton*. His articles have appeared in numerous periodicals including *National Review, Newsday*, and the *New York Daily News*. A lifelong resident of New York, Mr. Marlin resides with his wife, Barbara, in Nassau County.